LORDS OF THE HORIZONS

LORDS OF THE HORIZONS

A History of the Ottoman Empire

JASON GOODWIN

A JOHN MACRAE / OWL BOOK
Henry Holt and Company
New York

Henry Holt and Company, LLC
Publishers since 1866
115 West 18th Street
New York, New York 10011

Henry Holt® is a registered trademark
of Henry Holt and Company, LLC.

Library of Congress Cataloging-in-Publication Data
Goodwin, Jason, 1964–
Lords of the horizons: a history of the
Ottoman Empire / Jason Goodwin.
p. cm.
Originally published: London: Chatto & Windus, 1998.
Includes bibliographical references (p.) and index.
ISBN 0-8050-6342-0
1. Turkey—History—Ottoman Empire, 1288–1918. I. Title.
DR486.G66 1999 98-41601
956.1'015—dc21 CIP

Henry Holt books are available for special promotions and
premiums. For details contact: Director, Special Markets.

Originally published in Great Britain
in 1998 by Chatto & Windus

First published in the United States in 1999
by Henry Holt and Company

First Owl Books Edition 2000

A John Macrae / Owl Book

Frontispiece: Gentile Bellini's portrait of Mehmet II

Printed in the United States of America

1 3 5 7 9 10 8 6 4 2

Contents

Map of the Ottoman Empire viii

Prologue xi

Part I *Curves and Arabesques*

1. Origins 3
2. The Balkans 12
3. Thunderbolt 22
4. The Siege 29
5. The Centre 44
6. The Palace 50
7. War 65
8. Suleyman the Magnificent 79
9. Order 90
10. Cities 110
11. The Sea 121
12. Rhythms 130

Part II *The Turkish Time*

13. The Turkish Time 149
14. Stalemate 158
15. The Cage 164
16. The Spiral 173
17. The Empire 185

Part III *Hoards*

18. Hoards 209
19. Koprulu and Vienna 221
20. Austria and Russia 237
21. Ayan 245
22. Shamming 256
23. Borderlands 269
24. The Auspicious Event 289
25. The Bankrupt 301

Epilogue 322

Ottoman Sultans 327
An Ottoman Chronology 329
Glossary 333
Gazetteer 336
Bibliography 337
Acknowledgements 342
Index 343

These songs will not be to everyone's taste, for there is little variation among them, all of them containing the same words, such as: hero, knight, horseman, galley slave, serpent, dragon, wolf, lion, falcon, eagle, falcon's nest and sword, sabres, lances, Kraljevic, Kobilic, Zdrinovic, necklets, medallions, decrees, heads chopped off, slaves carried away, etc. May those who find them pleasing sing them; may those who do not, go off to sleep.

Andrija Kacic-Miosic,
The Pleasant Conversation
of the Slavic People,
Venice, 1756

N
R. Dnestr
(Dniester)
R. Dnep
(Dnieper)
VIENNA
BUDA
PEST
R. Po
R. Sava
BELGRADE
(captured in 1521)
BUCHAREST
BLAC
FLORENCE
R. Danube
RAGUSA
SOFIA
ROME
EDIRNE
ISTANBUL
BURSA
ATHENS
CANDIA
MEDITERRANEAN SEA
TRIPOLI
BENGHAZI
ALEXANDRIA
CAIRO
R. Nile

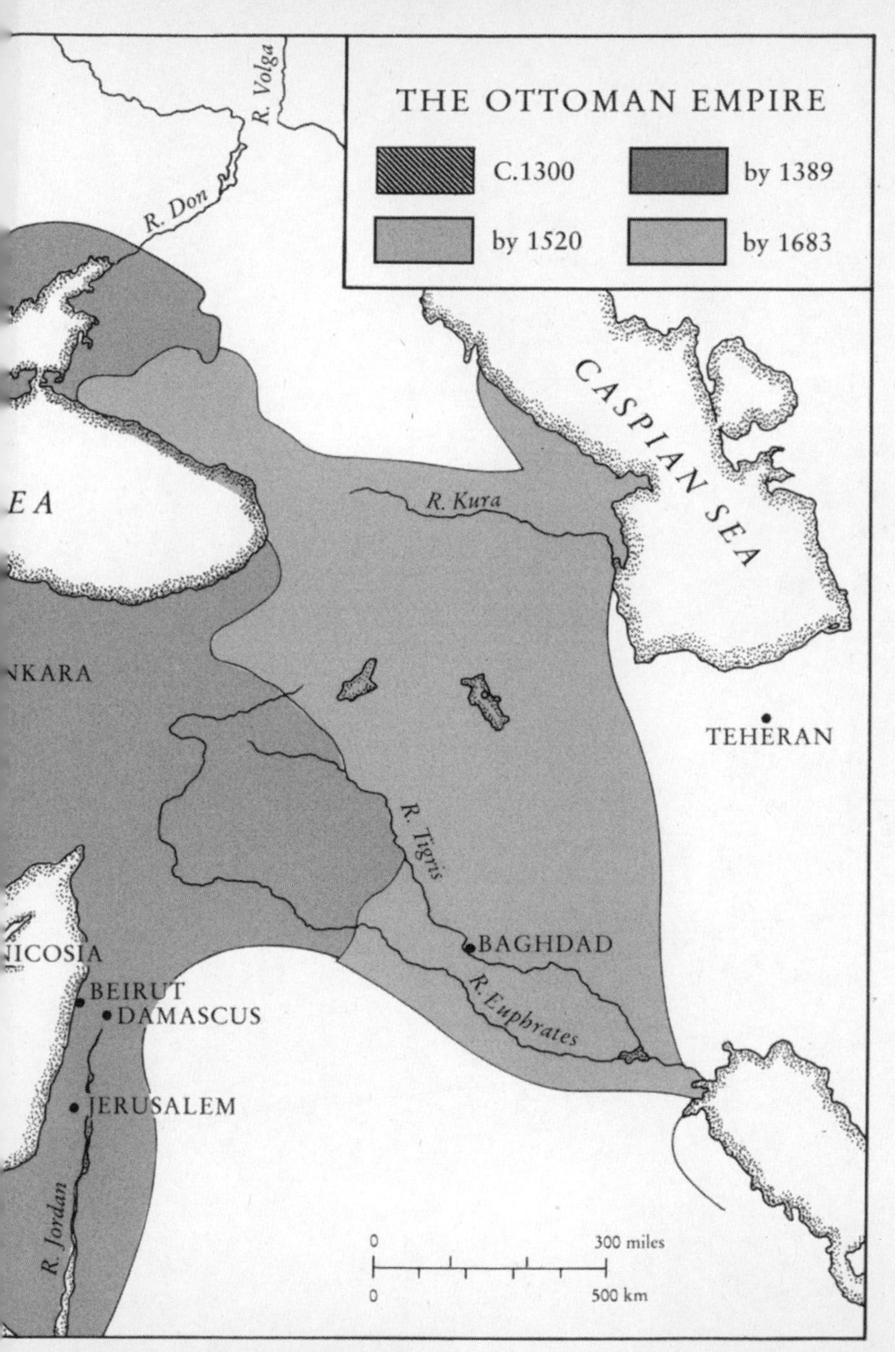
THE OTTOMAN EMPIRE
C.1300
by 1389
by 1520
by 1683
R. Volga
R. Don
CASPIAN SEA
EA
R. Kura
NKARA
TEHERAN
R. Tigris
NICOSIA
BAGHDAD
BEIRUT
DAMASCUS
R. Euphrates
JERUSALEM
R. Jordan
0
300 miles
0
500 km

Prologue

At the back of the Bayezit Mosque in Istanbul, close to the walls of the Great Bazaar, stand the ruins of an old Byzantine chapel. Beneath its vaulted roof is a tumbledown café. Horn lanterns hanging from the wall cast a dim light on the clientele, while the open door affords a glimpse – beyond the gigantic cypress which grows in the courtyard of the Bayezit Mosque, past the porphyry columns – into the sanctuary of the mosque itself, where the faithful kneel in prayer.

In the café a little orchestra – flute, two drums, a viola and a triangle – is playing in one corner; a backlit sheet is stretched across another. Armchairs are taken by several elderly pashas, some in uniform, some in Stamboulines and fezzes, all of them supporting armfuls of grandchildren. Behind them sit a handful of solemn old men in turbans, smoking pipes; a clutch of Greek and Armenian women, swathed to invisibility in black shawls; and a couple of Cook's tourists, in tweeds, hoping for an insight.

For in a moment Karagoz and Hacivat will skitter across the sheet, heroes of the shadow play, the Pantaloon and Harlequin of the Ottoman stage: jointed silhouettes, cut from dried camel leather, painted up and oiled for translucency. The original Karagoz, hunchbacked and foul-mouthed, and his straight man, Hacivat, are supposed to have developed their knockabout routines on a building site in 1396, where their antics proved so irresistible that work on Sultan Bayezit's Great Mosque in Bursa ground to a halt, and the Sultan had them put to death. Others say Constantinople (Istanbul) always had its Karagoz and Hacivat, even in the days of the Roman emperors. Some think

The Bayezit Mosque

that the pair of them are offshoots of an ancient wisdom, dressed in a corrupted version of the licensed finery of the Sufi and the shaman and the bard.

In the semi-ruinous café they are worked by an Armenian, who is a mimic and comedian rolled up in a newspaper – a five-, six-, even seven-tasselled puppeteer. His is a very old, wandering profession. Over the years he has been in Hungary, setting garrisons in a roar, or in Egypt, raising a pasha's smile; he has carried his cut-outs, lamp and little screen to Iraq and the Crimea; to the neighbourhood of Venice in the army's van, and with the fleets to

Algiers. The Cook's tourists have been told to watch for his scurrilous take-off of a foreigner speaking Turkish. The orchestra wails and squeaks; the Armenian ladies giggle; the children squirm; and a constant supply of coffee cups moves about the room, borne by Circassian youths in 'the good old costume': which is baggy trousers, waistcoats, and coils of coloured linen piled on their shaven heads.

This book is about a people who do not exist. The word 'Ottoman' does not describe a place. Nobody nowadays speaks their language. Only a few professors can begin to understand their poetry – 'We have no classics,' snapped a Turkish poet in 1964 at a poetry symposium in Sofia, when asked to acquaint the group with examples of classical Ottoman verse.

For six hundred years the Ottoman Empire swelled and declined. It advanced from a dusty *beylik* in the foothills of Anatolia at the start of the fourteenth century to conquer the relics and successors of Byzantium, including the entire Balkan peninsula from the Adriatic to the Black Sea, Greece, Serbia, Bulgaria, and the so-called Principalities of Wallachia and Moldavia north of the Danube. It took Anatolia. The submission of the Crimean Tartars in the fifteenth century, along with the capture of Constantinople in 1453, completed its control of the Black Sea. In 1517 it swept up the heartlands of Islam – Syria, Arabia, and Egypt, along with the Holy Cities of Mecca and Medina. Controlling the thoroughfares which linked Europe to the Middle East, the Ottoman Empire stretched from the Danube to the Nile.

The empire in those years was Islamic, martial, civilised and tolerant. To those who lived outside its boundaries, in lands known, by Islamic custom, as Dar ul-Harb, 'Abode of War', it was an irritant and a terror. To its own subject peoples, however, it belonged in the Dar ul-Islam, or 'Abode of Peace', and was such a prodigy of pep, so vigorous and so well-ordered, such a miracle of human ingenuity, that contemporaries felt it was helped into being by powers not quite human – diabolical or divine, depending on their point of view.

But at the start of the seventeenth century the Ottomans faltered. The Mediterranean Sea was relegated to second-division status, the Islamic spirit seemed to stagnate. The nations of the West were querulous and disunited, but their very squabbles proved vigorous and progressive. In the Ottoman, Islamic world the battles were already won, the arguments suppressed; the law was written, and the Ottomans cleaved ever more rigidly to the past in a spirit of narcissistic pride.

For the next three hundred years, the empire defied prognostications of its imminent collapse. Fractious and ramshackle, its politics riddled with corruption, its purposes furred by sloth, it was a miracle of a kind, too, a prodigy of decay. 'It has become like an old body, crazed through with many vices, which remain when the youth and strength is decayed,' wrote Sir Thomas Roe in 1621. The crazed old body survived him by almost three centuries; outlived its fiercest enemies, the Russian Tsar, and the Habsburg Emperor, by a full four years. Not until 1878 were the Ottomans dislodged from Bosnia; not until 1882 did the Sultan cease to rule, in title anyway, over Egypt. Albania, on the Adriatic coast, was one of the toughest provinces the Ottomans ever sought to subdue in the fifteenth century; but the Albanians were still sending parliamentary deputies to Constantinople in 1909.

This was an Islamic empire, though many of its subjects were not Muslim, and it made no effort to convert them. It controlled the thoroughfares between East and West, but it was not very interested in trade. It was, by common consent, a Turkish empire, but most of its dignitaries and officers, and its shock troops, too, were Balkan Slavs. Its ceremonial was Byzantine, its dignity Persian, its wealth Egyptian, its letters Arabic. The Ottomans were not accounted builders by contemporaries – even though one grim old Grand Vizier was remembered as the man who built more churches than Justinian. They came with no schemes of agricultural improvement, although production soared in the lands they conquered in Europe. They were not religious fanatics as a rule; Sunni Muslims, they followed the moderate Hanefi school of Koranic interpretation. Sultans read the life of Alexander, but they were not particularly interested in the past.* But the young Ivan the Terrible took the life of Mehmet the Conqueror as his primer, and the Venetians, who always liked to know the way things ran, fiercely admired the system of government which Mehmet had devised, and found in it a Palladian quality, of harmony and handsome proportion.

The empire outlived its grandeur, famously. By the time Napoleon landed in Egypt the empire seemed to the world as weak as Spain, as decayed in ancient pomp as Venice. Rich in talents still, the empire no longer provided a glittering stage for their expression. Its most brilliant sailors were all Greek. Its canniest merchants were Armenian. Its soldiers were ineptly led, while everywhere admired for their courage. Imperial statesmen operated at home in an atmosphere of intolerable suspicion. Yet the empire lingered into the twentieth century with no white cliffs to shield it, like England; no single language to unite it, like France. Unlike Spain, the empire was wedded to no illusions of religious purity; and it never discovered gold, or Atlantic trade, or steam. The Ottomans seemed to stand, in their final years, for negotiation over decision, for tradition over innovation, and for a dry understanding of the world's ways over all that was thrusting and progressive about the western world.

Never, perhaps, did a power fall so low, in such a glare of publicity – the Crimean War of 1856, in which Turkey fought Russia with French and British aid, was the first war in history covered by journalists. Tsar Alexander called the Ottoman Empire 'the Sick Man of Europe'. The Victorians referred to it impersonally as 'the Eastern Question', to which an answer, by implication, was to be supplied by muscular Christian gentlemen. To many westerners, of course, what was no longer an object of fear became an object of curiosity, and even admiration: certainly

* Posterity concerned them, of course. Abdi was Sultan Mehmet IV's court historian (1648–87). 'The Sultan kept him always near his person, and charged him with the special duty of writing the annals of his reign. One evening Mahomet [i.e. Mehmet] asked of him, "What hast thou written to-day?" Abdi incautiously answered that nothing sufficiently remarkable to write about had happened that day. The Sultan darted a hunting-spear at the unobservant companion of royalty, wounded him sharply, and exclaimed, "*Now* thou hast something to write about" ' (Creasy).

no one could deny the beauty of a traditional society, and painters found a ready market for their depictions of Levantine life. In the nineteenth century the empire made a valiant attempt to remodel itself along western lines, to enjoy, as everyone hoped, some of the western magic; but the convulsion killed it, for by then the heart was weak.

Karagoz is put in a coffin and buried at the end of the play, but just before the light goes out he pushes up the lid, hops out and sits on the coffin, roaring with laughter. The Armenian puppeteer puts out his lamp. The little orchestra, after a timpanic crescendo, lay down their instruments. The Circassian boys who have been handing refreshments round now pass amongst the audience for coins, and the pashas' little girls, who have giggled through some improper dialogue, wriggle out.

The grave old master behind all the moves and bustle of that prodigious performance known as the Ottoman Empire moves on, packs up his puppets, extinguishes his lamp, and leaves only the screen behind: the hills, plains and declivities of the Balkans, the plateaux and coasts of Anatolia, the Holy Cities Mecca and Medina, the sands of Egypt, the grasslands of Hungary, and the grey, grey waters of the Bosphorus, which slap at the pilings of the Galata bridge.

PART I

Curves and Arabesques

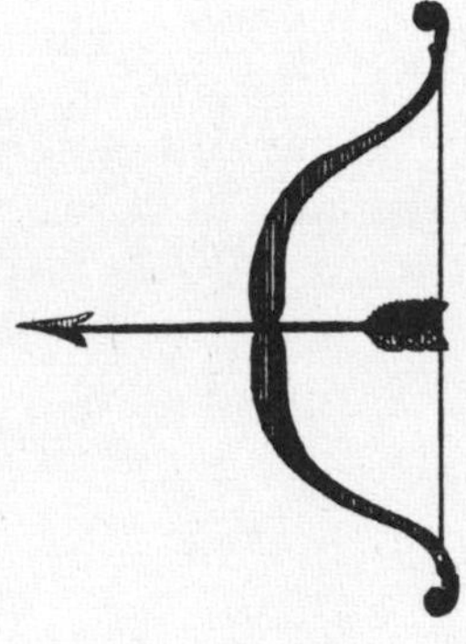

I

Origins

The great Eurasian steppe is a region of scrub and feathery grasses which stretches from the borders of China to the shore of the Black Sea. To the north, it gives way to conifer forests and permafrost; south, it is belted generally by deserts. Steppe grass is too tough, and the weather too variable for cultivation. There is little running water to speak of, and in the last fifty years, since the Soviets brought in machinery to plough the steppe, the rivers have begun running dry, so that the Caspian Sea – landlocked, enormous, a watery reflection of the dry steppe itself – has started to recede.

Steppe dwellers range the grasslands with their flocks, living in tents, and riding the short, hardy Turkish pony of the steppe – here, sometime in the third millennium BC, the horse was tamed for the first time. These people are broadly known as 'Turkmen', divided into tribes, or clans. Over the centuries, thanks to the strength and craft of neighbouring states, the area of their distribution has contracted; their sway was at its height in the eleventh century.

In times of famine, when peasants die more or less where they stand, nomads look for a way out, and climate probably explains the tendency of the steppe to produce now and then a torrent of warriors which would pour out of the steppe and into the settled lands beyond.

Shocks passed like waves across this great dry ocean; often the people who descended on the ploughman were not themselves the victims of famine, but rather people displaced by some distant explosion way down the line. This is how the Turks were shunted west in the eighth century, first against the settled empires of Iran and Iraq through the gap in the mountains known as Transoxania, and then beyond, sometimes slipping over the borders one by one, sometimes advancing *en masse*; acting as soldiers for the states and sometimes, too, usurping power.

Between age-old fortresses with wells and markets, domes and minarets, and lemon groves where learned men rehearse theological points worn smooth like pebbles in the handling, the turkmen come riding upon embroidered saddles, with stirrups like metal galoshes. Their wiry ponies, short-legged and high-backed, are so intelligent and beloved that sometimes it is hard to say whether the migration is of men riding horses, or of horses carrying men. 'The people of the Sublime State', an Ottoman dignitary was to inform the Russians in 1775, 'have been on familiar terms with horse and saddle for a *very* long time.' The Turks used a horsetail, raised on a standard, as the symbol of authority. The Turks could make a horse cry, or teach it to pick up a sword from the ground with its teeth and pass it to its rider. A Turkish horse had his tail dyed red, his wounds healed with chestnut bark, and enjoyed the same right as a man to a decent burial. Horses earned fame in their own right, like Karavulik, the Black Wolf, who galloped young Prince Selim to safety after his abortive rebellion in 1505. Their riders could hurl the *gerit* from a galloping horse so that it gained an incredible momentum and pierced sheet iron. They could fire arrows backwards from the saddle at a moving target, at a rate of three a second, and their archery was so accurate that as late as the nineteenth century, when the Turkish Sultan wore a frock coat and spoke passable

French, it is said he placed an arrow at 800 yards between the legs of a doubting American ambassador.

'Islam,' said the essayist Essad Bey, 'is the desert.' Unlike the two other great monotheistic faiths, Judaism and Christianity, Islam has no priesthood. The nomad can vanish for weeks on end but the all-powerful, all-seeing God goes with him: five times a day he must clear his mind and wash his hands and call on God. Islam is a powerful weapon in the struggle against uncertainty and change, for people who are not quite sure where they will be, or who they will be with, from one moment to the next, and its rules are firm. There is no God but God, and Muhammad is his prophet. The five daily prayers must be said. Pork and wine are forbidden. Alms must be given. The believer must tirelessly combat unbelief, but peaceably, unless provoked. The Koran is not a scripture but the law, dropped, as it were, flaming from the mind of God; and if it is safe from the mumbo-jumbo of priests it is consequently beset by the cold and legalistic wrangles of Islamic jurists, the *ulema*, who debate the meaning of the rules.

Islam was forged on a frontier. There have always been Muslim peasants, creatures of habit with nowhere else to go, who must do as they are told: the Ottomans recognised them, like the Christian peasants of the Balkans, as a special charge, defenceless tillers of the soil who composed the *reaya*, or flock, that horsemen were born to manage. Islam's genius has been reserved for townsmen and nomads, those quicker and less predictable communities which at bottom despise the peasant life. Islam was spread by caravan through the cities of the Middle East, and by the sword, as well, wielded by those Muslim conquerors who called themselves *gazi*, warriors of the faith, and who rode out of Arabia in the seventh century, contemptuous of distance, swooping down the north African shore, sweeping up to the barrier of the steppe, making Islam, the Abode of Peace, from the Pillars of Hercules to the deserts of Iran, and turning the Mediterranean into an Islamic lake.

Their impetus eventually petered out. The gazi spirit began to flag. The Gates of Interpretation closed in the ninth century. Islam settled down, losing some of its old dash, but gaining in charm, as it blossomed into the Muslim civilisations of Iran, Egypt, Spain, where the scholar and juror advanced over the soldier, to the murmur of plashing water, and the rustle of old texts. The fierce conviction and simplicity of the early Muslims gave way to subtle dialogues between the followers of divine revelation and the exponents of Aristotelian exegesis. In the twelfth century the Christian crusades disturbed the Abode of Peace, so that Palestine and even Jerusalem were lost for a time; Norman – Viking – warriors loosened the Islamic hold on the Mediterranean world; the splendours of Moorish Spain were already succumbing to the Christian advance; but the classical unity of Islam under one caliph had anyway been shattered by the Shi'ite controversy. Shi'as believe that the descendants of Ali, the Prophet's son-in-law, are the senior line; Sunnis that the grace descends through Fatima, his daughter. Under the pressure of this dispute, the Abode of Peace was riven by internecine wars, fought not by those who controlled the arguments but by armies of slaves recruited from the Turkic nomads of the steppe.

Islam's genius for movement, all the same, remained lively and ceremonious. By the caravans threading their way across the Islamic world, carrying sacks of spices and bags of gold, bales of silk and bundles of furs, most of the luxuries of the known world were handled by Muslim merchants. There was the extraordinary event known as the Haj, the Pilgrimage, enjoined on every believer, which the Ottomans were destined to control, that huge annual movement of men and women to the Holy Cities of Mecca and Medina across the waterless deserts of Arabia. Islam honoured travellers, too, and when Ibn Battuta, an elderly Moroccan scholar, completed the Haj in 1329, he pressed on to Jerusalem and then, passed by the guilds across Anatolia, saw for himself the gallery of 'Turkish kings' who upheld his faith in this rough borderland.

Among the Turks, it seemed, Islam had recovered some of its original swing. Battuta called Orhan, son of Osman, the greatest king of the lot – prophetically, for in the 1330s Orhan's estate was not so very large. Orhan captured cities with his troops, and provided them with mosques and schools as an Islamic ruler should, but he summered in his tents and was perpetually on the move, just as the old Moroccan remembered him, making a circuit of one hundred fine castles, with an energy that seemed lusty and barbaric, and mesmerising to a visitor from the languid heartlands of the faith.

When they quit the steppe in the ninth century, the turkmen had taken service with the Abbasid caliphs of Baghdad, who taught them Islam. From the Persians they learnt statecraft, and some founded Middle Eastern empires of their own. But the horsemen, herding sheep, moved on; tinged with Islam in many colours, and contemptuous of statecraft and settlement and taxation. The imperial powers of the Middle East ushered them on enthusiastically; for nomads are dangerous to villagers who pay tax.

They were drawn into the rhino's head of Anatolia by the backwash of declining Byzantine power: after the battle of Manzikert in 1071 the eastern borders of Byzantium were soft as yoghurt, which the nomads liked to eat. They were pushed by the Mongols in the thirteenth century, who left devastation in their wake. Pushed or pulled, they always moved west.

By the end of the thirteenth century the Turks had reached the eastern shores of the Mediterranean Sea. Behind them lay a gridlock of emirates, or principalities, which had grown up in the holy war against Byzantium and then, as the frontier swept on, lost touch with their enemies and the nomadic style, and settled instead to tax and cultivation. These little states hustled new arrivals on towards the west quite as eagerly as had the big empires of the interior; so the frontier was continually replenished by new blood. The more venturesome began to build themselves ships, bristling with hemp ropes and cutlasses, to explore the Aegean and wage holy war – on a tiny scale, but of the richest sort – as they plundered the vessels of Christian traders, and raided the coasts of Greece and Thrace.

Osman of Bithynia led the next advance, at the beginning of the fourteenth century. His state was minuscule, and his title of *bey*, or lord, the lowest, but he stood at the crumbling ledge of

Byzantine power – on the very sword-point of Islam, close to the Christian Orthodox city of Bursa, overlooking the Sea of Marmara. At the first sign of success footloose warriors came to join him: hard-bitten pastoralists, shepherds-in-arms, adventurers, Sufis, misfits, landless peasants, runaways; men clambering across the rubble of Byzantine rule, families escaping the cruelty of the Mongols, and warriors impatient with the passivity of the emirs. Even Greek border guards, neglected by the Byzantine authorities, came over to the winning side. They lent Osman a force out of all proportion to the size of his estates, drawing his family destiny on to rule over two seas, two continents and the Holy Cities.

Osman himself, by the rough democracy of the borderlands, was only first among equals. His origins are obscure. His right to the lands he held is shrouded in myth, and he did not report to the nominal Mongol suzerain of Turkic Anatolia. The scant records of the age mention brothers and uncles and sons and cousins, sharing, in the Turkish way, something of Osman's own shadowy authority. Osman summered in his tents, befriended Greeks, and attended mixed marriages. He stood to martial music, as did his sons and their great-grandsons, out of respect – so they said – for the vanished Shepherd Kings, the Seljuks, whose crumbling empire the Mongols had swept away, and whose last delinquent avatar died in Osman's lifetime without anyone troubling to record the date. He fed his followers for nothing, and to each of them he is said to have presented a cup after the manner of the chivalric *futuwwa* brotherhoods whose rules laced Anatolia together at the time. He promised booty and good grazing and joined his force to struggles not especially his own; by night he produced extravagant dreams which reinforced his claim to leadership. With a Greek border warrior as his best man – Michael of the Pointed Beard, who had once rescued him from an attempted murder – he married the daughter of a local seer, Sheikh Edebali.

It was a love-match, by all accounts; but it also wedded Osman to the spiritual energies which lit up the fourteenth-century borderlands. Picking their way across the Islamic civilisations of the Middle East, the Turks had mingled the old steppe traditions of animism and shamanism with Islam of a stripped-down, low-slung, racing sort.

Remote from the great metropolitan centres of Islamic orthodoxy, and encountering much that was strange and heretical, faith on the frontier had an idiosyncratic, rebellious air. As rough country people whose women went unveiled, they preferred holy men who knew how to keep up to the supple intellectuals of the old cities. Tramps and wanderers they liked, fierce talk and wild habits; madmen with their plausible but unexpected utterances, whose ravings were the scorching words of God, direct and necessarily hard to understand.*

Osman's role was to cast the gnostic utterances of the *baba* or holy man into a plan of action, leading his people to better grazing lands, or plunder; otherwise he was no more than one warrior amongst the rest who respected his judgement.

Charismatic sects, chivalric orders, brotherhoods and guilds imposed codes of behaviour which maintained a kind of order in areas where authority such as Osman's was weak. These never quite died away, however orthodox and authoritarian the empire outwardly became. Some turned official, like the Bektashi order of dervishes who later built up a following in the janissary regiments, who drank wine and whose women were unveiled, and eased for many Christians the process of conversion. Others, like the Melami, were to be bitterly proscribed, preaching contempt for the illusions of the world.† Their theme overall was the mystery of life, and the divinity of change: a popular theme for the borders. 'Everything is in process of creation and destruction,' wrote the great frontier mystic Bedreddin. 'There is no here or hereafter; everything is a single moment.' He himself abandoned a prosperous career on the ladder of orthodox Islam to plunge

* Long after the frontier had been joined to empire, and empire had become the respectable guardian of the faith, when the mullahs with a single, outraged voice condemned the syncretic poetry of Mysri Effendi, you could still buy a copy of his poems, issued with this health warning: 'The Mufti has committed them to the Flames, and hath passed this *fetwah*: Whoever speaks and believes as Mysri Effendi, ought to be burnt, except Mysri Effendi alone: for no *fetwah* can be passed upon those that are possessed of Enthusiasm.'

† One anti-state branch of the Bayram order went underground, and ran secret courts and secret prisons.

into the esoteric tumult of the borderland, where he became a great guru, championing the wild freedom of frontier society and convincing many people, Christians among them, that he was the Mahdi, the Coming of the End of the World; so that the Ottomans, who had grown imperial, hanged him from a tree in Serres in 1416.

Contemptuous of authority, certain of victory, with their tents and their sheep and their families in camp, the turks' good fortune can seem like a blind conspiracy of nature, egged on by history. The very old Turkish historians explained their success as the work of greatness running in the blood, and could prove that Osman was related to Noah through fifty-two generations.* It might bear out the old saying that nomads move dreamlike towards the setting sun. Mehmet II thought that the selflessness of men who 'treated their bodies as though they belonged to someone else, as far as pain and danger was concerned' had brought his forebears their perpetual victory; and he shared this belief with his own troops on the eve of the great assault on Constantinople. Gibbon ascribed Ottoman success to the effeminacy of the Greeks. An Englishman during the First World War said that most of the early Ottomans *were* Greeks, and that the Ottoman conquest had therefore the quality of a *risorgimento*, or at least a reformation. A Turk, lecturing in Paris in the 1920s, dismissed the canard and called them Turks, and ultra-Turkish tribal Turks, to boot. A German in the 1930s developed the *gazi* theme, of warriors of the faith imbued with a mystic vision of their enterprise, citing in evidence a very ancient poem and better still a dated inscription on the mosque at Bursa: 'Orhan, son of Osman, gazi, sultan of the gazi, Lord of the Horizons, Burgrave of the Whole World.' The archaeologists announced that the inscription was a pious fraud, and dated it later than the German had supposed, but perhaps what we see in the swirl and swoop of the mounted men is the love of faith, and the pride of truth. Islam collapsed the huge distances which the steppe had pointed

* They proved it in thirty-six before they lost confidence in their reasoning.

up, proclaiming a single God and a single law. As the gazi won their way across Europe their leader had only to bestride his horse to be Lord of the Horizons already; for there was no future not telescoped into the moment at hand, and the ultimate victory of Islam was a reality which waited only for the world to catch up.

2

The Balkans

Between 1320 and the 1390s the Ottomans moved like a ripple through the shallows of Byzantine power, beyond Bursa and Nicaea in Anatolia, and across the Dardanelles into Europe; to Bulgarian Plovdiv, in the Maritsa valley; to Varna on the Black Sea coast, and the isthmus of Greece, and through Nis, the gateway to the upper Balkans; right up to the banks of Central Europe's great defining river, the Danube. They moved so fast, and so suddenly, that they swerved beneath the eye of chroniclers, and no single battle can be dated with precision before 15 June 1389, when they shattered the Serbs at Kosovo, on the Blackbird Field.

South-eastern Europe, the homeland of Byzantine Orthodoxy, was looking for a conqueror. For more than a thousand years the Byzantine Empire had ruled half the known world from Constantinople, and her blend of Christianity, Roman law, and Greek culture had held sway from Ravenna to the Euphrates. Byzantium had made the Balkans what they were: finding a homeland for the Bulgars and the Magyars, allowing other tribes of Pechenegs and Cumans and Avars to disappear, dictating terms to the Slavonic tribes, settling them to her service, binding them up with

Orthodoxy, and teaching them to write. She slapped them down, too, when they grew uppity.

In 1056 the simmering animosity between the Pope in Rome and the Emperor in the East had erupted into the full-blown schism which divides the Orthodox and the Catholic church to this day. Time hardened the dislike. Finally Constantinople was sacked by the army of the Fourth Crusade, diverted for the purpose on its way to the Holy Land by her jealous pander, Venice. On Easter Day 1204, the crusaders, drunk and spattered with Christian blood, placed a prostitute on the patriarchal throne in St Sophia, and danced around her hand in hand. Everything went, the notorious glitter and artifice of the place, the accretions of a thousand years of plunder and piety and civilisation: holy bones lost to France and Florence, sacred icons to the flames, offerings and artworks stolen to adorn the diadems of western European marquises; the jewels of ancient crowns, gold worked by master smiths in the so-called Dark Ages, sacred objects fashioned by Christ's companions, with bits of their hair, and fragments of their teeth, and a feather from Gabriel's wing, which had dropped in the middle of the Annunciation, and the Ark of the Covenant, and the veil of the Temple; St Peter's chains, and the nails used to make the cross, and the trumpets which the priests blew to bring down the walls of Jericho; and splinters of the True Cross. An incalculable store of books had perished in the flames, spreading doubt and mystery through the world. Order was gone; prestige was dimmed. The empire's luck had fled with the famous bronze horses which had graced the Hippodrome for a thousand years, and now pawed at the soft Venetian air of the Piazza San Marco across the sea.

For sixty years, Constantinople was run as a Latin city. One branch of the Byzantine imperial family, the Comneni, withdrew to Trebizond, on the Black Sea coast, to be succoured by Italian trade and protected for centuries to come by those celebrated towers. Another, the Paleologi, watched its opportunity from Nicaea, until in 1267 they had returned, finding Constantinople half in ruins, its land empire lost forever to a rabble of Frankish lords, Venetian providatores, Genoese mahonas and local strongmen. The city itself stood behind its massive walls; its Orthodoxy was maintained; its rulers were still titular Emperors of the Romans; but the wealth was gone, the menace – half holy, and half martial – which lay behind all its diplomatic genius was dispelled. Evocative as candlesmoke, more valuable than gold leaf, a millennial layer of old myth had been scraped away.

Constantinople mouldered after that. The Italian city states – Venice, Genoa, Florence – used the city as a godown in which to store the fruits of their lucrative Black Sea trade. They housed themselves in Pera across the Golden Horn ('as may be compared to Sothwarke from London'); from where they could watch, if they cared, Byzantine emperors bow themselves out in a welter of mutual blindings, insults, rebellions and trickery.

The Byzantine Empire, consequently, was in poor shape for its coming encounter with the Turks. Byzantine Burse fell in 1327, following a decade of harrassment and a hard siege which left the city streets strewn with corpses. Nicaea, where the Creed had been regulated in 325, surrendered in 1329, after five years vainly scanning the horizons for the dust-cloud of a relieving army. The Turks moved on with providential ease. Muslim Karesi wrangled with itself, faltered, and slipped into Ottoman hands in 1344–5, giving Orhan, Osman's son and heir, the southern shores of Marmara. For centuries, where the little Sea of Marmara, swollen with the Black Sea's overflow, bursts through narrow straits into the eastern Aegean, the fortress at Gallipoli on the European side had guarded the seaward approaches to Constantinople. Asia and Europe almost touch across the Dardanelles, the Hellespont of the Greeks, where Helle of myth, fleeing her jealous stepmother, slipped from the back of the Golden Ram and drowned. The Byzantine Greeks had long since enlisted Turkish warriors to help them fight their civil wars, and in 1354, just across these straits, a Byzantine regent plunged into a rebellion against his young imperial charge. The rebel Cantacuzenos applied to Orhan, the nearest Turkish bey, or general, for troops. It seemed as though the Ottomans, having reached the Hellespont, had only to gaze with a little longing at Gallipoli across the straits before the Byzantines proposed to ferry them into Europe.

Orhan's warriors crossed from Asia Minor into Europe in 1354, and no sooner had they discovered Thrace than the hand of Providence intervened again. On the night of 4 March 1356, Gallipoli was struck by an earthquake, just as an Ottoman war party was passing by on its way back to Asia. The Greek castle which guarded the straits fell down like a camel sinking to its knees; the Turks promptly occupied the ruins; and henceforward squadrons of Christian ships, Genoese or Venetian or Byzantine, hovered like taxis to carry them back and forth.

Cantacuzenos' successors were left to cope with the sour fruit of his Ottoman alliance, as a stream of men, women, sheep, children, saints, horses and tents came flooding into Thrace. Flying columns of Turkish horsemen made their way up the Balkan valleys, discovering a shepherd's paradise of cooling water, greenery and shade. Turkish beys began to set themselves up in Thracian fiefdoms when their Ottoman leader was off the scene, defending his dominions in Asia Minor. Dervishes established themselves in lodges, Turkish peasants awarded themselves farmsteads or grazing grounds, and within a generation Thrace had become a country of Turkish settlement. Edirne, the region's capital, the Adrianople of the Greeks, fell to them in 1362.

Successive Byzantine emperors made efforts to secure western aid against the encircling menace of the Turks, even to trading their religious principles for it: but the nap had long gone on the velvet glove, and there was no mailed fist underneath. The aid they sought was never very forthcoming, the conversions they promised were never very sincere, and the citizens themselves ignored the complicated submissions made by their Emperor to the Roman Pope. When Cantacuzenos, now Emperor John V, visited Louis the Great in Buda in 1366, in a fruitless attempt to make him fight the Turks, the Bulgars kidnapped him on his way home. When he toured western capitals four years later to raise men and money for the struggle, the Venetians imprisoned him for debt. Orhan demanded a Byzantine princess from him in 1356.

A gala flotilla of thirty ships carried Theodora away to that stylish barbarian wedding only sixty miles from home. Twenty years later, when the Turks conquered Macedonia, the Byzantines came and begged for food.

The Turks were not the only people with designs on the fading Byzantine Empire in Europe. A hotchpotch of local warlords swaggered in its afterglow, dusting off splendiferous old titles which had languished for centuries in hock to the Greeks: khan and kraal, tsar, voivode, ban and despot. They ruled states as multifarious as their titles, from rickety empires to walled cities. All of them marched to the fading drumbeat of Byzantine civilisation, bolstering their pretensions with strong draughts of fantasy. Shortly before the Turks arrived, Steven Dusan, Kraal of Greater Serbia, 'Emperor of the Rumelians, the Macedonian Christ-loving Tsar', built up an empire along the old trade routes between Ragusa, Adrianople, Belgrade and Salonica. He pampered the magnates at the expense of the peasants, and gathered in their petty realms, but his empire proved to be as loosely strung together as his title. In 1356, obedient to the call of the Byzantine legend, he set out to conquer Constantinople. He died on the march, and the Greater Serbia he had constructed, short-lived but long-shadowed, fell into a host of tiny statelets and six larger principalities. The Ottomans annihilated two of them in 1371 when they first broke into the Maritsa valley. At Nis in 1387, and at Kosovo in 1389 Serb nobles failed to halt the Turks' advance, or Serbia's collapse. The splintered kingdom accepted Turkish vassalage, before it was abolished altogether in 1448.

The Bulgars were fatally driven to pursue the memory of their eleventh-century empire. The Hungarians, sniffing advantage, set up a Ban in the rump of Bulgaria which lasted seven years (although the Hungarians remained the Ottomans' only serious rivals for influence in the region, until 1526). A decadent fantasy ultimately possessed one of the Peloponnesian Despots to establish a platonic court at Mistra. A brigade of Catalan mercenaries ran amok at the beginning of the fourteenth century, and supposed they could conquer Anatolia. Elsewhere bands of Orthodox monks roamed the countryside who believed they could win their way to heaven by bearing arms, and killing people. Impartially, the Ottomans swept them all aside, philosopher-kings and mailed knights, for the Ottomans lived their dreams out on the spot, sword in hand. 'There was no prince or leader: there was no redeemer or saviour amongst the people. The brave hearts of heroic men became the weak hearts of women. Rightly,' wrote a Macedonian monk, with all too real despair, for the Turks stood at the gates of Skopje (Uskub): 'rightly were the dead envied by the living.'

Native rulers had long lived by shift and negotiation, and they fatally underestimated the Ottomans' firmness of purpose, discounting the vast reserves of men the Ottomans could draw on across the Hellespont. Balkan rulers greeted the Turks as a useful source of mercenary troops, as indeed they often were; but they generally failed to recognise the dynastic ambitions of the Ottoman family. One by one, as the Ottomans advanced, the Balkan rulers sought vassalage, and learned too late that it was a one-way street. Shishman of Bulgaria took vassalage with Orhan's son Murad in 1372; but in 1388, encouraged by King Tvrtko's defeat of an Ottoman army which had come to seize Bosnia, he refused to do homage. Within a year Shishman was attacked, defeated, and thoroughly humiliated; his best troops were sent into Anatolia to do battle against Karaman – using firearms for the first time, according to the tradition; and seven years later the Turks had him executed (although his son bore no grudge, turned Muslim and became Ottoman governor of Samsun on the Black Sea). As for King Tvrtko of Bosnia, he proved wilier than them all, for though he had won his battle, he conceded victory.

When the Byzantines asked to have Gallipoli returned to them, the Ottoman Prince Suleyman regretted that Islam knew nothing of retreat. Ottoman confidence was infectious. Citizens came tumbling forward with the keys to castles and towns. Soldiers Christian as well as Muslim asked to join up. In Athens, the Latin Duke accused the Orthodox Metropolitan of plotting a Turkish invasion in 1393. In Salonica in 1374 a jealous son of the Byzantine Emperor took up the governorship and adopted anti-Turkism as the chief plank of his policy; but the Salonicans, totting up the cost of his belligerence, promptly threw him out.*

The very presence of the Ottoman frontier had a melting effect on the lands beyond. At the Turks' approach people fled with all their goods and beasts, leaving behind a sort of frontier wilderness which slid into Turkish hands almost by osmosis. Many of their great victories were reactive, and their advance seemed ordained. Seldom did they pick a vulgar quarrel, or ignore a challenge. Kosovo was the result of a Serb rebellion. Sixty years later, in 1448, the battle was fought again, this time against a Hungarian-backed Serbian army, which had broken a solemn truce and was advancing towards Edirne; Kosovo 1448, like Kosovo 1389, was a far-reaching Ottoman victory.

In 1356 a travelling bishop was shipwrecked on the southern shores of the Sea of Marmara. He was taken to Orhan's summer camp, and royally entertained; but the Turks told him that they were divine instruments whose good fortune proved the truth of Islam; God was their aid, they explained, as Islam went travelling from east to west. A hundred years later a Venetian visitor was informed by the Sultan himself that 'times have changed, so that he would go from the east to the west, as the westerners had gone to the east. The empire of the world must be one faith and one kingdom.' So hypnotic was the Turks' advance, so rascally, duplicitous and divided were their enemies, so beguilingly gentle was the way they tickled their vassals to the halter, so otherworldly did their success appear, that two centuries later Luther himself made the same deduction, and wondered piously aloud whether they should be opposed at all.

The Ottoman Turks were never assimilated by the people they conquered. They won control too fast, their habits were too engrained, their faith too proud, their organisation too advanced, for Balkan Christianity to have anything left to teach them. As for their own people – that swirl of beys and men obeying a call they

* Poor Manuel! For fear of the Turks, the Byzantine Emperor John V in Constantinople refused him shelter within the walls of the ancient city. There was nowhere else for him to go but to the Ottomans themselves, for whom he worked faithfully until 1394.

could barely have pretended to control – the young Ottoman dynasts soon moved away from the rough old notions of equality that characterised the borderlands, and crabwise, from nothing, made sovereignty for themselves. Osman was named in the Friday prayers, a traditional signal of rulership; and the name of Orhan his son appeared on coins. Their dreams gained currency among the frontiersmen. Osman and Orhan ate with their men, saw to the shoeing of their own horses, and dressed so quietly that as late as the beginning of the fifteenth century a stranger at the funeral of Murad II's mother had to have the Sultan pointed out to him. But the authority of the Ottoman princes kept pace with the Turkish conquest. The Danishmends, another Turkish clan, which had flourished in the thirteenth century, had been gazis, too, and had conquered Byzantine cities on the Pontic coast; but when Murad, Orhan's son, had their history translated from the Persian, it was only to hear (for he was illiterate) how they had eventually run themselves into the ground, like a river on the steppe.

Murad I evolved strategies to maintain his rule even while he himself was absent, playing the beys off against each other, moving them on if they showed signs of entrenching themselves in particular regions. Murad consulted experts on rulership, clerics from the old Muslim world.

> When the ulema came to the Ottoman princes, they filled the world with all kinds of trickery. Before them nothing had been known of accounts or cadasters. They also introduced the practice of accumulating money and creating a treasury.

So wrote the gazi chronicler, in disgust. Clerics from the older, orthodox Muslim world, teachers and theologians who could smell success as surely as the Turcomans, came flocking into the Ottoman cities, bringing their mosques and medreses, their Arabic script and orthodox pieties. They brought the tools of sovereignty with them, too. All land, they instructed, belonged to the Sultan; a fifth of all booty. The *spahi*, or horseman, might receive an income from the Sultan's lands, commensurate with his prowess, but not ownership, and he could be moved on at a nod.

In the years before the Ottoman conquest, Balkan society had been quietly feudalising itself: Dusan of Serbia had let his lords exact two days' labour a week from their peasants. Under the Ottomans, peasants – the *reaya* – were only expected to work three days a year for the local spahi; beyond that small impost, and the tithe they paid as Christians amounting to ten per cent of their income, they were undisturbed in either their religion or their cultivation. Those who worked the land were to be protected, like sheep. Peasants came trickling back, if they had ever really left, to discover that all the weight of Balkan feudalism – the requisitions, corvées, serfdom, droit de seigneur – the whole bitter panoply of warriors in their castles and helpless villages clustered at their foot, had been swept away. Turkish overlordship came even to the Orthodox as a kind of liberation.

Between 1300 and 1375 the rank of the Ottoman leader rose from bey to emir, from emir to sultan. Their military renown pulled in fresh Anatolian recruits, eager for plunder and glory under their standard. The Ottomans moved against their Muslim neighbours by marriage, purchase, and often outright war, so that their holdings in Anatolia reached Ankara by the 1380s; they saw to it that jealous emirs in their rear could always be accused, if it came to blows, of undermining the sacred enterprise upon the frontier. Their advance through the Balkans, and against their Anatolian hinterland, pushed them upwards inexorably. They were expected to deal with feudal rulers, and to slap their inky palms to treaty documents,* to marry Balkan princesses, accept emperors as their vassals, and take in defeated Christian troops. When Balkan politicians sought out a representative among the invaders, to deal with this great movement of Islam into the

* The early Ottoman leaders, before Bayezit I, were illiterate. Murad I (r. 1356–89) dipped his thumb and three fingers in the ink, and pressed them to the page. From this simple cognomen, it is said, the Ottomans developed the beautiful calligraphic emblems of subsequent rulers, the *tughras* which followed this basic pattern: a large, ballooning oval at the left to represent the thumb, and three wavy lines above, the marks of the fingers. In 1916 the original Ottoman treaty with Ragusa (Dubrovnik), with Sultan Murad's print on it, could be seen in the museum of the Communal Palace at Dubrovnik.

Balkans, it was the Ottoman ruler they forever wooed, the Ottoman ruler whom they made kingly.

Ottoman power in its early days was a family affair, with sovereignty shared, to a degree, by brothers, uncles, cousins and even female relatives; and when Murad I in 1365 founded the janissaries, the *jeni ceri*, or 'new troop', he extended his family in a remarkable way. Osman and Orhan had taken their fifth of booty, as the Koran permits a leader to do, in the form of land and gold; Murad took up his fifth of the captives, too. Slave armies were common in the old Islamic world, and the men of the frontier knew just where to pin the blame. 'It was a pair of theologians who introduced this innovation,' says the early Turkish chronicler, gazi to his marrow; and we can almost hear, across the centuries, his windy sigh of exasperation.

By the time of Kosovo, 1389, Sofia and Nis and the outskirts of Varna on the Black Sea coast were in Turkish hands, and Murad's vassals ruled to the banks of the Danube, their loyalty burnished by the presence of Turkish garrisons at Nicopolis and Sumen.

In the Sultan's tent at Kosovo in 1389 a Serb called Milosh Obravitch, long since immortalised in ballad, drew a dagger and stabbed Murad, wounding him fatally. Three times the assassin made an effort to regain his horse before they hacked him down. And when Murad's two sons returned to camp, Prince Bayezit promptly had his brother executed and took up the sultanate on the spot.

3

Thunderbolt

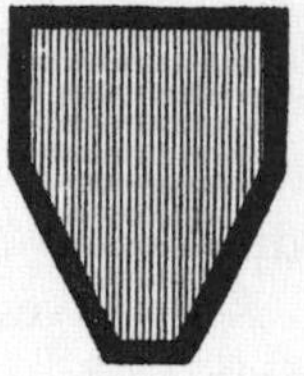

Bayezit is known in Turkish history as Yilderim, 'Thunderbolt', though whether because of his lightning marches, or the speed with which he seized the sultanate, or his ferocious temper, nobody is sure. He opened his reign with a succession of dazzling exploits. He pushed back a coalition of Anatolian beys. In the Holy City of Constantinople the Byzantine Emperor, now his vassal, gave over one of the churches to be a mosque, surrounded by a Muslim merchant quarter, equipped with its own religious judge, a *kadi*.

Murad had been the illiterate son of an emir. Bayezit was the son of a sultan. His mother was a Byzantine princess, born of that city where imperial grandeur and its assumptions had been ingrained for a thousand years. The ulema mistrusted him. He named his children after major religions. The Pope opened a correspondence with him, though he might have been surprised by Bayezit's ambition to make the high altar of St Peter's a manger for his horse. Bayezit grubbed up the buffer state between his domains and Hungary by executing Shishman of Bulgaria; he dressed like a Greek, practised buggery like one; drank wine; and asked the Caliph in Cairo to make him Sultan of Rum. He seems to have enjoyed having enemies. 'For this I was born – ' he told a shrinking Jean de Nevers, hefting his scimitar, 'to bear arms and to conquer whatever is before me,' and he bundled emirs from their emirates until he could claim to rule from the banks of the Danube to the far Euphrates.

In 1396 he laid siege to Constantinople, with 10,000 vassal troops. News reached him there of the arrival of a foreign army on his Danubian frontier, and he swiftly raised the siege and marched north-west to combat what proved to be the last European crusade to the East.

An army of mainly French crusaders had set out in imitation of their knightly forebears two centuries earlier, to drive Islam from Europe.* In Buda they joined up with the Teutonic Knights and the Hungarian army of young King Sigismund. A month later they were all at Nicopolis on the Danube, boasting they could hold up the sky with their lances. The Ottoman garrison commander refused to yield; perhaps he had learned of the massacre of the garrison which surrendered at Widdin days earlier. The crusaders settled down to a siege. Bayezit, someone suggested, was far away; 'in Cairo in Babylon'. They prepared to wait for him, and ordered the tables spread.

The knights had drunk deep by the time scouts reported the appearance of a Turkish army in the vicinity. The Hungarians knew their enemy. With the support of the French commander, Sigismund proposed a cautious advance led by the Hungarian infantry; but the mass of knights had never much trusted the Hungarians, whom they now suspected of devising a stratagem to rob them of the honours of victory. Before anyone could change their minds 6,000 knights were charging uphill, and laying into a swarm of barbarous horsemen who wilted and parted at their thunderous advance.

A very old Turkish trick. Somewhere ahead, the French supposed, lay the undefended Turkish camp. 'They said, "Aha!

* The old Duke of Bavaria advised his son not to 'carry arms against people and countries which have never done anything to us, with no reason to go there but vainglory', but to go into Friesland if he wanted to travel and conquer his inheritance.

Aha!" ' recalled the Rabbi Joseph, drily, 'but their joy was quickly gone.'

Having far outstripped the Hungarian infantry, the knights crested the rise and found themselves face to face with a force of 60,000 men. Their charge took them crashing and stumbling into the centre. The Turkish wings rolled them up, 'the horse of Bayezit and his hosts and chariots'; the light horsemen closed in from behind, and grim janissaries of the royal guard plucked them from the saddle one by one.

Later the French blamed the Hungarians for having struck a defensive attitude from the first. The Hungarians accused the French of hastiness. Schiltberger, a German infantryman who was captured and turned Turk, serving thirty years as a janissary before escaping home to Germany, thought Sigismund had been advancing when the Voivode of Wallachia chose suddenly to desert him, and the Ottoman side was bolstered by a detachment of Serbian troops. But it was a very academic post-mortem.

A lucky few got away. King Sigismund and the Grand Master of the Knights of St John fled to a Venetian galley on the Danube, which plied its oars for the Black Sea; others struggled across the river and thence north on foot into the Carpathian mountains, where they were robbed and beaten. In Paris that winter a few bedraggled, half-wild men who entered the capital in ones and twos were told to shut their mouths, or hang. It was solemnly declared that Nicopolis should not be mentioned in the King's Council, for the rumours were terrifying. Not until Christmas Eve did a French negotiator, Jacques de Helly, arrive at the palace with incontrovertible proof.

The crusaders had butchered their own Turkish prisoners blithely enough on the morning of the battle. Bayezit, grimly surveying his casualties on the field, ordered a massacre of his own, sparing only twenty-four of the richest dressed knights for ransom, and a handful of boys for his own army. Marshal Boucicault was given the grisly privilege of choosing two more men to be spared out of the hundreds of knights who were led before the Sultan; the commoners were dispatched without review. Blood flowed until vespers, and when the Sultan agreed to hear pleas of clemency from his own men, 10,000 prisoners had already been decapitated. A detachment of the Ottoman army was sent into Wallachia to punish its prince, a vassal of the Sultan, while the light horsemen who had lured the knights to their doom followed the Danube up its course without fear of opposition, and raided as far as Styria in Austria, taking 16,000 captives.

The survivors were marched over the Balkans to that castle at Gallipoli which became their prison; and one day they were all brought out and lined up along the shore to watch a Venetian galley row by, carrying the King of Hungary into the Mediterranean, and safety. The Turks shouted at him to come and rescue his men, 'but they did not do him any harm, and so he went away'.

Bayezit's own fantastic doom was sealed in a decade. Headstrong and arrogant, he never quite understood the natural limits which his forebears had been careful to respect. They had loaded up their conquests east and west like saddlebags, careful to secure one front before campaigning on the other, keeping their enemies anxious and divided. Murad by 1389 held 101,000 square miles of territory, almost exactly divided between the two continents; but Bayezit gobbled such huge tracts of Anatolia that by 1402 he ruled over 267,000 square miles, of which two-thirds were in Asia. He made many enemies among the old ruling families he displaced, and he was careless of the loyalty of the men he took into his service.

Nemesis sprang upon him in the shape of a Tartar warrior whose power and energy surpassed his own. Tamerlane the Great, Marlowe's Tamburlaine, was born in Samarkand in 1346, and by the age of forty he ruled an empire which stretched across Central Asia. Marching south to the invasion of Syria in 1398 he was met by a deputation of exiled Anatolian emirs, along with ambassadors from Constantinople, Genoa, Venice and even Charles VI of France, who urged him to attack the Ottoman Empire. This he refused to do; but he did pluck a few border cities from it *en passant*.

It was not in Bayezit's nature to swallow the insult. He wrote fiery, scornful letters to Tamerlane, his own name in a golden flourish, with Tamerlane's below, very small and black; and rashly promised support for his ally Kara Yusuf, Lord of the Black Sheep, who had placed himself beyond the reach of mercy by attacking the caravan for Mecca. Tamerlane, on taking Sivas, had the Ottoman garrison and Bayezit's eldest son executed in 1399; three thousand Christian Armenian soldiers of the town were buried alive.

A confrontation was inevitable. Bayezit sought battle eagerly enough. Tamerlane approached the conflict with relative indifference, but total concentration. Bayezit disposed his troops with sullen carelessness on the day of battle, outside Ankara in 1402. Tamerlane's army was twice the size of his, and had recently been paid; with it were emirs who knew the terrain well. Bayezit, though, preferred to save his coin, 'reserving it for Tamerlane', as one of his generals bitterly remarked, 'as surely as if the head of that monarch were stamped on it all already'; and on the morning of battle he led his men on a huge hunting expedition in which 6,000 men were said to have perished from fatigue. Returning to their camp, they found that Tamerlane had shrewdly occupied it in their absence, seizing the only local water-source. Out of sheer thirst Bayezit's shattered troops were forced to give battle right away.

His Anatolian troops and Tartars deserted to their emirs at Tamerlane's side as soon as the battle began. Fighting into the sun, choked with dust beaten up from the arid ground by the hooves of hundreds of thousands of Mongol horsemen, shaken by the onslaught of Tamerlane's Indian elephant corps, hopelessly outnumbered, his own right wing now turning upon him, the Sultan with his janissaries and vassal troops fought until nightfall on a patch of rising ground. His vizier swept up Suleyman, Bayezit's chosen heir, and the trusty Serbs covered their retreat. His other sons Isa and Musa saved themselves, with their personal troops. Mehmet was carried to Amasya by its old emir. At dusk the Sultan made an effort to escape, but he was spotted and ridden down by the Titular Khan of Jagetai. Only Mustafa, among Bayezit's sons, was unaccounted for. Tamerlane ordered a close inspection of the battlefield, but his corpse was never found, and his fate remained a mystery. 'On whose account,' wrote the historian, 'thirty men of that name perished.'

Tamerlane used his captive magnanimously until Bayezit's prickly hauteur proved too much for him, and he was placed in a cage, too small for standing upright, and dragged in the wake of Tamerlane's retinue. His wife Despina was made to serve naked at the victor's table. Nobody offered to ransom the prisoners, and perhaps no one was sorry when Bayezit eventually dashed out his brains on the bars of his cage.

Before he left the area, Tamerlane made a lunge at Bursa which sent Prince Suleyman scurrying for cover in Europe. The conqueror took Izmir, the western Anatolian base of the Knights of St John, which Bayezit had never managed to do; and there, finding the pyramid he built with the severed heads of the garrison and the population combined too small, he had the heap repacked, with alternate layers of heads and mud. As he left the region the nervous citizens of Ephesus sent their children to meet him, singing, but the gruesome Tartar growled, 'What is this noise?' and had his cavalry ride them all down; then he went on his way, and he managed to die with his boots on, heading for China, in his seventy-first year.

The young Ottoman Empire could have collapsed. The emirs, exulting, galloped back to their palaces, rentrolls, and old feuds. The gazis returned to their old frontier freedoms. The Christians of the west, on news of Bayezit's defeat, relaxed and forgot about the Turks. Byzantium heaved a sigh of relief, and bustled about diplomatically to regain some of her lost domains. The surviving Ottoman brothers began to fight out a devious civil war amongst themselves, prodded on by the emirs, the gazis, the money men of Bursa, the theologians, the Byzantines, and the Italian city-states, all eager to prolong the conflict. Over the next ten years a brother would now and then be thrashed and executed, and Prince Suleyman, who once used three battalions of dead Serbs as a table for his banquet, and whose chances looked the best, was the very first to go. Somewhere Isa disappeared. The emirates overplayed their hand; backed Mehmet as the weakling; found him more powerful than they had hoped, tried to back off, but all too late.

Bayezit's fate, and the interregnum which had followed, revealed both the strengths and weaknesses of the Ottoman state. Bayezit's authority still descended from the stirrup. But the empire had outgrown the ability of a single man to govern it personally, and the larger it grew, the more local loyalties threatened to prevail over loyalty to the new dynasty. Physically it was hard for the Sultan to meet threats as they arose on distant borders, and the journey between them was long and hard.

On the other hand, his enemies were no more united than before, and nobody proved very capable of taking advantage of Ottoman disarray. The idea of Ottoman dominion had taken root, and the easy rhythm of Turkish conquest soon resumed under Mehmet I and his son Murad II. By 1430 the sultans had restored the empire Bayezit had gambled away thirty years before. The Ottomans did not often repeat their mistakes. 'I am bound to be equal to the needs of both continents,' Murad's son Mehmet II reminded the Byzantines, whose city, of course, lay between them, like a hinge.

4

The Siege

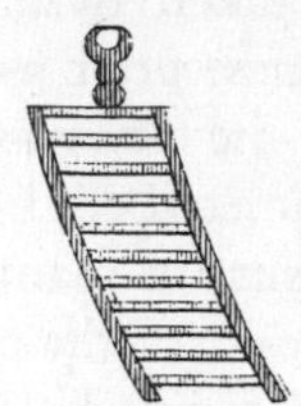

The Turks seized Constantinople from the Greeks in 1453. For more than a century the Ottomans had been extending their rule over most of Balkan Europe and the western reaches of Anatolia. They controlled the straits through which the Black Sea syphons into the Mediterranean, and the problem of ferrying their forces to and fro to meet threats in the east or the west no longer troubled them. They had at times relied on other navies to ferry them across; but neither Genoa, Venice nor the Byzantines themselves, when the moment came, had been willing to forgo the benefits that might bring. Lately, with the assembly of a fleet, and a few well-placed castles capable of stopping with cannon anyone who braved the straits without permission, the conquest of Constantinople itself had become technically superfluous. The Ottomans had enveloped the city like an oyster its grit.

In 1452, against much opposition, the new young Sultan Mehmet II proposed the siege. For Mehmet the risk of failure was high. The young Sultan was not popular. His reputation was already tarnished. Turkish assaults on the city had failed before, baffled mostly by the strength of the walls and the difficulty of isolating a place so easily succoured from the sea. The gazis mistrusted the plan, for Constantinople was an imperial centre of the sort they most detested and despised, an administrative capital with a thousand-year-old log-book. Candarli Halil, a long-serving vizier whose family had monopolised the vizierate for years, liked to remind the young Sultan of his father's friendly relations with the Byzantines. Halil was nicknamed 'the Greek' and the story went round that he had taken Byzantine bribes. It is hard to imagine what the Byzantines, poor as church mice, might have bribed him with; but after the city was taken he was executed.

Constantinople, as Mehmet II told his men, was 'no longer a city but in name, an enclosure of plants and vineyards, worthless houses and empty walls, most of them in ruins'; it was living on ceremonial and borrowed time. There were sixty churches in Constantinople on the eve of the conquest, from the still magnificent cathedral of St Sophia to roofless chapels in half-abandoned parishes in remote corners within the walls, where once teeming streets were turned under the plough. Byzantium had witnessed, in its proud poverty, a wondrous rekindling of intellectual life, and its libraries were still interesting; but there was a brain drain to Italy and the point at which it could afford to arm for its own defence had long passed. There were just 4,983 men, including monks, capable of bearing arms – a figure so lamentable that the Emperor Constantine was obliged to keep it secret; and the outcome of the assault seems, in retrospect, a foregone conclusion.

Mehmet, though, sensed the city's power. Perhaps, he warned, she might rouse 'the whole west against us, from the ocean and Marseilles, and the western Gauls, the inhabitants of the Pyrenees and Spain, from the Rhine river, the Celts and the Cantiberians and the Germans'. Certainly the Byzantines were to discover, at the eleventh hour, all the pride and determination of their finest years, under an emperor, the last, whose nobility almost effaced the memories of indignity and squalor; and they fought for the city as they had never fought for the empire.

It was rash of the Byzantines, though, to remind the young Sultan of the stipend his father had always paid for the maintenance of a pretender in their city. Mehmet promptly stopped the pension, and had all Greeks expelled from the cities of the lower Struma. On 15 April 1452, he began building a castle on the Bosphorus, on land that was still technically Byzantine, designing it and even helping the workmen build it himself. Greek protests were dismissed. Mehmet paid no attention when the Greeks imprisoned all the Turks who could be found in Constantinople; he paid no attention when they were released. He ignored an embassy laden with gifts, which begged that at least the Byzantine villages on the Bosphorus should not be harmed. When his castle was finished, on 31 August 1452, he spent three days encamped by the walls of Constantinople, examining its fortifications. He dubbed his castle Rumeli Hisar, 'the Strait Cutter', and promptly sank a Venetian ship which defied his order to stop: the crew were decapitated, but its captain, Antonio Rizzi, was impaled, and his body exposed at the roadside. As Rizzi's body mouldered in the rain, the Byzantines made their last, desperate appeals to the west.

Venice, Genoa and Ragusa were too deeply involved in Ottoman trade, too much at daggers drawn themselves, to offer much assistance. Venice told her commanders in the Levant to protect Christians, but to offer no provocation to the Turks. The Podesta of the Genoese community in Pera, across the Golden Horn, was told to act as he thought best, but at all events to avoid antagonising the Turks. The Ragusans let it be known, *sotto voce*, that if a grand coalition could be raised, they would certainly join it; but the possibility seemed remote. The King of Naples, with all sorts of Greek entanglements and ambitions, sent ten ships into the Aegean which cruised there for several months, and then went home again. The Pope persuaded the Holy Roman Emperor, when he came to be crowned in Rome in 1452, to issue a stern ultimatum to the Sultan; but the only real ultimatum at the time was the one Mehmet sent to the Byzantines on 5 March 1453, demanding the immediate surrender of the city.

Looking down over their ancient city walls, the Byzantines counted 300,000 men, at the very least, encamped around them. Mehmet brought the whole of his empire out to the assault. For months the craftsmen of the empire had been making helmets, shields, armour, javelins, swords, arrows. Engineers made ballistas and battering-rams. All leave was cancelled; thousands of irregular troops were enrolled; a Serbian detachment was brought up to the walls; the 12,000 janissaries were stationed around the Sultan himself; the Sea of Marmara was patrolled by a Turkish fleet, hurriedly assembled, some of it new, much of it recaulked and old, but its very existence a surprise to the defenders, low-lying triremes, the smaller biremes, the yet smaller and lighter long-boats, the oared great galleys, the heavy sailing barges used for transport, and a host of messenger vessels, sloops and cutters.

In front of the Sultan's tents stood the new-fangled machine whose appearance changed the nature of medieval warfare, and had possibly tipped the scales in favour of this assault on the battle-scarred old city. In the summer of 1452 a Transylvanian cannon-founder had offered his services to the Emperor, who could neither afford the salary he sought, nor provide him with the material he needed. Urban then went to Mehmet who offered him four times as much and every assistance, too; and in three months he cast the cannon which sank the Venetian ship from the walls of Rumeli Hisar. The monster he unveiled in January at Edirne was twice as big: 28 feet long, the bronze of the barrel 8 inches thick, firing balls which weighed 12 cwt, which had to be dragged, attended by seven hundred men, on a special carriage drawn by thirty oxen. When it was first tested, the citizens of Edirne were told to expect a loud bang, and not to panic: the ball travelled a mile and sank six feet into the ground. Two hundred men immediately went to level the road to Constantinople. The bridges were strengthened. The numbers of oxen were doubled. On 7 February 1453, it was settled in place, this stone-thrower 'of the newest kind, a strange sort, unbelievable when told of, but as experience demonstrated, able to accomplish anything', to await the Byzantine answer to Mehmet's ultimatum.

The Byzantines had cleared the moats, repaired the walls, gathered together all the city's arms. There were still some Catalans about, who organised themselves under their consul, and roped in some Catalan sailors, too. A Castilian nobleman with a claim to imperial descent arrived, calling the Emperor cousin, and a German, doubtless 'from the Rhine river' as Mehmet had predicted, calling himself Johannes Grant. There was even a full-blown Turk – the Ottoman pretender, Mehmet's uncle Orhan, who offered the services of his entire household.

The Venetians in the city put themselves at the Emperor's disposal in spite of their Senate's equivocal orders, 'for the honour of God and the honour of all Christendom', as a merchant captain bluffly told the Emperor. Various Genoese, too, made their way to the city; and Giovanni Giustiniani Longo, of one of the republic's best families, arrived in January with 700 men and a reputation which induced the Emperor to make him putative lord of Lemnos. With more immediate effect he was appointed to command the defence of the whole of Constantinople's land walls.

There were land walls and sea walls to this city. Constantinople resembled the head of a dog, pointing east on a triangular peninsula. Over its nose the channel of the Golden Horn meets the Bosphorus; its throat is caressed by the Sea of Marmara; and the land walls erected by Theodosius in the fifth century are slung across as a sort of huge loose collar from ear to chest. The waterside walls were of single thickness: those of the Marmara shore reared up abruptly from the sea, dotted with reefs and shoals, pierced here and there by gates, and opening into two fortified harbours; those of the Golden Horn skirted by a foreshore which had built up over the centuries, covered with godowns, but protected from all possibility of assault by a massive chain – a chain to all chains what Urban's monster was to cannon – which could be hooked up across the mouth of the Horn to prevent the entry of any ship. From this harbour seven ships, six from Crete, one from Venice, slipped perfidiously away one February night, taking with them 700 Italians. The rest, mainly sailing ships without oars, rode stolidly at anchor, twenty-six equipped for fighting; on the northern side the Peran merchant ships were anchored beneath the walls of the Genoese colony, which remained strictly neutral throughout the siege.

These walls, the chain, the reefs and the speed of the currents made a seaborne attack unlikely. The massive collar on the landward side defied assault by its very bulk. A little nub of territory like the dog's ear jutted out from the walls where they climbed steeply uphill from the Golden Horn, and comprised the old suburb of Blachernae, long since incorporated into the city and strengthened by the fortifications of the royal palace which were built up into it. From there the walls ran unbroken to the Marmara side of the peninsula, treble walls, if you counted the crenellated breastwork which ran the whole distance, and divided the 60-foot-wide fosse, or moat – for it could in parts be flooded – from the outer wall, 25 feet high, and studded with square towers. Behind this a clear space of 40 to 60 feet divided the outer from the inner walls, fully 40 feet in height, with 60-foot-high towers, some of them square, some octagonal, but all cunningly staggered to fall between the towers of the outer wall.

If this monstrous system of defence had any weakness at all, it was generally supposed to be somewhere about the Lycus valley, where the ground dropped about a hundred feet to a little river feeding into the city through a conduit under the walls; and it was here that the Sultan's tents were spread, the janissaries were grouped, and the great cannon peered with its Cyclopean eye at the Venetian sailors, in their distinctive costumes, parading the battlements at the Emperor's request to remind the Sultan that Venetians, too, had mobilised for the city's defence, and meant to stick it out.

The Ottomans, for their part, dug in against the whole length of the land walls behind a trench and an earthen wall, topped with a palisade. Baltoghlu, a Bulgarian renegade in command of the fleet, was ordered to see that nobody reached the city on the Marmara side, and above all to force a passage through the chain that covered the entrance to the Golden Horn.

On 6 April the guns roared for the first time, with a noise that made women faint, and brought down a small section of the walls, which the defenders managed to repair overnight. Two small castles still held by the Greeks were bombarded into submission: the survivors, both those who surrendered, and those who were captured in the smoking ruins, were impaled as a warning to the men on the city walls, while a castle on one of the largest islands in the Sea of Marmara was burnt, its garrison put to death, and all the inhabitants of the island rounded up and sold into slavery, which Baltoghlu deemed to be their proper punishment for permitting resistance on their soil.

Mehmet's big cannons could be fired only seven times a day; they slipped in the mud and rolled from their carriages; but with constant attention they kept up their work of demolition for six weeks. After initial setbacks on the Golden Horn, where ten Christian ships guarded the boom and actually made a sally upon Baltoghlu's fleet, Ottoman cannon placed on Pera Point sank one galley with a single shot, and the ships bustled away from the boom, further up the Horn, for safety.

The defenders worked round the clock, soldiers, civilians, women, to repair the damage done to the outer walls, stockading it in ruinous parts with planks and sacks of earth, using barrels as crenellations, everywhere heaving bales of wool over the walls, and draping them in sheets of leather, to muffle the effects of the cannonballs. A night assault in which the rush of janissaries, archers and javelin-throwers was lit by flares, whipped up by the crash of cymbals and the beat of drums, was repulsed in four hours' hand-to-hand fighting in which the Christians did not lose a single man, so stout was their armour.

A convoy of three papal galleys hired from Genoa, with a Byzantine transport laden with Sicilian corn, took advantage of a fair southerly wind, and the preoccupation of the Turks with the boom across the Horn, to run in towards the city across the Sea of Marmara. The defenders spotted them at the same time as the Turks themselves, and everyone was in a position to view the engagement that soon ensued. By afternoon the high-built Christian ships were gaining against the whole of the Turkish fleet, shouldering the low galleys aside as they made the most of a full wind which had carried them almost round the point, to the mouth of the Horn, when it suddenly dropped. Their sails flapped; one of the weird eddies of the Bosphorus began to drag them, slowly but surely, away from the walls of Constantinople, and towards the Pera shore, where the Sultan himself – now urging his horse into the water, now bellowing instructions to his admiral, now encouraging, now cursing – seemed ready to take the ships on personally.

Still the struggle continued, the sea so thick with Turkish vessels that its course was sometimes hard to gauge. By mid-afternoon the stricken ships had collected a positive infestation of Turkish vessels, clinging to their sides with grappling irons and hooks, aiming to carry them by assault or fire. One Genoese ship was surrounded by five triremes, another by thirty longboats, the third by forty troopships; but the lumbering Byzantine galleass, made more for corn than war, seemed to concentrate the Turks' efforts. Baltoghlu himself ran his ship into the prow of the big transport, and around her the fighting seemed fiercest, wave after wave of boarders steadily repulsed, the Byzantine weapon of Greek fire – the equivalent of napalm – used to deadly effect, the Turkish galleys forever entangling their oars, or losing them to missiles dropped from overhead by the much higher Christian vessels. The Genoese wore excellent armour, and had provided themselves with great tuns of water to extinguish fires, and by late afternoon, perceiving the especial danger to the Byzantine transport, which was less well armed, and running low on weapons, the Genoese commanders managed somehow to form a sort of floating, four-towered fortress by lashing their ships together. They were still fighting when evening came, but the hearts of the Byzantines on the walls sank as they saw yet more Turkish ships move in to take their place against the heaving, splintered, drifting knot of Christian ships. Even the Sultan seemed to regain some of his calm as the end approached.

Just as the sun began to set, the wind regathered from the north – and the sails of the Christian ships billowed out, the ties were slipped, and one by one they crashed again through the mêlée of galleys, and at last into the safety of the boom.

One of the sheikhs wrote immediately to Mehmet, warning him that the humiliation of defeat was already encouraging people to say that he lacked authority and judgement. Baltoghlu was publicly condemned as a traitor, a coward and a fool, and was saved from execution only by the testimony of his officers, who bore witness to his resolution and bravery, so that he was merely bastinadoed, stripped of all his offices, deprived of all his worldly goods, and sent, half-blinded by a stone hurled from one of his own ships, to obscure exile. Mehmet had now to achieve some bold success: it was his bad luck not to be present when a large chunk of wall collapsed, over which, the defenders thought, a general assault ordered immediately would surely have succeeded; but it was his forethought which made possible a miraculous stroke against the city, from which it was doomed never to recover.

At the outset of the siege, Mehmet had begun to prepare a road running round the back of the Genoese colony at Pera, over the hill from the Bosphorus to the Valley of the Springs on the northern shore of the Golden Horn. With the failure of the fleet uppermost in his mind, Mehmet ordered the work to be speeded up; cannon played harder on the boom, workmen carried on their tasks by firelight, and the black smoke which drifted across the Bosphorus concealed all his activity until it was too late.

When the stratagem was finally revealed, a sort of groan went up from the watchers on the walls above the Horn. Over the hill on the opposite shore came the first of the Ottoman ships, a small *fusta*, or longboat, its oars meticulously sweeping the thin air in time to the beat, its sails spread; while to the wail of fifes, the screech of metal wheels, the creak of the massive cradles, the cracking of whips and lowing of oxen, seventy ships followed her down the hill and splashed into the waters of the Horn.

The city's flank was turned. A squabble between the Venetians, who had proposed a lightning assault on the Turkish fleet by night, and the Genoese, who heard of it and insisted on joining in, postponed the attack until all secrecy had been lost, and it was rebuffed by a well-prepared barrage which sank two Christian ships and cost her ninety sailors – some of whom, swimming ashore, were beheaded in full view of the defenders, who beheaded 260 Turkish prisoners on the walls in reply. The Italians' rivalry became so intense that the Emperor summoned the Venetian and Genoese leaders, and told them that 'the war outside our gates is enough for us'.

A huge tower was erected overnight, and inched forward across the fosse while men underneath worked to fill it up; although the defenders managed to fire the tower and clean out the ditch again, the towers mushroomed around their walls. More invisibly, a detachment of Serbs from the silver mines of Nrvo Brdo began to tunnel beneath the walls in various places, their activities countered by the imperturbable Johannes Grant, who flooded the tunnels and fired their props. The mining stopped when several Serbs were caught and tortured to reveal the positions of a number of tunnels around the walls, at least one of which, its entrance cunningly concealed by one of those wooden towers, might never have been found otherwise; and the headless bodies were hoicked over the walls.

A tiny brigantine came dodging in across the boom: at first the defenders took her for the vanguard of the relieving fleet once promised from the West, but she was only a ship that had sailed out, disguised as a Turkish vessel, twenty days before, to look for help: and she had found none. Her captain had then asked the crew what they wished to do, and one dissenter was silenced by the others, who told him that their duty was to return to the Emperor, and give him the news. Constantine wept as he thanked them.

But Mehmet, of course, seven weeks already into his siege, could not know the news the Venetian brigantine had brought; indeed, there were rumours that a Venetian fleet was already in Chios. An embassy from Hungary informed him that the three-year armistice he had signed was no longer to be considered binding after a change of regent there. In seven weeks not a wall had been crossed, and if the defenders were weak and tired – so weak and tired that the Emperor himself actually fainted during an interview in which his ministers urged him to escape, and organise resistance from outside the doomed city – the troops were growing restive, and Mehmet's prestige was in decline. He had been clever to engineer the swoop of the fleet into the Golden Horn; but the boom was still in place; no landing had been effected; Constantinople remained unseized. It was the very nightmare which Greek Halil had predicted months before.

On 25 May, Mehmet offered to raise the siege if the Byzantines would pay him 100,000 gold bezants as annual tribute, or if they preferred, leave with all the baggage they could carry under a guarantee of safe conduct. To the Byzantines the sum was too great; the guarantee, it was felt, too slender, and the Emperor offered instead to hand over everything he owned, barring Constantinople itself. It was all he did own, as it happened, and the Sultan replied that the choice between surrender, death, or conversion to Islam now lay with the Byzantines. In a council the Grand Vizier Halil Pasha demanded an end to the siege, on the grounds of the risk its continuation carried for the young Sultan and his empire. But Zaganos Pasha, and many of the younger beys, argued him down, as Mehmet wished. He told Zaganos to go among the troops and gauge their mood: and Zaganos returned shortly with the news that everyone wanted an immediate all-out attack.

For two nights the Turkish armies worked by flares to fill up the fosse, to the skirl of fifes and trumpets. At midnight on Sunday, the lights went out, and silence fell on the camp. Monday was spent in prayer and preparation, while the Sultan toured the camp, encouraging his men. There would be the three days of looting, as enjoined by Koranic law upon warriors of the faith who took a city by the sword after it had refused the customary demand to surrender. Mehmet swore by eternal God and His Prophet and by the four thousand prophets and by the souls of his father and his children, that the treasure would be fairly shared out. The city was not impregnable – did not the Tradition declare: 'They shall conquer Qostantinya, glory be to the prince and to the army that shall achieve it'? The enemy now were exhausted and few, he said, and low on ammunition and food; while the Italians would not die for a country not their own. His officers must be brave, and maintain order, for tomorrow he would send wave upon wave of gazis to the attack. He told the commanders to rest in their tents, and he outlined the plan of battle to his generals. Then he ate, and went to bed.

All the while as Mehmet carefully marshalled his army round the walls, and Constantine, as carefully, disposed his meagre troops within them, the assembled talismans of the city's fortunes, those which had escaped the sack of 1204, united in proclaiming the city's desolation. Icons were observed to weep and the holy picture of the Mother of God, carried in procession, slipped into the mud where it defied every effort to raise it again. Sudden storms blew in off the sea. The gutters ran blood red. God removed Himself from the city which was, perhaps even more than Rome, dedicated to His image: He stole away under cover of a thick and unseasonal fog which enveloped the entire peninsula in early March. When the fog lifted, everyone saw light play fitfully around the dome of the Church of the Holy Wisdom, so that the citizens were disturbed, and Mehmet sought reassurances from holy men. From the walls, the defenders saw lights which never were explained, bobbing about in the dark distance beyond the Turkish camp. They did not prove to be the campfires of a Hungarian army. On 23 May the full moon suffered a partial eclipse and shone like a crescent in the night sky.

On the eve of the planned assault, a sweeter, sadder miracle occurred within the old Church of the Holy Wisdom, where for months, by the terms of Constantine's last appeal for western help, clergy devoted to the Latin rite had held sway, so that no Greek of conscience had been able to bring himself to enter its defiled portals. In the evening, after the Emperor had thanked the Italians, and reminded the Greeks of their duty to Emperor, family, faith and country, a service was held, and everyone came, Catalan and Orthodox Greek, schismatic bishops and the unionist cardinal, Catholic and Orthodox priests, and all the people who were not at the walls received communion from whoever chose to administer it, and made confession, to whoever was ready to hear it.

But this impromptu and emotional reunion of the churches could do nothing to deflect the city's fate. Three hours before dawn, three pashas at the head of 50,000 men apiece led separate attacks, met by a thin line of defenders. All the bells of the city were rung, and even nuns came to the walls with stones and water, while many people made their way back to the Church of Holy Wisdom, praying for the fulfilment of an old prophecy. For it had been said that though an infidel army would enter the city and reach the church itself, there an angel would appear and beat them back.

Mehmet flung his irregulars first against the walls, a horde of Turks, Slavs, Hungarians, Kurds, Yuruks, Germans, even Italians and Greeks, who were urged on with whips and maces while the janissaries closed ranks behind them, to cut down anyone who tried to run away. For two hours they obeyed the Sultan's promise to wear the defenders down, before they were retired in favour of professional Anatolian infantry, each of them eager to be the first believer onto the walls. Like the irregulars, they suffered from crowding – so many could be flung from toppling ladders at once, or maimed by a single stone dropped from above; and even when a breach was suddenly opened in the stockade by a roar from the great cannon, the Anatolians pouring in were surrounded by Byzantine troops with the Emperor at their head, and beaten back in that confined space with terrible slaughter.

So the honour would fall to the Sultan's men, the janissaries. They advanced now at the double, but in perfect order, their bands so loud that they could be heard across the Bosphorus, Mehmet himself going with them to the fosse. From there he urged them on, as line by line added to the preparations for scaling the walls, and retired neatly.

Giustiniani – proud, energetic, brilliant Giustiniani – 'what would I not give,' the Sultan had exclaimed, 'to have that man in my service?' – was shot through the breastplate at close range, and in great pain and fear of death, he insisted – despite the pleas of the Emperor himself, who rushed to his side – on being carried back to his ship. The Genoese saw him go, and fell back too, in utter confusion. 'The city is ours!' Mehmet cried, and the janissaries crowded to the walls.

The outer wall was lost. Greeks pulling back got trapped under the inner wall in a deadly fusillade from the janissaries overhead. The Turks were already clambering onto the inner walls when they saw their flag flying from a tower in the northern sector of the walls – for chance had led to the discovery of a postern gate, left open after a sally; and it was through this little unguarded crack in the walls that fifty Turks broke through, as if ordained.

The Emperor tried to rally his men streaming back through the gates in the inner wall; but everyone's thought was to reach his family, and nothing further could be done. Constantine held the approach himself for a few last minutes, but the tide against them was much too strong. The last Emperor of Byzantium flung off his imperial insignia, and with that splendid Castilian nobleman who had called him cousin at his side, plunged into the fray sword in hand, never to be seen again.

Mehmet rode into the city on the morning of the first day, and called a halt to the plundering in defiance of Islamic law: perhaps it was a reflection of the poverty of the city that nobody seemed to mind, for all the plunder was already taken. At the threshhold of St Sophia he dismounted, and sprinkled a scoop of dirt over his turban as a sign of humility. The scene in Hagia Sophia as Mehmet first entered was fairly bestial – indeed, halfway up one of the finest columns of the cathedral, on the south-east side, very clear-sighted visitors can still see the image of a hand, supposedly left by the Conqueror as he reached out to steady himself while clambering on his white charger up a huge pile of the slain. It is said that even as the priests were being hacked to bits, and the nuns were being ravished on the altar, and the women, children, patricians and plebeians who had crowded in were being trussed up for slavery, a priest in the middle of saying Mass took his chalice and his consecrated host, and at the point of the Turkish scimitars he slipped into the very walls of the church, which sealed him up.* Mehmet is supposed to have rounded on a soldier he saw hacking piously at the marble floors – 'the gold is thine, the building mine.' Then he rode to Blachernae, the palace of the emperors, where Constantine, after the holy sacrament two nights before, had stood a moment before going to the last defence of his city. Mehmet spent some time wandering among its empty

* Not to reopen, of course, until the cross replaced the crescent on the dome. Now it is a museum.

halls, murmuring the lines of an old Persian poem: 'An owl hoots in the towers of Afrasiab, / The spider spins his web in the palace of the Caesars.'

There were hiccups. Lucas Notarias, the highest ranking Byzantine captive, who had once famously declared that better the Sultan's turban than the bishop's mitre, was put to the sword with his entire family for refusing to sacrifice his son to the Sultan's lust; there had been talk of setting him up in office. Conceivably Mehmet was at first discouraged by the devastation of the city, its streets and shops blown out after the looting, its buildings strangely sooty and black, its fields and hedgerows very melancholy as they went to seed, for he continued with work on a great palace at Edirne as if nothing had happened.

5

The Centre

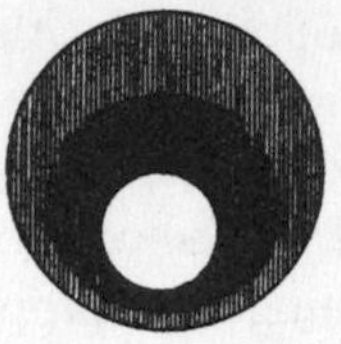

Mehmet had been obstinate as a boy, and his learning had apparently to be beaten into him. At the age of twelve he had been made Regent of Rumelia while Murad went to fight the Emir of Karamania in his rear. A fearsome Christian coalition army, in defiance of treaties sworn on the Bible and the Koran, burst into the Balkans in 1444. Murad came back, gathered his troops, and went to defeat them decisively at Varna on the Black Sea coast, charging the Christian ranks with a copy of the violated treaty stuck on a lance. Murad promptly abdicated, until two years later Halil had him reinstated in a sort of bloodless *coup d'état*. Mehmet, whom the janissaries despised, was exiled to Manisa. When Murad died in the winter of 1451,* Mehmet leapt vigorously into the saddle with the cry 'Let all who love me, follow me!' but exhortation was not enough, he was not well loved, and Mehmet became the first Sultan to issue an accession donative to the troops.

The fall of Constantinople changed all that. Everyone – the Venetians, the Genoese, the Ragusans – rushed to offer their congratulations and, where appropriate, agreed to raise the

* On New Year's Day 855, by Islamic reckoning.

amount of tribute they already paid. The Knights of Rhodes were congratulatory, too, even though they could not pay tribute, they said, without reference to the Pope. Mehmet basked in the prestige he gained in the Islamic world, as well, making quite sure of it by sending Constantine's supposed head on a tour of Islamic potentates. It is conceivable that Mehmet was discouraged by the city's dilapidation; but he had an eye for pattern, and the lineaments were strong beneath the soot and rubble.

Constantinople remained the finest city in the world. Christians had torn themselves and the city apart in their efforts to possess it: crusaders, pretenders, ambitious Serb princes, Bulgar khans with long and bitter memories who drank from their enemies' gilded skulls. In a thousand years Constantinople had suffered twenty-nine assaults. It had repulsed twenty-one of them. The King of Naples coveted it still; and as the last of the Byzantine dynasty were dying, Charles II of Anjou bought up their claims and titles and made, in that faded purple, a feint into Italy which disturbed even the Sultan.

It was as if some tilt of geography or politics had always destined this to be the first city of the world. The Byzantines had thought it the navel of the world. The Venetians toyed with the idea of moving Venice there, lock, stock and barrel, after they captured it in 1204; but perhaps their own city on the Veneto was so stuffed with looted treasures from Byzantium that the business of shipping it all back seemed too much trouble. In 1503, fifty years after the Ottoman conquest, Andrea Gritti – who learned his merchanting in Istanbul and later became a doge – wrote that 'its climate, its two seas protecting it on both sides, the beauty of its neighbouring lands, give this city what is thought to be the most beautiful and the most favoured site not only in all of Asia but in all the world', a site, Busbecq noted a century later, 'created by nature to be the capital of the world'.* Another Venetian, Benedetto Ramberti, wrung his hands over the beauty

* A year under house arrest in the capital of the world, though, changed his tone. 'What I enjoy is the country, not the city,' he later wrote. 'Especially a city which is almost falling to pieces . . .'

of it all. 'The situation of Constantinople is not only beyond description, but it can hardly be grasped in thought because of its loveliness,' he said; and the Roman traveller della Valle, who came in the seventeenth century, described the cascade of buildings with their huge spreading eaves, the big shuttered verandas under the eaves, their shade, the snow-white buildings and green cypresses as a 'sight so beautiful that I do not think there is any city to be found that looks better than this from the outside'. Years later, seeking an image of absolute loveliness to decorate the dome of an Albanian mosque or to brighten the walls of a Greek merchant's house, it was to the eye of empire that people instinctively turned, the kiosks and cypresses of the Golden Horn that people painted, the domes of Istanbul. The poet Nabi wrote: 'Because its beauty is so rare a sight / The sea has clasped it in an embrace.' 'What a city!' wrote Tursun Bey:* 'For an aspre you may be rowed from Asia into Europe.'

Asia came to Europe, the church became a mosque; and Turkish women asked to wear the Byzantine veil in place of the linen hood, with holes for eyes. Mehmed's world-conquering ambitions were crystallised in the new imperial capital. When he rode to Hagia Sophia and the Imam called the faithful there to prayer it was enough, in the rough conquistadorial spirit of the faith, to consecrate the edifice as a mosque. But a hunt was made among the captive Greeks for the fierce old theologian Gennadius the Scholar, the most implacable opponent of the Roman church. They found him in Edirne, in the house of a merchant who had bought him in a job lot, at a knockdown price, at the post-conquest sales, and was now bemusedly according him the courtesy due to his evident dignity and learning. Mehmet invested Gennadius with the robes and honour of the patriarchal office, and he was consecrated by the Archbishop of Heraclea; while thirty-six churches including the Church of the Holy Apostles, whose plan the Venetians had copied at St Mark's, were preserved for his ministers in the city alone.* The Chief Rabbi was called

* Turkish historian under Mehmet's successor, Bayezit II.

* Six years later the Serbian church, with its own patriarch in Pec, was suppressed in the name of Greek unity.

to the city from Jerusalem. The Armenian Patriarch was roped in from Bursa. The Sultan's share of captives were released and resettled, and everywhere the Sultan went in the coming years, when laying siege to cities in Greece and the Balkans, he dispatched his share of the captives to populate his capital.

All the while his troops laboured in the summer heat to repair the ravages of centuries of neglect, repairing cisterns and aqueducts, rodding drains, laying paving stones. Motion returned to the fossilised city: ships loading in the roadsteads, lighters bustling about the harbour, processions winding through the streets, the sound of hammers as the streets of the artisans came alive. Greeks sniffed the wind. Kritovolos compared Mehmet to Alexander the Great, and George of Trebizond wrote him a letter: 'No one doubts you are Emperor of the Romans. Whoever holds by right the centre of the Empire is emperor and the centre of the Roman Empire is Constantinople.'

Constantinople was the spot where the long trajectory of the gazi's fortunes fell to earth. Its conquest blew off the beys, just as they had feared; for Mehmet used it to build the edifice of Ottoman power, in which craggy individualists had no place. As the empire began to push against tougher enemies than before, unity was needed if conquest was to proceed at the old rate.

Mehmet followed up the conquest of Constantinople with the subjection of the whole Greek-speaking world. From Trebizond to the Peloponnese, he wound up all the Byzantine despots, rivals, and dependants. Kritovolos was a judge on the island of Imbros, the only Byzantine not to run away; he explained the new situation to the papal fleet when it cruised past, was given the governorship of the island, and eventually wrote a convincing history based on Greek and Turkish sources, in which the Sultan was the hero and the Greeks, for all their tragic loss, were urged to reconcile themselves. George Amouritzes negotiated the surrender of Trebizond, by which the Trapuzuntine Emperor David agreed to take his family to exile in Istanbul, and all the men of the city were enslaved.* The old Byzantine Emperor's brothers, the Peloponnesian despots Thomas and Demetrius, betrayed their cause by their faithlessness and opportunism, squabbling when Mehmet urged brotherly love, and making war when he urged peace, so that in 1460 he crossed the Gulf of Corinth and finished them off, while the cities of the Peloponnese fell to him one by one. Thomas died in Rome, and his sons never prospered: one married a Roman courtesan and died poor in the city, while the other returned rather hopelessly to Constantinople, dying as a pensioner of the state, and perhaps a Muslim, too. His uncle Demetrius died in Edirne in 1470, last of the Paleologi. Only Thomas's daughter Zoë got away: she married the Russian Grand Duke Ivan III in 1472, taking with her the old Caesaro-papist claims, and the double-headed eagle of Byzantium.

In 1456 Mehmet stormed up the Danube with his battle-hardened army of veterans, heroes of Constantinople and Sofia. His objective was an island at the confluence of the Sava and the Danube, the key to all Central Europe, named by the Ottomans Dar-ne-jihad, 'Battlefield of Holy War', and known to us as Belgrade, the White City. At the first news of his approach Janos Hunyadi, the military champion of Hungary, dashed across country to the island citidel with a welcome addition of musketeers, squeaking in just days before the siege commenced. Hunyadi cleared the houses round the ramparts for a clear field fo fire, and strung up a few Belgrade citizens who had been seen to be friendly with the enemy; but Mehmet's cannon did its work and on 13 August the janissaries advanced through a smoking breach in the walls, trampling over the corpses which lay piled up in the moat.

There was no resistance as they fanned out through the deserted streets and crooked lanes which ran up towards the citadel. Cautiously at first, then more boldly, they pressed through the alleyways, chalking houses for looting later – when a clarion call from the citadel brought the defenders out of their holes. They

* In 1463 the Comneni were put to death in the Castle of the Seven Towers: the Empress Helena buried them 'little by little' with her own hands. She donned a hair shirt and died in a thatched hut nearby.

rose from the ground like the sheeted dead – bounding out of cellars, springing down from rooftops – to fall upon the divided columns of Turkish soldiers. Taken completely by surprise, the janissaries fell back on their fellows streaming through the breach. The defenders chased after them, clearing the trenches with their slashing pikes, and the Turks fled in tumultuous disarray. Not even the exhortations of their Sultan, who must have seen better than they how close to victory his army was, and how easily they could turn the tables on the outnumbered defenders if they would only stand and fight; not even the furious bellowing of the *aga* of the janissaries, or the skirling of the janissary bands urging attack, could stem the rout. The Sultan cut down his generals with his own hand, and at his furious reproach the aga, handling his reins at the Sultan's right, did the decent thing and plunged into the fray, where he was soon cut down.

For Hunyadi, Belgrade restored a reputation tarnished after an earlier débâcle at Varna; and to cap it all he died there twenty days after the siege was lifted, weaving the indomitable legends of the city and the warrior together. The Turks would hush their babies' crying by mentioning his name, and eighty years after his death they broke through to Alba Iulia in Transylvania where he lay buried, and chipped at his effigy with a kind of respectful hatred, solicitous of his memory, and damaging to his nose.

Mehmet failed to take Belgrade, and failed to take Rhodes; but he scoured the Black Sea and the Genoese were booted out of their colonies there: Kaffa, the Little Constantinople, fell in 1475, and fifteen hundred young Genoese nobles were enrolled in the janissary regiments. In the year 1456 he rested his troops; but he spent the summer reading the classical geographer Ptolemy, whose concentric vision of the world matched his own. The Venetians from their rooftops watched the glow of burning villages as the Ottomans swept to the banks of the Piave. In 1480 Mehmet's general Ahmed the Broken-Mouthed, Grand Vizier and conqueror of the Crimea, landed unopposed on the southern shores of Italy, and seized Otranto, then considered the key to Italy, with terrifying slaughter, and it was only Mehmet's death that called him back.

6

The Palace

Every storm must have its eye, where the winds sound without a breeze, and in whose still, flat air you can feel the whole of its sullen energy. For Islam itself, the centre was the Kaaba of Mecca, the weird stone cube which Adam, some people thought, had erected precisely beneath an identical building in heaven and which others supposed to have been raised by God before he built Mecca round it and, encircling the city with holy ground, proceeded to the creation of the world. The whole building was covered in a thick black cloth, embroidered with verses of the Koran, and in its south-eastern corner was set the Black Stone, God's eye on earth, which bestowed blessings on anyone who touched it – and which pilgrims kissed seven times as they proceeded widdershins around the Kaaba itself.

For the common man, the centre was perhaps a tree. 'Cursed be the man who injures a fruit-bearing tree,' the Prophet said, and the idea of the tree – the shaman's tree, the tree of the Old Religion – was firmly rooted in Ottoman life. Osman's earliest dream was of a tree of destiny, which grew from his breast and whose leaves pointed at Christendom like spears. A tree grew gnarled and bent in the dusty square of every imperial town and village, where the men could sit to exchange the gossip of the day; so at the centre of the Hippodrome, in the middle of Constantinople, in the heart of the empire, stood a tree known as the Janissary Tree. From it, centuries later, in their days of arrogance and praetorian power, the janissaries liked to administer rough justice, and form their mutinous assemblies: 'a tree,' said a visitor in 1810, 'the enormous branches of which are often so thickly hung with strangled men that it is a sickening sight to look on'.

Within the political geography of the empire, too, an absolute stillness reigned at the very centre of the whole design – the 'more than Pythagorean silence', as Cantemir called it, 'of the Othman inner court', the dwelling place of the Sultan. Out on the frontier the Ottoman world might spin at a fantastic rate, gathering in treasure, and men, and countries, in ever widening circles, its bands a-screech, its troops rushing forward with horrible cries; to the clash of arms, and the groans of the dying, the boom of cannon and slither of rubble; but at the centre you would detect hardly any movement at all.

Mehmet did not repair the ruins of Constantine's Great Palace, or move into the half-fortified Blachernae Palace on the Golden Horn: they were dead men's shoes, and his power was more than a renovation. Shortly after the completion of the Old Palace in Constantinople in 1458 Mehmet erected a new one, Topkapi, on the promontory on which the Acropolis had stood. While on campaign in Greece he had asked permission to pay a visit to the legendary City of the Wise. With Mehmet's army only miles away the Athenians asked him in. For three days he studied the defences of the place, all the better to conquer it seven years later; but he also admired the many relics of antiquity, the splendour of the Acropolis, and the principles of its siting.

The Acropolis in Constantinople had views of the two seas, the waters of the Bosphorus, and the Golden Horn. Mehmet had the site stepped and levelled before he began building, taking the advice of Persian princes as well as Italian architects. The sixteenth-century historian Mustafa Ali wrote that 'the world-raising sultan must build his palace on a site vast as a desert, so that he can show off and boast', and Topkapi Palace today resembles the petrified encampment of some defeated army. Even in its heyday foreigners seldom saw the point of it exactly: Mustafa Ali's sixteenth-century contemporary, Salomon Schweigger, complained that the small low buildings looked as if they had fallen out of a bag. It was not as if the Ottomans were incapable of erecting great buildings, as certain visitors myopically or spitefully supposed: across the empire great mosques, medreses, asylums, hospitals, baths, inns and libraries testified to the Turkish talent for achieving symmetry and grandiloquence in stone.

The palace lacked the sculptural finality of pure architecture. It was a series of enclosures, a ceremonial ordering of space. Visitors, told to wait hours in the second court, perceived that the walls were lined, not with sculptured caryatids, but with living men who never moved a muscle. The experience was almost hallucinatory; certainly unnerving. It was an expression, not merely of wealth, but of will.

There were three courts. In the first court the business of the palace and the city mixed. The second, scarcely grander than the first, contained the offices of state, the archives and the nearby divan-room where the Sultan's viziers met, so that documents could be summoned up for consultation without delay. The divan met four times a week; a light pilaff was served for which the Grand Vizier paid. The Sultan would remain aloof, listening, if he so desired, to the vizierial deliberations through a small curtained grille – the Eye of the Sultan – which gave onto his private apartments in the third and most restricted enclosure, the Seraglio, which was approached through the Gate of Felicity. The name Abode of Felicity was not a coy reference to the legions of pretty women who lived there, but signified the sheer happiness of a place honoured by the presence of the Sultan Caliph.

In the outer courts, Ottoman marriages, circumcisions, and births were celebrated. The heads of traitors were displayed on poles; pay was issued, foreign envoys were received and, when the divan met, messengers and clerks scurried to and fro like medieval electrons. Yet the Sultan was able to impose, at will, moments of silence, and areas of peace. To proceed from court to court was to experience a muffling of sound, from the filtered hurly burly of the outer court, through the gardens and gazelles of the second court, to the quiet of the inner sanctum, where 'no man speaks unless ordered to, no talking to one another, neither doth any person dare so much as to sneeze or cough'. Here Sultan Suleyman in the 1520s introduced *ixarette*, the sign language of the deaf and dumb.

Silence was reinforced by solemnity. The Sultan's horse, which carried him the short distance through the streets to Friday prayers, was suspended from straps the night before to ensure that it walked with halting gravity. The Sultan was expected to move slowly – which 'shews something of Majesty' – in the palace; everyone else, from scullion to Grand Vizier, moved at the double; and in going through the corridors a harem girl who had not been selected for the Sultan's bed was warned to flee noiselessly from the tap of the Sultan's silver-studded slippers in the night.*

George Sandys watched the Friday procession to the mosque at the beginning of the seventeenth century, and he made a rather creepy discovery as the gorgeous cavalade passed by – the Sultan on that unfortunate horse, his viziers riding at a respectful distance behind him, the Sheikh ul-Islam in a great turban, the janissaries in arms, the mounted cavalry, the crowd pressing close to glimpse their Padishah in the flesh. You had only to shut your eyes in the crowd, Sandys says, 'as had you but onely eares, [and] you might supose (except when they salute him by a soft and short murmur) that men were folded in sleepe, and the World in midnight'.

The government took the name Sublime Porte, or 'High Gate', in the 1650s. Men clustered at the palace gates, and justice was dispensed there; gateways, too, provided each slightly featureless court with a focus towards the next; and whether they opened or remained shut to a man defined his role and status. The same principle operated in the simplest nomadic camp, where a chief could convey rank, perhaps, or disapproval, through ceremony and gesture, in his manner of receiving guests, rising or not, widening the ring of seated guests, or allowing the newcomer

* For which slippers an entire nation – albeit a very small one – paid a special poll tax, an event no Montenegrin could remember without shame centuries later.

to remain standing. By the end of the sixteenth century foreign ambassadors given an audience with the Sultan were frogmarched by officials to the foot of the throne, and conducted their entire interview with their arms pinned to their sides: not, as some thought, because the Sultan feared assassination, but to preserve the stranger from collapse.

The palace in motion expressed, by repetition, a universal and transcendent order. The Sultan's power radiated outwards, from the empire as it was to the empire as it was to be, world-conquering; from court to court, from the palace to the city, away from the city down the roads and passes that led to the borderlands. At the centre of the palace stood the Mansion of Justice, the Sultan's eye, from where he might look into the hearts of men, and assure himself of the justice of his rule.

But the Sultan, and not the palace, was the true eye of the empire. Wherever he went, to the old palace in Edirne, to the wars, striking camp after camp on the Maritsa or the Bursa road, or wintering in Topkapi itself, he was surrounded by the same familiar layout, the same faces, the same order of precedence, whether in canvas or in stone. The Sultan was everywhere: not only, by the law of pattern, doubled and redoubled across his empire, but sometimes actually in the midst of things, slipping incognito through the bazaars – Mehmet queerly stabbing anyone who recognised him, on the eve of the Conquest, Sultan Suleyman disguised as a spahi, Sultan Mehmet IV as a Sufi (and so impressed by the smart opinions of a baker that the very next morning he made him Grand Vizier), Sultan Selim the Sot, it is said, honouring the barfly who first showed him the route to paradise, in a bottle, and Murad IV befriending, to his own ruin, one Bekri Mustafa, whom he found in the market quarter, 'wallowing in the dirt dead drunk'.

Turnstile of the continents, seal of empires, geomantic paradise, Constantinople was a place of absolutes. It was either very hot, or very cold. Here Europe and Asia met. Here the seas joined. The palace stood like a city within a city, and the Sultan lived in the palace like Narcissus, Blaise de Vigenère said; but Mustafa

Ali, his more respectful subject, compared him to an oyster in its shell.

The conquest of Konstantiniyye, as the city was to be formally known,* was the fulfilment of a prophecy running like a thread through Islamic history, that 'a just prince' would conquer the

Constantinople, from Scheder's Chronicle, *1493*

Red Apple of Islamic myth. Under the Turks it became the largest city in the world. The hungriest, too, so that it was fed on army rules. Its presence at the hub of the Ottoman Empire, with mosques and fountains, schools and charities, was the realisation of Mehmet's will. In *kanuns*, or laws, issued from the palace in his name, came the terrible ordinance that would ensure that only one man could ever rule the empire at a time: the fratricidal law. Justified, rather tendentiously, by the Koranic verse 'what is the death of a prince to the loss of a province?' it allowed sultans to execute their brothers (and nephews) to prevent power struggles (primogeniture was unknown). When a rough old Turk burst in upon the divan and asked which of the gentlemen present was the fortunate Sultan, the shame, apparently, was so acute that it gave Mehmet an excuse to stop attending the council, as a creature half-divine. He had Halil, the gazi spokesman, executed, and he

* Istanbul, its popular Turkish name, may be a contraction of the Greek *eis tin polis*, 'to the city'. This is the best of a number of feeble theories. Under the Ottomans the city remained Konstantiniyye on coins and documents.

erased all pretensions other than his own. In his kanun of ceremonies, he abolished the old easy practices of sultans past, who ate with their men, and stood to martial music in remembrance of a fudged old tradition of fealty to the vanished Shepherd Kings. Mehmet said bluntly that those kings were dead. 'It is my will that the Sultan dines alone,' he explained, as he made the Ottoman custom of breaking bread with the men into a biennial event.

'We light our lamp with oil taken from the hearts of the infidels,' Mehmet once wrote, to describe the single institution which made the Ottoman Empire so fantastically strange, and so peculiarly itself. Nothing in the rolling tide of conquest so nearly approached fluidity as the ceaseless production, elevation and disappearance of the highest in the state, the very Ottomans themselves, the Sultan's *kul*, his slaves.

Most sovereign states discovered ways to devolve power, without giving it all away. The Romans and Persians used eunuchs, the kings of Europe unmarried clergy, and the Chinese used their famous exam system to enrol humble but eager scholars into the ranks of the ruling caste.

Murad II introduced the boy tribute system in 1432. Mehmet carried it to a logical conclusion. Every three years or so, a tribute officer went into the villages of Greece and the Balkans to select the finest Christian youths for the Sultan's service, consulting parish rolls provided by the local priest or elder. After the march to Istanbul, every youth was sent to work on an Anatolian farm, to build up his muscles, and learn Turkish; and from there, having formally converted to Islam, he went to the schools. His competence, his looks ('a corrupt and sordid Soul can scarce inhabit in a serene and ingenuous Aspect'), his bearing, his liveliness, intelligence, piety, strength, were tested to assess his suitability for particular branches of the Sultan's service, and from now until his death, watched and assessed at every step, he was the Sultan's slave.

These youths and their predecessors formed, under the Sultan their master, a commonwealth of slaves. Since no born Muslim could be enslaved, their own sons were barred from joining it. So there was no dynastic servitude – Mehmet II tightened the system up when he executed Greek Halil, bringing his family's longstanding hold on the vizierate to its inglorious end – no dynastic threat, no 'empire building' to take place beneath the Grand Turk's nose. After Halil's death, thirty-four of the next thirty-six Grand Viziers, though Muslim converts themselves, were not Muslim-born, and in all Europe the Ottoman Empire alone possessed no hereditary nobility. A *kapikulu* was cut off from his true parents by the gulf of faith and place; he was severed from his children because they were free, and his career could never beat a path for theirs.

The boys gave up little when they were enrolled as the Sultan's slaves. Priests were rare in their highland villages, and then as ignorant as their flock, at least as poor, and prone to abuse their position. Churches were scarce. The villagers had a bellyful of sprites, elves, vampires, tree spirits and such, who could be propitiated, moved on or deflected by charms, amulets, magical cures, muttered invocations, scraps of paper with writing on them, ceremonies of renewal with water jugs, feasts marked by sacrifice and meat, to everyone's relish; and the tribute boys' arrival in Anatolia probably marked their first contact with religion of a formal sort. The Bektashi order, to which the janissaries were officially attached from 1543, dispensed altogether with some of Islam's striking peculiarities like the veiling of women, or the prohibition on wine. Insincere conversions didn't bother the Turks, because they supposed that a man who followed the outward forms would come to believe soon enough, and they felt that they were bringing children back to the faith into which they were born – for every child, according to the founder of the janissaries Kara Halil Chendereli, comes into the world with the beginnings of Islam.*

What could rival the experience of being drawn from a life of drudgery and obscurity into a world of exhilarating novelty, from a narrow parochial society into the cosmopolitan one of empire, from poverty to all the possibilities of wealth, from the flock to the ranks of rulers, soldiers, wielders of power? If a boy had the

* The curious white flap which janissaries wore on their hats commemorated the founder's sleeve as he touched their heads in benediction.

qualities the selectors sought, he might be enrolled immediately in one of the palace schools, where boys were trained as pages under the sway of the terrible Chief White Eunuch, whose cruelty Rycaut supposed to be either envy of men, or 'their nearness to the condition of the cruel sex'. There was nothing effete about the boys: they studied, they practised martial arts, and emerged strong as well as handsome, versed in a dozen branches of learning, frequently displaying some special talent, such as singing, or architecture, or folding turbans (no mean art) and steeped by now in the traditions and mores of the palace – reverence and silence being the first things that new recruits were made to learn. They bent their energy to the practice of obedience; and when their beards grew and they were sent out to fill positions of responsibility in the provinces, 'none know so well how to govern', said the Turks, 'as those who have learned to obey'. Others graduated at the same time into the Noble Guard or, in far greater numbers, joined the royal order of chivalry, the Spahi of the Porte, who formed the Sultan's regular cavalry.

Ambassador's janissary

The janissaries, who sprang from the same stock, were less cultivated. Out of this brawny second stream came the gardeners, the gate keepers, the scullions and woodcutters, the navvies and shipwrights and marines and infantry. At any point a youth could be selected for the palace schools, if some aptitude had been overlooked. They too received a corporate training, ate and slept together, and had the traditions of the regiment dunned into them from the start, swearing loyalty to their fellows on a tray containing salt, the Koran, and a sword. The bedding reserved for new boys was famously lousy. They had to look lively, and wash and cook for their elders. Even fully fledged janissaries were not allowed to marry: the regiment was their family. They wore its uniform, and had marching bands with martial music, long before the West copied them; music grave and sonorous for the march, and cymbals clashing and eerie for the attack, so that enemies quailed, and their horses shied with fright, while the janissaries were vastly encouraged, and fled if it stopped.

When western observers understood the principle, it made their hair stand on end. The boy tribute fulfilled the logic of an empire geared for war: just as war booty financed the next assault, so the borderlands could be made to furnish the men who, being raised to perfection in the capital, were turned out again to rule the empire and to expand the frontiers of the state. Worse still, it cut clean across the hereditary principle which western visitors held so dear. Again and again, the Ottomans proved that birth had nothing to do with it. 'The Turks care not whether these boys are the children of noblemen or of fishermen or shepherds.' The Venetians saw that boy tribute worked, which was enough for them to admire it – Morosini confessing that 'their major officials are all good-looking and impressive', though 'their manners are uncouth'.

Just as terrifying was the nonsense the system made of supposed Christian superiority: the apostasy was seldom forced. Western visitors liked to suppose that the crosses they saw tattooed on the hands, or foreheads, of Balkan boys were there to render them unfit for selection; but many other motifs, including crescents, came down with the habit itself from the days of the Old Religion. The janissaries liked to be tattooed with the symbol of their regiment on the leg and on the shoulder. Evidence that the tribute was resisted is patchy; though the tribute gatherer gave plenty of warning of his coming, and the Balkans offered countless avenues for escape. The tribute was collected implacably, but not blindly or with malice. The Turks left widows with their boys, and did not trouble families with a single son. As the convoy wound its way across Muslim Bosnia it had to be heavily guarded to prevent parents from substituting their own offspring. For their own part, they avoided boys who already spoke Turkish, or had learned a trade, or had lived in the city; they refused orphans, too, who were too wily, and had learned too young to fend for themselves.

The Venetians perceived that the Palladian harmony absent in Ottoman buildings was most handsomely revealed, instead, in the architecture of power itself; and their *relazzioni*, the reports given by returning ambassadors to the senate, were not only literary productions of a high order, obeying countless Venetian rules of taste and order, but were so eagerly sought after by the world at large that, although secret, they were available in Rome at fifteen paoli per hundred pages, and found their way into the courts and libraries of Europe. A sixteenth-century observer described the entire kul system as a ruthless meritocracy. 'Each has his good and real fortune in his hand. Being all slaves of a single lord, from whom alone they hope for greatness, honour and riches, and from whom alone on the other hand they fear punishment and death, what wonder is it that in his presence, and in rivalry with one another, they will do stupendous things?' 'They care for men,' Busbecq* reported, 'as we care for our horses. This is why they lord it over others, and are daily extending the bounds of their empire. These are not our ideas; with us there is no opening left for merit; birth is the standard for everything; the prestige of birth is the sole key to advancement in the public service.' 'One of the most Politick Constitutions in the world, and none of the meanest supports of the Ottoman Emire,' Rycaut wrote soberly.

The kul were certainly the Sultan's slaves, but the translation is inexact. The Sultan's absolute authority over his kul, his power of

* Ogier Ghiselin de Busbecq, a Flemish nobleman, wrote four superb *Turkish Letters* while on an ambassadorial mission to Constantinople between 1554 and 1562. A distinguished diplomat, he was also a botanist, a linguist, an antiquarian, a scholar and a zoologist, and his delightful letters, translated from Latin in 1927 by E. S. Forster, are among the best anecdotal sources of information on the empire in the sixteenth century. He also brought back the lilac, the tulip, the most famous of all Latin inscriptions, the *Monumentum Ancyranum*, 240 classical manuscripts and a great collection of old coins, as well as an irreplaceable Crim-Gothic vocabulary. He was always fresh, appreciative and funny. He died in 1592.

life and death, and possession of all their wealth, never resembled plantation slavery in America. No opprobrium attached to their position. They could not be bought or sold. Nor – for all their power – did they resemble an aristocracy. Not only were their functions non-hereditary, but their wealth was only a reflection of their status within the hierarchy, and if they stepped out of it – by banishment or death – their wealth stayed with the system,

Ottoman official

not the man. 'On their death,' says Baron Wratislaw, 'the Emperor will say: "Thou hast been my man, thou hast gained wealth from me; it is a proper thing that after thy death it should be returned back again to me".' Absolutely obedient to the Sultan's will, without right of appeal, dependent on him for favour and maintenance, they were no more than the Sultan's extended and adopted family, obedient to a patriarch – the son of a slave himself – who enjoyed few practical rights which a father of the time would not possess over his own children. Far from carrying a stigma, the proudest boast of an Ottoman was that he was the slave of the Sultan.

They gave up everything to reach the pinnacle of power; but like the janissary who for all the collegiate self-abnegation of his life still strutted through the streets of Istanbul, they knew they were the best. A miracle had pulled them, as it seemed, through an invisible door in the Balkan pasturelands.* The training which they received, and the rigorous selection procedure which they had surmounted to reach the top, must have left them with a grandeur of purpose and a breadth of view without parallel in any ruling group in history; observers liked to call them 'wide awake'. Theirs was pride of the most splendid and forgivable sort; for they were fitted to rule. The western baron knew his region, of course, but his talents depended on the lottery of birth; and the Kapikulu had not only studied the arts of government, he knew his people intimately. He often retained a sympathy for the humble. In 1599 a rough peasant with a grievance approached the Grand Vizier's office, in his skins and sandals, with a live ewe hefted over his shoulder: he arrived just when an embassy from the Holy Roman Empire was preparing to negotiate a cessation of hostilities; and he walked right in, ahead of them all.

Through his slaves the Sultan's power was transfused throughout the empire. They were the Sultan's eyes and ears and hands – the word *vizier* meant 'the Sultan's foot' – and when they had risen far, close to riches and the strangler's bowstring, even their deaths were encompassed in the active mood: 'Whereas for such or such Facts thou deservest to die, it is our pleasure that . . . thou deliver thy Head to this our Messenger,' the Kapikulu was told, as he might have been asked to fetch the Sultan's slippers or subdue a province in happier times. There were occasionally muffled scuffles, and at least one vizier, when the *chaush*, or

* In 1512 the first tribute was levied in Anatolia; the great architect Sinan was a product of that levy.

imperial equerry, reached him in his Cypriot exile, died of fright before the cord touched him; while Elias Haneschi sketches a lurid picture of a resistant pasha – 'the executioner, who has made himself expert at his office, in throwing up apples into the air, and cutting them in halves as they descend, aims at the neck as well as he can, but missing his mark, makes dreadful havoc in destroying his victim.' But most would respond with the same dignified obedience with which they carried out any of the Sultan's commands. 'Then I must die?' said Kara Mustafa. 'So be it.' He washed his hands, and bared his own neck, and when the silken cord had finished him off, his head was struck from his shoulders, and duly sent to the palace in a velvet bag.

In 1524, shortly before Sultan Suleyman launched his brilliant and successful assault on the island of Rhodes, the supposedly impregnable bastion of the crusading Order of the Knights of St John, his attention was caught by a page at his court. A year older than Suleyman, Ibrahim was the son of a Greek sailor. Captured by pirates as a boy, sold to a widow of Magnesia, educated by her and seconded to the Sultan's retinue, this handsome and quick-witted young man grew up speaking Turkish, Persian, Greek and Italian, playing the viol, and reading histories and romances. He was a foil to the young Sultan, who made him Grand Vizier in a skip and a jump.

Ibrahim worked hard. Suleyman accorded him the insignia of high authority: six horsetails, to his own seven and the four traditionally given to grand viziers. The two young men became inseparable. They campaigned together, ate together, even shared a tent. In 1523 the governor of Egypt, who had been expecting the post that Ibrahim took, rebelled. Ibrahim was dispatched to pacify the province, doing it so well, so carefully weighing his checks and his balances, so skilfully marshalling the vast resources of this country that Egypt remained quiet for a century and a half, and the system was applied in later years to almost any province that would bear it. He weighed janissary garrisons against their treasury paymasters, and Ottoman governors against muftis; he saw to it that commanders and treasurers were appointed by, and reported to, Istanbul, and enacted laws ensuring that, while Mamelukes might hold office, they might hold it anywhere but in Egypt. He made the most prudent fiscal arrangements, whereby the whole revenue of the state was collected, not by this man and that, but by tax farmers, with fixed sums to produce, and the rest their profit. On his return in 1524 he married the Sultan's sister, and six years later, after Suleyman had thrown a party for the circumcision of his sons, he asked Ibrahim which ceremony had been more magnificent, Ibrahim's wedding or this. 'My wedding,' Ibrahim retorted smartly. 'Your Majesty had no guest equal to mine, for I was honoured by the presence of the Emperor of Mecca and Medina, the Solomon of our time.'

Poor Ibrahim! This line of talk between friends shows the way the wind was blowing. Ibrahim led a campaign into Persia, where he allowed the army to flounder through a land laid waste by the Shah's tactical retreat until the situation was rescued by Suleyman in person. Westerners were subsequently astonished to hear Ibrahim declare that he was, in matters of negotiation, Sultan himself. One morning in March 1536, in his bedroom next to the Sultan's own, Ibrahim was found dead. The bailio, or Venetian ambassador, of the day, Alvise Gritti, was unimpressed. Ibrahim had forgotten, he said, that if the Sultan sent his cook to finish him off, nothing Ibrahim could do would prevent the killing.

7

War

The Ottoman Empire lived for war. Every governor in this empire was a general; every policeman was a janissary; every mountain pass had its guards, and every road a military destination. The most willowy and doe-eyed pageboy was a dab hand with the gerit or the bow, and well versed in wrestling, the king of Ottoman sports. At the siege of Baghdad in 1683, when the Persians demanded the contest be decided by single combat, they put up a Herculean warrior from their ranks, and Sultan Mehmet IV took him on himself, splitting the Persian champion's mailed head in two with a single blow. Even madmen had a regiment, the *deli*, or loons, Riskers of their Souls, who were used, since they did not object, as human battering rams, or human bridges (and in the eighteenth century another regiment, 'the lost children', took their place). Outbreaks of peace caused trouble at home, as men clamoured for the profit and the glory. Georgius de Hungaria was one of the first westerners to observe the Ottoman army at first hand; he was captured by them in 1438 and remained among them twenty years.

> When recruiting for the army is begun, they gather with such readiness and speed you might think they are invited to a wedding and not to war. They gather within a month in the order they are summoned, the infantrymen separately from the calvarymen, all of them with their appointed chiefs, in the same order which they use at encampments and when preparing for battle . . . with such enthusiasm that men put themselves forward in place of their neighbours, and those left at home feel that an injustice has been done to them. They claim they will be happier if they die on the battlefield among the spears and arrows of the enemy than at home among the tears and slavering of the old women. Those who die in war like this are not mourned but are hailed as saints and victors, to be set as an example and given high respect.

'For this was I born, to bear arms,' Bayezit had said; and when a Frenchman, Bertrand de la Brocquière, got a chance to review Mehmet II's army in the field in 1462, he saw no reason why such a splendid troop should not conquer all Europe if it chose. In 1576 a Venetian witness echoed him, declaring that Christendom should fear a great extermination. 'The empire's forces are of two kinds,' he added helpfully, 'those of the land and those of the sea, and both are terrifying.' The empire's land forces were of two principal kinds, too, the light, fleet, patrician cavalrymen, and the stolid heavyweights of the infantry, each representing, perhaps, a particular strand of imperial virtue.

The janissaries formed the empire's standing infantry, drawn from the boy tribute of the Balkans, with some of the strengths and limitations of the peasant, keeping their eyes on the soil, to capture ground, or hold it against fearsome odds. They dreamed of food in an earthy way, and so grumbling and insistent were their regimental bellies that they adopted titles of rank from the kitchen: their commanders were called soup-men, cooks, head scullions, water-carrier and Black Scullion. To lose the regimental standard in battle was disgraceful; but the loss of the regimental cauldron warranted the dismissal of all officers. A janissary strolling through the streets of Istanbul was a man of privilege, not rich but splendidly attired, and bearing himself with all the pride of a soldier who had earned his position in the world, with immunity from the common courts, like a peer of the realm. But no hearthside pleasures for him. From the crown of his pure white linen hat to the tips of his tough red boots he was a one-man fighting machine. The English ambassador once laughed at the little trowels hanging at their waists and said they looked more like diggers than soldiers; his wiser companion laughed too, and reminded him that 'it was just with weapons of that sort, rather than with arquebuses and guns, that they had taken from the rest of us the strongholds of Rhodes, Agrigento, Chios and many other famous fortresses. Since there may be a hundred or more thousand men, all working together like that, with shovel and spade under the walls of a fortress, I cannot imagine what force or skill is able to defend it.'

The spahi, or cavalryman, was invariably a Muslim Turk, descended figuratively and literally from the old gazis. Give him his horse, hand him his bow, din in his ears his commander's roar – 'Come on, my wolves!' – and you had, if not the first centaur to bear arms since the days of myth, then a man at any rate hard to tell apart from his horse (and swift, too, as a missile). Unhorsed, he could only stand helplessly by the campaign road, holding his saddle on his head, mutely imploring the charity of some great man to give him a new mount.

The spahis were scattered across the empire, always on the move, from billet to billet, from billet to the front. They retained to the end some of the wildness of the gazis. They wore skins. They practised by galloping at full tilt past a suspended brass ball and swivelling in the saddle to fire an arrow at it, like nomads of the steppe; and they came prancing and curvetting to the Edirne Gate, or the shores of Scutari, in answer to the horsetails' summons. When a cavalryman was sentenced to death for allowing his horse to trample crops at the roadside, rider and mount were executed together.

It was every horseman's dream to enrol in the permanent army with that billet or stipend known as a *timar*, to free him for the task of war. The sick, Rycaut* says, came to war on their beds, and infant timariots in their cradles. The timar was strictly a direct and convenient form of pay in return for military service, by which the timariot was entitled to collect a certain number of imperial taxes himself, according to his merits. The Ottoman Sultan owned all the land, and claimed all its taxes, but he lent some of its revenues directly to his men in return for service. A cavalryman might enjoy the revenues of a timar, a small village, say. A commander might be assigned a *ziamet* – the revenue perhaps of several small villages, and even a market. High provincial officials would be awarded their *hass*, compounded of various revenues from the region they governed in the Sultan's name, potentially scattered across it, but generally the sort of revenues they could more conveniently reach, lodged in the city as they were – urban dues of various kinds, bridge tolls, market receipts, hearth taxes. All were expected to muster with a number of armed men, too: the timariot just one or two, the ziamet five or so, and the bey his whole household, pages, horsemen, slaves and all.

None were ever possessors of their land; never owner of the peasants; only the collectors, by appointment, of the precise dues to which they were entitled, whose value could be made up anywhere in the empire if they needed to be moved on. A timariot's sons inherited nothing from him but the natural predisposition of the commanders to favour them by virtue of their father's service; and the eldest son, when he was old enough, was generally granted a timar worth about a third as much as his father's. When the frontier moved forward, the spahi might be moved forward with it; for signal valour he would be rewarded; but he remained through and through the Sultan's man, and the wealth he disposed of remained the Sultan's, too.

In each generation the resources of the empire would be sur-

* Sir Paul Rycaut (1628–1700) was an English factor, or merchant, in Smyrna, much liked and respected by almost everyone who met him. He wrote several books on the empire and its religions. His *History* was issued in 1679, as a follow-up to Knolles's *History of the Turkes* of 1604 – Rycault regretted seeing his work 'Crouded into 50 sheetes, and to become an appendix to an old Obscure author'; but the book was well received throughout Europe. He later traded in Hamburg, from where he introduced the duvet to England.

veyed. Taxes, tolls, every customary charge or grant of labour, all market dues, the value of lands, the wealth of villages were recorded for the construction and adjustment of the empire's military fiefs, the timars. 'Take a Turk from the saddle', it has been said, 'and he becomes a bureaucrat'; but every bureaucrat in the empire still felt, metaphorically at least, the saddle under him,

and from the humblest copyist in the chancellery of the empire to the two highest judges in the land, the *kadi askers* – one for the troops of Anatolia, one for the soldiers of Rumelia – whosoever took the Sultan's asper believed himself to be contributing to his military success.

From Buda to Baghdad the revenues of the empire were geared to endless predation upon the frontier, bringing booty for all,*

* The lure of booty cannot be overestimated: Hungary lost whole trees and even flowers, stolen not destroyed.

new sources of tax, new timars for the men, and new pashaliks for the mighty, too. The Ottomans were the first state to maintain a standing army in Europe since Roman days, paid, fed, and unleashed through insurpassable feats of organisation. In 1683, when the Ottoman army marched up the Maritsa towards Vienna, 200,000 men on the move got fresh bread every evening; and in 1548, when they marched on the Persian Shah – hurried along, we are told, in case the local Shias infected them with heresy – they sprang upon the enemy with cannons charged and already ablaze, such contraptions, as they well knew, never having been seen by the Persians before; the entire army so well-provisioned, and the transport of all the necessities of life so carefully organised, that they had marched imperturbably for weeks through a landscape laid waste by the scorched-earth retreat of the Shah.

Western camps were babels of disorder, drunkenness and debauchery. The Ottoman camp was a tea party disturbed by nothing louder than the sound of mallet on tent peg, the camels' cough, the bubbling of the cauldrons filled with rice. 'I think there is no prince', wrote the Byzantine chronicler Chalcocondyle, 'who has his armies and camps in better order, both in abundance of victuals and in the beautiful order they use in encamping without any confusion or embarrassment.' When an Italian traveller in the eighteenth century, the Comte de Marsigli, observed that the Ottomans still lay under the influence of their nomadic past, he was thinking principally of their tents. The Ottoman world was full of them. There were tents which gave shelter from desert sun, or Balkan rains. The Prophet had used a tent, and Sufi saints had pitched theirs in the sky. The real foundation of the empire came with Topkapi, or the casting of a tent in stone. The real power of the empire was its capacity to fling itself forward, so that at the last siege of Vienna, for example, it erected a canvas city beside the Austrian capital, but bigger than Vienna, and much better ordered, with neat rows of tented streets, and an orchard and garden for the Grand Vizier. 'Ottoman order', Tursun Bey called the army's camp, when with miraculous speed and enviable precision it was unfolded at the end of a day's march, so that within an hour a whole city had risen up in the fields. The dusk was lit by the companiable fires of the janissary messes, and the approach to the royal tent was arranged with supplicants, messengers and officials exactly according to their degree. It dazzled Busbecq in the fifteenth century; and in the eighteenth, when the empire could seldom rattle a scimitar with conviction, it astonished Lady Mary Wortley Montagu, who otherwise found militaria perfectly dull.

The bureaucracy of government was schematically represented by four tent poles: the Grand Vizier, the treasurers, the judges, and the chancellery; while every sultan ordered himself an accession tent, which took years to make, like the one of pure satin which Galland saw, pitched on the Hippodrome for everyone to admire, supported on sixteen poles, and richly embroidered with stylised foliage of red and green.

The army bivouacked for five months every year, and the excellent order of their camp not only delivered them fresh to the battlefield, but also served as a sort of collapsible castle, for it was a cat's cradle of guy-ropes pegged out everywhere, protecting the camp from a sudden assault. An early witness thought that the Ottomans 'lodge more grandly in the field than at home', while their tents – red or yellow for high officials, purple for the Grand Vizier – reflects the evanescence of power amongst those who were the Sultan's slaves. The circumference of the Grand Vizier's own tent, the traveller della Valle said, was half a mile; before it lay a vast piazza, much resembling the palace courts, and you entered by way of a 'large, tented rotunda, high pitched, under whose shade stayed the servants and other retainers'; the piazza itself was screened by a circle of green tents – the better, della Valle thought, to camouflage themselves in grass. Internal columns were painted red and hung with imitation lamps. The covered way was spread with huge carpets; thronged with persons of the lesser quality, squatting at the edges, who would all rise and salute a dignitary, in utter silence. From the inner pavilion, you glimpsed other tents making apartments, all of gold-embroidered silk. Even stables were erected in canvas – with 'all the conveniences a great palace can possess'.

A cavalry perk was the right to sell off worn-out tents. When the janissaries, slumped in barracks in Istanbul, wanted to signal their dissatisfaction, they overturned their cauldrons and refused the Sultan's food; but on campaign, mutiny was declared when the ropes of the commander's tent were cut, and gorgeous satins fluttered in the mud.

The Venetian Morosini, with scant desire to admire the empire, grudgingly confessed that their system allowed the Ottomans 'to maintain armies larger than another ruler could have if he paid them ten and a half million gold ducats a year'. While western feudal rulers would be cajoling and threatening their vassals, pleading with over-mighty magnates, perhaps, or the citizens of free towns, or frantically raising loans to raise troops, the Ottoman armies would be assembling like clockwork, paid up and signed on. 'They never show the least concern for their lives in battle, and they can live a long time without bread or wine, content with barley and water', the sort of food a western soldier would give to his horse. Their camels gave them a great advantage over western armies, too, in carrying war to the enemy, for a camel could carry 250 kilos, twice as much as a horse; only one in every four, not one in two, was required to carry the beasts' own fodder.

The Ottomans carefully analysed the problems of war. No source of intelligence was overlooked, and a well-developed spy network brought accurate assessments of enemy strength and movements, and of strategic entanglements which the Sultan's forces might exploit. Each winter the last campaign would be subject to a minute post-mortem, with new techniques, tactics or weapons perhaps added to the Ottoman arsenal. Weaknesses would be noted, both in their own performance and in their enemies' defences. Orders for the next campaign were already out – 30,000 camels from the Maghreb, tunics from the Salonica cotton weavers – as governors along the line of march began to organise stockpiles of food, commanding the nomads to deliver their tax in the form of sheep, and setting the local villagers to mending roads and bridges in lieu of tax (although the army also had a corps whose job was to prepare the road; a corps to pitch the tents ahead; a corps to bake the bread). The reserve would be deployed to keep order in the rear, while the garrison men, the servants of the frontier, were stirred up to raids on the borders, to soften up the enemy while the main army was still on the march.

Ottoman morale was splendidly high, for Ottoman society was sustained by hope, a very refreshing air, especially when expectations were so readily fulfilled. On 23 April – St George's Day* – each year the palace itself got underway, and like a merchantman suddenly dropping concealed gun ports and running up the Jolly Roger, turned itself into a mobile fighting machine. The Halberdiers of the Tresses, whose long hair fell over their eyes like blinkers when they carried wood into the harem apartments, fanned out as foragers along the line of march. Palace tailors, shoemakers, doctors, holy men bundled up the tools of their trade, ready to unwrap them again at every camp. The dog handlers, the falconers, the gardeners and the oarsmen of the royal pinnace assembled under banners like the janissaries they really were, and prepared to march. The head gardener resumed his seasonal office of executioner, ready for any man infringing the fabled order of march. The learned pageboys whose task over the winter had been, perhaps, to keep a taper alight in the Sultan's room at night, or to chant from the Koran, or dress the Sultan in the morning, sprang onto Arab steeds, snatched up their weapons and formed themselves in a troop around their lord. The pashas, the kadi askers of Rumelia and Anatolia, took to the saddle. The kadi of Istanbul prepared to take over the government of the city. The pasha of Erzerum led an army out into the plains, within striking distance of the borders, to maintain order. The fleet cruised in the Dardanelles. Somebody thrust the horsetails into the ground, and as they streamed in the Scutari wind, or at the Belgrade Gate, to signal the direction of the campaign, not only the governed but the entire government, too, set off; and everyone, everywhere, slipped into their position, as the empire prepared for the task it performed best, and apparently enjoyed the most – going to war.

* The Turks were amused to see St George represented in Greek churches: they thought of him as their own.

As that army marched into Europe up the old military road to Belgrade, it would be joined in perfect order by any number of special auxiliaries – Slav voynuk bands on horseback, inherited from the old Balkan rulers; professional marauders, mostly Christian, who also worked in garrisons and for the river fleet;

The beylerbeyi

taciturn *derbendcis*, who manned the straits and the mountain passes; mounted Vlach shepherds, a man for every five families in the hills. All along the marching route men sprang to, Christians mainly, mining, quarrying, towing boats, manufacturing arms and gunpowder, coming to swell an army of perhaps 100,000 men; and still others might pour down from the north to join up, Tartars from the Crimea, the vassal troops of Wallachia and Moldavia, the mustachioed warriors of Transylvania. They came at a whistle, and for free, while the enemy would be scrabbling for funds, and beseeching its men at arms to fight. 'It would seem a great Clog to the Gran Signor to be obliged to depend on the bounty of his Subjects, when he would make a War,' said Rycaut.

It was a sight to see, and few foreigners passed up the chance to witness the cavalcade pass out of the city. Della Valle saw them go in 1615, preceded by flags, yellow and red, borne on lances; chaushes on horseback, two by two; gunners, in pairs, with arquebuses and scimitars. Then came a body of infantry carrying wooden weapons, the insignia, della Valle thought, of government and justice, followed by the spahis of Rumelia, with bows and arrows but no lances, since they were not detailed to participate in this campaign, swathed in animal skins like Greek heroes.

Behind them marched the trainee janissaries and their aga, or commander, a white eunuch who went on foot. Then came all the janissary banners, followed by mounted janissary captains. The janissaries themselves, marching out of line in a dense pack, took a long time passing.* 'They had no defensive arms of any sort, and no weapons of attack save for scimitars, arquebuses, and some little hatchets or spades at their wrists . . . for digging the ground and cutting wood rather than for fighting: yet arms to be respected for their use in assailing and storming cities.'

The cavalcade acknowledged the watching crowd with a display of wooden weapons, wooden artillery, little galleys stuffed with dolls in western hats, huge globes with hatchets suspended significantly over them, a camel, and a large number of footmen shouting praises to the pasha and army. The aga of the janissaries came accompanied by four big furled flags and companies of dervishes, all singing and leaping and whirling, followed by the green flag of the emirs, attended by green turbaned emirs without weapons and on horseback. The kadis, or Islamic judges, of Constantinople, rode past, and the six chief porters of the palace. Next came the royal standards, three with a horsetail, more banners, the flag of the Prophet, green and 'odd shaped' – then the Grand Vizier's horses, all caparisoned to the ground, attended by

* Marching in step went out with the Roman road, and returned with tarmacadam.

pageboys in matching livery, some leading, some riding, with bows and arrows and chain-mail coats under their clothes, mail on their heads too, and a little hat. Then legal dignitaries. Then the viziers who, with the Grand Vizier, made up the Sultan's council, the divan. Then the Chief White Eunuch, who controlled the palace officials and who, as the Grand Vizier's deputy in his absence, had on this occasion engineered the Grand Vizier's departure in the first place. With him was the highest Islamic dignitary, the Mufti, 'the finest looking man with the most splendid and venerable beard I have ever seen in my life,' della Valle recalled, adding that 'by a man's presence and his beard' the Turks 'tend to deduce his valour and brains'.

Surrounded by footsoldiers, the Grand Vizier himself, with his heron plume on his turban, smiling and bowing to right and left (a privilege reserved to himself and the Sultan) was pursued by further squadrons of spahis with unhilted lances like spears, bows and arrows and, for some, light mail coats. Behind them rode the Grand Vizier's cavalry, in the same gear but bearing different pennants, and wearing mail coats and helmets without visors, golden stirrups, and carrying bucklers, on horses decked to the ground in cloth of gold. This, our witness thought, had been the most attractive display of all, as the whole army embarked, amid salvoes, for Asia.

It seemed like the grandest caravan in the world, bound to reap surefire profits from the far corners of the empire, to return laden with booty in the autumn. When the Sultan himself rode out, he was surrounded by his household cavalry, the men stationed on his right flank all left handed, to draw their arrows from the quiver like a mirror image of the squadron on his left. At their back, on the march, came a vast troop of beasts of burden: thousands of horses; thousands of camels led by muffled Bedouin; buffaloes pulling the heavy cannon; and already the janissaries had begun letting their beards grow, to show their hardness.

In the van of the army rode a mob of volunteers, kicking up a cloud of yellow dust, prepared to live on what they could pillage in enemy territory and hoping to be rewarded for their skill by promotion to the ranks – in one terrible assault, so Rycaut tells us, a single timar was awarded, and re-awarded, eight times. Mostly from Anatolia, their service, which was free, was indispensable to a good campaign, for these *akinci* bands roamed far and wide, showing themselves in Styria, in Saxony and Bavaria; some reached the Rhine and burnt crops; and their presence in the enemy's rear – torching a soldier's farm, cutting an army's lines – was very demoralising.

In pitched battle, as in sieges, these cannon fodder proved their worth, flying at the enemy like dust, battering defences with their bare hands, sapping the enemy's strength long before real battle commenced. At Belgrade, the janissaries stormed the walls over a moat filled up by dead akinci. Again and again, attacking and then wheeling in apparent flight, they lured their over-eager opponents into traps.

Hungary's effort to contain the Turks on the lower Danube had failed at Nicopolis in 1396; but only Hungary could hope to check the Turks in Central Europe. In recognition of the fact the Serbs handed them Belgrade in 1426, to be the centerpiece of a southern defence line. For a century, Hungary was in constant dynastic alliance with Bohemia, Poland or Austria; but the costs of defence could not so easily be spread, and even though the brilliant general Hunyadi saved Belgrade in 1456 and came within an ace of marching on Edirne in 1451, he was always fatally strapped for cash and arms. His son Matthias, who became King of Hungary in 1458, was at best able to organise a coherent system of home defence.

The Ottomans, by then, were rolling the Balkans up. Serbia was incorporated in 1459; Bosnia in 1463. The Peloponnese fell in 1460. Albania succumbed after the death of her heroic warrior Scanderbeg in 1468. Moldavia followed Wallachia, and became a fee-paying vassal of the Sultan in 1455: neither of these storehouses of grain, timber, honey and furs could defend itself against the Turks, who occupied Wallachia's Danube frontier in the late fourteenth century, Moldavia's less than a century later. Against both they could unleash at will the terrible fury of the Crimean Tartars, whose khan had become a vassal of the empire in 1475.

With Hungary struggling to defend herself – Smederovo and Galamboc on the Hungarian frontier were taken by the Turks in 1439 – the physical occupation of the Danubian Principalities seemed unnecessary. Their rulers became Ottoman vassals and, much later, appointees.

By the end of the fifteenth century the Ottomans had brought their dominion to a comfortable point: their borders lapping against Hungary on the middle Danube, against the steppe in the north, against Iran and the Arab states in the Middle East. It was this latter region which held out the fattest promise: take Arabia, even Egypt, and the Ottoman monopoly over trade routes from the East into the Mediterranean world would be complete.

So it was that in 1514 this brave Ottoman troop turned east. The horsetails were planted on the Scutari shore, and the cannon and chains which protected the camp from cavalry attack were rumbled forward. Within three years Sultan Selim (1511–21), known to history as Selim the Grim, had made himself master of Iran, Iraq and Egypt, the heartlands of his faith, and the Sherif of Mecca handed him the keys to the holiest city of Islam.

8

Suleyman the Magnificent

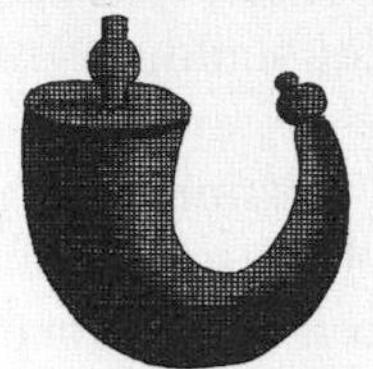

On 18 July 1520, Sultan Selim left Constantinople to join his army assembling near Edirne, a hundred miles to the west. All Selim's campaigns to date had been into Persia, and Arabia, and Egypt; but for the first time in his eight-year reign the horsetails stood at the Edirne Gate; old symbols of Turkish authority, they announced to the world, and the mustering troops, that the pride of Ottoman arms was moving west, towards Europe. Only halfway to Edirne, on 21 September, Selim died, a chronicler wrote, 'of an infected boil, and thereby Hungary was spared'.

The traditions which governed Ottoman succession moved smoothly into operation. Selim's Grand Vizier kept the news of his master's death secret in the camp, while the fastest messenger service in the world carried word to Selim's only son, Suleyman, currently acting as military governor of Manisa across the Dardanelles. Because Suleyman had no brothers, on this occasion the empire would escape the conflict which usually marred Ottoman succession by the implementation of the law of fratricide.

Suleyman, then twenty-six years old, reached Constantinople on Sunday 30 September, within eight days of his father's death. There he was escorted to the mosque and tomb at Eyup, on the upper reaches of the Golden Horn, outside the city walls. To Ottoman believers, this was the third holiest site in the world, after Mecca and Jerusalem, the spot where Eyup Ensari, the Prophet's friend and standard bearer, had been buried during the first Arab siege of Constantinople, which took place between AD 674 and 678. The siege had failed, the burial site was lost, and Constantinople remained in Christian hands for another eight centuries; but during the successful Ottoman siege of the city in 1453 Eyup's tomb was miraculously rediscovered, and Mehmet the Conqueror had a *kulliye*, or mosque complex, erected there. After his own death, it became the custom for all succeeding sultans to be girded with the sword of their illustrious ancestor, Osman Gazi, at Eyup's tomb, and then to visit the tomb of the Conqueror himself, in the great kulliye* he had built in the middle of Constantinople, over the old Byzantine Church of the Holy Apostles.

At dawn the following day – Monday 1 October 1520 – he received the homage of the high officials at the gate of the third court, in the Topkapi Palace. In the afternoon he met his father's funeral procession at the Edirne Gate, and escorted the body to its burial place: his first official decree was to order the erection of a kulliye in Selim's honour. Two days later he distributed the now customary donative, or bakshish, to the Janissary Corps: a larger sum, it was noted, than his father had thought necessary to give them eight years before. He also gave money to the other household troops, and various palace functionaries. To demonstrate his own regard for mercy and justice he decreed that some Cairene intellectuals Selim had brought to Constantinople by force should be allowed home; a boycott of Iranian goods was lifted, with compensation; and a few persistent evildoers were executed.

'He is tall, but wiry, and of a delicate complexion. His neck is a little too long, his face thin, and his nose aquiline . . . a pleasant mien, though his skin tends to pallor. He is said to be a wise lord,

* This was constructed around the Fatih Camii, the Conqueror's Mosque, which was entirely rebuilt after an earthquake in 1766; the complex included eight theological schools, a hospice, a soup kitchen, a hospital, a caravanserai for visiting merchants, a primary school, library, public bath, market and graveyard.

fond of study, and all men hope for good from his rule.' So Bernardo Contarini summed up the new Sultan at his accession. Selim's conquests had given Europe a breathing space of some twenty years. 'A gentle lamb had succeeded a fierce lion,' Jovius wrote, while Pope Leo X had prayers sung all over Rome.

While the earliest Ottoman sultans had been dubbed 'Gran Turco' by the Italian city-states, later, as their prestige and power grew, they were referred to as 'Gran Signor'. For Suleyman the West reserved its highest commendation. Suleyman the Magnificent signed himself ruler of thirty-seven kingdoms, lord of

> the realms of the Romans, and the Persians and the Arabs,
> hero of all that is, pride of the arena of earth and time!
> Of the Mediterranean and the Black Sea;
> Of the glorified Kaaba and the illumined Medina, the noble Jerusalem and the throne of Egypt, that rarity of the age;
> Of the province of Yemen, and Aden and Sana, and of Baghdad the abode of rectitude, and Basra and al-Hasa and the Cities of Nushirivan;
> Of the lands of Algiers and Azerbaijan, the steppes of the Kipchak and the land of Tartars;
> Of Kurdistan and Luristan, and of the countries of Rumelia and Anatolia and Karaman and Wallachia and Moldavia and Hungary all together, and of many more worthy kingdoms and countries:
> Sultan and Padishah.

Suleyman was sometimes known as Suleyman II, in coy deference to his biblical namesake. He was to be styled 'the Perfecter of the Perfect Number', for his whole existence was hedged about with the number of good fortune, ten – the number of the Commandments, the number of Muhammad's disciples, of the parts and variants of the Koran, of the toes, the fingers, and the astronomical heavens of Islam. Sultan Suleyman was the tenth ruler of his house, born at the beginning of the tenth century, the year 900 of the Hegira, AD 1493.

Successive Venetian ambassadors at his court found themselves dealing with a sovereign who could put 100,000 men into the field at no visible cost, whose borders ran for 8,000 miles, who was so exalted that he only gave audience in profile, and then did not deign to speak. In their reports they were puzzled as how best to describe his powers, whether geographically, classically, politically, numerically or financially – so that one pictured his empire in near fantastical terms, saying its borders ran with Spain, Persia and the empire of Prester John.*

Under no other sultan would the Ottoman Empire be so universally admired or feared. Suleyman's corsairs plundered the ports of Spain. Indian rajahs begged his aid. So did the King of France, who once had letters smuggled to the Sultan from an Italian prison cell, hidden in the heel of his envoy's shoe. The Iranians burnt their country on his account. The Hungarians lost their nobility at a stroke. 'He roars like a lion along our frontier,' wrote one foreign ambassador, and even the Habsburgs gave him tribute. His reputation was so splendid and magnanimous that twenty years after his death the English begged his successors for a fleet to help them tackle the Spanish Armada. Thirty years later a Neapolitan traveller went to admire his sepulchre in Constantinople, 'for surely though he was a Turk, the least I could do was to look at his coffin with feeling, for the valorous deeds he accomplished when alive'. When he went to war – thirteen times on major campaigns, endlessly on stiletto raids – foreign descriptions of the cavalcade ran to chapters. The flight of the Knights of Rhodes to Malta in 1526 made the eastern Mediterranean Ottoman; and the coast of North Africa right up to Algiers was ruled by the Barbary corsairs in the Sultan's name. When Suleyman went to sleep, four pages watched the candles for him. When he rode through the city or into battle or out hunting, they went with him, as one of the overwhelmed Venetian ambassadors reported, 'one to carry his arms, another his rain clothes, the third a pitcher full of an iced drink, and the fourth something else'.

Better known in Turkish history as Suleyman Kanuni, 'the

* Habsburg Central Europe was, of course, an extension of the power of Habsburg Spain; Egypt lay close to the fabled Christian 'empire' of Abyssinia.

Lawgiver', Suleyman oversaw the most detailed codification of sultanic and Koranic law that had ever been known in an Islamic state, surpassed only by the work of Justinian, in the same city of Constantinople, almost a thousand years before. The law fixed the duties and rights of all the Sultan's subjects, in accordance with Islamic precepts, established the relationship between non-Muslims and Muslims, and laid out the codes by which society was to understand and comport itself, down to the clothes which different people were to wear.

He ruled so long that he became something of an Ottoman Queen Victoria, the very embodiment of his state. Fantastically impassive, for example, was his reaction to news of a great naval victory over the Holy Roman Emperor, King of Bohemia and the Low Countries and Emperor Elect of all the Germanies, Charles V, whom Suleyman referred to as 'the King of Spain'. When the Ottoman admiral sailed his fleet up the Horn, a little pinnace ran ahead trailing the high standard of Spain in the water from her stern. The admiral's flagship was laden with high-born Christians, including a Spanish commander-in-chief. A long line of captured vessels, dismasted and rudderless, bobbed along behind like ducks, while forty-seven other ships of the Christian fleet – ships of Naples, Florence, Genoa, Sicily and Malta (all fitted up by the Pope himself) – were now sunk in the shallows off the Tunisian coast. The Spanish were chastened by their attempt on North Africa. Their greatest admiral, Andrea Doria, was lucky to escape to Italy with his life. Suleyman went down to a kiosk on the water's edge to give his Kapudan Pasha the honour of his attendance; but not for a second did his expression change, 'the same severity and gravity as if the victory had nothing concerned him, so capable was the heart of that old sire of any fortune, were it never so great'.

He fell in love magnificently, and to the astonishment of the whole world he not only married the slave girl Roxelana, but was faithful to her; and everyone – the French, the Italians, the Russians – unabashedly claimed her as their own. He seldom wore the same clothes twice. He was majestic enough to stock his court with an unusual number of buffoons, dwarves, mutes, astrologers, and silent janissaries; lofty enough to enrol in a janissary regiment, and draw pay with them; and so rich that one bailio advised the Serenissima that it was no longer the value of presents that counted at court, but only their volume, for nobody even bothered to look at them.

Suleyman's first move in 1521 was to offer to suspend Turkish raids against Hungary in return for tribute. The Hungarians clipped the ears and nose of his envoy and sent him back. An envoy of their own was sent to Worms, where so many princes of the Holy Roman Empire had assembled in diet, to seek allies in the coming war. 'Who prevented the unbridled madness of the Turks from raging further?' the envoy demanded, with magificent flourish. 'The Hungarians!' The princes had not come to hear him, though; just the day before, Charles V had condemned Luther as a heretic, and the Holy Roman Empire was about to fall part.

So while the cream of Hungarian society attended a wedding in Pressburg, the gentle lamb took Belgrade. The loss of Belgrade punctured the southern Hungarian defence line: Busbecq was thinking of this when he described the Turks as 'mighty rivers, swollen with rain, which, if they can trickle through at any point in the banks, spread through the breach and cause infinite destruction'. This, and Suleyman's attack on Rhodes, brilliantly marshalled and so relentlessly pursued that he had his war tent rebuilt in stone to represent his adamantine determination, signalled the return of the Ottomans to Europe.

For two hundred years the Knights of the Order of St John on Rhodes had been preying on Muslim shipping, sheltering Christian pirates, and massacring their prisoners. (An Englishwoman *en route* for Jerusalem in 1320 had supposedly purged her soul by dispatching a thousand saracens herself.) Their presence as a hostile island in the Sultan's seas imperilled the passage of Egyptian grain and Egyptian cash to Istanbul, and those shipbound pilgrims to Mecca whom the Sultan was newly bound to protect. Their fortress was considered impregnable. They had 60,000 men, one of whom had invented a giant cowhide stethoscope to hear where the enemy were digging mines; another was the son of Suleyman's great-uncle Cem; he was a Christian who fought with the knights. When Suleyman took the surrender of the place he asked for them both. The knights pretended the stethoscope man was dead and smuggled him out; but Cem's son was handed over to be killed along with his family. In an audience given on Christmas Day, Suleyman praised the Grand Master of the order for his gallant defence. It caused him great sorrow, he whispered aside, to make this Christian in his old age abandon his home and his belongings. The knights left on New Year's Day 1523, and ten years later they established themselves again on Malta, further to the west, leaving the eastern Mediterranean to the Ottomans.

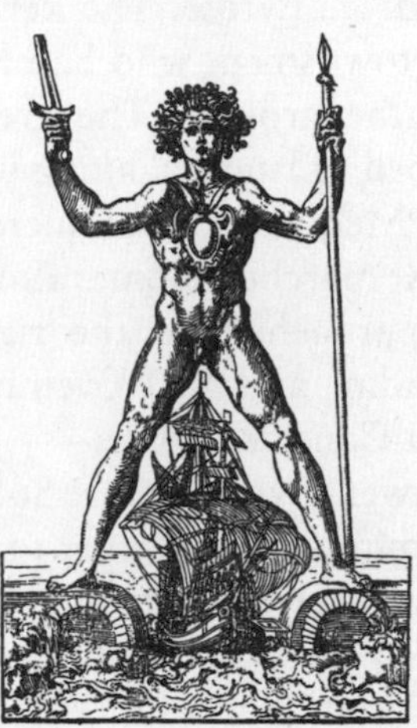

Sixteenth century image of Colossus of Rhodes

In Hungary, the collapse of the southern defences coincided with the shattering of the country's political strength. A young Polish king had been elected. Louis was ten when they crowned him: born too soon, married too soon, king too soon, died too soon, they quipped afterwards. Four years later, in 1526, when the magnates were at last driven to make common cause with the crown, they moaned that the royal policy of going forward to meet the enemy was an expense better avoided, and insisted on camping at Mohacs, between a marsh and a river. All the errors the French had committed at Nicopolis the Hungarians now repeated. The nobility clamoured for battle. They refused to fall back and gather in a Transylvanian army, or to wait for the Bohemians; and they haughtily dismissed the suggestion of a Polish mercenary that they entrench behind fortified waggons, as the Bohemian Hussites had done to such effect against cavalry at the battle of the White Mountain. They died just as the French at Nicopolis had done, driving too far into the enemy centre and enclosed by the Turkish wings like a fly in a trap. Hungary died at Mohacs: two archbishops, five bishops, most of its magnates and knights. As for the little king himself, Suleyman wept to see his corpse; but his chronicler reflected the general satisfaction. 'A nation of impious men has been extirpated! Praise be to God!' he wrote. The keys to Buda were offered up by the common townsmen, who had lost their leaders, and the city was razed to the ground. The great library of Matthias Corvinus was shipped to Istanbul along with two enormous cannons, abandoned by Mehmet the Conqueror at the siege of Belgrade in 1456. The army marched home along the left bank of the Danube, having approached on the right, taking booty all the way to Peterwaradin; and in November the Sultan made a triumphal entry into Constantinople.

It was twenty years before Suleyman formally annexed Hungary to his dominions, preferring to see the region buffeted by squabbles between rival claimants to the throne while he turned his attention to Persia and the Mediterranean. Little Louis II had died childless; John Zapolya, Voivode of Transylvania, claimed the throne with Ottoman support by the election of his peers. Ferdinand, Duke of Austria, and brother to Charles V, advanced his candidacy through marriage. 'No king, only a little man of Vienna,' the Ottomans called him, but he had the Habsburg doggedness and by 1538 he had persuaded Zapolya, who had neither wife nor child, to make him his heir.

Zapolya promptly married a Polish princess, Isabella, who bore him a son two weeks before he died, annulling as far as he was concerned his earlier agreement with Ferdinand. It was such a fortuitous event that Suleyman even sent a chaush to witness for himself the queen suckling the infant. Ferdinand of Austria, without the money to press his claim very forcibly, was thwarted; but really it all made very little difference. In 1541 Suleyman arrived at Buda, which Isabella had been defending against Ferdinand's attacks, and lifted it from her with an oath to return it when her baby came of age. Ferdinand was granted a peace a few years later, which allowed him to keep a little corner of north-eastern Hungary in return for 30,000 ducats in tribute; and the queen, when the moment came, was persuaded to accept estates in southern Poland.

But although Suleyman consistently treated Ferdinand with withering contempt, that 'little man of Vienna' kept resolute possession of his capital. Vienna, by rights, should have long since fallen to the Sultan. As early as 1529, three years after Mohacs and the capture of Buda, a surprisingly rapid series of victories in Hungary had brought Suleyman's army to Vienna's walls. 'Tell him that I will look for him on the field of Mohacs, or even in Pest,' Suleyman had told the Archduke's envoys; 'and if he fails to meet me there I will offer him battle beneath the walls of Vienna itself.' Now those walls were pierced; the suburbs were burnt; and the city itself, according to its defenders, was on the point of giving way, when Suleyman abruptly announced his decision to withdraw on 14 October 1529. He spent, that year, 201 days on the march, and a mere nineteen on the siege.

In 1532 he came back, with an army primed for the assault – perhaps as many as 300,000 men, including those who swung into place as they marched through Hungary in July and August. The Holy Roman Emperor Charles V, King of Spain and her colonies, was this time in Vienna, as Suleyman knew. For a moment Charles had quieted his bickering princes, allowing him to raise an army in Germany and visit the battlefront in person. Charles V and Sultan Suleyman were, each in his respective sphere, the lords of the age. Upon Charles's victory hung the future of his own house, of course, with that of the lands he ruled, Spain, the Netherlands, much of Italy and the whole of Germany, from the Baltic to Bohemia. In all Christendom only the French, everywhere squeezed between Habsburg satraps, were eager to see him beaten.

The weather, which was bad when the Ottoman army left Edirne in May, became atrocious by mid-June, when they reached the little town of Guns, some seventy miles south-east of Vienna on the River Raab (the modern Koeszegh). The incessant rain had forced the abandonment of the unwieldy big cannon, drawn by oxen who slipped and slithered in the mud and slowed down the pace of the whole army, while Guns itself was so small that the besieging force was never able to deploy its numerical advantage to best effect. The tiny garrison, of course, had no business holding out: their defence was foolhardy and gallant. Repeated assaults, similar to those which had battered the walls and exhausted the defences of Constantinople, did finally force the surrender of the citadel. The Ottomans allowed the garrison to march out with full military honours but the progress of the Ottoman army had been checked by a month. The campaign season was too far advanced for a full-scale siege of Vienna to have much chance of success; Suleyman must have hoped, instead, that the Habsburg army would come out to meet him. It refused him that satisfaction.

Charles V and Suleyman the Magnificent had much in common; and though each made much of the other's failure to give battle, and declared himself victor by default, both were perhaps relieved that the gigantic edifices which they carried on their backs had not been hazarded in a day's battle.* And for Suleyman it was not a defeat; not by any means. Yet a succession of victories like these gave him pause for thought. In 1537 he led the first campaign in the Ottoman annals to return without booty; and almost twenty years later, after his failure against the Knights of Malta in 1556, he brought the fleet home by night, and wandered the streets of Istanbul incognito to hear what the people said.

Suleyman's high aspirations warred with his suspicious, gloomy, passionate nature. His long reign is flawed by tragedy more subtle

* If anything, Lutheranism was the victor of the non-event: the incursions of Suleyman's akinci, and Charles V's first and only brush with the Turks on land, convinced the Emperor at last of the gravity of the threat, and of the need to reconcile himself with the Lutheran princes of Germany. Without this, the young faith might have been successfully suppressed.

than the hubris which had overcome his ancestor Bayezit the Thunderbolt; more consequential than the gilded misery reserved for later sultans. The higher men rose in the empire, the closer they got to the bowstring; and the reign of Suleyman seems in retrospect coiled round with a silken garotte.

On 31 August 1526 – that buoyant year for Ottoman arms, when the Sultan carried the day at Mohacs, annihilating Hungarian opposition – he penned this most depressing diary entry: 'Rain falls in torrents. 2,000 prisoners executed.' In his lifetime he pushed the borders of the empire further than ever before, but he may have realised, before he died, that he had found their limits, too. He was a poet and a fighter, a patron of the faith, and of the arts and sciences, a monarch who understood his duty, but he was more ruthless within his own borders than in enemy territory. He had his best friend murdered. On the death of one of his children he threw his turban on the ground, ripped off his jewels, stripped all the decorations from the walls of the palace and turned the carpets upside down, before he followed the coffin to its grave in a chariot drawn by weeping horses. Yet his son Mustafa was strangled by mutes whiles Suleyman watched from behind a screen: he had been given to believe that Mustafa was plotting a coup. Another son, Bayezit, saw the writing on the wall; he mounted the coup, was defeated, and fled to Persia from where, after negotiation, the Shah delivered him to Suleyman's executioner. Suleyman left the empire to Selim, a drunkard, but Roxelana's child. In his last years, his instinctive morbidity crowded out the high hopes and generosity of his youth – he dressed plainly, dined off earthenware platters, and fostered the triumph of orthodox Islam, making the wisest mullah, the Grand Mufti of Constantinople, into a sort of Muslim Patriarch, in command of a new Islamic hierarchy. But when the Austrian ambassador took leave of Suleyman in his old age, it was scarcely a living being he described, but a sort of metaphor of empire, rotting and majestic, fat, made up, and suffering from an ulcerous leg.

9

Order

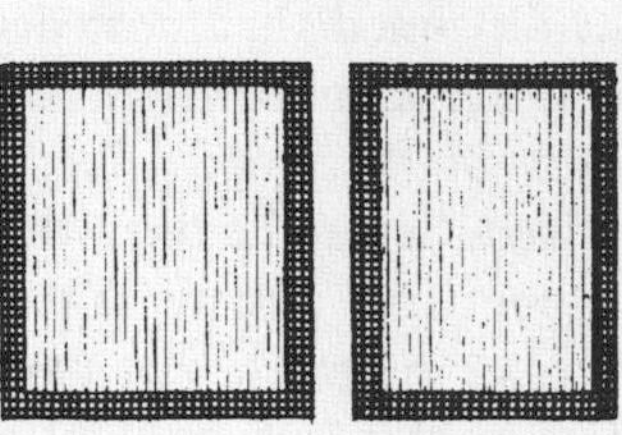

In battle, said Kritovolos, men 'slaughtered each other and mercilessly cut each other to pieces, charging and being charged, wounding and being wounded, killing and being killed, shouting, blaspheming, swearing, hardly conscious of anything that was happening or of what they were doing, just like madmen'. But the frenzy of battle is short-lived; soldiers are often the mildest of men; and the Ottomans themselves were not a confrontational people. They had no programme to implement beyond arranging for their own upkeep. They didn't demand conversions to their faith. They didn't insist on their own language. 'The whole Policie is enlargement,' a sixteenth-century observer deduced; and unlike a host of later imperialists, the Turks never asked themselves why other people could not be more like them.

For the Ottomans knew the answer. Soon enough the Mahdi who was to usher in the end of the world would come, correct the prevalence of unbelief, and prove them right; until then it was enough to keep order, and patiently expand the Abode of Peace, holding the world in trust.

For all their tolerance towards the habits and beliefs of people of the book, however, they loathed the Shias with an anxious passion, for the Shi'ite heresy threatened their complacent expectations. The followers of Ali tended to mysticism, in contrast to the worldly Sunni princes, and conventional authorities perceived them as a challenge. Selim the Grim was terrible to the Shi'ite *kisilbas*, literally 'red-heads', who wore red turbans and were seen as a danger to the state; he hunted them down in their thousands through eastern Anatolia. There was a general known simply as 'the Butcher', who massacred heretics wherever he met them, and whenever their core assumptions were challenged, whenever they felt truly frightened, the Ottomans seemed to lose control. Otherwise they could put up with a great deal. David Urquhart* in the 1830s once watched a little boy tormenting his janissary father in the porch of his house, astonished that for all the old soldier's furious remonstrances he never lifted a finger in self-defence. At last he asked the man why he didn't just give the boy a beating.

'Ah!' said the soldier. 'What clever people you Franks are!'

The Ottomans waged war hard, but they governed their conquests with a light hand. The very nature of the territory they inherited made it vital that people looked after themselves: it was one thing to marshal armies at a whistle and send them thundering up the border roads, quite another to penetrate into every nook and cranny of this remarkably corrugated empire and attend to all that was going on.

For all its glitter and martial energy, for all the riches which poured into Constantinople, the empire was pastoral at bottom. It was a land of mountains: the Pindus, the Carpathians; the impenetrable mountains of central Greece, Mount Olympus in Thessaly, the land of eagles itself, Albania. The name Balkan, meaning mountain, has grown to cover the whole region south of the Danube, in what was European Turkey; and geographers have never quite decided where one range of mountains ends and another one be-

* British consul in Constantinople 1834–6, he travelled widely in the European portion of the empire and wrote a penetrating and entertaining apologia for Turkish rule in *Spirit of the East*. He retired to a Moorish palace in Watford, where he entertained naked in a Turkish bath. Lear considered him 'very sufficiently mad'.

gins. Ottoman islands were often like Welsh bonnets, ports and settlers on the brim, herdsmen on the crown. In the east rose the Haemus, the Pontic and Taurus mountains of Anatolia, the jagged scree of Azerbaijan, the fastnesses of the Caucasus; and between the mountain pastures and the plains thousands of the empire's subjects roamed according to the seasons, and lived a nomadic or half-nomadic life. It was an empire of seasonal movement, where the shepherds who climbed to the plateaux in summer would die if they stayed over the winter; where ships only set out after the Patriarch had blessed the waters in the spring, and would have foundered if they attempted the journey earlier. Between October and April, the mountains and the seas closed down, like the bazaars at night; and the empire half slept, like a hibernatory beast.

Invisibility was the nomad's natural defence. Sometimes settled people, for a quiet life, pretended not to see them. Sometimes they melted into the shadows, the rocks and trees. It was the business of the state to flush them out and make them settle down for the convenience of tax officials; but Ottoman nomadism was a sort of constant, more enduring than the clutter settlers could gather around themselves.

The Ottomans had to recognise about thirty different tribal governments in the highlands of Armenia and Kurdistan. The old Gheg chieftains of northern Albania were semi-independent. The Yörük tribes who wandered in Anatolia dealt with the authorities on their own initiative. Some of them were Shi'ite, some were Sunni; often it was impossible to tell. They spoke a variety of Turkish dialects, identifying themselves by the flocks they tended, white sheep or black goats, or by a place of supposed origin. Their movements from summer to winter quarters and back again were carefully watched, and if they broke the rule against staying longer than three days anywhere on the route, or marauded, a special police guard was on hand to inflict immediate punishment.

Yörüks were clannish and married amongst themselves, unless they stole a girl from a neighbouring tribe. (Marriage as a theft was practised by semi-nomads all through the empire, while among settled people it was generally a stylised feature of the marriage ceremony. The Crimean Tartar custom was for the bridal party to chase the groom and his retinue right up to his tent flap, whereupon her friends implored her not to dismount and his family begged her to get down and give them all presents.) The tinker who fixed the tackle and retinned the pots was paid collectively with cheese and butter. Every wife had her own tent, where she would spin, weave, churn; she might tend the camels, or the goats, or forage for fuel and water; and she invariaby went unveiled.

The routes the Yörüks took were marked by the graves of their fellows and forebears, generally under some sacred tree; and as they passed they would throw a few stones on the grave, and tie rags and wooden spoons in the branches.

Against this order in motion, the gypsies were noted for dancing bears, for telling fortunes, for potions, and singing at weddings, for metalwork and horses, and they never seemed very subdued by the grave decorum of their wandering cousins. Nobody ever really knew very much about them; they were despised everywhere, and the cruellest thing that anyone could do was to lock a gypsy up in gaol.

As for the Vlachs, those Balkan shepherds who moved on foot, struck their goathair tents in the noonday sun, and spoke a Latin dialect like Romanian which inspired the romantic notion of their descent from Trajan's lost legionaries, they were Christian Orthodox, and the Ottomans employed them, now and then, to guard the passes and spy on enemy movements; but as often as not they passed easily from side to side, treating the border with contempt. 'Vlach' means a stranger. They ranged the hills, fierce men with their woven rain capes and their shaggy mastiffs, moving from one settlement to the next, buying and selling a little as they went, so that the Greeks maintained that five Vlachs made a market – and sneered at them too, for being so landlubberly that the very word 'Vlach' came to signify, in Greek, a man who had never seen the sea. Across the higher ranges of the Balkans lay a tangle of Vlachs – the limping Vlachs, Black Vlachs, Albano-Vlachs, Arumanians, the Sarakatsans who roamed deep into Anatolia; some who protested that they were not Vlachs at all, and others who pretended to be Vlachs; and some who gave wickedness a country, Klephtouria; and some barely recognised even in the 1940s, who covered both the Balkans and the highlands of Anatolia in their shepherd rounds, and spoke, it appears, the Greek of the ancient Greeks, unmixed by the speech of invaders since before Christ; and some who were thought dirtier than anyone in the world; and one (according to Eliot in the late nineteenth century), who built himself a summer residence in the hills, and proved to be so houseproud that he repaired a broken window with a new piece of glass, instead of a sheet of brown paper, 'a proceeding, I believe, unique in the Levant'.

It paid the nomads to appear fierce and truculent, and to hold themselves aloof; for they were notoriously hard to tax. Townsmen, though in principle afraid, were fascinated by them. When a Bedouin chief pitched camp near the walls of Damascus, he received a flood of visitors. Some of them, an English merchant recalled, got to spend the night in a tent. One made the chief a hot meat pie, although 'when he saw it cut up and opened, and perceived smoake to come out of it, he shrunke backe, fearing it had beene some engine to destroy him, and that the fire would follow after the smoake'. Eventually 'he was content to taste it, and highly commended it, as the daintiest dish that ever he tasted of in his life'.

The Ottomans were always interested in effective forms of self-government. They reissued the exemplary Saxon mining laws they inherited with the Balkan mines, as part of the Sultan's own kanun. They folded the old Serbian *voynuk* into the military organisation. 'They pay great respect to the customs of foreign nations,' it seemed to Busbecq, 'even to the detriment of their own religious scruples.'

The Ottomans demanded that every subject should belong to the retinue of some great man; or to one of the guilds which regulated the quality and price of a man's work, told him where to live, and protected him in hard times; or to a regiment, a religious fraternity, or just a village, as the responsibility of a headman. The affairs of the Muslim community were perfectly regulated by the Koran, which was law as much as faith; and while it was the Sultan's duty to ensure that Islamic law prevailed in any conflict between Muslims and unbelievers, Christians and Jews were expected to have their own laws, too. Everyone was organised in *millets*, based on faith, and as long as the millet did not come into conflict with Islamic organisation and society, provided it stumped up its taxes and kept the peace, its leaders were left to run their own affairs.

The authorities established the millets in law as simply as possible. The Orthodox Christians had recognised a number of independent churches before the Ottoman conquest, but Mehmet II abolished all rivals to the ecumenical Greek Patriarch of Constantinople, to whom he gave three horsetails, and wide-ranging clerical and secular powers over his flock. The Jews formed their own millet shortly afterwards. The Gregorian Patriarch ruled not only over the Armenian population within the empire, but over everyone else who had been left out, the gypsies, the Assyrians, the Monophysites of Syria and Egypt, and the Bogomils of Bulgaria. The Armenian millet was extremely useful, for its elasticity; and as time wore on it came to include the Maronites of Lebanon, who answered to the Pope in Rome, the Latin Catholics of Hungary, Croatia and northern Albania, and the uniate Armenians of Cilicia and Palestine.

Shielded from the bullies of the Counter-Reformation, Protestant doctrine spread through Ottoman Hungary: the boy levy, in fact, was never extended to Hungary, and in the Balkans, beyond this single imposition, no efforts were made to convert Christians to Islam. Sixteenth-century cadastral registers suggests that only about 300 families in the entire Balkan region converted in any year, and conversion was a feature of town life. The empire wanted tax-paying subjects, not Muslims: one function of the levy, which so outraged Christian spectators, was precisely to limit the number of converts. Mehmet the Conqueror would always meet the Greek Patriarch Gennadius at the church door, not for fear of polluting himself by entering an infidel place of worship but, conversely, for fear of consecrating it: wherever he placed his foot was hallowed ground,* and his followers could have seized upon his entry into the church as an excuse to turn it into a mosque.

Mehmet enacted sumptuary laws soon after the conquest, and the medley of costumes in the streets of a city indicated order. Greeks wore black trousers and slippers; the Armenians violet slippers and purple trousers; the Jews sky-blue trousers and slippers, and certain very privileged non-believers were allowed to wear yellow slippers and red trousers, like a Turk. Arsenal guards stuck knives in their belts. Dustmen had red leather smocks. Hajjis, who had completed the pilgrimage to Mecca, were entitled to a green turban. Important personages sported tall turbans, wound around a sort of witch's hat; holy men wound their turbans round a skullcap, so that they were wider and flatter, and wore black gowns. In the countryside every district and valley and mountain and profession had its own distinctive variant of dress. Travellers were slotted into the order of things through the rules of Ottoman hospitality, which placed responsibility for their conduct on their hosts. Visitors of the highest rank, ambassadors and their suites, were maintained at public expense;† others, by charity. Foreign merchants answered to their own representatives in Smyrna, perhaps, or Istanbul, and were to be chastised in their own courts (unless the offence was against a Muslim) just as the janissaries were brought to book in theirs.

* Like the roses which, the Albanians politely said, sprang up wherever Enver Hoxha trod.

† Which of course put them on an uneasy footing, as any ambassador slung into gaol at the outbreak of hostilities discovered. The leap from generosity to implacable enmity was well illustrated in the fate of Baron Wratislaw, a young Bohemian nobleman who accompanied the imperial ambassador to Istanbul in 1599. He was of an open mind, high-spirited, and for a year he enjoyed himself hugely, but war with Austria broke out in 1600 and he and other members of the embassy were first imprisoned in the Arsenal, manacled in pairs, then in the dreaded Black Tower, in a room without light, so poorly treated that when they found a way to make a porridge out of hoarded scraps of bread they found it 'extremely nice, especially when at times we procured some olive oil, made it rich for ourselves, and licked our fingers afterwards'. After hair-raising vicissitudes the party finally regained Prague, only narrowly escaping death as they blundered across the battlefields, and on their return the Emperor Rudolf personally listened to their tale, with tears in his eyes. 'Wir wollen tun!' he thundered when they asked him for some back pay, by way of compensation; but no doubt he was a busy man, for that was the last any of them heard of it.

Caste was much more important than class: no man was dishonourable who fulfilled the role he was born to play.* 'When a rich man meets an inferior in the street,' wrote Hobhouse in the early nineteenth century, 'he not only returns his salute but goes through the whole round of complimentary enquiries which are always usual on a casual encounter.' The easy familiarity of master and slave was a source of constant wonder to visitors from the West, but there was no shame or blame attached to slavery. It was another way of belonging. Busbecq wondered 'whether the man who first abolished slavery was really a public benefactor; there would not perhaps be need of so many gallows and gibbets to restrain those who possess nothing but their life and liberty, and whose want drives them to crimes of every kind', which he recognised as characteristic of his own country.

The citizens of Ragusa (modern Dubrovnik), with characteristic foresight, had petitioned the Pope for permission to trade with infidels right after the Turks' first serious victory in Europe, on the Maritsa in 1371; and by the fifteenth century the Ottomans had taken Ragusa under their wing, turning the bustling city-state on the Adriatic into their own Venice, to every doge's fury and despair. The Ragusans appear to have taught the Turks how to make guns in the 1390s, and though the Ottomans stopped the lucrative export of silver from Ragusa the city thrived, its income from Ottoman trade and transhipment always, at a pinch, exceeding the tribute it paid to Istanbul. The Ottomans kept Ragusa's merchants lean enough to follow at a whisper the flux of trade. Ragusans monopolised the salt trade and their councils – or *plazza* – were established in every major Ottoman town in Europe.

* Everyone, after all, was entitled to dignity. Edward Lear did a portrait of an Albanian merchant, and then one of his brother. For want of paper, he squeezed the second 'small but accurate portrait' onto the same sheet. 'O, canto cielo!' said the younger. 'It is true I am the youngest, but I am not smaller than my brother – what right have you to remind me of my inferior position? Why do you come into our house to act so insultingly?' The older brother, too, declared himself 'vexed and hurt . . . if you think that you win my esteem by a compliment paid at the expense of the affection of my brother, you are greatly mistaken.' The pair bowed him out, 'with looks of thunder'.

Power within the city lay firmly with the nobility, who decided in the Grand Council on tariffs and decrees. Policy was decided by a Legislative Council of fifty-one elected nobles, and the daily management of affairs entrusted to a Little Council of eleven. At the head of state stood a sort of doge, the Rector, or Knez. Most of these leaders, Paul Rycaut thought, were selected by a process even more extraordinary than anything Venice could devise – the Rector elected once a month, and lesser officers once a week, and a chatelain singled out by the senate in secret conclave, winked at in the street, blindfolded, and given command for exactly twenty-four hours. The Rector was allowed one term of office only. He lived his month out in the palace – indeed, he was barricaded into it by elaborate protocol and ceremonial – and while all the nobility treated him with enormous reverence, and to some 30,000 ordinary citizens he seemed like the very embodiment of the republic's power, he enjoyed not a whiff of it. Everything was decided by the Little Council. He was obliged to retire when his term was out, and was thereafter never allowed to display any emblem of his former rank until he died, when the regalia were placed on his coffin.

The Ragusans' behaviour was so mild and noble that they had erected a municipal old people's home by 1347, abolished all trafficking in slaves by the fifteenth century, forbidden torture, organised a dole, established a public health service, a town planning institute, and numerous schools; and perhaps once in a quarter-century when their courts were obliged to pass the death sentence they would import a Turkish executioner, and plunge the entire city into mourning. So commercially minded were the nobility who supervised the state that in 1428, at a time of misfortune and foreign threat, they sought to jolly the people by erecting a column dedicated to freedom; the figure they set at the top was of Orlando, a popular knight; but the expense of the undertaking was prudently carried by making his forearm an official measure of length, everywhere known as the Dubrovnik Elbow.

The Jews were expelled from Spain in 1492: a millet launched on the high seas. Sultan Bayezit II heard of their predicament and

Ragusa

ordered his governors to receive them with kindness and assistance. 'They say Ferdinand is a wise monarch,' he told his courtiers. 'How could he be, he who impoverishes his country to enrich mine!' The Spanish Jews after all knew everything, from how to card fine wool to how to manage funds at interest; and they had arrived with a useful knowledge of the ways of a world which the Ottomans fully expected to conquer. Some expected to return – on the back of Ottoman victory or not – and treasured huge old keys to Granadan spice vaults, to palaces with shady courtyards filled with the sound of running water, or to synagogues and banks. For generations, like the Moriscos of North Africa, they regaled their children with stories of the high old Spanish days. Yet in the empire they found themselves very well received; their religion was respected on a par with Christianity, and they were soon writing to friends, agents and acquaintances all across Europe, encouraging them to join them.

They established themselves in every major Balkan city, in Sarajevo, Zemun, Skopje, Belgrade, Monastir, Edirne and Sofia; but above all they settled in Salonica, Thessaloniki, the city to whose ancient Jews – established there, it is said, from the days of Alexander – St Paul had addressed his Epistles. Under the Byzantines, Salonica had been the second city of the empire, with half a million inhabitants; the Jews found it decayed to a kind of swollen village of seven thousand souls, littered with vestiges of Roman rule: not unlike Spain. So the exiled merchant bankers, teachers, officials, doctors, scholars and craftsmen turned Turkish Selanik into a Spanish city, where one could hear the accents of Catalonia and Valencia, Portuguese, the guttural Spanish of Galicia, fluid Castilian, the soft, half-Moorish tones of Andalucia.

The principle of collective responsibility was one of the conditions of Ottoman rule, like boy tribute, which the Chians tried to dodge when they surrendered their Aegean island to Ottoman sovereignty.

Chios had been a Genoese protectorate since the thirteenth century, and it was ruled as a family firm, in a manner which chimed exactly with the commercial instincts of Genoa itself. Power was concentrated in the hands of shareholders, the Mahona, all descendants of a single Genoese clan, the Giustiniani, who emigrated there *en masse* in 1346 and took up, as it were, a commercial franchise on the island. Giovanni Giustiniani, who so nearly saved Constaninople in 1453, was carried back there to die of a broken heart. So powerful were the Giustiniani that every newcomer automatically took their name, and so sensible that from 1407 they had paid the Turks a tribute every year, and so righteous that when Antonio, Bartolomeo, Britio, Cornelio, Filippino, Francesco, Giovanni, Hercole, Hippolito, Paolo, two Pasquales, Rafaelle, and Scipione Giustiniani, with four other Giustiniani boys whose names are lost, were sent to the Seraglio, they suffered martyrdom rather than change their faith, and one of them was so steadfast in his refusal to raise his index finger as a sign of apostasy that 'he clenched his fists so tightly that neither in life nor in death could they ever open them again'. The bulk of Chios's people, though, were Greek.

By 1566 the Ottomans, at the height of their power, were fed up with the Chians. Their tribute payments arrived late, if at all. They showed none of the respect to which the Ottomans, as overlords, were entitled; on the contrary their spies reported on Ottoman affairs, and passed intelligence to the West. They were full of trickery and deceit. The Grand Vizier had at one time threatened 'to blow the roofs off all the houses in Chios' because they had imprudently cultivated his predecessor, along with other enemies of his at court. As long as their primary allegiance was to Genoa, the Chian authorities were a menace to Ottoman power; and the Ottomans resolved to do something about it.

It was the custom for the imperial fleet to collect its tribute every year, making a tour of all the islands; and when the Chians spotted the Turkish sails 'the garrison sounded the tocsin to inform the government, and the inhabitants and the envoys in large boats richly decorated with costly hangings and dressed in the ancient style in long robes of crimson velvet, went to meet the fleet; and after welcoming the admiral with one salute from a gun, the other captains saluted the town in similar manner'. In 1566 the fleet, under the Chians' old friend Admiral Piali Pasha, chose to anchor, instead, outside the harbour mouth. The Mahonesi were debating anxiously what this deviation from routine could mean, when Piali ordered them aboard his flagship. There he warned them that they had placed themselves beyond the pale by their own misconduct, spying, hiding runaway slaves, sheltering Italian pirates, and not paying their dues. The elders replied that the

Sultan's ear had been bent by the malicious falsehoods of their enemies, that their so-called spies were merchants – 'it is impossible for our town to survive without trade' – and that the arrears were simply due to the fact that the Ottomans observed the lunar calendar, while they observed the solar one.

Meanwhile the Chian populace had gathered in the streets and drawn their own uncomfortable conclusions. From the shore came wailing and shrieking and cries for mercy which drowned out Piali Pasha's response. At last the Mahonesi heard him say that his duty brought him no pleasure; 'God knows how heavy is my heart and how I feel for you all.' The subsequent occupation of the island went exactly to plan. Ten thousand troops were landed, with scimitars concealed under their overcoats; for in order to quiet the populace it was given out that they had come to buy cloth for uniforms and canvas for sails, as they did every year. Their officers were ordered to prevent any molestation of the inhabitants, and to reassure the Chians that they had nothing to fear as the action was only aimed at those who had disobeyed the Gran Signor.

The infantry seized control of the fortress without resistance, commandeered all the munitions dumps, and ran up the Turkish flag in place of the standard of St George. Piali then came ashore in a white brocade uniform and rode through the town, where two soldiers who had molested inhabitants were instantly impaled as an example. Piali spent the night in town, while his troops patrolled the streets.

The following day, Piali ordered the destruction of idols in the churches, and had two of the best converted into mosques, although he left the Catholic bishop his cathedral. Five hundred non-resident aliens were arrested, including many Knights of Malta and some noblemen from Naples and Messina, who were placed in the Ottoman galleys, to be sold as slaves or held to ransom. In the governor's palace the admiral again received the terrified Mahonesi. He asked them to be seated and then sat down himself. In a curious and presumably ancient ceremony, he signalled the transfer of power from the Genoese to the Ottomans, holding a bow in one hand and three arrows in the other, demanding to know whether they submitted to the will of the Sultan. The Mahonesi replied that they had always been the Sultan's slaves and that his orders would remain graven on their brows. Piali then made the same reply to his own question, and the litany was thrice repeated. Then he stood up, handed the bow and arrows to a page, and quietly addressed them all. 'I knew nothing when I was handed the order. I had no time to make any counter representations, but had to bury my feelings and carry out the order. I have done so in the most lenient manner possible, and I swear by the head of my Lord and by the sword hanging by my side that I have not by a long way acted as I was instructed. Be of good cheer, therefore, and know that I shall not fail to do all in my power in your favour.'

The lives of the Mahonesi were spared, but the grander of them were sent into exile in Kaffa, a former Genoese colony on the Black Sea, while the lesser fry, to ransom themselves, sold their houses in the campos for nominal sums, by which the ancestral Chian properties passed into the hands of Turks, who kept them until the Greek army occupied the island in 1912. A garrison of a mere 700 men was placed in the castle – Chios was sufficiently close to Asia Minor for reinforcements to be rushed across, if either Genoa or, as was possible, the King of Spain attempted a counter-attack. Two months later, leaving behind a fully fledged Ottoman administration, headed by a Hungarian renegade, which he had brought with him from Istanbul,* the admiral set sail for Naxos, which he also occupied.

Piali Pasha's protestations of friendship, like the charges he was instructed to bring against the Mahona, seem to have been perfectly genuine. The Chians were guilty, and he saved their necks; yet in October 1566, nothing daunted, its leading citizens, Latin and Greek, sent an embassy to Constantinople to see whether they could negotiate their independence again. They counted on the help of the French ambassador in Istanbul, who considered

* Shortly afterwards, a Dominican friar started an irrepressible rumour that the Turks had handed rule of the island to two illiterate peasants; but he was an unreliable adventurer. He later changed his name to Paleologus and was ultimately beheaded in Rome by the Inquisition.

himself the protector of all the Roman Catholics in the empire, and their embassy was led by Mgr Timoteo Giustiniani, the Catholic bishop of the island. They first approached Piali Pasha, who proved very amenable to the project, and promised to promote it in the divan for a staggered fee of 25,000 ducats. Piali's enemy, though, the Grand Vizier, automatically vetoed the idea. 'Would to God that we had never had recourse to Piali Pasha,' one of the

Women of Chios

merchants wrote; while Piali very generously allowed them to try their hand directly instead, forgoing his fee. What they got – after some very tough negotiating – was not independence, but a series of privileges 'which are not to be scorned', for they amounted to the same commercial privileges enjoyed by the French.

The Chians' autonomy was increased when they renegotiated

the pact eleven years later – the Ottomans knew that toughness could be followed by concessions – so that the Chians found themselves not only free of the Giustiniani but enjoying, indeed, *imperium in imperio*. They were spared the boy tribute, and the application of collective responsibility. They were permitted to keep commercial colonies in the Levantine ports, and to maintain trading links with Italy and the West, and they stayed rich. Ottoman protection over Chian merchant vessels was surer and cheaper than the precarious protection offered by Genoa; yet in some ways the legacy of Genoa was preserved, as well. Right up to the twentieth century the Chians put salt in their babies' mouths, like Italians, and believed in fairies, and first-footed their neighbours on New Year's Eve. They stuck to the lunetted vault, and the peculiar sway of the Genoese staircase; and many went to Padua for their education. Their hospital was erected on a Florentine model; vaccination was invented by a Chian, Emmanuel Timoni; and Chians did especially well for themselves when they arrived, centuries later, in America. The Greeks of the island moved into administrative positions formerly denied them by the Giustiniani, and spearheaded the general movement of Greeks into the Ottoman administration, too, until it became proverbial that sensible men were as rare in Chios as green mice and green horses. In 1669 the Grand Vizier Ahmed Koprulu created for Panayoti, his secretary, who had been useful to him in Crete, the office of Dragoman of the Porte. He was succeeded by another Chian, Alex Mavrocordato, who was a signatory to the treaty of Karlowitz. The Chians maintained friendly relations with the Porte until 1822, when the frenzy born of terror and despair provoked an Ottoman massacre on the island.

'Better the Sultan's turban than the bishop's mitre,' the Byzantines had once declared, and again and again, as islands under Catholic rule had fallen to the Turks, the Greek inhabitants received them with guarded jubilation. They invariably preferred direct Turkish rule to that rabble of Normans, adventurers, Neapolitans, crusaders and, above all, Venetians who had lorded it over the islands since the sack of Constantinople in 1204, fighting and raiding and marrying each other, but never giving much thought to the Greeks who paid for it all with their labour, unless they meant to interfere with their religion. From time to time the Turks introduced goats onto the islands, which ate up the herbage, and one little island at the mouth of the Sea of Marmara was abandoned to hares of 'varying colours'; but an old Greek on Lemnos spoke for the entire region when he told Belon du Mans that 'never had the island been so well cultivated or so rich, and had as many people as now'.

Western merchants admired the Chians tremendously, because they were good at doing just what the westerners did; but the Chian case was not unique. There were any number of other *imperiae* in this *imperio*, plenty of niches where various people could find a firm and prosperous footing. The Turks reserved the bulk of war's glory for themselves, of course. But they did not make a monopoly of it, and wherever they met talent they gave it scope.

The savviest raiders were the Bosnian Muslims of the Hungarian border. Evliya Celebi describes a raid's aftermath, in 1666, when the slaves were thrown into the dungeons of Kanija, the raiders were given town hospitality, and a five-day auction of slaves and their goods began. Ten of the fifty slaves went to the pasha as the imperial one-fifth. After paying off the guides and the gatekeepers, giving alms, and buying the sheep to be sacrificed to the memory of the dead soldiers, 1,490 gazi divided the remainder of the spoils in the Sultan Mehmet III mosque. Evliya himself got four shares extra, two for his servants and two for seeing to all the paperwork, and he wound up business by reciting verses in his lovely voice while everyone joined in fervent prayers for Islam, the Prophet, the holy martyrs, the dead raiders and the saints.

There were not many who could mount a raid with such style, and conclude it with such adroitness. But for slaving wholesale, there were none like the Tartars of the Crimea, who had once been aloof but essentially harmless tradesmen, supplying up-country goods to the Italians on the Black Sea. They became the slave-runners of southern Russia, 'as jackal to the Turkish lion',

Rycaut described them, heads half-shaved, terrible mustachios flying in the wind, making raids into Poland and the Ukraine. From there they would drive their captives down to the coast – 10,000 slaves were exported from Jaffa every year. They marinaded their meat, notoriously, beneath the saddle, in horse's sweat.

If Tartars made the best slavers, then Circassians unquestionably made the best slaves. Russians* and Poles were esteemed in the galleys; Hungarians, Venetians and Germans 'are thought incapable of all drudgery, by reason of the softness of their Bodies, and the Women of giving pleasure proper to their Sex by the hardness of theirs', but a Circassian might go for 1,000 imperial crowns, and a German for a quarter of the price. At home, Cantemir reported, the Circassians were 'always devising something new in their Habits and Arms, in which they are so passionately followed by the Tartars, that they may well be called the French of the Tartars'. They had a morbid horror of obesity – nobody fat could be considered noble, and both boys and girls slept on hard boards to keep them thin. In the markets the Circassians were prized beyond a horse or a woman for their beauty, good proportions, modesty, and capacity for instruction; the boys were sharp-witted and made good artisans, while slave-farms were ultimately established in the Caucasus, turning out odalisques to supply a ready market.

The Albanians, like the Circassians, came from impenetrable and dirt-poor mountains, and had nothing to fall back on but their own bodies† – which they adorned as stylishly as the Circassians. Byron, who had himself painted in Albanian dress, thought their costume was 'the most magnificent in the world, consisting of a long white kilt, gold-worked cloak, crimson velvet gold-laced jacket and waistcoat, silver mounted pistols & daggers'. With their queer, bristling language,‡ they considered themselves to be

* Tartars stole Turkish children and passed them off as Russians.

† Or rather the bodies of their women: when Edward Lear was driven to exclaim at the sight of Albanian women bent double under enormous burdens, his guide hastened to explain that although women were, indeed, inferior to mules, they were really much better than asses, or even horses.

‡ Lear made out among 'the clatter of strange monosyllables – dort beer, dort bloo, dort hitch, hitch beer, blue beer, beer chak, dort gatch'.

among the oldest inhabitants of Europe, and by the nineteenth century they had five alphabets, one with more than fifty letters. Albania was incorporated into the empire in 1468, and Albanians rose fast in the military and bureaucracy; they were all crack shots; and in time they established a monopoly over certain branches of building and medicine. The white skull-caps of Albanians were

Albanians

familiar on building sites in the Balkans well into this century; and they were famous for their skill in building perfect aqueducts. 'Without any mathematical learning, precepts, or instruments, they make these Aqueducts, measure the height of mountains, distance of places, more exactly than a geometrician can, and judge very well of the quality and quantity of water. When they are asked the grounds of this art, they know not what you mean, nor can explain themselves.' Their surgical skill was uncanny, too, for they could operate on 'ruptures' and have the patient up and well in a fortnight.

Throughout the empire were regional specialisms the Ottomans were happy to exploit. In the equestrian world, everyone knew about the Bulgars, who raised horses in the plains of Thrace. No one could handle a camel better than the nomads of Arabia, who undertook to supply 30,000 of them every year when the army went to war. No one washed clothes whiter than the villagers of Kastamonu or made better paper than the papermakers of Constantinople, or drove a mule more stylishly than the muleteers of that city, who were so cocksure and inbred that they had a whole district of it to themselves. No rulers were so pliant and grovelling as the voivodes of Wallachia and Romania; no priests so otherworldly as the monks of Athos. The tilemakers of Iznik were legendary; and the work of Ragusan goldsmiths was as much in demand in Rome as in Constantinople. 'God preserve you from the Hebrews of Salonica, the Greeks of Athens, and the Turks of Euboia!' ran a proverb, honouring them respectively for their prowess in business, quarrelsomeness and strength. It was a very stable empire, and full of opportunity. Henry Holland, as late as the nineteenth century, observed that 'the modern Greeks, like their ancestors, are fond of discriminating the peculiar character of the population, even in small districts and towns'.

10

Cities

It has been said that every Ottoman city was a little Istanbul, with baths, mosques, covered bazaars, and a zoning law that kept the communities at arm's length, especially at night. Most Ottoman towns were built on slopes, like Constantinople, partly because most Ottoman land sloped, and partly because everyone was entitled to a view. While the bazaars were open there was a jostling and mingling of crowds, regardless of religion, and membership of most guilds was open to all. But come nightfall the centre of the city closed down like a modern shopping mall, patrolled by watchmen, and the people who worked there went home to their respective quartiers. There was little excuse for strangers to wander the streets, and crime was rare. Travellers had their needs met centrally, at the *han*, or hostel; and they were often greeted with suspicion when they started coming for no better reason than to please themselves. Edward Lear found himself embroiled in an ugly altercation when he began to sketch in Elbasan in 1848; people objected to being 'written down' and a crowd gathered, shouting that he was a devil. A green-turbaned greybeard shrieked it demagogically to the winds, 'Shaitan! Shaitan!' – until

Lear rather stiffly packed up his brushes and ran away, under a shower of stones.

Ottoman cities tended to reflect the demands of private, not public, life: they lacked the architectural embellishment of the piazza, where private and public intersect, and if there was an open space, a *meydan*, it was a rough field for the pitching of tents, or sports. Whole districts were discrete – the migrant working men of Istanbul were locked in at night, as was the street of prostitutes – and every home was screened as far as possible from the road. In Syrian cities the streets were full of blank walls, and dead ends; in Hungary, on the whole, the downstairs windows were boarded up. Each Muslim home, of course, had its public and private areas, the reception room where visitors took coffee or smoked the nargile, and the harem, reserved for the family, where even policemen in search of a criminal were forbidden to go. With its hugger-mugger domesticity, the Turkish ideal of a home was very seductive; and in late-nineteenth-century Pera, although the Greeks might walk abroad in western dress, 'one is obscurely conscious that the whole business is a ceremony and a show . . . confirmed by those rare peeps into domestic mysteries which fall to a foreigner's lot – passing visions of inner rooms where there are more divans than chairs, men in slippers and dressing gowns, and numerous elderly, black-robed female relatives who attend to the household duties, and do not appear in society'. In Smyrna, the domestic scene was given spice by the *tandour*, a stove under a table covered with a quilt; the women would 'draw the quilt up to their chins, which makes them look as if they were all in bed together'.

Muslim features tended to dominate city life. Most Balkan cities, if not first founded by the Turks, were settled by Muslims after the native population fled; Christian townsmen were often latecomers moving back on Turkish terms, behaving so much *à la mode* that western travellers frequently supposed towns with a varied population to be entirely Turkish – if they recognised them as towns at all, for queerest of all, to western eyes, was the look of a city from afar, without walls or a citadel. Pax Ottomanica rendered them superfluous.

*

Every city seemed to distil some quality of Ottoman dominion. Damascus's wealth and industry bore the legacy of the classical Islamic world. Bursa, where the Silk Road ended, was their first capital, City of the Theologians, and the city to which members of the Ottoman dynasty returned to be buried in a garden overlooking the domes and minarets, with a silver-ribboned plain beyond, and the snowy cap of Mount Olympus to one side, and to the other a cataract of the clearest water, which fed half the cisterns of the town.

The Green Mosque at Bursa

Belgrade was the empire martial, crenellated, bastioned, violent: so that as late as 1848, when a German visitor crossed the Danube (a one-and-a-half-hour journey, in such stormy weather that the Austrian boatmen refused to make the crossing and recommended him to a loitering party of Turks, who being a courageous and fatalistic people, they said, would ferry a man across even if the waves reached the ramparts of Belgrade castle) his first impression of the city was of the castle, in a state of serious disrepair, but still garrisoned by Turks, though the whole country around was self-governing Serbia.

Suleyman the Magnificent had used its capture in 1520 to signal the return of the Turks to Europe, after two decades fighting in the East, and it became the base for operations further up the Danube. Mohacs followed, when the flower of Hungarian chivalry fell; then Buda itself; and Belgrade became the bastion of Turkey in Europe, as it had been of Hungary in the Balkans.

It remained, in consequence, rather grim. Whenever the army approached from the south-east, at least every other year, officers arrived to close the wine shops in advance; the huge troop encamped at Zemun, across the Sava. Here armies coming from Anatolia via Gallipoli met the armies marching up the Danube, and the levies of the Principalities. Civilians could be brought up smartish by a rapped-out order in the street, as they scuttled by; and most of them, anyway, worked for the army, sewing, nailing, polishing, butchering, so that they lived always with the dread of requisitions, and earned themselves a reputation for fly behaviour and artificial poverty which did nothing to improve the city's appearance.

Kara Mustafa, fleeing back in 1683 with a hundred excuses for his failure to take Vienna, was bowstrung in Belgrade by the Sultan's messengers. In the great Austrian push which followed Kara Mustafa's defeat Belgrade was at last taken by the Duke of Bavaria in 1688. Six years later, when the Austrian garrison which held the island of Orsona on the Danube negotiated their surrender to the Turks, the governor stipulated that he and his people should be given transport, and safe conduct, to the city. The Turks politely advised him to choose a better destination, telling the governor that Belgrade was in Turkish hands again; but such was the city's reputation that the governor refused to believe them. He and his 600 men, women and children did go to Belgrade, as they had wished, and were put in a fort for a day or two, then disarmed, chained and sold into slavery, while the youths were shaved and circumcised and sent to join the army.

In 1717 the brilliant Prince Eugene retook the city for Austria, but his military successors lost it again in 1739. After half a century of peace, the Ottomans surrendered the city in 1789, but then two years later it was surrendered back to them. It was still a bunker in 1804, though meaner, and dirtier, and more cruel, pinched by want and pricked on by greed, when the janissaries solemnised their affection for the place, and made it the base of a sort of janissary junta, ruling over Serbia in defiance of everybody else: of Constantinople, which had complex treaty obligations to carry out, involving their removal; of the Turkish cavalrymen, who tended to live on their Serbian estates, and whose rivalry with the janissaries stretched back centuries, like the factions of ancient Rome, sharpened by the prospect of carving up Serbia for themselves; of the Serbs, led by the janissary turned rebel, Kara George, at the head of a national uprising. Belgrade and the janissaries had a lot in common: both decayed and immovable. Kara George and his Serbs finally took Belgrade in 1806; in the process he dealt a death blow to the janissary junta, and a more regular Ottoman army retook it in 1813.

A semi-autonomous Serbian state was declared around it in 1814, but still the Ottomans refused to recognise their loss of Belgrade, and while the city developed in its own way, an Ottoman garrison bunkered in the citadel and the green flag of the empire fluttered from its pale tower until 1867.

If Belgrade was all martial punch, Sarajevo expressed the Ottoman instinct for gentle hospitality. It was in Sarajevo that the camel caravans from Anatolia and beyond terminated, and their goods were transferred to mules and horses, for after Sarajevo the camels tended to fall ill.* The Sarajevans were widely noted for their gentleness and their learning; 'everyone befriended us', writes M. Quiclet, who passed through in 1658; their fame reached Syria. Lying on the east–west route from Ragusa into the empire, it grew into a city of wealth and industry, well able to afford, in later years, a sort of dashing semi-independence from the Porte, whose pashas at times found it hard to enter the city at all, and were reduced, in the end, to spending three nights a year there. A trading town as Belgrade was a garrison town, multifarious as Belgrade was monolithic, by the sixteenth century it expressed all that was liveliest in a region of expanding wealth, with a growing population. Sarajevo was full of parks, Sephardim, gypsies, Muslims, and members of old Bosnian families who had turned

* In the museum you could inspect a long silver tube, which was used for giving camels their medicine.

Turk to keep their estates; and perhaps it derived its kindliness from the sense of well-being that prompted the Sarajevans to count their blessings so punctiliously. Never before the days of Soviet tour guides were statistics so freely trotted out as they were to visitors to Sarajevo. The traveller Evliya Celebi rhapsodised over its bustle and piety, with 1,080 shops selling goods from India and Bohemia, more than a thousand 'elderly people' in excellent health, and 17,000 houses; while Quiclet admired every one of the city's 169 fountains. In October 1697 Prince Eugene, drawing up his troops on a ridge overlooking the town, was able to admire its size, its openness and its 120 fine mosques before he burnt it to the ground.

Of all the cities of the empire, Constantinople was the largest, wealthiest, greediest, and most influential. Topkapi, the city palace, expressed the principle of unity which bound up this sprawling empire. The city's position was the soldered joint which bound the bell of Ottoman Asia to the balloon of Ottoman Europe. Its barracks housed the only standing army in Europe, the notorious janissaries, whose lives were dedicated to war. Its Arsenal witnessed the industry which sustained – for a giddy moment – Ottoman claims to command the Black Sea and the White. The highest religious authorities in Mehmet's day were the kadi askers, judges in the army, one for Rumelia, and one for Anatolia; but so centrist and singular was the influence of the Constantinople court that less than a century later the Grand Mufti of Constantinople was without question the empire's leading Muslim dignitary, pictured by visitors as a sort of Islamic pontiff.*

Just as the army, passing through the countryside, was able to feed and supply itself without reference to the surrounding lands, so Constantinople seemed to float free of its immediate environs, and spread its networks to the furthest reaches of the empire. By the mid-seventeenth century, 250 tons of bread were baked there every day; 18,000 oxen were slaughtered a month; seven million

* An error scrupulously avoided by the Sultans, one of whom was to depress the pretensions of a mufti who claimed infallibility by remarking that he recognised only one pope.

sheep and lambs a year – a tenth of it all went to the palace alone. Two thousand ships sailed in with foodstuffs each year. Nothing in Istanbul was left to chance, and so great was the city's appetite that while it was the Venetians, famously, who discerned and pursued the pattern of trade in the eastern Mediterranean, it was really the Turks who willed that pattern into being, controlling it by fiat and regulation.

Like every city in the empire, Constantinople's markets were patrolled by a kadi with summary powers. He knew the true price of tripe soup, and kept an eye on the brain vendors in case they substituted suet. He inspected cooking vessels to see that they were properly tinned; ensured that there were three grades of high boot; and demanded that shoes should last two days for every asper the buyer gave for them. Profit was generally limited to ten per cent, although the profit on goods brought from afar was hard to gauge. For reasons which have never been quite explained, the butcher's trade in the capital was a ruinous one before the seventeenth century, and was forced upon rich men as a form of punishment. 'False weight is what the civil policy prosecute and punish with the utmost rigour, and it is not uncommon, as you pass the streets, to run against a pendent Baker's body for three days consecutively', Porter recalled.

So rich were the marts of Constantinople that the Georgians, who were very poor, began sending their children as slave tribute to the city, while the Georgian ambassador would recoup the cost of his visit by selling off his entire retinue, right up to his steward and his secretary, slipping home with no more than an interpreter and a contribution to the public treasury.

Trade was the one area of civil life where the Ottomans felt obliged to interfere, to maintain the efficiency of their armies, and the security of the city streets. By Islamic tradition, a just ruler should be a prosperous one, open-handed with his people, never suffering them to want; and Islamic cities had a proud old tradition of grain revolts when the ruler failed to deliver. The prosperity of the artisan depended on him receiving a fair price for his work, and this was enshrined in guild legislation. The people had to be protected from overcharging and scarcity.

Biscuit seller; every trade had its guild with specific dress

Once the dust of Ottoman conquest settled, everyone seemed to get richer by the year. The population of the empire doubled in the sixteenth century. Everybody had something to do, and everywhere teemed with life and activity, not only the markets of the capital, or the roadsteads of the Bosphorus. Morosini thought the empire so busy and prosperous that its security no longer depended on the number or the quality of its fortresses – 'of which they have few' – but 'on the abundance it has of all the necessities of life. Not only is there enough for the daily needs of her people, but great quantites of foods and other goods are exported . . . There could be even more if there were additional people to cultivate the fields.' Moldavia and Wallachia, Sandys added, 'doe serve them with Beeves and Muttons; and as for Fish, the adjoyning Seas yeeld store and variety . . .' 'Everywhere in the woods of Mingrelia,' Busbecq reported, 'under the shade of wide-spreading trees, you can see the common people reclining in groups and keeping holiday with wine and dance and song.'

Even in the hinterlands, people moved round in a purposeful way: timariots travelling light to new timars, bureaucrats bustling round with their registers, the Kapudan Pasha setting out with the fleet to raise the tribute from the islands, nomads heading up for the hills and green pastures; the Sultan splendidly processing to winter quarters in Edirne, where he would hunt in the royal parks until the frogs' croakings became a nuisance. Trade was conducted on an imperial scale. Bertrand de la Brocquière was in Damascus when a caravan came in from the desert, and it took two nights, and three days, to settle in. In Belgrade's shops in the mid-sixteenth century a German visitor found 'everything as in the most advanced cities of Italy and Germany'.

Bazaars constructed in every Ottoman town offered goods (produced under the watchful eye of the guilds) that were hard to resist. A decent bow was made from a maple wand taken at Kastomonu, buffalo sinew, boiled horn, and glue from a resin found at the Danube's mouth. Matured for a year, and fed linseed oil, it would last two centuries. The horsehair bowstring was steeped in beeswax, resin and fish glue. Arrow flights were made of tortoiseshell or ivory, of swan, eagle or cormorant feathers;

their tips were goat-bone, their shafts pine. 'Exquisitely made,' a French visitor exclaimed, 'and *so* durable.' Cheap, too; although many items were forbidden to foreigners – Salonica cotton, for example, was made to a special grade for janissary uniforms. Much was smuggled. Nile linen was available, Bursan brocades and velours, mohair, coarse woollens from Plovdiv, fine woollen yarns from Edirne and Salonica which were made by the Spanish Jews; silk and carpets. Foreigners came for spices from the Far East, scents, soaps and drugs; Iznik tileware, Istanbul paper, Hebron glass; in return the Europeans traded woollens, paper, English steel, and a lot of silver. The Ottomans, in turn, were indebted to their east – against which, oddly enough, they erected the same kind of barrier, part psychological and hygienic, part physical watch-towers, as western Europe was erecting against them. They took musk, rhubarb and porcelain from the Chinese, and furs, which were important ceremonial items, from the Muscovites, as well as birds of prey, amber and mercury; the Tartars supplied them with bows and arrows, bucklers and caviar, with leather from Kazan, and white slaves; while the Sudan sent them gold, and black slaves.

When Rycaut wrote that 'all the delightful Fields of Asia, the pleasant Plains of Tempe and Thrace, all the Plenty of Egypt, and Fruitfulness of the Nile, the Luxury of Corinth, the Substance of Peloponnesus, Athens, Lemnos, Scio and Mitylene, with other Isles of the Aegean Sea, the Spices of Arabia, and the Riches of a great part of Persia, all Armenia, the Provinces of Pontus, Galatia, Bithynia, Phrygia, Lycia, Pamphylia, Palestine, Coelosyria and Phoenicia, Colchis, and a great part of Georgia, the Tributary Principalities of Moldavia and Wallachia, Romania, Bulgaria, and Servia, and the best part of Hungary, concur all together to satisfie the appetite of one single Person'.

Within Mehmet II's lifetime the hapless rulers of the principalities had remade their coinage on Ottoman models, the better to facilitate exchange; and when Moldavia became a vassal state, its boyars launched the process of supplying the Istanbul markets which led to the enserfment of the population. On the Moldavian hillsides and the upper slopes of the Carpathians, no shepherd might sell his flock until the imperial commissioners had made their purchases, at the stipulated price. As the shores of the Black Sea were drawn into the Ottoman world, by threat and conquest, there were nuts and fruits for Constantinople and timber for fleets, while the Bulgars reared horses, and the Greeks of the islands crushed olives, and the fishermen cast their nets, and from the shores of Lake Ohrid, sanctified and blue in the mountains of Macedonia, imperial messengers hotfooted it to the place with buckets of celestial trout.

The Ottomans did not engage in much trade themselves but they taxed it, exports like imports, and would give their Ottoman equivalent of favoured nation status, called capitulations, to anyone who promised to supply the markets with regularity. The first such treaty, made with the French in 1534, allowed them to buy a limited quantity of Ottoman stuff and to import whatever they chose at preferential rates. To avoid friction, the French were given rights of extraterritoriality, which was effectively the same principle of collective responsibility the Ottomans applied to every subject community. Police yourselves, the Ottomans said, or suffer the consequences together. Other nations soon clamoured for capitulations of their own: the English in 1567, the Dutch five years later. The busiest foreign presence in the ports was Venice, of course, which more than once endured treaties which were politically crushing but commercially advantageous, using brisk, cheap warfare as a last resort, to be dropped as soon as a point was gained, before diving into the sea of diplomacy.

11

The Sea

The landscape was puckered by mountains, but it was washed, as well, by seas: dark and turbulent when the winds that every Mediterranean race detests howled from the water into the hills; brisk when the imperial fleet set out to make its circuit of the islands, the Mecca pilgrims crowded the sea lanes of the eastern Mediterranean, and the grain ships from Egypt came lumbering up to Istanbul.

Under the early Arabs, the Mediterranean had been in Islam's pocket. By the fifteenth century, the Turks had resolved to put it back there. The assembly of a fleet allowed Mehmet to take Constantinople. His pious successor, Bayezit the Sufi, laid the foundations of Ottoman maritime power, renovating the Arsenal to launch a fleet capable of sustaining war with Venice, the supreme maritime power of the age.

Genoa suffered most from Ottoman conquest. The humble effort the Genoese had made, in 1423, to butter up their future conquerors by inviting the Sultan to put his mark on the tower they were building in Pera, and the neutrality they had observed during the siege of Constantinople, came to nothing. The fall of

Constantinople closed up her access to the Black Sea, and shortly afterwards Genoa sold all her interests in her prosperous trading colonies in the Crimea and Trebizond to a joint stock company, the Company of St John. It proved to be a bad investment. In twenty years the Genoese were swept from the Black Sea, leaving their ship designs and their naval titles fixed in the Ottoman mind, so that an Ottoman admiral was called Kapudan Pasha, and the Ottoman navy constructed galleons with heavy cannon after the Genoese model, and galleys, too, the most effective and terrible of Mediterranean ships, in which men worked the oars in chains, and whose presence could be smelled from a mile away over the water.

Swept from the sea, her company bankrupted, her colonies wasted, her retreat unmourned, Genoa hung on at Pera, and her galleys drifted through the Bosphorus; but her trade was very much reduced, and the Genoese were so disgusted by the loss of their Black Sea colonies, and by the fall of their islands in the Aegean between 1456 and 1462, that they were driven to make a clean break, and served the Spaniards as Venice serviced the Porte, giving Spain the Genoese sailor Columbus.

Venice, famously, never made a break at all. She pursued her eastern trade, as ever mingling war with negotiation – 'procureur de Mahomet', as one Frenchman called her, 'précurseur d'Antichrist' – fending off the Turkish advance as long as she could, and losing her stepping stones to the Levant gradually, one by one – in 1499 she lost Lepanto, the first of her pearls, Coron and Modon in 1503, Nauplia in 1540, Cyprus in 1570. She had no illusions as to the cost of an all-out war with the Turks, and she made treaties which, however embarrassing politically, were commercially sound.

'My Lord, you dwell in a city whose benefactor is the sea. If the sea is not safe no ships will come, and if no ships come Istanbul perishes,' Selim I was once advised. Selim took Egypt, and Suleyman Rhodes, so that the eastern Mediterranean was secure, and relations with Venice were in practical terms an internal affair. 'Write immediately to your Signoria,' Suleyman commanded the Venetian bailio in 1533, 'for it can find out what the fish are doing at the bottom of the sea, and also about the fleet which Spain is preparing . . .' Andrea Gritti, who was Doge in 1523, learned his merchanting skills in Constantinople, and sired four bastards by an Ottoman concubine. He gave them a Renaissance education in Venice; but when their illegitimacy prevented them

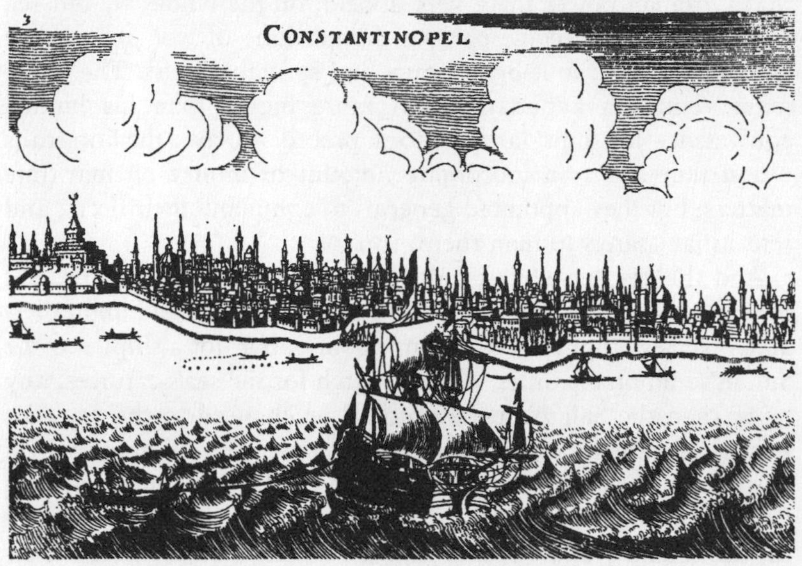

Constantinople, seventeenth-century woodcut

from taking office there, his favourite son, a graduate of Padua and Venice, went to Constantinople, befriended Ibrahim the Grand Vizier, was made the godson of the Gran Signor, and the keeper of Suleyman's jewels. He amassed a fortune, maintained his own court and seraglio, and fed a thousand mouths. Suleyman even came to his house. He had the revenues from a Hungarian duchy, fought in the Hungarian campaign of 1528, and was present at the first siege of Vienna, even while his father was Doge of Venice. In 1530 he commanded an Ottoman army defending Buda. In 1534, while leading 3,000 men into the Principalities, this son of a doge and godson of a sultan, half-Venetian, half-Ottoman, was captured by Transylvanians and beheaded.

*

Alexander Kinglake was wrong when he called the sea the Doge's blushing bride, but the Sultan's bowing slave. The Black Sea fell to the Turks by default, once they controlled its shores and stopped up its entrance by capturing Constantinople. In the Mediterranean they were only too eager to franchise the business, so that Ottoman power there was upheld, on the whole, by old sea dogs who never became part of the machine of war proper, but who were bound to it by honours and special favours. The Ottomans ranked a kapudan pasha more highly than his landed equivalent – his ships' lanterns took precedence over the horsetails – and they spent an inordinate amount of money on maritime matters; but they appointed generals to command their fleets, and sent in janissaries to man them, too.

And the sea herself resisted systems. She was changeable and treacherous, a place of cruel winds, sudden squalls and unpredictable reverses. Topkapi was a tent of sorts, but not a ship; and the Sultan's immutable order was no match for the sea's caprices, any more than the Sultan's person could be chanced to the vagaries of weather, enemies, corsairs, or the restrictive vulnerability of a battleship. 'God had made the earth for their Dominion, and Enjoyment,' the Ottomans privately confessed, 'and the sea only for Christians'; and Muslim sailors would actually delay their sailing until after the Patriarch had blessed the sea in the spring. Only the Barbary corsairs, Rycaut believed, ever lost sight of dry land, and Ottoman maritime operations always lagged several years behind land campaigns. It was only after they had captured Greece that they began to pick on Venice's islands and her ports in the Levant, beginning with Bayezit's capture of Lepanto in 1499. The great naval clashes of the sixteenth century were an extension of landed enmity, the Turks striking at Spain to weaken her hold on Austria. Spanish fleets disputed all the forts of North Africa – Algiers, Tunis, Oran, Bizerta and Tripoli. The Turks threatened southern Italy, Sicily and Corsica. Neither, in the end, could quite make good their threats.

This was, after all, an astonishingly broad frontier, and Mediterranean society had a tang of its own. Every seafarer was bound into one fraternity, with its own rules and rumours and scores to settle; every ship afloat flirted with piracy, and often succumbed; while sailors were always changing sides, so that Mediterranean sea battles are frequently shrouded in mystery, as fleets ostensibly bringing relief stand off, and admirals negotiate covertly with their enemies.

The Bosphorus, engraving by Antoine Melling, a German artist to the Court of Selim III

There was Cigalazade Yusuf Sinan Pasha, who at the age of sixteen had been captured by corsairs with his father, an Italian nobleman (and freebooter). The father paid a ransom to escape, and was 'sent home so carefully that he died within three days'; but he left his son to try his fortune with the Turks. Cigalazade became Kapudan Pasha in time, and notoriously hard on Christians, so that Baron Wratislaw shifted uneasily before his scowl when he met him in 1599. He used to take his fleet to Messina, where his father had commanded a Spanish squadron, and go ashore to visit his old mother in her mantilla.* A Calabrian-born admiral, Kilic Ali Pasha, was the only commander to extricate

* For a reverse incident, see footnote on page 226, on Padre Ottomano.

himself with any honour from the débâcle off Lepanto in 1571, bringing off his ships to form the nucleus of a reconstituted fleet, and carrying in his hold the prisoner Cervantes, who was courteously treated.

In the nest of pirates, nominally under Ottoman suzerainty, that was Algiers, full of swarthy men with daggers in their teeth, and vaults heaped with jewels, with harems filled with European heiresses and willowy Nubian girls, where the air was thick with musk and sweat, and the plight of prisoners grotesquely miserable, there swaggered the terrible corsair chieftains, among whom once were counted six Greeks, an Armenian, and a face as Dutch as an Edam cheese, red rind and all. Algiers remained a hotbed of piracy well into the nineteenth century, when even the Americans primly demanded an end to the pirates' activities. The Porte hardly dared admit that it had no control. The men of Algiers retained their worldly cynicism, and were anxious not to be thought anyone's fool, so that when in 1815 Consul Broughton brought the Dey of Algiers a musical snuffbox with a clasp garnished with emeralds and brilliants, the Dey looked at it and asked if the English king 'took him for a child to be pleased with the ting ting thing!' – although as Broughton observed, the ting ting thing had cost fifteen hundred pounds.

The corsairs took sobriquets in Old Sabar, the Latinate lingua franca of the Mediterranean, which stank of wickedness and the frisky plank. Among them were Mortamama, whose name hinted at hideous crimes, with his agonising 'fistula in ano' and so fat that his only exercise was the rolling of his ship; and Barbarossa's henchman, Cacca Diabolo. The Danube fleet was well captained in the 1690s when Mezzomorto ('Halfdead') Kara Huseyn Pasha was seconded there from a Mediterranean command. Barbarossa, a buccaneering showman even in his sixty-seventh year when he brought his gala fleet up the Golden Horn and into the Sultan's service, did not have a red beard at all, but lifted the name from his elder brother, who had been a promising young pirate himself before his death.

In 1534 Barbarossa was made Kapudan Pasha, and he brought to the Ottoman world, weighed down by thoughts of Hungary and Persia, a huge new range. With a fleet of eighty-four ships, sixty-one of them new built at the Arsenal, he set sail for the Italian coast, where he made strenuous efforts to abduct Julia Gonzaga, the beauty of her day, for service in the Sultan's harem. His galleys were black, and low-lying, so that they might lie invisibly out at sea, waiting for nightfall to make a surprise attack on the coast. Barbarossa landed his men stealthily in the night, and raided Fondi, where the lady was asleep. That very night she was plucked to safety in her negligee by an Italian cavalier, who managed to gallop her out of the city.*

In 1543 Barbarossa sailed for Toulon with the fleet. The war against Charles V, who constantly eluded Suleyman on land (although, as Suleyman tartly observed, 'the provinces of kings are as their very wives, and if these are left by their fugitive husbands as a prey to foreigners, it is an extraordinary and a disgraceful thing') could now be carried into the western Mediterranean. Thanks to Barbarossa, the southern coasts were already under Ottoman sway; and Charles's disastrous failure to seize Tunis opened up an excellent opportunity for revenge.

The alliance between France and the Porte against the Habsburgs, which was always vague on land, became a reality at sea. Barbarossa had been looking for a western base in which to winter his fleet. The French evacuated the city of Toulon, the Turks marched in, and in a trice, said a visitor, it looked like an oriental city, complete with mosques. Some say the inhabitants eventually returned to find their homes intact; others say Toulon was pillaged,† and certainly the King of France granted the Toulonese ten years' tax freedom.

On the return voyage to Istanbul, Barbarossa ravaged the coasts of Italy, with a fleet of eighty galleys, holding 1,000 spahis and 6,000 janissaries, as well as various French officers and an English doctor, Alban Hill. Barbarossa's first task was to assist the French in the reduction of Nice: an operation which taught him contempt of the French navy. No resistance was made to a landing at Elba;

* She had him murdered for the impropriety.

† And pillaged, too, on account of the very poor biscuit the French provided, which prompted Barbarossa to demand fresh corn.

Orbetello was taken, with the loss of five lives, and a harvest of 140 slaves. At Giglio, 30 Turks were killed but the city's notables were beheaded and 632 prisoners chained. Ischia was wasted, for 2,040 prisoners. Lipari was tough, and it took almost a fortnight, at the cost of 343 lives, to take the town; but it provided 10,000 slaves, and after it had been stripped of all booty it was burnt, and the elderly had their gallstones removed, to make into charms. At Reggio, Barbarossa bargained for his prisoners' ransom. The fleet put in at the Venetian port of Zante for supplies, and then sailed back to the Bosphorus.

As long as Barbarossa led the fleet, victory followed victory. But he died in 1546 and the naval supremacy of the Turks succumbed, in the same century, to the cost and waste. When the great battle of Lepanto was fought, in 1571, it looked like a splendid victory for the West – the first of any magnitude that Christendom had ever won. In practice, it was nobody's victory. The Christians were quite incapable of following up the blow, and the Ottomans were perfectly capable of restoring their fleet. 'There is a great difference between our loss and yours. You have shaved our chin; but our beard is growing again. We have lopped off your arm, and you can never replace it,' the Grand Vizier told the Venetians, when after Lepanto they sued for peace. The Arsenal worked overtime that winter, and the following year a whole new fleet, built from a forest of Pontic timber, was launched to the Christians' consternation. So fast did the Turks recover, in fact, that a sort of titter ran round Europe at the Emperor's expense.

The huge expense of naval wars, with so little to show for it, made both sides wary of engagements after Lepanto; and the Mediterranean galleys were no match for the gigantic Dutch and English ships fitted up for the Atlantic. In 1607 Sir Thomas Sherley said that an English warship could defeat ten Turkish galleys; and the Ottomans, who had always so carefully followed innovations in the Mediterranean – even careening prize ships in the Arsenal – moved very slowly into the age of galleons. They were afraid of the monstrous taxes that would have to be raised to fit out a first-rate fleet capable of tackling Christendom, for adventures merely Mediterranean.

So with few exceptions the history of the Ottoman navy is one of accelerated decline. Warships rotted in the Arsenal, for lack of funds and knowledgeable crew. Only the corsairs understood the sea, and they preferred to work independently rather than nail their colours to the falling mast. As a result the Ottomans suffered sudden rude shocks. The Black Sea was never really a lake, Ottoman or otherwise; and Cossacks raided Sinope in 1614. In 1654, through a mixture of bungling and bad luck, the Ottomans were blockaded in the Dardanelles by Venice. In 1787 they were thunderstruck by the arrival of a Russian fleet off Greece which had not come through the Bosphorus – and so ignorant of geography that they sternly rebuked the Venetians for allowing the fleet to slip through, via, as they supposed, a secret channel to the Adriatic.

12

Rhythms

An Ottoman was not born, but made, passing through the imperial schools, following the requisite course of studies, learning obedience and a language so hi-falutin that nobody else could speak it; a language which could elegantly express every nuance of meaning, every shade of emphasis in single words, but which lacked a word for 'interesting'. Amusing, astonishing, useful, important – all these qualities they recognised; but there were no grey states of mind. As the cosmos between heaven and earth, so the visible world was split between the Abode of Peace, Dar ul-Islam, and the Abode of War, Dar ul-Harb. The Lord of the Horizon, Burgrave of the World, was also Sultan of the Two Continents, Emperor of the Black Sea and the White, the shadow of God in this world and the next, the Favourite of God on the Two Horizons. Two imaginary characters, Husein and Hasan (like the shadow puppets Karagoz and Hacivet), clarified Ottoman law. Anyone could go to a mullah well versed in Koranic law and present him with a purely hypothetical case concerning Husein and Hasan. The mullah's response, his fatwa, was either Yes or No, and on the strength of it the plaintiff might proceed to court, or not. When the war against the Persians was at its height, the

Chief Mufti was asked whether the death of a single heretic was worthy in the same degree as the death of seventy Christians; and the Mufti, after calculations, thought it was. Ottoman poetry was written in couplets. The Ottoman home was divided between harem and *selamlik* (and in the late nineteenth century between western and oriental styles, with grandfather clocks in the hall, robes and sofas in the interior). Ottoman people were either *reaya*, flock, or servants of the state; and the historians have generally seen Ottoman dominion divided, very neatly, between the Muslim Institution of the law, and the Slave Institution of the administration.

But the puppets Karagoz and Hacivet depend on the third, rogue, element for their comedies: a gaggle of ladies, the unworldly Sufi, a blustering janissary, or a Frank. When Dmitri Cantemir* wrote up Ottoman history in the eighteenth century, he perceived it as a parabola, an arch which sprang from victory to defeat; and in an empire's rise and fall, each curve sustains that murky force, or stress, where seeds of failure are sown in the midst of triumph, and some of the lineaments of greatness survive in the ignominy of defeat.

That graceful curve was not only drawn through Ottoman history, but streamlined every area of Ottoman life. A sixteenth-century ambassador from Germany was so impressed by the modest gravity of Ottoman dress, which fell in graceful folds like the mantles of the ancients, that he began to dread going out in a puff-waisted doublet and his knobbly hose. Over 'the arch of

* Dmitri Cantemir (1673–1723) belonged to the Greek-speaking aristocracy of the Principalities. He arrived in Istanbul from Moldavia at the age of fifteen, and for twenty-two years held court in his palace at Fethiye, or in his mansion at Ortakoy, by the Bosphorus, where he first notated Turkish music. In 1710 he was appointed Voivode of Moldavia; his dreams of independence were foiled by the Ottoman defeat of Peter the Great on the Pruth in 1711. Cantemir escaped Ottoman vengeance by hiding in the Tsar's coach; his successor was a Phanariot Greek from Constantinople. Brought into a comfortable Russian exile – fifty villages, 50,000 serfs – as a royal counsellor, he excised his nostalgia for Istanbul by writing his *History of the Turks* in 1714–16, the standard work on the subject before von Hammer in the nineteenth century. Conceiving the history as an arc of rise and decline, the book was partly written to justify his treachery. As his story unfolds, his footnotes, crammed with personal observations, ideas and interpretations, start to take over the text in a very entertaining way. The book was first published in England, where his son was Russian ambassador. It was rapidly translated: Voltaire praised it; the German edition was dedicated to Maria Theresa. Gibbon quoted it. Byron and Shelley used it.

our sabres', one pasha was pleased to report, enemies 'leaped into the abyss of defeat'. Ottoman script was cursive, and Ottoman mustachios were twirled; their swords were curved, their symbol of faith a crescent moon; their public baths and mosques were domed, and often round as well; and a woman – or a page – was a beauty whose eyebrows arched like twin bows (all the lovelier if she swayed as she walked, like a goose, as the Serbians said approvingly). It is said that Ottoman builders never used a plumb-line. The janissaries formed a standing army with uniforms and marching bands long before such things were thought of in the West. But they never marched in step, the roads were much too bad, and they had a special swaying walk instead, like models, or sailors.

The Chinese had identified the Turks as a people on their borders in the fourth century. For a thousand years they were on the move, learning the nomad's instinctive reserve – discretion was the surest guarantee of privacy in camp – and to the end the Turks were notorious for gravity, and *politesse*. If the empire they built became almost legendary in its immobility, in detail it remained in a state of constant graceful movement, its arcs forever being drawn, its flourishes incessantly produced, its white-hatted and mustachioed janissary soldiers, visitors said, magnificently offering you their bouquets.

Their movement was always economical. Turks never got used to the sight of western merchants pacing up and down in conversation, and one of the greatest of grand viziers, Fazil Ahmet Koprulu, was as well remembered for his queer habit of walking about while sunk in thought, as for his administrative and military genius. Mrs A. J. Harvey found Turkish women amused by westerners constantly raising their top hats, and in her *Turkish Harems* of 1871 she records this spritely curse: 'May your fatigued and hated soul find no more rest in purgatory than a Giaour's hat enjoys on earth!' And when an Ottoman ambassador to the court of France was introduced to the child King Louis XIII, he was so astonished by Richelieu instructing the boy to run up and down for his guest that for half a moment he could not even speak (but he recovered himself, and winged the incident diplomatically, praising Allah).

The Ottomans felt the geomancer's horror of hard lines, dead spaces and sharp angles. For all their bravery on the battlefield, at home they were afraid of dark corners: imps would gather in them, as they did around still water (iron worked, though, and even the word for iron, *timur*, had some effect when it was shouted into a corner). They built low sofas into the angles of a room, or concealed them with corner cupboards; or even sliced them off, by opening them into doorways, on the slant. For centuries the powerhouse of the empire was known as the divan, where viziers sat cross-legged, handling half a dozen separate matters all at once with perfect fluency; and even in the nineteenth century, when western furniture was the rule, pashas sometimes sat tailor-fashion on their desks, while their underlings squatted on the armchair seats.

An Ottoman did not particularly like to view all his possessions foursquare around him; he preferred things gathered in bags, slung over a hook* – indeed, anything too flat, or fixed, or straight bore the odour of death, the stamp of the Final Immobility. Ottoman mores considered even direct questions discourteous. When an Ottoman ambassador to a western court was asked how the Turks made love he replied, with a flash of reproachful wit: 'We do not make love. We purchase it ready-made.' They avoided straight compliments at all costs, as carrying the *jettatura*, the Evil Eye. Praise a thing, and as often as not it would be pressed into your hands: for the Eye was on it, and it would only bring bad luck to the owner if it was kept (the glassy blue eyes of Franks were considered especially sinister and malign). 'There is no colour, no flower, no weed, no fruit, herb, pebble or feather that has not a verse belonging to it,' Lady Mary Wortley Montagu discovered in the early eighteenth century, 'and you may quarrel, reproach or send letters of passion, friendship or civility, or even of news, without ever inking your fingers.'† When an Ottoman

* The Germans call the Turks *Sackenleute*, 'bag-people'.

† This language of flowers was briefly fashionable in the West as a result of her research.

smoked, he reclined with the graceful nargile, which coiled from the lips to the floor – where the clumsy western visitor often trod them underfoot. Even their courtesies were elliptical, as Edward Lear discovered when he apologised for trampling those pipes; for the pasha merely waved a hand. 'The breaking of such a pipe-bowl would indeed, under ordinary circumstances, be disagreeable,' he said; 'but in a friend every action has its charm!'

'There is no past, there is no hereafter, everything is in a process of becoming,' wrote the Turkish mystic Bedreddin. Mysticism of this sort is a form of practicality. If it were desired that at an Ottoman funeral even the horses should be seen to weep, the Turks could make them weep. They pioneered inoculation. The gardens of the royal palace in Constantinople produced an abundance of vegetables which were sold at market to defray the cost of the Sultan's food – 'well acquired moneys,' Menavino said, 'and not from the sweat of poor men.' After one particular massacre in an Italian square they extracted all the gallstones they could find to make a preparation for gout. They considered any shelter sufficient for a traveller, though assiduous in stabling and feeding his horse. In their own houses they seldom allotted rooms a single function. 'You sit in a room,' Eliot explained; 'and when you are hungry you call; a little table is brought in and you eat; when you want to go to bed a pile of rugs is laid in a corner and you go to sleep in it.' And deep inside the warren of the palace lies a suite of very tiny rooms. Many researchers assumed they were storage. They were the quarters of the palace dwarves.

Ottomans could, as need arose, bridge a river in spate in record time; bivouac in winter; march on a handful of rice; or unerringly lay their hand upon facts and figures out of an astonishing collection of reports, censuses, registers and surveys. The Ottomans simply bound good laws, when they met them, in with the rest, so that the Ottoman police superintendent of Chios drew his salary from a tax on prostitutes, just as his Genoese predecessor had done. This talent for practical organisation survived the empire's decline, and must account for its longevity. When the ambassador to Russia in 1775 was fitted out, he took a letter to the Tsarina written on special paper, in special ink. He drew his tent, stores, gifts and dining utensils, his horse tackle and his petty cash, soup ladles and wagon wheels, from the relevant department of the palace, following to the last spoon and pot the example set on record by his predecessor; and he signed them all out on chits.*

Mostar Bridge

Probably only an English tea planter, kitting up in the Army and Navy Stores for his first five-year stint in India, could draw so exactly and methodically on the accumulated experience of his forebears.

Lovely bridges were raised across the empire, like the bridge at Mostar, high-arched and hump-backed, only destroyed in 1993

* Twenty years later, an ambassador complained that his stuff was mere copper and brass, which, he said, depreciated his mission and reflected poorly on the grandeur of the Ottoman state. Selim III told him that the honour and glory of the state did not depend on whether Mustafa Rasih Pasha had utensils made of silver.

because for four hundred years it had linked the Muslim with the Christian side of town; or the bridge of Scutari in Albania, which could only be built when a woman had been immured in its foundations, into whose cell a tiny vent was introduced, through which she continued to suckle her infant (in a Vlach version of the story, though, it was the bridge of Arta, and the poor mother was deprived even of her vent). Some bridges were military, like the Danube bridge at Giurgiu, or the massive timber bridge across the Sava marshes at Osijek in Yugoslavia, which was five miles long and supported a string of wooden towers – the gateway into Hungary from the south, on the campaign trail. Others were for trade, like the bridge of Buda, and the bridge for livestock at Vac. In Monastir there were innumerable bridges, some flanked with rows of shops, 'forming a broad covered bazaar'. Had he never built mosques, Sinan, the greatest architect the Ottomans ever produced, would have been remembered for his bridges. Sultan Suleyman, his patron, nearly drowned while out hunting in the marshes of the Marmara coast in 1563: Sinan flung no less than four bridges from one island to the next across the treacherous estuary at Buyukcekmice, wide enough for caravans to pass each other. Bridges going nowhere at all were flung across steep and broken ground, to provide a level building surface – the entire side of Topkapi facing Istanbul, for instance, is carried on a series of bridges, and at Urfa a street crosses a gulley over high arches. The transverse ravines of the Pontic coast were made passable by teetering rope bridges and breathtaking single arches made of stone, still in use today; and across the empire you find little packhorse bridges without parapets placed on the drovers' roads, their common horseshoe design humbly expressive of the unity, and utility, of empire.

The bridge that Ibrahim, in 1526, flung across the Sava in four days, which his engineers had told him would take three months to build, signalled the apogee of the empire – he went on to build a pontoon bridge across the Danube at Buda, too, weighted with the bells of the city churches in all the insolence of victory. When, later that century, a bridge collapsed with fatal consequences just when the pasha of Bosnia was riding over it – to the undisguised amusement of the Austrians, whose derision so offended the Porte that war was only averted by a timely gift of flowers – the existence of a bridge so unsafe could be said to have presaged the empire's imminent decline, until a day was reached when a traveller, with business in another town, could be told, 'There are many bridges on that road,' as a reason for taking another.

The Ottomans did not burden the world with monuments to their own magnificence, and it is this, perhaps, which makes them seem so distant, as though their empire had flourished many centuries ago, on other continents. Besma Sultan ran out of money for the second minaret on the Yeni Valideh Cammi at the Akseray; and when her son offered her the money to finish it she said, 'No, one minaret is enough to call the people to prayer, and another would only glorify me; the poor need a fountain.' You will search in vain for the familiar memorials of empire – for statuary, triumphal arches or obelisks, of the rewards which imperialists tend to discover for themselves – comfy lodgings in up-country stations, sprawling villas on the latifundia, or great country houses lapped by manicured lawns. The palaces of the great were invariably lost in the winding byways of the city, and in the evening of empire the local governor's *konak*, or residence, in any Balkan town, was always a sort of barracks, dirty white, where half a dozen irregular-looking men with broken teeth and oily rifles milled about.* *Konak* described the governor's residence, but also any ordinary wooden house; and its first meaning was a halt on the caravan route.

You might conclude that this was a very modest empire, for there was certainly a delicacy, a tact, in the way people provided for themselves. However much an Ottoman city might be admired from afar, on close inspection it generally proved to be a warren of closely packed wooden buildings 'built on the bare earth', which in every city in the empire – but especially Istanbul – was

* An exception was the palace which Suleyman's Grand Vizier Ibrahim erected for himself. Outside its gates he set two statues looted after the fall of Buda, one of Apollo, the other of Diana. The people understood them to be the King and Queen of Hungary.

regularly swept by plague, and consumed by fire.* 'If anyone is asked his age,' said Baron de Tott, a Frenchman who ran an artillery school in Constantinople in the eighteenth century, 'the answer will always refer to the year of some plague or famine, some rebellion or conflagration', while Thackeray, who witnessed fifteen major fires in a month in Pera, could only regret that none of them had lasted long enough to oblige the Sultan to attend them in person.

The eye was drawn to the city from a long way off. The minarets of Sarajevo, it used to be said, could be seen from Bosanski Novi, in the far north-west corner of Bosnia, seventy miles away. In Eger, northern Hungary, the solitary pencil of a minaret rises above a dusty square, shorn of its mosque, its schools, and soup kitchens, but, as anyone there will tell you, it was the northernmost minaret in Europe until modern times. Vlore's perfect little mosque was sinisterly preserved as a museum of superstition, lonely between the serried blocks of flats of a vanished socialist utopia. In Tirana, which the Ottomans founded, the mosque of Sultan Ahmet graces the corner of the presidential square like a rash of poppies on a building site; its dome within is ablaze with visions of the Bosphorus, and when the imam, in a flat cap and tweed coat, gets you sliding your feet nervously onto the parapet of the minaret, he will murmur the call to prayer confidingly, just to show you how the thing is done.

It used to be said that Ottoman mosques were journeyman copies of the cathedral erected by Justinian a thousand years earlier, but Ottomans sought light.† The taste for abstractions which the Ottomans brought to the empire's European regions followed

* 'Because its beauty is so rare a sight / The sea has clasped it in an embrace', wrote Nabi, but he continued: 'Were it not for all kinds of diseases / Were it not for the accursed plague / Who would ever leave this place like paradise / This grief-dispelling city? / If only its weather were more equable / Who would ever look at any other place?'

† Probably the Byzantines gave the Ottomans little directly. A troop of warriors attending the Emperor, whose spleens had been removed for reasons even the Byzantines had forgotten, the Turks superstitiously maintained. For women, a Byzantine gauze veil replaced sackcloth; but that was town sophistication, and the fact that Byzantine women were veiled at all suggests how far the cultures were already intertwined.

the old invasion route taken by monotheism, by sterner forms of spiritual Christianity, abstract Islam, numerals and alphabets, geometry and algebra, disdain for the gross illusions of the flesh, Platonic ideals of a transcendent universe. Islam had seized upon the work of the early Greek geometricians and algebrists with glee, and made them its own.

In their mosques, the Ottomans made structural use of the dome and semi-dome, spinning them heavenwards so that the central dome floated upon a cascade of structures which became more slender, numerous and small as they reached the ground, like a fountain rising within from solidity to translucency, and cascading down in a widening shower of droplets. Karoly Kos felt that the silhouette of a mosque could be a reflection of the circular nomadic tent; and one historian took a step further, and claimed to see inside every bare unfurnished mosque a reminder 'of the vast wastes of the sunlit deserts of Arabia'.

The tracery filling a mosque window, set with fragments of coloured glass, light and dark marble or stones on the façade, geometric designs carved on the monumental doors, mother-of-pearl inlay, bore the same gift for pattern as armies which sought the imprint of last year's camp on which to pitch their tents; the carpets of Anatolia, the tiles of Iznik, the maps of Piri Reis,* or the imperial household revolving around the Sultan like stars around the earth. A Circle of Felicity dominated Near-Eastern political thought:

> In order to hold a land one needs troops and men,
> In order to keep troops one must divide out property,

* In 1513, heralding an explosion of Ottoman geographies and travel books, Piri Reis, corsair and later Admiral of the Red Sea Fleet, produced a two-fold map of the world: the western portion has survived. People still speculate on how he was able to include the New World, which Columbus had discovered only twenty years before; some put it down to information from a Spanish seaman captured at Valencia in a raid by Piri Reis's uncle; others argue for arcane knowledge. Piri Reis engaged the Portuguese with considerable success around the Persian Gulf, and was instrumental in bringing southern Arabia under direct Ottoman control in the 1540s. His successor, Seydi Ali Reis, was driven off by the Portuguese in 1554; he escaped to India, reaching Constantinople in May 1557 after an epic land voyage through India, Afghanistan, Central Asia and Iran, recorded in his *Mirror of the Lands*.

In order to have property one needs a rich people.
Only laws create the richness of a people.
If one of these is lacking all four are lacking:
If all four are lacking, the dominion goes to pieces.

Patterns are light, but strong. Tamerlane's name means approximately 'man of iron': but *timur* was not actually iron itself, rather the quality of hardness which made it so difficult to bend. Most calligraphic inscriptions contained an outer and an inward meaning, to be read by the initiated; and when that historian claimed to see, in every Ottoman mosque, an echo of the sunlit spaces of the steppe, he pointed the way to the inner quality of this empire as it rose to power, and acknowledged the lightness that was its genius. At its heart was the pattern which rose almost to nothingness, the rippling Arabic so abstract that meaning itself was jettisoned, the mantra, repeated towards infinity, which emptied the Sufi's mind and let it fill with God's.

William Biddulph, an English factor in Smyrna in the seventeenth century, once took the trouble to weigh his drinking water, and promptly discovered why it was so good: it was lighter than English water, he said, by four ounces in the pound. Christendom produced, by way of cloth, heavy woollens; the Ottoman Empire gave the world its silk, muslin, and cottons. The Christian nations clamped down hard on trade, and from the sixteenth century their policy of mercantilism, favouring exports and their own ships, grimly made trade a battering ram to riches. The Ottomans freely summoned to their empire all the products of the world.

The defence of Christendom was an armadillo affair: towering castles, armoured knights, mail, breastplates, maces so heavy they can hardly be lifted with two modern hands. A German mercenary of the sixteenth century might be festooned with bullets and powder horns and bowed beneath his six-foot musket; but Ottoman armies moved like tides, and travelled light, with simple wants and few possessions. The janissaries took to guns, but the spahis baulked at the muskets first tried out on them in Persia in 1556. Their companions derided their horns, pouches, ramrods, and bandoliers, and mocked them as mounted apothecaries; the guns jammed and fell apart, and when they were fired, the discharge covered their beautiful clothes with soot. Before long the spahis were begging for their bows and arrows. Outmoded chivalry, perhaps: but boys spent years learning to flex a light bow, long before they were allowed to draw it, and in the spahi's hands the bow was more accurate, more manoeuvrable, cleaner, lighter and more effective than the early firearms. Having judged the musket for what it was, they lost interest. The West improved its workings. The spahis ignored it.

The organisation of western faith was ponderous and hierarchical: Christian divines hunkered in their cells; Christian monks built themselves vast monasteries; and the domes of an Orthodox church can appear earth-bound, clustered like cowpats beside the aspiring minaret. In the East holy men removed themselves so far from the gross world that they sat on pillars for years; or walked on flaming coals. Evliya Celebi describes how a Sufi who could only have passed bodily through the wall once visited him and the Grand Vizier; Lady Mary Wortley Montagu knew of a teacher who moved with his entire family into the branches of a tree; and the pet holy man of the higher Ottoman ranks was always the Mevlevi 'whirling' dervish, whose performance left spectators gasping for breath. 'The rapidity with which they whisked around became amazing,' wrote Chandler, who witnessed a performance of the rite in the Athenian Tower of the Winds; 'their long hair not touching their shoulders, but flying off.' Afterwards the visitors were given coffee and pipes, with the chief dervish 'as cool and placid as if he had been only a looker-on'.

Mevlevi Whirling Dervish

An enormous amount of the empire's wealth, and almost a third of its land, found its way out of the tax system altogether, and into charitable foundations. Islam was a powerful provider, and most of the memorials of empire were charitable. Charity, said the poet

Jami, was like musk, 'which may be hidden but is discovered by the grateful odour it diffuses'.

Bridges were often erected as an act of piety, and maintained by endowments. Endowments, or *vakif*, were enshrined in Islamic law, and supplied a great range of public services in perpetuity. The sick could get free treatment at the mosque, and the traveller three free nights, with food, in a *han*, or hostel. The mentally ill – if not kept as the village idiot – were cared for in asylums. When the antiquarian Postel was sent by Louis XIV to seek out old manuscripts in the bazaars he fell on hard times, whereupon the janissaries cordially enrolled him into their mess. Before the seventeenth century at least, foreigners often commented on the absence of beggars; later they had a guild to maintain their position in society like everyone else. Eliot, in the nineteenth century, remembered the legless beggar of Therapia, who saluted passers-by with a graceful bow, and 'received with the dignity of a courteous tax collector the alms which his persuasive tongue never failed to elicit'. He was said to have become quite rich, and when ambassadors left Therapia at the onset of winter he left, too, taking a first-class ticket to Mitylene, to spend the winter with his eleven blind sisters. Endowments proved, tangentially, to be a useful way for a wealthy man to leave something to his heirs, for every great man could set up some foundation and appoint his heirs as its perpetual guardians, permitted to sustain themselves from its revenues.

There were shops in Bulgaria whose rents were taken to feed the poor of Medina. Some shop rents went to the maintenance of nearby bridges, or drinking fountains. So many hans were set up on the Edirne road, providing travellers with food and lodging, that the Sultan actually forbade any more to be established. When Mehmet II issued a kanun abolishing a large number of vakif, and at a stroke brought 20,000 villages into the sultanic fisc, he was regarded like a modern politician who raids the pension fund: within a year he was dead, amid rumours that he had been poisoned. Islamic civic society, in consequence, was marvellously insulated from the vagaries of politics, going its own collective way; its clubs, guilds, secret societies, religious cults, trading networks cast a net of mutual support across the empire. So much was dedicated to God, the Eternal, the coming of paradise on earth: for the Ottomans lived on the brink, as they thought, of a golden age.

'The dog barks, the caravan moves on,' goes an old saying; and the annals of the empire do now and then exude an air of expectation. In Anatolia the arrival of the Mahdi who was to usher in the end of the world was forever being celebrated by a rabble of peasants who moved toward the capital, overturning everything in their path, suffering delusions of immense joy.* Baron Wratislaw's gaoler in the Seven Towers once brought him the news that Raab had fallen to the Turks, a fact which the gaoler understood to mean, not the loss of a fortress, but the long-awaited collapse of all Christendom. He even advised his prisoners to convert, since now they had nowhere else to go.

The Ottomans were born to move, and this fact had made them warriors: for upon the frontiers of the empire, movement inevitably meant war. They accepted death and disappointment fatalistically, as they accepted without question the burdens of their caste. 'There is nothing wonderful in emperors being defeated and made prisoners,' wrote Suleyman consolingly to the King of France, who languished in an Italian prison cell. The customary response of an Ottoman pasha to his own death warrant was never indignation, but surprise – grimly comical, at times – followed by resignation. It has been said that the incessant westward movement of the frontier represented not so much an urge to subjugate as an urge for consummation: a desire to belong. The sultans were always to be found visiting the borders of their empire, the whole panoply of state going west to the Danube, or east to the Euphrates. Christendom seemed to shrink from

* As late as 1785 one of the oddest marching Mahdis approached Smyrna and Sivas with his followers. An Italian born in Montferrat, he became a notorious seducer and then a fiercely proselytising Dominican friar. Sent to take up a sensitive post in Mosul, his zeal for converts actually earned him excommunication from the church. Subsequently he became a Muslim, then a self-proclaimed Mahdi, and with Persian backing launched his mission on the empire. At the height of his success he inexplicably agreed to fight for Catherine the Great. Four years later the Turks captured him. They kindly gave him a pension and in 1798 he retreated into an Armenian monastery.

contact. It was the West which at last attempted a lock-out, erecting its *Militärgrenze*, with forts, and establishing quarantine stations, through which every traveller from the empire had to pass; twenty days or more in one of those lazarettos which *Murray's Handbook* called 'prison, with a chance of catching the plague'.

The Ottoman urge to motion craved satisfaction. The kul could leave nothing to their sons, and their status required continual display. Power, like the grandeur of the palace, could not be still; it could not be stored, as it was in the palaces of the West, or in the bloodlines of European aristocracy. The Venetians understood this: for years, as their real power waned, they fought tooth and nail to maintain the precise detail of their bailio's reception at the palace, and again and again, in their *relazioni*, scrupulously described the entire rigmarole; while Lady Mary Wortley Montagu confessed she could not be bothered to write about it at all. Everything about a pasha was indicated by his clothes, and where he went, and the size of the retinue he maintained: Ottoman society concentrated fiercely on the act. Presents were handed out at every meeting; prayers had to be said regularly by everyone, to affirm belief.

PART II

The Turkish Time

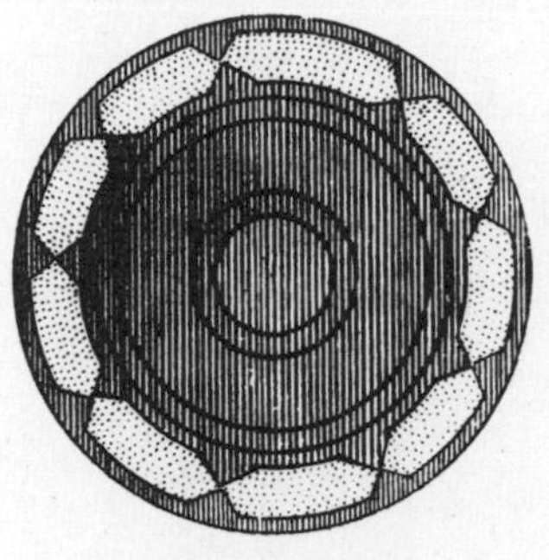

13

The Turkish Time

'The Turks,' wrote Busbecq, 'have no hours to mark the time, just as they have no milestones to mark distances.' Nobody thought to count the hours, or to reckon the days, or to quail before any of the distances to be covered – neither the soldier setting out from Istanbul, nor the ploughman squaring up to his stony slopes, nor the pasha, rising to the business of the day. People lived, did and died: everyone knew that.

The unfolding pattern of Ottoman conquest resembled a truth revealed, not created; and the early Ottomans dealt with time in a lordly way, as nomads do. A day was appointed for their deaths, as it was for victory. They never looked back, or calculated risk. A janissary giant called Hasan was the first onto the walls of Constantinople; and although Hasan was cut down by the defenders, every Turkish assault threw up its Hasan, charging bull-necked into the breach, ready to claim in an instant his martyrdom, and all the houris due to him in paradise. When the Turks dodged the chronicler and his dates; and Bayezit earned the nickname 'Thunderbolt' for the rapidity of his marches; and they sliced new roads through barren mountains to fall, with horrid suddenness, on some enemy – 'Woe! thunderation! What an army!' cried poor Uzan Hasan in 1461, as he watched Mehmet's forces spread from the hills like lava, before seizing, in a twinkle, the age-old empire of Trebizond; then time seemed flat and immeasurable like the steppe, encouraging great speed. Foreigners envied the speed of law; and Ottoman horsemen rode like the very wind, astonishing one nineteenth-century traveller who reckoned 30 miles in a day good going for a man on horseback. Here, he said, '100 is fast travelling; 150 the fastest; 600 miles in four days and a half, and 1,200 in ten, are indeed, feats, but not very uncommon ones.'

The idea that the whole world would be subsumed within a single commonwealth belonged to the framework of European thought until at least the seventeenth century, but few could back the pretension with quite the same wide-eyed confidence or resources as the Ottoman state. The fifteenth-century inscription on the Bursa mosque – 'Lord of the Horizons, Burgrave of the Whole World' – may have been, in narrow terms, a fraud; but it was the fraud of an optimistic age. Every new sultan, girded with the sword of Orhan – the particularly Ottoman version of coronation – bent his lips to the ear of the janissary aga and whispered, 'Let us meet at the Red Apple,' by which he meant whatever will'-o'-the-wisp lay beyond Islam's grasp: Constantinople, Rome, Vienna. Bayezit fully intended to conquer Austria, and be in France next; he meant to stable his horse in St Peter's. Mehmet the Conquerer, says Kritovolos, 'immediately overran the whole world in his calculations', taking Constantinople for its centre; and in gloomy moments the Venetians – who knew the Ottoman world better than any other Christian power, and could calculate that the Sultan's receipts exceeded his expenses – would judge the Ottomans to be sure victors in the eschatalogical project of achieving world empire. For when they effused over Constantinople's position, it was not the disinterested praise of the traveller, nor even entirely the businessman's assessment: it was mostly the suspicion that the propaganda that had issued from the place ever since Constantine founded it in AD 376 was true, and Constantinople was created by nature, ordained by history, to be the centre of the world. There was a belief that an emperor would usher in the Second Coming, and a familiar prophecy that four empires were to rule before the Kingdom of God was established on earth. There was a strong indication, however you looked at it, that the Ottomans, and Islam, had everything on their side, and that 'to fight,' as one Barbero wrote in 1573, was 'useless'.

Ottomans judged themselves against no yardstick of progress. The notion was blasphemous; in the Sayings of the Prophet one might read that 'Every novelty is an innovation, every innovation is an error, every error leads to Hellfire.' Time was circular, not linear. When Evliya Celebi went raiding in Podolia in 1684, he found himself looting in the very house he had looted in 1683: and when he opened a closet in the bedroom he was able to retrieve, as the most natural thing in the world, the little hatchet he had left behind.*

The hillmen of Albania or the Caucasus were as much given to vendetta as Sardinians. An offence remained as fresh as on the day it was given; vengeance was bequeathed; honour could be satisfied by a well-aimed shot in the back forty, or sixty, or even a hundred years after the offence. Earlier this century Edith Durham travelled rough through Albania, and everywhere she was greeted with effortless courtesy by these fierce and independent people, for the grisliest Arnaut was a gentleman (some of the women, as it happened, were gentlemen too: they dressed like men, and farmed and fought their corner as members of a beardless bachelor sorority). They lived, she found, like birds, who sleep at dusk and rise at dawn, summer and winter. No Albanian would admit that their summer nights were shorter than those of any other season of the year. They had twenty-four hours in a day like anyone else;

* Evliya delightfully encapsulates the contempt for time which infused the Ottoman world. An indefatigable traveller, scholar and musician, he wrote a book with more than a whiff of *Tristram Shandy* (including a description of his own birth), mingled with reportage, fantasy, political diatribes, and personal recollections: chapter CCCLXX sprawls across sixty-two folios, or several hundred pages of print. His sweet singing voice caught the attention of Murad III, but he saw no urgency to get on and chose to go travelling instead, in a world he revealed to be crammed with dreams and miracles, glimpses taken across the rings of time.

but twelve to night, and twelve to light. Durham yawned, and nodded in her chair; at dusk she was allowed to crawl to bed; but at dawn her hosts awoke refreshed, congratulating themselves on having had a really good night's sleep.

Du Fresne, a young Huguenot who joined an ambassadorial suite to Istanbul in 1623, claimed there was then just one public clock in the whole of the Ottoman empire; it was at Skopje, it tolled the hours *à la française*, and its survival, or erection, was considered something of a marvel, for bells and public clocks were generally outlawed in the empire. The Grand Vizier Ibrahim had proudly taken the title Breaker of the Bells of the Pagans when he had anchored his pontoon bridge across the Danube with the assembled peal of Buda. A sixteenth-century visitor had been irked by his janissary escort's habit of waking him hours before they were due to start, which he discovered was because they were unable to tell the time correctly; he showed them his watch and bade them rest easy, which at first they found hard to do; but after a few days' sleeping with one eye open they began to trust him, and all agreed that the watch was a wonderful thing for getting a good night's rest.* When Busbecq praised the Turks for their unique readiness to adopt the useful inventions of others, he made an exception of clocks and printing, both which might, he thought, challenge the dominion of the mullahs.

The moon governed the caravans from which Islam sprang, for desert journeys were made by night (the Turks call the morning star Kervan Kiran, or 'the caravan breaking'). The moon was the symbol of the faith; and the dread hour of the Muslim world was not midnight, but high noon. At that flat moment the devil took the world on his horns and prepared to make off with it, before he was blasted in his triumph by the cry 'God is most great', deliberately called from the minarets a few seconds after midday.

The attachment to a lunar calendar gave the empire a peculiar feeling of transcendence – allowed it to function at a remove from

* On the way home, though, he cheered up his janissaries by feeding them zabaglione, after which they promised to carry him to Buda if necessary.

the rough material world, inhabited by the reaya, the peasants, and their interminable harvests. The Islamic year spun faster than the sun: so Ramadan falling in summer is the fiercest hardship for the faithful, who may not swallow so much as their own spittle between sunrise and sundown, a time of fraying tempers. But the ecstasy of Ramadan surpasses all conventions, and for a month the days are like nights, and the nights like day. The sun is always a disc, but the moon curves, swells, declines – and returns. She indicates the essentially illusory nature of time itself, for her phases are only apparent, and her substance never changes.

The matter of time was one of those things like horse-breeding, or pastry, for which everyone relied on experts. The holy men knew how time should be used. There were water-clocks and sundials in certain mosques to indicate the hours of prayer, tended by a class of men called talismans. The ulema issued almanacs to the lunar year of 354 days, noting in columns the prayer times, the solar and lunar months and days, phases of the moon, sunsets and sunrise, and the timing of Greek festivals, too. These gave guidance to propitious and ill-starred days – days good for petitioning, bad for buying horses. The 9th of Safer 1593, for example, was a good day to invite people for dinner; the 16th very bad for travelling.

Alongside the Holy Koran, the law of the land was given in the Sultan's *kanun*, decrees which operated over areas of life for which the Prophet had made no explicit provision; and they had the force of the old Turkic *adet*, the utterances of the pre-Islamic chiefs. The Ottomans sought moments in the cosmic pattern – Suleyman made his entrance into Buda after consulting astrologers as a matter of course, but once when he considered it more important to maintain his army's strength than to observe the letter of the Law, he publicly ate a lunch during the fast of Ramadan as an example to his troops.

God Himself, the arbiter of fate, made time and space irrelevant; the ulema attended to the mysteries of time's calibration; but the very longevity of the royal line – the empire's only hereditary power – seemed like a material expression of eternities, and lent every sultan a transcendent dignity and importance. The Sultan bound time to himself, as he bound all the powers and currents of the empire into his own hands, just as he dyed his beard and hair, never allowing a telltale streak of grey to disturb the illusion that about him time stood still. So carefully did Suleyman the Magnificent tend the link between his person and the cycle of renewal, that he never wore the same clothes twice, but appeared each day anew, like the sun.

Each new sultan affected to act as if his predecessor had bequeathed him nothing. He bought the troops anew, with an accession donative. He sent away the old harem and imported his own; and he executed those playmates of his early youth, his brothers, leaving him with no male relatives but his own sons. He ratified laws and treaties as if they had never been ratified before, and a fresh census, as complete as the Domesday Book, but bigger, was made of dues and obligations. (Portents were expected at this time. In 1574 Murad III, making his first remark as Sultan, said 'I am hungry – let me have something to eat.' It could only mean famine. Murad was superstitious himself. On the morning of 16 January 1595 he was perturbed by his musicians playing the tune to a song whose first line he was prompted to murmur: 'Come and keep watch by me tonight, O Death!'; later that day he died of shock when a pane of glass was shattered by the noisy salute of Egyptian ships sailing into harbour – such was the intolerable tension which Mehmet and Suleyman bequeathed to their successors in the silent court.)

Between one sultan's death and the girding of the next, ambitions and jealousies locked into a framework of devotion and obedience came tumbling out like stones from a capless arch, and it was flat noon, the moment of misrule and devilry in the state. Those privy to the old Sultan's death strove to keep the news secret while they sent word to the favoured heir – for succession was one area in which Islam refused to legislate. 'Princes will follow me: render them your obedience,' the Prophet said; but it left the details to the imagination. Turkic tradition was no help, either, because it was clan based, awarding hereditary power, if at all, to whole families. With power as ruthlessly individual as the Ottoman, such traditions added up to nothing more than a weaselly injunction to let the best man win.

In a period which would be short, decisive, and end in blood, people were deft about it, urged on by anxiety. In 1421 Mehmet I's corpse was propped up in a litter and presented to the suspicious troops; the masterstroke was to make the Sultan gravely stroke his beard, while under the litter a cunning official worked the dead man's arm with a concoction of gears and string. The sons of a reigning sultan jockeyed for governorships as close as possible to Constantinople; a prince given a province far from the centre knew that his chances of succeeding were slim and prepared, as best he could, to save his own life; Cihangir, Suleyman the Magnificent's crippled child, went mad when he heard how Suleyman had executed his brother in 1553. 'Let those who love me, follow me!' cried Mehmet when he received the news of his father's death; while on *his* death in 1481 there was jubilation at Manisa, where his son Bayezit had established a gloomy and reverent court, so opposed to Mehmet's statist policies that it was supposed Bayezit had poisoned him.

Bayezit II took seventy days to seize control of Constantinople. The soldiers admired his brother, Cem. Bayezit loved Cem, too, but 'a sultan knows no blood relations', he said; and, to his brother's proposal that they divide the empire between them, he replied: 'Empire is a bride whose favours cannot be shared.' From Mameluke Egypt Cem led an abortive invasion in 1482. In desperation he appealed to the Knights of Rhodes to carry him into Europe, to try a rebellion there. The scheme was accepted by the knights, and Cem was ferried to Rhodes with a small retinue of some thirty men. He promised the knights an advantageous treaty in the event of his becoming Sultan, but Bayezit offered them more – peace, free trade and 45,000 ducats a year, ostensibly for his brother's maintenance. It became impossible then for the knights to give Cem up. Supposedly for his own safety he was carried to Nice, which he admired, all the while expressing his urgent desire to travel on, into Rumelia. Being on French territory, he was told, he should visit the King; but the messenger he sent to arrange the meeting was at last tactfully given up for dead.

A plague in Nice gave the knights the excuse they had sought to move their royal prize to one of their inland commanderies, detaching him from his retinue; first Roussillon, then le Puy, then Sassenage, where he fell in love with the commander's daughter, Philippine Helena, and wrote a lament:

> Ah, for the time when my star rode triumphant,
> good-fortune its mount,
> Keeping abreast with the dream of your fleetly elusive
> embrace! . . .
> Ah, for the time when your threshold was residence, also,
> for Cem!
> How good a time it was we never knew until lost
> without trace.

The knights had meanwhile built a special tower for Cem, seven storeys high, where he might languish above the kitchens and the servants, and beneath the guards. He begged for freedom and attempted to escape; while the knights milked his brother, and even managed to extract 20,000 ducats more from his wife and mother, living in Cairo, with the promise of his imminent release.

In 1489 the knights struck a deal with the King of France and the Pope. The Grand Master was made a cardinal. Cem was brought to Rome; saluted the Pope with a kiss on the shoulder, like a cardinal, and had an interview with Innocent VIII which reduced the pontiff to tears. Cem soon discovered how his family in Cairo had been tricked. An Ottoman ambassador arrived with various relics of the Crucifixion, and negotiated a 40,000 ducat pension to be paid to the Pope. Innocent was succeeded by Alexander Borgia, who sent the only ever papal ambassador to the Ottoman court, and got the 40,000 ducats continued, as well as a promise of 300,000 ducats as a one-off payment if Cem should die; but he also took a shine to his captive and would dress up *à la turque*, and ride about Rome with him. In 1495 Charles VIII took Rome; Borgia took Cem with him into the Castel Sant' Angelo. Negotiations followed; Cem was transferred and taken by Charles to the siege of Naples. Borgia, bilked of his income, opted for the second option; and the deed was done, so the story goes, by a Greek renegade acting as Cem's barber, who nicked him with a poisoned razor, and much later became Grand Vizier. It is striking how gingerly Bayezit II had set to work as long as the possibility of a rival had existed; even the excellent position the army had secured for itself in southern Italy, at Otranto, had to be abandoned when Bayezit recalled Ahmet Keduk to defeat his brother. But when Cem died at thirty-six, after thirteen years' captivity, his body was returned to Bursa for burial, with all due pomp; and Bayezit ruled more easily, and began a war with Venice.*

The elevation of a new sultan returned the empire to its cyclical patterns. The state had withered and died in the winter of the interregnum; the arrival of a new sultan, steered by the hand of God through all its dangers and alarms, signalled the return of spring.

'In divan poetry,' wrote a Turkish critic in 1932, 'nature has the lack of perspective of a Persian miniature. Trees cling to man, birds to the sky. There is no wind, and everything seemes frozen.'

Out went the armies. Up went the nomads to the hills. Fleets cruised on the seas, caravans wended their way across the sands, the peasants sowed and reaped, and in the palace grave old men ran lightly to and fro, on stockinged feet, like boys.

* The odour of sanctity never left Bayezit, though. His son and successor, Selim the Grim, once commented on a portrait of him in the Marble Kiosk on Seraglio Point, in Constantinople. The painter, he said, 'has not been able to capture his likeness. The deceased used to make us sit on his blessed lap in our childhood; his noble countenance is still in our memory: he was falcon-nosed.' Strange words from a sultan whose martial valour so appealed to the troops that he was able to depose his father, and then poison him.

14

Stalemate

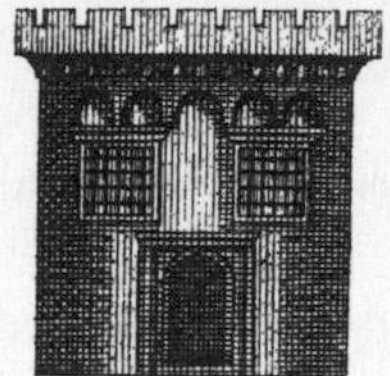

Suleyman ruled for forty-seven years, and thirty of them he spent on campaign, tireless and resolute, plodding from one project to the next – Egypt and the Rhodes trouble, Belgrade and Hungary, Tabriz, Baghdad, Vienna. 'What! Suleyman still here? What a drag!' wrote the Christian-born poet Yaga Beg, successfully chancing his reputation on very thin ice; and the soldiers, too, grew tired of their leader in his later years. On the Persian front in 1553 the army was murmuring that the Sultan was too old to march – he was fifty-nine. The soldiers wanted to make Suleyman's eldest son Sultan. Suleyman invited Mustafa to his tent, and had him strangled there.

But in gobbets of Balkan mud, and in the smouldering deserts of Iran time began to establish its dominion over his empire. These were regions a sultan could not cross before his army chafed to be home again for harvest. Suleyman ventured out from Edirne or Bursa year after year with an army larger than any he had amassed before, his grandeur concealing intimations of decline, his reign a feast of ambiguous victories.

Suleyman's last campaign in 1566 proved little more than a monstrous *razzia* into Austrian-held territory, for his enemies eluded him, as ever. The Ottoman army spent ninety-seven days on the march before besieging Szigetvar. On 7 September 1566 Suleyman died among his troops, in the midst of a siege, in his campaign tent pitched in the mud of Hungary. His Grand Vizier concealed his death from the army and brought the siege to its successful conclusion. The body was embalmed, dressed, and propped up in the litter as if it were alive until the army was almost home. Meanwhile messengers started from the camp to reach Suleyman's surviving son, Selim.

The poet Baki, who had been the Sultan's friend and correspondent, mourned:

> That master rider of the realm of bliss
> For whose careering steed the field of the world was narrow.
> The infidels of Hungary bowed their heads to the temper of his blade,
> The Frank admired the grain of his sword.
> He laid his face to the ground, graciously, like a fresh rose petal,
> The treasurer of time put him in the coffer, like a jewel.

The treasurer of time was measuring up the Ottoman Empire, too. The three great Mediterranean powers, Venice, Spain, and the empire itself, all soon toppled into a decline as protracted as it was profound, and a note of exhaustion stole across the whole Mediterranean world. The Venetians heard it, sung softly at dusk beneath the Venetian Rector's window in Split, 'a song on everyone's lips . . . and it says in this song that the Turk is running water that erodes, and that the Doge is a sandbank which has been carried away little by little by the river.'

In 1570 Suleyman's old Grand Vizier, Sokullu Mehmet, took the island of Cyprus for the worthless Selim, who died in 1574. It was much against his better judgement, for Sokullu believed that the empire was tired, and needed a period of caution and repose; but an attack on Venetian Cyprus was the price he paid to hang onto power. It proved to be a turning-point for the empire.

There was nothing wonderful about the Turks having a crack at Cyprus. It rounded off their control of the eastern Mediterranean; it swept out a nest or two of pirates. The Greeks of Cyprus welcomed the invaders, as Greek islanders frequently did. Fifty thousand Turks died in the effort to capture Fermagusta; but Ottoman wars were traditionally free with lives. The Venetian commander Bragadino, surrendering at last with full military honours and guarantees of safe-conduct for his troops, was treacherously seized, horribly mangled, and at last flayed alive; the Turkish fleet returned to Constantinople in triumph with his skin stuffed with straw and hanging from a yard arm. It was a gruesome but not unprecedented end, and the Turks had no monopoly on the manner of it.

What distinguished the Ottoman assault from preceding adventures of the kind was the world's reaction. The attack was perceived, on all sides, as an unwarranted disturbance, as though Turkish conquest was no longer something to be expected but an outrageous upheaval in the natural order. The impetus for the attack was certainly all wrong – the whim of a drunkard, egged on by a Jew, said the western powers bitterly – and it was steeped in palace intrigue. Sultan Selim, the Sot, had a passion for Cyprus wine; his boon companion, Joseph Nasi, a refugee from Spain who had become the court banker, and who as Duke of Naxos was the first Jew to be ennobled for over a thousand years, even hoped to turn Cyprus into a homeland for Jewish refugees from Europe; but to Selim he suggested that the toper should master the source of his good cheer. New powers, too, could be seen stirring in the palace now. Suleyman's marriage to Roxelana brought the Sultan's harem out of the Old Palace and into his private apartments in Topkapi, opening a period of harem influence, the so-called Sultanate of the Women, which was to endure until the 1650s and introduced all sorts of political cross-currents into the management of imperial affairs. Don Joseph's case for Cyprus was supported from the harem by the Jewish-born Nur Banu Sultan, mother of the future Murad III. It was opposed by Selim's Venetian-born wife, Safiye Sultan.

Cyprus fell, and the drunkard got his wine tax-free. But new powers were stirring in the West. The fall of Cyprus prompted the formation of a Holy League against the Ottomans. Spain, Venice, the Knights of Malta, and various Italian states under the lead of the papacy, put together a fleet under the command of Don Juan of Austria, a bastard son of Charles V. On 7 October 1571 he sighted the Ottoman fleet in the Gulf of Lepanto, and moved to the attack.

Sokullu Mehmet Pasha possessed superlative powers of imagination, brilliant sources of intelligence, and excellent maps, out of which he concocted a plan to maintain the momentum of Ottoman conquest. His intention was to dig a canal to link the Black Sea and the Caspian, over territories increasingly troubled by Russian Cossack raids. Here the Don and the Volga converge as they flow south over hundreds of miles, until a mere thirty miles divide them as they each turn and debouch into their separate seas. Had the Ottomans been able to launch a fleet through the canal and into the Caspian, they could have struck at Tabriz, the Persian capital, from its rear, avoiding the miserable overland approach through the arid mountains of Upper Armenia and Azerbaijan; gained direct access to the Silk Road from Central Asia for themselves; and erected a barricade against Russian and Cossack encroachments from the north-east, just as the Danube had formed their breastwork in the north-west. Dig the canal, open the Caspian to Ottoman ships and arms, and with a bound the empire might be free.

European discoveries were turning the eastern Mediterranean into a backwater, and the lines of trade and wealth which had lately converged on Constantinople now seemed to be moving away. At the end of the fifteenth century the Portuguese had discovered the route to the Indies round the Cape: they began trading straight away, bringing peppercorns to Europe in bulk, and cheap. Soon they had added silk, calicoes, and all kinds of spices to their cargoes, directly challenging the ancient caravan routes through the Middle East. The effect on the empire's revenues was not immediate, and coffee even substituted for spice in the Cairo trade. In the East itself, while some rulers had of course been delighted to see the Portuguese, others felt threatened and petitioned the empire to do something about it. In 1552 a naval expedition, under Piri Reis, had entered the Red Sea and driven the infidels, with difficulty, back to the mouth of the Persian Gulf; but the Portuguese still throttled off the Egyptian trade routes. (In the seventeenth century the establishment of Dutch and British power in Asia, and their decisive redirection of trade routes to the open ocean, was to deprive Turkey of most of her foreign commerce. In London 'nabobs' replaced 'pashas' as objects of envy and derision.) In 1580 Murad III was advised by a geographer to dig a Suez canal and 'capture the ports of Hind and Sind and drive away the infidels'. The Suez project never got beyond the planning stage, for the region was engulfed by a rebellion.

Work began on the Caspian canal, though, in the spring of 1570. Ten thousand troops, and 6,000 labourers, assembled at Kaffa in the Crimea; munitions and supplies were stockpiled at Azov; 500 men led the artillery up the Don and made camp at Perekop. Digging did not begin before the end of August. The Khan of the Crimean Tartars, Devlet Giray, sent 3,000 riders as guards and guides – not many, given the hordes at his control; they proved rather demoralising, describing to the Turkish troops the impossibility of righteous men surviving a Russian summer, when the sun never truly set, and the first and last prayer of the day could never be said. He withdrew them when progress on the canal began to be made. Almost a third had been dug by October, when the fierce steppe winds and the cold nights descended, and the general, 'Circassian' Kasim Pasha, broke off to secure the region for the spring, and better weather. One part of his force he sent to Astrakhan, to hold the mouth of the Volga on the Caspian; another he sent back to Azov, where the Don pours into the little sea of that name. The assault on Astrakhan, which was still held by the Russians, was repulsed by a sally; the troops at Azov were surprised by a small Russian army, the supplies went up in flames, and the Russians took their first Turkish war trophies. Disobeying orders, Kasim Pasha abandoned the whole ill-fated enterprise, and embarked his troops; but the flotilla was assailed by storms, and only 7,000 men returned to

Istanbul. It seems that the border guards, the Crimean Tartars, preferred to keep their enemies to themselves; and a year after the Ottomans withdrew they demonstrated their own ability in superb style, riding through to Moscow and firing the city, herding 200,000 captives back to Azov.

Distant Lepanto in 1571 brought the Ottomans a defeat which ruled out a return to the steppe. It was the largest battle ever waged in the Mediterranean – 487 ships took part, and 200 of the 245 Turkish ships were sunk. It was the first major defeat the Ottomans had suffered in two centuries, and was remembered by Cervantes, who took part in the battle, as 'that day so fortunate to Christendom, when all nations were undeceived of their error in believing that the Turks were invincible'. Depictions of the day became a stock-in-trade of western painters, and even G. K. Chesterton wrote a rousing poem about it 350 years later. But it was only the insults which remained full-rigged when the smoke of battle had cleared away; and the sheer costs of the engagement, to both sides, signalled an end to the struggle for the Mediterranean.

Sokullu himself weathered the death of his master Selim the Sot in 1574, and continued as Grand Vizier under the superstitious Murad III. But on 12 October 1579 he was struck down by an assassin's dagger as he walked through the palace to the divan. The killer's motives remain obscure: perhaps he was an agent of the Sultan, perhaps a religious maniac. The tide of everlasting victory, the unbarred tide of time, was beginning to turn back, setting up curious whorls and dangerous eddies; and violence and bitterness at the heart of state were grim portents of things to come.

15

The Cage

1591–2 was the thousandth year of the Hegira, the Islamic millennium. In the far west prudent families moved over the border, telling the Venetians that rumours of impending doom were common currency in the empire. And when the world did not end, nor the Mahdi come, the Ottomans seemed suddenly very weary, as if age-old expectations had been put aside, and replaced by a sense of time more nervously realistic, such as strikes a person approaching forty.

In the 1590s war broke out on two fronts at once, a situation rulers had always been very careful to avoid. The so-called Long War with Austria ran until 1606, when, as a French wag noted, the crescent strained to become a full moon. Simultaneously a twenty years' war with Iran surged back and forth into Azerbaijan and the Caucasus in a riot of propaganda, and with a severity which seemed to crystallise in the so-called Battle of the Torches, where the armies fought each other in a kind of dream, battling on through the night, and the following day, and into the night again. A rebellion in which Michael the Brave sought to unite Moldavia and Wallachia was not ended by Ottoman intervention, but by hit-men sent by the Habsburgs, who resented his growing power. In the increasing obsolescence of the cavalry, in the flight from the land, in the collapse of the register, the need for cash, the sudden and inexplicable effect of cheap American silver, and in the low calibre of Suleyman's successors, there was a sense of the empire slowing down.

Hajji Khalifa (1608–57) felt it; he thought wars were fatal to empires which had reached old age. The Venetians noticed it, as they always did. The bailio Lorenzo Bernardo made a return visit to Constantinople in 1593, and what he saw prompted him to say that everything had a youth, a maturity and a decline. Busbecq, in 1543, had been refused permission to move from Constantinople during an epidemic; but Bernardo now saw that Stambouliots chose to avoid the plague, and that even the Grand Mufti had lately fled from an outbreak in the city, setting at naught the old belief that every man's fate was written on his forehead.

Fatalism had been the ballast of Ottoman valour; but having learned the lesson of the plague, they applied it also to wars, and sought to avoid war wherever possible. Bernardo sensed widespread cynicism: 'I have known many of these renegades who had no religious beliefs, and said religions were invented by men for political reasons.' Now that everyone from the Sultan down preferred to stay at home, they busied themselves – Bernardo half-incredulously reported – with details of furniture, and food, clothes, even wine. The kul had gone soft in his lifetime, and no longer was a pasha 'happy with bread and rice, a carpet and a cushion'; nor 'showed his importance only by having many slaves and horses with which he could better serve his ruler'.

The inevitable result, Bernardo foresaw, was disobedience and then disunion, especially now that the higher-ups 'have no other goal but to oppose each other bitterly'. They were marrying into the royal family, he noticed, widening the scope for intrigue. Served with such an example, disobedience was rising among soldiers. The janissaries had collapsed Osman Pasha's tent upon him for higher pay in Persia. The spahis had rebelled in Istanbul; they had called for the heads of two officials, and 'no gifts of money, no command from the Sultan would shut them up until they had their way. They took the heads and brutally hurled them along the city streets with horrible cries.'

At the back of it all, the bailio thought, lay the indolence of the Sultan. Once every sultan had struggled to surpass the valour of his forebears, and the only territory the Ottomans had ever lost was Cephalonia to Venice in 1500. When the Sultan campaigned, men had struggled to perform great things in his service, but Selim, father of the present Sultan Murad III, had preferred his wine to war, and the empire's 'decline may now be underway. It seems quite possible', Bernardo wrote, 'that no sultan would ever go in person on campaigns, but that they would leave them to their slaves, which would certainly start their empire on a downward path.'

In 1596, three years after Bernardo's warning, Mehmet III conceived the idea that he would go to war, perhaps mindful of the decline of Ottoman prowess, and linking it to the fact that no sultan had accompanied his troops since the death of Suleyman thirty years before. The palace resisted, because it was cheaper to keep sultans at home; but 'it has been found impossible to delay much further the departure of the Sultan for the [Austrian] war,' the bailio reported. 'The Sultana Mother . . . persuaded a girl of singular beauty, with whom he is desperately in love, to beg him as a favour that he would not go. She did so one day when they were together in a garden; but the Sultan's love suddenly changed to fury, and drawing a dagger, he slew the girl. Since then no one has dared to approach the subject.'

Mehmet did go to Hungary, presiding over a royal disaster on the Tisza where he dazedly watched his troops cut to pieces by Prince Eugene's Habsburg army as they struggled to re-form across the river. The following year, the bailio noted, 'The doctors declared that the Sultan cannot leave for the war on account of his bad health, produced by excesses of eating and drinking.'

Ten years later, in May 1606, Sultan Ahmet I went to review his troops assembling in answer to the horsetails' summons at Scutari. 'It is now too late for a campaign,' the seventeen-year-old Sultan informed the divan, as the court historian Naima recalled.

'Provisions are scarce and dear. Is it not better to put off the expedition till next year?' The astonished assembly was silent until the Mufti, who vainly wished that Ahmet would follow the example of the great Suleyman, said, 'Would it, then, be fitting to carry back the horsetails, that have been planted in the sight of so many foreign ambassadors? Let the troops at least be marched to Aleppo to winter there, and collect stores of provisions.'

The Sultan interposed, 'What is the use of a march to Aleppo?' 'It is of use,' answered the Mufti, firmly, 'to save the honour of our tents which have been pitched.'

The Sultan was prevailed upon to allow Ferhad Pasha to take the army on. ' "Will he receive the money necessary for the purchase of provisions?" asked the Mufti. The Sultan replied, "The public treasury is empty. Whence am I to draw the money?" "From the Treasury of Egypt." "That," said the Sultan, "belongs to my private purse." "Sire," was the rejoinder, "your great ancestor, Sultan Suleyman, before the campaign at Szigeth, sent all his own treasures of gold and silver to the public mint."

'Sultan Ahmet knit his brows, and said, "Effendi, thou understandest not. Times are changed. What was fitting then is not convenient now." The result was, that Ferhad Pasha did set off with a part of the army without pay or supplies. The troops mutinied on their march, and were routed by the first band of rebels whom they encountered in Asia Minor.'* Ahmet himself soon sank into the oblivion of his harem, where the Jewish procuress Mme La Quira, also known as the Sultana Sporca, consoled him with hugely fat black girls.†

Any yardstick will signal the better fortune of the first ten rulers of the dynasty, from Osman Bey to Sultan Suleyman the Magnificent, who died in 1566. The old sultans had prepared their sons for rulership by making them governors of provinces, and surrounding them with advisers. These ten reigned an average of twenty-seven years apiece; campaigned with the troops, won

* From Naima, via Creasy.

† Mme La Quira was rewarded with jobs for all her family, and was eventually strangled at the insistence of the mob.

battles, and earned sobriquets like Grim, Magnificent, and Conqueror. In the century which followed, sultans averaged twelve years on the throne: out of the next ten sultans, five were deposed, and two assassinated. Of the twenty-six sultans who followed Suleyman the Magnificent, Selim was to be known as the Sot, Ibrahim as the Mad, Abdulhamid (at least in the European yellow press) as the Damned. Many of them seemed to be mentally unstable – a fact which could hardly be put down to the dangers of in-breeding which affected aristocracies in the West, but is easily explained by the atrocious conditions in which they were raised.

When Mehmet III took the throne in 1595 nineteen princely corpses had been carried from the Gate in obedience to the law of sultanic fratricide. The youths had been 'brought to him, one by one. They say that the eldest, a beautiful lad and of excellent parts, exclaimed: "My lord and brother, now to me as a father, let not my days be ended thus, in this my tender age"; the Sultan tore his beard with every sign of grief, but answered never a word.' The sight of the terrible cortège passing through the streets moved even Istanbul – all Mehmet's sisters died, too, for good measure; but the city wept less for them.

None of the early sultans had any living male relatives, other than their own sons: the fratricidal law ensured that they had no uncles, no cousins, no nephews to challenge their authority, or weaken their position as the sole representative of the House of Osman. Mehmet's successor, Ahmet I, broke with fratricidal law. After his accession in 1603, Ottoman princes were no longer killed as a matter of routine. But they never left the harem either. Uncles and brothers began to pool in the harem quarters, and the iron law of descent to the ablest son gave way to the right of the eldest living male to inherit the sultanate.

The princes-in-waiting were confined to the inner sanctum of the harem, the so-called Cage, or *kafes*, to await a sudden or natural death, or coronation, dragging out their existence in a state of suspended animation, amused by concubines whose sterility was guaranteed, withdrawn from the flow of life. Not even high potentates could predict how many princes might be found when turbulent soldiery broke down the palace doors and looked about for a suitable candidate for the throne. Men in advancing states of delirium and fear had to be raised from dungeons at the end of a rope, or let out of a dark attic through a trapdoor, before power was thrust upon them. It is said that Murad IV ordered the death of his brother Ibrahim while he himself lay dying in 1640; that he struggled to rise, to view the corpse, and 'grinned horrible a ghastly smile' in the belief that he was the last of his line. But Ibrahim had been preserved, in a furious harem struggle between the departing Valide Sultan and his mother, to rule as the very maddest of this increasingly mad and morbid family.

High office was dangerous. 'May you be vizier to Selim the Grim!' an old curse ran, and it is said that Selim I's viziers carried their wills in their bosom at all times. Generally, a Grand Vizier's chance of survival was only ten to one, so that one Grand Vizier compared himself to an ant, 'to whom God gives wings for their speedier destruction'. But 'paradise and sovereignty are never united', as the saying went, and the sultans themselves ran risks as grave as any of their slaves. Thirty-six sultans were girded with Osman's sword; seventeen of them were deposed. Westerners were learning to accuse Ottoman sultans of absolute tyranny, at the very moment that sultans were proving remarkably susceptible to defeat. Louis XIV, for one, was never held to account for French disasters on the battlefield, but the supposed tyrants of the Ottoman Empire seemed incapable of surviving military reverses once fresh princes were stockpiled in the kafes.

An admirer had once described the Sultan as an oyster in his shell; but the artful mechanisms by which Mehmet and his successors enforced their majesty soon clicked shut. Ixarette, sign language, was introduced to the Seraglio by two mute brothers, and Suleyman encouraged its use, believing that silence enhanced the Sultan's dignity. When Suleyman's rebellious son Bayezit fled to Persia in 1565, Shah Tahmasp's courtiers found him incapable of maintaining the light and easy flow of learned conversation that was proper to a gentleman in their eyes; probably with some relief they handed this awkward uninvited guest back to his father's executioner. Suleyman's weaker successors found ixarette suffocating, and in 1617 poor mad Sultan Mustafa refused to learn it. He was brought to book by a menacing discussion of the issue in divan; it was not proper, the viziers informed him, that the Padishah should speak in the language of copers and thieves, but he should maintain a gravity to make men tremble. Mustafa's little rebellion finished him off. Du Fresne, for his part, was very struck by the Sultan's attempt to respond to the ambassador, before the Grand Vizier cut him off – 'lui dit qu'il ne seyait pas à la majesté d'un si grand roi de trop parler avec les ambassadeurs, prit la parole et déclara brièvement ce qu'il avait à répondre'; and he hit on a resonant image of loneliness when he observed how, in the Sultan's lovely gardens, 'the alleys are lined with cypresses so high that their sight excites admiration; but they are narrow, for the Grand Seigneur always walks alone'.

Osman II, girded with the sword at Eyup in 1618, attempted a *coup d'état* against his own servants, 'the Drones that eat up his estate'. He meant to escape from Istanbul, raise a new army in Anatolia, and seize the empire afresh as master of a Turkish, Muslim state, but an angry crowd gathered outside the palace gates; the Grand Vizier sent out to calm them was torn to pieces; and Osman himself was finally taken into custody by the janissaries. His fate was sealed when a search was made of the harem for male relatives, turning up a few brothers; and the soldiers drew his starving, raving uncle out of a dungeon by a rope and made him Sultan. The new Grand Vizier walked into the room where Osman was asleep. Osman, we are told, woke up, and defended himself desperately; but the fabled training of the Sultan's kul won out when Davut Pasha put him to death 'by the compression of his testicles', Evliya Celebi records; adding that this was 'a mode of execution reserved by custom to the Ottoman sultans'.

His successor was his uncle, Mustafa. When Mustafa was returned to the Cage in favour of Osman in 1618, he twice escaped strangulation by a hair's breadth, and was imprisoned in a tiny room over a sunless courtyard tucked away behind the quarters of the harem favourites. The experience had not been of much help to him. Insane enough before, his restoration was brief, and the janissaries were so perturbed by his madness that they agreed to let Murad IV accede without paying the accession donative.

Murad IV was thirteen when he came to the throne, and he was dominated for many years by his mother, the Valide Sultan Kosem. A military riot in the capital turned on the palace in November 1631; the Grand Vizier, Grand Mufti, and fifteen courtiers and advisers including Murad's favourite page, Musa Celebi, were ripped apart by the mob, who forced the Sultan to appoint one Topal Recep Pasha as Grand Vizier, and proceeded to loot and murder in the streets of Constantinople. Six months later, exploiting popular outrage against the soldiers' depredations, Murad had Topal strangled. With a new Grand Vizier, he fell upon the mutineers, killing 20,000; tobacco, coffee, alcohol and boza, the unfermented millet beverage the janissaries loved, were banned; and he led, in person, a grand campaign against Iran, capturing Erevan and Tabriz in the summer of 1635. The kadi of Izmit was beheaded for letting the roads fall into disrepair, and that year, with all the ulema turning against him, Murad had the Grand Mufti executed with his son. He instilled terror in his men and recovered something of the old ways of the state – for he retook Baghdad on Christmas Day 1638, digging the trenches with his own hands; but even he was able to achieve only one reform, and that one dear to the officials' hearts: the formal abolition of the boy tribute. In every other field he found himself treacled in by the soft resistance of the palace functionaries, and he finally died of drink, which he discovered late, overwhelmed by alcoholic manias, 'running through the streets barefoot,' Cantemir recalls, 'with only a loose gown around him, like a madman, [he] killed whoever came in his way. Frequently from the windows . . . he shot with arrows such as accidentally passed by . . .'

Murad IV was the last sultan to rule, rather than merely reign, for a century and a half – and he died, as we saw, believing Ibrahim was dead. Among his successors, Osman III had spent fifty years in the Cage, with his deaf mutes and barren women; Selim III, the reformer, fifteen; and for many months after they were brought out, both apparently found it very hard to frame their words. Suleyman II had been in the Cage for thirty-nine years, copying and illuminating the Koran; he reigned for just thirty months, and often asked, in that time, to be allowed to return to his prison.

Machiavelli had described the Ottoman state as one which would be hard to conquer, but easy to hold. It turned out, though, that the conquest was internal, as power slid from the sultans to their slaves.

16

The Spiral

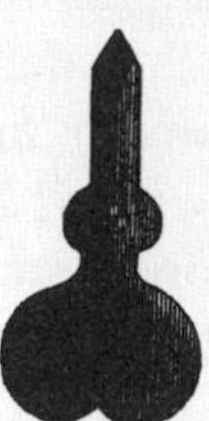

Power was a slippery thing in the early 1600s. The pashas were caught up in the crisis of the closing frontier. New jobs grew scarce. The state had encouraged provincial governors to enrol militias to keep order in these tumultuous times; but they were tempted to use them to defy the Porte, defraying their cost by raising local taxes on their own initiative. The Porte winked at this, for without the levies it might have no army. Assailed on the one hand by the demands of the new breed of warrior, the professional musketeer, and the rise of inflation on the other, the state was forced into massive tax-gathering efforts which increased the burden on the peasantry.

Ipsir Mustafa Pasha, governor of Aleppo, was offered the grand vizierate in 1651. Local rebellions, he replied, made it impossible for him to leave his post. 'I have mustered 40,000 musketeers,' he assured the Porte. 'I am prepared to come with this company and to rub my face on the Imperial Threshold.' The Imperial Threshold was not sure whether this rubbing would be quite what it liked; but still Ipsir Mustafa Pasha delayed, reluctant to exchange his quasi-independent position for the uncertainties of palace life, and suspicious of the motives that lay behind his summons. When he finally came to negotiate terms and sound out the mood of the city, he covered his approach with the support of an army of 'seasoned warriors, fully armed and accoutred, from the lands of the Arabs and the Turks and the Kurds, each one a walking armoury, uppity Segban and Sarica vermin, clad in mail and armour and helmets and link-mail neckbands and shields and felts, each one having ready in his hands and at his waist five or six double-barrelled lead-shot muskets with double wick, like so many salamanders in Nimrod's fire, marching in close formation and brandishing their weapons as though they were entering a skirmish. The Istanbul troops shook like Autumn leaves.'

The biographies of most seventeenth-century pashas make for sombre reading. The kul suffered from overcrowding, like everyone and everything else: between 1640 and 1656 the numbers of salaried officials jumped from 60,000 to 100,000. One Omar Pasha, for example, spent two years waiting for a new post, maintaining the retinue which his rank demanded by borrowing money from his sister. Two jobs were offered to him in this period, but in each case the incumbent refused to budge. A war, in which he and his retinue were bound to participate, sent his debts soaring. He desperately needed a job, with the chance to recoup his losses. Once again, the pasha he was detailed to relieve was in no mood to change places with him. A battle had to be fought, and Omar died in it. The victor made his apologies to the Porte, regretted the confusion, and hung onto his job. Survivors like him became rich, larded with gifts, so that the higher echelons of government were choked with presents and finery and officials laid their hands, in desperation, on any available source of revenue. Men lower down were pushed to the bottom of the heap. 'No one can afford the old establishments,' lamented one memorialist.

Inflation was much to blame. It first arrived in 1584, stealing in with American silver which the Genoese first brought into the eastern Mediterranean. Spanish-American silver undermined the value of the currency in Genoa in 1580, and in Ragusa soon after. Its effects were particularly severe in the Ottoman world because the lunar metal silver, not gold, was the standard measure of value; one of its effects was to make Ottoman gold seem ludicrously cheap, so that bullion ships began clustering round the Horn, putting in cheap reals in return for gold.

In Suleyman's day the soldiers received their pay by weight, so that no one cared if the coin itself was clipped or light. More astonishingly they received it, Busbecq said, 'not on the day it falls due but on the day previous'. In the 1590s they began to experience arrears, as did thousands of salaried functionaries, palace men, and provincial bureaucrats, clerks and kadis. Corruption and the habit of selling every service rose. The Ottomans' little silver asper had remained remarkably stable in value for most of the sixteenth century – 58 aspers bought one gold coin in 1507, 62 in 1589. But by 1600 this 'gypsy money', or 'tavern money', stood at around 280 aspers to gold. By then the fiscal premise on which a long view of time could be supported, the security of knowing that, as the empire grew, so it would get richer every day, had been completely overturned, and the calm, self-regulating pattern of Ottoman life, with all its felicitious connections and dependencies, the little springs and triggers which ensured that the entire mechanism pulled in a single direction, was thrown into disarray. Aspers, said a contemporary Turkish historian, 'were as light as the leaves on an almond tree and as worthless as dew drops'.

Money inflation brought inflation of another kind. More and more people sought refuge in state service: if the salary was inadequate, at least every service could be sold. The Venetian bailio kept on hand a list of the bribes he gave palace servants; a register explaining who might receive what in future; and a *ragionateria* stuffed with potential *douceurs* – from which one learns that the chief dragoman, or interpreter, had received fifty-six robes, seven *picchi* of saglia rubin, three watches, two boxes of perfumes, three mirrors, a cooling chest, a silver chocolate service, three glass cabinets, fifty pieces of glass, glass for twenty windows, twelve locks, four canaries, fruit, vegetables, Piacenza cheese, chocolate, candy, and miscellaneous articles.

It was as if the men in power had peeped into that register for themselves, too, for they were perfectly aware of their own value, and not afraid to complain if the *douceur* was the wrong colour, or too short, or (worse of all) less valuable than the last. When the Reis Effendi (a sort of foreign minister) chose to lament that he had not yet had the pleasure of wearing one of the fine Venetian gold capes he had heard so much about, he was sure to receive the very thing later that afternoon. The Venetians fretted at the escalating expense, and despaired, like the incorrigible cost analysts they were, of getting value for money. 'In Constantinople,' a bailio complained, 'one has to lavish respects and favours on everyone, even on the marioli [Cretan adventurers rounded up in taverns for the Ottoman navy] because there is a perpetual wheel of fortune that the Signor causes to rise and fall according to the spins of his caprice.'

Shake-ups were profitable for office sellers, ultimately located in this period in the harem, under the control of the Chief Black Eunuch. The ceremonious order of the empire which turned like the heavens became jerky and confused. Sultans had once ruled seven, eleven, twenty years but now averaged only five or six. In the Principalities, the Hospodars were rolled over every year, rather than every three.

The terrible period which signalled the apogee of the Sultanate of the Women, between 1644 and 1656, saw eighteen grand viziers (four were executed, eleven dismissed, two resigned and one died naturally); twelve sheikh ul-Islams, and eighteen kapudan pashas. The old system of maintaining retinues concomitant with rank made the turmoil all the fiercer, for each high official had a shoal of small fry to put into place; and they worked hard to advance themselves, by any means,* since their terms of office seemed likely to be short.

As never before the Ottomans learned to watch the clock, mesmerised by the inexorable passage of time. Ottoman technology never advanced beyond the water clock, but European clocks began to exert a fatal fascination over all classes of society.

* Ibrahim Metin Kunt notes that between 1568 and 1574 half all appointees could expect terms of three or more years; by 1632–41 the proportion was one in ten.

It was whispered that the very same Grand Mufti who first learned to flee the plague, and fate, 'much delighteth in clocks and watches, whereof, as some say, he hath not so few as a thousand'. Ornate clocks, gilded, golden, machicolated, glazed, but always replete with curious movements, such as buglers blowing and lions raging, were carried by well-advised ambassadors as gifts for pashas. A century later Prince Ypsilanti, one of the Phanariot aristocracy who claimed descent from the Byzantine emperors through the female line, crammed his saloon with two hundred clocks, eighty of them grandfather clocks – western visitors sniggered, a bit uneasily, when they were ushered in. One ambassador heading for Istanbul in 1599 with his suite of attendants was held up for a day while his jeweller was taken back to Nis to fix a clock 'shaped like a Turkish turban, upon which stood a chamois, which turned its eyes backwards and forwards, and when the hour struck pawed with its foot and opened its mouth, and under this gilt serpents and scorpions twisted about'. It was a clock the ambassador had presented to the Beylerbey of Greece in Nis the day before; and the pasha had madly overwound it, as if trying to squeeze more time out of it.

The end of the sixteenth century had brought the so-called Long War, with Austria. Time was also short for the army, the backbone of the Ottoman enterprise. Gone were the days when the Ottoman cavalry surging up the passes and thundering across the plains of south-east Europe could demolish the chivalry of nations they invaded at a stroke. The wilder horsemen might still spread devastation far and wide, and gather slaves; and the Tartars still performed their horrid loop from home, riding out with incredible speed, driving harmlessly but deep into enemy territory before suddenly wheeling about to loot and burn and put their enemies to death on the long ride back. But Ottoman armies as a whole could scarcely reach the borderlands within the campaign season. The enemy retired to their strongholds, and each small advance meant reducing fortresses, one by one, and returning the fire of those monstrously accoutred, grimly expert musketeers, whose job it was to hold them.

Warfare became a drag. The so-called Long War with Austria, at the end of the sixteenth century was seemingly unwinnable. Back and forth the armies marched across Hungary, year after year, with thrust and counter-thrust, sieges and sallies. Finally exhaustion overwhelmed the combatants, and the long war was concluded with a hasty peace, clapped up there and then on the field at Zsitvatorok in 1606, leaving matters standing much as they were before the war began.

But there was a crucial difference. The Ottomans traditionally dealt with supplicant ambassadors to the Sultan's court, where they could grant peace as a favour, and generally in return for tribute. At Zsitvatorok, exhausted, they were forced to drop their guard, and admit the Emperor of Austria as an equal. Inscribing the Emperor's title and claims upon the treaty document was tantamount to an admission of defeat. The ideal of a universal commonwealth was put aside, for sovereignty of this earth was divided, after all; and with that shattering admission the great old conductors of imperial affairs seemed to take their place, very humbly, in the concert of European diplomacy.

The armies had grown with every passing year: Mehmed the Conqueror's 10,000 spahi had become almost 30,000 by Suleyman's day. The janissary rolls leaped from five to twenty-five thousand men. Fighting on frontiers far from the home base, the empire had less call for horsemen. It needed infantry and sappers and artillerymen, trained at barracks, not scattered through the empire like the spahis. Instead of rewarding men with fiefs, and seeing that they were parcelled out with care, the treasury had to find cash to pay the wages of men who spent half the year in barracks. By 1595, it was paying 48,000 soldiers. By 1652 the number had doubled to 85,000.

The swelling wage bill put enormous strain on the finances of the empire at a time when the rewards of constant warfare were beginning to dry up. No new timars were being conquered for the spahis, no new sources of revenue discovered with which to pay the janissaries. The Treasury's accounting system had been established in those centuries of conquest and success when the

Ottomans had scorned to count the hours. Salaries, traditionally, were paid out by the lunar year of 354 days. But the taxes – largely agrarian, raised from the sale of harvest crops – came in seasonally, or according to the solar calendar. Between the money coming in and the salaries going out, the Treasury faced a shortfall of eleven days each year: or every thirty-two income years the state undertook to pay thirty-three annual salaries. Some historians have seen this cycle as the base-note of unrest in the empire, as the Ottomans were driven to extraordinary levies and expedients to bridge the gap – many of which, having been tried once, became permanent burdens on the people.

The simplest answer to the problem of raising cash was to use timars as a source of tax, instead of men; but the social consequences of undermining the old system proved disastrous, triggering a vicious circle of discontent. Many timariots, disgruntled and insecure, began to regard the state as a threat, rather than the be-all and end-all of their existence. Failing to be promoted, finding their children unprovided for, they moved into the cities, or took to the highways. Brigandage spread, for men who might have hoped to win their spurs on the borderlands had nowhere to go, and in the early seventeenth century all Anatolia was engulfed in rebellions, known as Celali revolts.

Rarely, however, did they join forces with the janissaries, who were undergoing difficulties of their own. The janissaries loathed the cavalry, Rycaut's 'gentry of the Ottoman Empire'. The janissaries were conscious of their standing as the Sultan's permanent army. Every regiment, originally, was autonomous, in order to operate neatly in the field: each had its cooks, bakers, tailors, padre, tent-makers, and so on. They performed various crucial tasks in the off-season: they put out fires, they patrolled the streets, and supplied the city with two corps of detectives, credited with a remarkably good success rate, and especially skilled at recovering stolen goods through their shadier links with the guild of thieves. For punishment they were beaten on their bottoms, to save their feet for the march: the spahis were bastinadoed, on the feet. The janissaries jeered at the horsemen, and frequently accused them of cowardice; but people laughed at the janissaries for having good eyes and good legs – to spot if the cavalry were wavering, and to run away.

As early as 1523 they had sought permission to marry. By the end of the century, with families to support, the janissaries' devalued pay encouraged them to practise their military trades off-season in the civil sphere. Their commanders, enrolling phantom

Janissary of Grand Vizier in camp

soldiers in the army to increase the payroll, began selling vacant janissary positions to tradesmen and artisans facing janissary competition. More and more janissaries appeared on the books, less and less effective as a fighting force. The old swaggering janissary trooper, proud veteran of countless engagements with the infidel, gave way to the artisan janissary, who feared for his business and his family and hoped never to see a battle in his life, but who enjoyed all his predecessor's well-earned rewards.

*

The state still needed troops equipped with guns, as cheaply as they could be found. Anatolian Muslims, willingly drawn from the distressed countryside, were speedily enrolled in the Ottoman armies, only to be discharged at the end of the season, gun in hand, to support themselves as best they could by brigandry, or in the retinues of provincial governors.

The janissaries, meanwhile, made the most of their ancient privileges – only a janissary court could judge them, and military authorities have always taken a lenient view of high jinks. As the rewards of war began drying up, legally or otherwise they took what they could at home. They became notorious fire-raisers. Istanbul was a city of wooden buildings always prone to burning, and the janissaries were magnificent extortionists. People paid them not to burn their homes and businesses, then they paid them to come and put the fires out. When the janissaries had to select areas for demolition, as a windbreak, people paid them to create the windbreak somewhere else. And at the end of it all, the janissaries looted the ruined homes. For the janissaries, fire in the city was the sack of Constantinople all over again.

They were quick to take advantage, slow to appreciate long-term consequences. They were not all buffoons and cowards; some wrote elegant poetry, but their impositions were frequently niggardly, like the tooth rent they demanded for chewing stolen food; and their grand rebellions had all the viciousness and ultimate purposelessness of any peasant uprising. Their demands of the moment were invariably met, and many a pasha, after kissing the hem of the sultanic robe, was to stride out as a sacrifice to the blood-lust of the troop. But they were only the tools of intrigue in the palace, and when a rebellion had run its course its leaders were invariably taken out and slipped into the waters of the Bosphorus at night.

The janissaries came to feel little more than an oily, self-interested sentimental attachment for the Sultan, their Little Father; and like all such attachments it was dangerous when it was broken. No doubt they blubbed and called the Sultan a good fellow who melted the plate to pay their donative; but woe betide the sultan who failed to provide one. Small wonder that the years

1623–56 have been called the Sultanate of the Agas, the janissary commanders.

Nobody knew that the borders had closed, or understood that the empire had reached its geographical limit – victories and conquests were still being made and one might expect more to come – yet the chaos demanded an explanation. A traditional view suggested men had shrunk. We like to think that people used to be smaller, but in the seventeenth century people believed, a little wistfully, the evidence of their own eyes – Pietro della Valle visited the pyramids and concluded from the size of the sarcophagi he found there that they had been raised by a race of giants. Men shook their heads and agreed that no one could draw a bow like the men of old, or nodded sagely at the stele set up on the Atmaidan* in Constantinople, recording incredible feats of hurling the javelin.

The ulema believed that moral fibre had declined. You had only to look at the markets and bazaars, they said, to see that people were less straight and honest than they had been in the days of the Prophet, when no one had thought of fixing prices by law; if the religious judges undertook the business now, it was only in sorrowful acknowledgement of moral decline. Wherever you looked you might find people behaving badly. Peasants were trying to squeeze their way into the army, a serious challenge to the clear old delineations between warrior and reaya.† Sultans were apparently trying to squeeze out, preferring to chase skirts or go hunting, though it was sultans at the head of their armies who had won the great battles of the past. The janissaries were disobedient. Prices were too high. Too many ne'er-do-wells infested the capital, like the rabble of French soldiers seconded to the Habsburgs who defected in Hungary in 1599 and made trouble in Constantinople: they were put into ships and sent against enemies in the Black Sea, but some returned and had to be dealt with by the ambassador. Too many Jews hung about the palace.

* Twenty can still be seen.

† The trouble seems to have been exacerbated by Ottoman conquests in Azerbaijan and the Caucasus in the early seventeenth century; Anatolian peasant immigrants considered themselves timariots. Balkan opportunities had dried up.

Too many pashas clung to their offices without permission. And everyone in the bureaucracy could finger someone, or some clique, who put their own interests before the interests of the state, and offered bad advice, and took outrageous bribes. Sokullu Mehmet himself had been guilty of rampant nepotism (though spite is quixotic: his predecessor, Rustem, was nicknamed Louse for cutting his own father).* And because the Ottomans were used to victory, the loss of a battle, or an unfavourable treaty, provoked accusations of incompetence, or treachery.

It was hard for anyone to put their finger exactly on the source of the trouble; they could only lament the passing of the old days, and the old ways, before the reaya took to arms, and obedience was lost. 'All acted as they pleased,' lamented the old historian Selaniki. 'As tyranny and injustice increased, people . . . began to flee to Istanbul. The old order and harmony departed.'

Once the tendency had been for all elements of the empire to pull together; the tendency for them to fall apart was now strong. In 1651 the Valide Sultan Kosem, mother of two sultans, and a wily survivor of harem politics and intrigue, finally lost her grip on power. She was hunted down in her private apartments and discovered, after a long search, hiding under a pile of quilts.

> Assaulted by furious young men, greedy of Riches; she was in a moment despoiled of her Garments; her Furs were torn off into small pieces; and being stript of her rings, Bracelets, Garters and other things; she was left naked without a Rag to cover her, and dragged by the feet to the Cushana: and being at the place of her execution, the young Officers found themselves unprovided of a Cord to strangle her, so that crying out for a Cord, one ran to the Chappel Royal, and thence took the Cord that upheld the great Antiport of the Mosch, which being twined about the Queen's Neck, the

* At least according to one interpretation. Another suggests that Rustem's enemies attempted to forestall his marriage to the Princess Mihrimah by accusing him of leprosy; the doctors who examined him, though, found only lice – supposedly incapable of infesting lepers. The wedding went ahead, proof of the old Turkish proverb, 'When a man has his luck in place, even a louse can bring him good fortune.'

> aforesaid Dogangi getting upon her back, pitched her neck with his hands, whilst the others drew the Cord. The Queen, though she were by this time besides her Senses, and worn out with age, being above 80 Years old, and without Teeth; yet she with her Gums only did bite the Thumb of his left Hand, which by chance came into her Mouth, so hard, that he could not deliver himself until with the haft of his Poniard he struck her on the Forehead near her right Eye. There were four that strangled her, but being young Executioners, laboured long to dispatch her, till at length the Queen leaving to struggle, lay stretched out, and was supposed to be dead, and so crying she is dead, she is dead, ran to carry the news thereof to his Majesty; but being scarce out of sight, the Queen raised herself up, and turned her Head about; upon which the Executioners being again called back, the Cord was a second time applied, and wrung so hard with the haft of a hatchet, that at length she was dispatched . . .

So Paul Rycaut describes the scene, and he goes on to say that upon that frightful murder the smooth functionaries of the court forgot years of careful training in their panic and terror. 'The ears of witnesses were assailed by a tumult of different voices and tongues. Some shouted in Georgian, some in Albanian, some in Bosnian, some in Mingrelian, others in Turkish or Italian', and in their robes of office, sporting the turbans of their rank, stuck with the aigrettes and feathers and seals indicative of their position in this seamless enterprise, all yammered helplessly at one another, unable to understand what anyone else was saying.

17

The Empire

'It is no unpleasant sight, to behold a new scene of the World, and unknown face of things, in habits, Dyet, Manners, Customs and Language,' wrote the traveller Edward Brown in the summer of 1669. 'A man seems to take leave of our world, when he hath passed a day's journey from Raab: and, before he cometh to Buda, seems to enter upon a new stage of the world, quite different from that of the Western countrys: for he then bids adieu to hair on the head, bands, Cuffes, Hats, Gloves, Beds, Beer.' Brown was writing for generations of western visitors who invariably felt, as they crossed the threshold of the Dar ul-Islam, that they had entered another world.

The empire never really had a shape, except as a sort of figure of eight, intersecting at Istanbul; but when you came across the Danube at Raab, or over the high passes of the Dalmatian coast, or by sea – thirty-six days from Venice to Constantinople in the 1650s – from Italy or Marseilles, even the oxygen of the place was foreign. 'Do you not breathe the Gran Signor's air?' a seventeenth-century vizier demanded, as he squeezed the foreign merchants. 'And will you pay him nothing for it?'

The border, by then, was not a lively place itself. The Christians had ringed the border with their forts and quarantine stations, the Turks had dotted it with garrisons, and it had the hackneyed air of a place forgotten, stirred up now and then by the passage of armies, and raiding bands. Ottoman merchants seldom bothered to come this far; the quarantine, if not the insecurity of the Christian lands beyond, discouraged them. From the west this great divide, this cultural fault line running through Europe, brought a nip of the energy stored up there by the men who had pushed the frontiers out – to the Adriatic coast, and the Hungarian plains, to the banks of the Danube and the Dnieper, the shores of the Caspian and the deserts of the Maghreb – in the days when the Ottoman frontier was alive. 'After that,' William Makepiece Thackeray reported, 'there is nothing. The wonder is gone, and the thrill of that delightful shock.'

Everyone had their premonitory moment. For the young English traveller Alexander Kinglake in 1846 it came when his bags were snatched up, fought over, and finally carried up from the river bank at Esen by an improbably large number of colourfully dressed men. For the young Czech nobleman Baron Wratislaw in the summer of 1599 it was finding people offering the tiniest of services for payment – the Turks, he advised, are very 'calmed' by money. Frenchmen noticed that boots, gaiters, doublet and hose, or whatever European fashion was then in vogue, had been left behind for a battery of different hats, and the simplest sort of flowing robes. It was the moment, a sixteenth-century philosopher who had never been there explained, that the traveller from Venice would feel he had left a city and entered a sheepfold. You had arrived in the empire when the soldiers presented you with flowers and a kiss. You were there when a splendid retinue of mounted spahis, their lances pennanted, their chests draped with the skins of wild beasts, their turbans gleaming white, their faces dark and weatherbeaten, bows strung, arrows aquiver, galloped up in a cloud of dust to supply you with an escort. In 1599 the English merchant George Sandys knew he was about to get there when the crew of his Greek-run ship began to behave oddly and, claiming it was death to bring in wine, 'they loth to poure such good liquor into the sea, drank it: the captain seems half the time dead, and the other, lively and violent; a blind man striked the air with his cane and toppled into the sea; the captain, as if of a sodaine restored to life, lays about him with a cutlass, so everyone dives off the boat.'

Hard, humped and crowded up were the mountains of the Balkans, with steep defiles and snow-bound passes, miserable villages which looked like the rubbish thrown out by a town, whole nations tucked up so safely in their high lairs that they might only be approached on hands and knees, and only then if you avoided looking down. Dark and enveloping was the canopy of oaks which spread over your head as you entered Serbian-speaking country, and which marched with you for days on end to the superstitious dread of your janissary attendant. Green and wet were the paddy fields of the Maritsa, in Bulgaria. Very dry and hot were the corrugated folds of Thrace, fit only for goats. The empire's springs were sulphurous, travellers said, and none of its towns had clocks or walls, and anyone making the three-day crossing by sea, from Bari to Durresi across the Adriatic, invariably met with a storm, and fetched up anywhere he could, after a fortnight at sea, thin and bewildered.

The people of one valley in Bosnia all had goitres, and wore sandals. The farmers of Bulgaria were invariably respectful. The herdsmen of the Pindus were always wild. In the Dalmatian mountains lived a race of giants, whose guns were longer than the giants were tall. If the Jews of Thessalonica could still show you the keys to old houses and godowns in Granada, to which they meant shortly to return, then the Albanians could point out the eagles from whom they were descended. The girls of a village outside Plovdiv were all princesses of Byzantine blood, as Busbecq fancied he could tell by their fine carriage, and smouldering good looks.

For food 'on a rimmed tray, a dish of boiled barley or rice, soupy, and large piece of mutton. Around the dish nice-looking bread. Also a dish of honey or piece of comb,' one traveller recalled; another described fetta as 'a beastly kind of unpressed Cheese that lyeth in a lump'. Europeans grumbled about folding their legs and sitting on the floor; by the nineteenth century grown men were filling whole pages of their travel books with semi-comic descriptions of the pain. Instead of a jolly Christian inn, the traveller might shack up in some dismal, bug-infested han – 'a range of rotten shanties surrounding a manure-heap', in a humid windowless chamber where you lay down to sleep on a pile of straw. When a han was no good, it was really awful: the straw second-hand, the rooms freezing, bugs abundant, alarming fellow guests, and a solitary attendant behind a 'small door bolted, barred and barricaded; the little grated window secured the cage of the prisoner within, who dealt out garlic, salt, cheese, olives', and sometimes a bottle of nasty Greek wine, like an off-licence in a jittery neighbourhood. Busbecq preferred to tidy up a local shed, screen off the fire with his tent canvas, set up his table and chair, and 'live as happy as the King of Persia'. Lord Harry Cavendish in 1589, as a Genoese agent, slept in a succession of haystacks, a peasant's cart, a church porch and a hen-coop. 'O khans of Albania! Alas! the night is not yet worn through!' wailed Edward Lear, three centuries later; 'Numberless fleas . . . Bulky spiders, allured by the warmth, fall thick and frequent from the raftered ceiling. O khans of Tyrana! Big frizzly moths, bustling into my eyes and face!' But with luck, the visitor was carried to some magnificent caravanserai, part bazaar, part refuge, where a merchant's goods could be stored in vaults with massive barred gates, and the horses tethered in proper stables, and the upstairs rooms around the courtyard were at the disposal of travellers, each with a fireplace, some private and some dormitory, but provided with bathrooms and lavatories; where the traveller was entitled to three days' food and lodging, free of charge.

Crossing overland from the west you bade 'to Christian tongues a long adieu', Byron said – Hungarian, Mingrelian, Serbo-Croat, Greek, Bulgarian – and Castilian Spanish, if you landed at Salonica. If you sailed up to Constantinople through the Dardanelles you were met in Turkish, Greek, Hebrew, Armenian, Arabic, Persian, Russian, Slavonian, Wallachian, German, Dutch, French, English, Italian, Hungarian ('there is ten of these languages spoke in my own family,' wrote Lady Mary Wortley

Montagu, forgetting Georgian). Some low-life character might finger your sleeve and address you in his native French, and a helpful seaman would put you on your way in the familiar dialect of the Veneto, and you might even hear the scowling Admiral of the Ottoman fleets, a kapudan pasha famously intolerant of Christians, and plainly weighing every one he met for the frisky plank, half-suppress a native Italian oath.

It was a country of queer distortions and half-echoes. In Salonica, in 1814, a smart Greek girl sang a popular patriotic song which suddenly carried Henry Holland back 'to the shores of the Faxe-Fiord in Iceland; where two years before I had unexpectedly caught the sounds of this very air, played on the chords of the Icelandic langspiel'. What an outlandish brand of familiarity! In the Albanians Byron recognised some forgotten link to his own Highlanders, for 'their very mountains seemed Caledonian; ... the kilt, though white, the spare active form; their dialect, Celtic in its sound, and their hardy habits, all carried me back to Morven,' he wrote in 1809. Other visitors felt more bewildered. 'In every one of their customs they do exactly the contrary of what Christians do,' wrote a seventeenth-century Venetian diplomat. 'One would think that this is what their legislator intended when he decreed their ceremonies. Few Turks are adept at operating machinery; they do not cultivate the land ... play neither handball or football ... do not fire cannonballs ...' Ottoman Jews were so free of ghetto pallor as to be practically unrecognisable to western Europeans, who were baffled by the Ottoman's religious tolerance. For Christians in a supposedly Muslim empire some Hungarian stockholders looked fat and well dressed; and it was hard to credit that the men lining up for free soup in the shadow of the mosque were all Muslim, and dirt-poor. The peasantry seemed to wear their hats upside down, narrow at the bottom and wide and teetering on top; while several travellers remarked on the way they dressed hot on top and thin around the legs, both summer and winter. It was much the same with houses, all of which, Eliot believed, were 'constructed entirely with a view to the summer, and the advent of winter ...

seems a constant source of surprise. The inhabitants huddle into one room heated by an iron stove or open brazier, and leave empty the rest of the house which cannot be warmed.' The fishing boats of Ohrid were rowed by three men all on one side, near the front. 'The result of their labour is actually to make the boat turn round in a circle, and movement in a straight line is rendered possible only by the counteracting force of an old man who sits in the stern and steers with an oar. It is one of the most perfect contrivances for wasting labour and obtaining a minimum of result from a maximum of exertion ever invented.'

J. F. Fraser (whose account of the Balkans in 1906 is illustrated by grainy photographs of atrocities, with a dotted line close to the fold, and the instruction: 'This page can be torn out and destroyed by those who find the pictures too horrible') claimed that the Ottomans wrote backwards, moved the wood against the saw, and feathered their oars upside down; their officers saluted soldiers, and even bus conductors punched tickets for your boarding stop instead of your destination.

Newcomers often met with unexpected drama. Baron Wratislaw – who was still in his teens, and liked the food – crossed the border in the summer of 1599. A day or so out from Istanbul he gave his ambassadorial suite the slip and went for a paddle in the Sea of Marmara. Being Czech, he had never seen the sea before. He began collecting stripy shells, watched the dolphins sport, and admired a ship which was running in towards the beach; but when his janissaries suddenly caught Wratislaw up and swept him away from the shore, exchanging fire with the sailors, he understood he had narrowly avoided being seized by pirates. They had spotted him from a long way off, and were even now tacking furiously out to open sea in a storm of arrows and curses.* Paul Rycaut had to spend a night among some very tough-looking nomads on the plains of Pergamum: they fed and sheltered him, and sent him on his way next morning, refusing his money and

* His infuriated master, the ambassador, wanted to beat him with a horsewhip in lieu of birch twigs (for there was no birch about – a quaint Bohemian problem); but the Turks successfully spoke for him, and pleaded the folly of youth.

asking him only 'to speak well, wheresoever I came, of such poor Men, who led their Lives in the Fields, who were instructed in these Principles, viz. to hurt none, and to be humane and helpful to all Mankind'.

Some travellers were amused, some appalled, to discover that their janissary would turn a peasant Greek or Serbian family out

Janissaries

of their house for the benefit of the traveller, and demand not only food and wine for himself and his charge, but tooth-rent, too, for the wear and tear of consuming it; and others were shocked by the spectacle of public execution, its methods as grisly as they were impressive; so that one concluded, *sotto voce*, that 'the Turks do not jest with malefactors'.

*

The sheer breadth and complexity of the empire around the dawn of the seventeenth century was unparalleled, outgrowing the medieval systems that had been devised to regulate it.

Not since the days of ancient Rome had any state attempted to maintain a standing army, a palace and a bureaucracy on taxes levied on subsistence-level agriculture. At the start of the seventeenth century the Anatolian hinterlands seethed in a state of near-rebellion. The frontiers bristled with enemies. In Jerusalem the Ottomans controlled a city revered by every religionist in the known world, friend or foe. In Mecca and Medina they protected the wellsprings of Islam. In the ports of the eastern Mediterranean they bound up the strands of the biggest trade routes of the age. In the Haj they had the biggest organisational headache before Thomas Cook. Of all the nations that the Ottomans ruled – thirty-six, at a conservative count – the Bedouin were the most intractable, the Greeks the craftiest, the Egyptians the most urbane, the Serbs the most vicious, the Hungarians the most wearisomely litigious and the Albanians the only people in the empire whom the Ottomans recognised as a race in their own right – one that seemed to include every pirate, ruffian, cut-throat or swindler under Ottoman rule.

Nearer to home had gathered perhaps the most troublesome student population in the world, and the most intractable soldiery. It was true that the early Ottomans had always welcomed strangers, but one could grow weary of open house; and the man who described the city as full of 'men with no religion and no faith, tricksters and topers and city riff-raff of no known nation or religion, Turcomans, gypsies, tats, Kurds, foreigners, Lazes, nomads, muleteers and camel-drivers, porters, syrup-vendors, footpads and cutpurses and all kinds of others' was only gruffly expressing the unease which lay behind the elegant, anxious memoranda served up with growing frequency to the Porte on the causes of decline.

The millet ordered all people by their faith, but regions half-gazi by geography remained in a state of near-permanent local warfare, like Albania, Bosnia or Crete. Metropolitan Sunni orthodoxy could no longer impose itself on the borderlands as squarely as it had done in the days of Selim the Grim and Suleyman. Constantinople exiled its mystics to such places, and there suffered their enthusiasm; so that through the medium of a more warm-hearted, if heterodox, Islam, conversions to the faith – in Montenegro, too, and among the Bulgars of the Rhodopes, the so-called Pomaks – took place *en bloc* in the later seventeenth century. Crete became a powerful Islamic centre, and almost the entire population had turned Muslim within a century of the Ottoman conquest. By the eighteenth century some Albanians had become so confused that they 'declare they are utterly unable to judge which is best, and go to the mosque on Fridays and the church on Sundays'.

This sliding between religions was very common. In the old town of Charrah, in Syria, the Christians shared their church of St Nicholas with the Turks, each taking an aisle apiece; 'though Turks don't pay for the oil in the lamps they sedulously burn'. Muslims were so impressed by the ritual cleansing that accompanied a Christian baptism that they frequently sent their lepers to undergo it – 'acceding to Christian rites, as so often, in case they were useful, or had some good in them'. From a cave on Lemnos, the Greeks dug their 'Lemnian Earth', or Goat's Seal, on the feast of the Transfiguration, 6 August. They made it into cakes, stamped with characters, and used it as a cure for dysentery, snake-bites, and a salve for wounds. 'This custom', Busbecq wrote, 'the Turks observe, and they wish the service to be performed today just as the Greek priest has always performed it there, while they themselves remain at a distance as spectators only. If you ask them why they do this, they reply that many customs have survived from antiquity, the utility of which has been proved by long experience, though they do not know the reason; the ancients, they say, knew and could see more than they can, and customs which they approved ought not to be wantonly disturbed.' In Athens when the rains had failed, the Turks would go up to the old temple of Olympian Zeus and pray, and if the drought persisted, they would bring up a flock, separate the ewes from the lambs, and there begin 'a loud and general supplication in the most pathetic tones', backed up by the 'plaintiff bleating' of the sheep, designed to 'give greater effect to the petition and move the pity of heaven'. Once when the case was really hard the pagan negroes who dwelt on good terms with everyone in the caves and ruins under the Acropolis were asked to beseech their gods, as well.

In the spirit of animism which underlay all faiths, Albanian songs allowed a pillow to tell a woman where her husband had gone, or a ship to stop in its tracks, horrified by the groans of a prisoner. The common people held writing in very high regard; they would pick up waste paper and thrust it into a chink in the wall, in case it contained Koranic verses, for there was a legend that on the fiery path to heaven your feet would be protected by all the paper you had saved in your lifetime. Busbecq's janissaries were very upset by the use his entourage put paper to. Mottoes – 'O God', 'O Protector' – were inscribed on buildings, and men and animals wore amulets containing little scraps of paper with effective words, such as the ninety-nine names of God, and other tried and tested talismans.

The weather, too, was more than a single polity could reasonably expect to bear. Lovely as the Balkan slopes might look in summer, a Balkan winter froze men as they stood. Hungary was full of autumn mud, as was Istanbul itself in winter; though in summer there people strained for the light airs that might play through their kiosks on the water's edge. In 1894 barely a tree was in leaf in Istanbul before the second week in May, when it suddenly became terrifically hot. In 1428 the ice in the Sea of Marmara and the Golden Horn was so thick it broke down the sea walls. In Arabia, where the temperature could reach 120°F by day, it would drop to a little above freezing when the sun went down. Newcomers to Greece might be warned against sniffing the hyacinths and narcissi, whose fragrance was 'so strong as to hurt those not used to it'. (Hundreds of our garden plants and flowers were rifled from the hills and gardens of the Ottoman Empire: roses, tulips, narcissi.)

The Mediterranean was beset by weird and vicious winds with old names, by sudden squalls and atrocious winters, though it maintained, much of the time, a placid appearance, all the better to tempt and deceive. Arabia was the most pitiless of deserts. Egypt was five regions in a single year, according to Amrou, for out of the Nile's 'prolific slime' came 'a powdery desert, a liquid and silvery plain, a black and slimy marsh, a green and waving meadow, a garden blooming with flowers, or a field covered with yellow harvests'. In the Sultan's own backyard, Anatolia, there were frozen peaks and scorching plains and coasts whose cliffs dropped, not only sheer and buckled and scored by rivers, but black, too, into the sea.

No river journey was as hair-raising as the journey down the Danube – 'this method of travelling will some day prove disastrous', Busbecq queerly said when he was sent in 1554 to negotiate an end to wars which had left the region strewn with corpses. No border was as convoluted as that of the Ottoman Empire, no garrison since Hadrian built his wall and staffed it with Spaniards so lonely as the Hungarian one; no conflict so ingrown as that between the Sultan and the Shah, whose respective borders, unbeknownst to them, were fixed for ever in 1615, with the *casus belli* so far forgotten in the mists of time that in the eighteenth century Cantemir understood it to be the horrible Persian habit of rubbing their feet with their dry hands first thing in the morning rather than washing them. No encounter in history was more deceptively ingenuous than the arrival of the first Russian ambassador bearing furs, and hoping for trade relations; no barber, Edward Brown believed, so versatile as the barber of Edirne, who could do a man's hair just the way he liked to wear it: 'The Greeks preserve a ring of hair on the centre of their heads, and shave the rest. The Croatian has one side of his head shaved, and the other grows as it will. The Hungarian shaves his whole head, except his foretop. The Polander has his hair cut short. The Turk shaves his whole head, save a lock. The Franks wear their hair long amongst friends, and in public tuck it up under their caps.' The Tartar horseman had thick useful hair which protected him against weapons and bad weather, without the need for a hat.

The Ottomans had a genius for pageantry – for all that was

improvised and evanescent. 'I think', wrote Ambassador Porter, 'that the dignity of our position is marred by the juniors' constant running after shows etc.' Mean and crabbed the streets of the capital might seem to the visitor; very disappointing after that first thrilling view from afar; but the Turks put far more effort into temporary displays than into solid architecture, and at festival times the city transformed itself. A triumph of arms might be celebrated by the bazaars staying open all night for a week, and at Ramadan, when the fasting was over, the city exploded into merry life. Swingboats were put up under canvas, decorated with leaves, flowers, festoons and tinsel, and to the tinkling of bells and music men would swing you 'high into the air, to touch the stars; and this is surely a mad sport . . .' There were festive gates erected over streets, and jousts, and contests in which youths shot arrows and flung javelins on the fields of the Atmaidan, and tried to surpass the mark. The seventeenth-century traveller della Valle, seated up on one of the gaudy beribboned swings, gyrated so wildly from side to side that the people cried out for his safety; and he was forced to pretend that it was all deliberate, and to swing even more crazily to impress the ladies, before the spectators grabbed his legs. 'I believe they play like this', he said, 'because, as they say, the angels do so.'

Going down to the Atmaidan, young Baron Wratislaw fell in with a bunch of Turkish youths trying their hand at archery and the javelin – 'very merry fellows', he recalled. Here is Evliya Celebi, scribbling the last of his 735 descriptions of the procession of the Constantinople guilds – 'By the Lord of all the Prophets, God be Praised that I have overcome the task of describing the guilds and corporations of Constantinople!' – which Murad IV ordered to parade before him in 1638:

> All these guilds pass in waggons or on foot, with the instruments of their handicraft, and are busy with great noise at their work. The Carpenters prepare wooden houses, the Builders raise walls, the Woodcutters pass with loads of trees, the Sawyers pass sawing them, the Masons whiten their shops, the Chalk-Makers crunch chalk and whiten their faces,

> playing one thousand tricks . . . The Bakers pass working at their trade, some baking and throwing small loaves among the crowd. They also make for this occasion enormous loaves the size of the cupola of a hamam, covered in sesame and fennel, carried on waggons which are dragged along by seventy to eighty pairs of oxen. . . . These guilds pass before the Alay Kosku with a thousand tricks and fits, which it is impossible to describe, and behind them walk their sheikhs followed by their pages playing the eightfold turkish music.

On and on the guilds come, showering the spectators with their gifts of tamarinds and ambergris, of confectionery and little fish; even the gravediggers pass, 'with shovels and hoes in their hands, asking the spectators where they shall dig their graves'. Even the thieves, the beggars and the lunatics go by, followed, as the lowest of the low, by the tavern keepers, disguised in suits of armour, the Jewish tavern keepers 'all masked and wearing the most precious dresses bedecked with jewels, carrying in their hands crystal and porcelain cups, out of which they pour sherbert instead of wine for the spectators'.

Even the women of the harem could look forward to celebrations and feasts to mark every significant event; and via illuminations, shadow plays and processions, the palace was linked to the city, and the city came to the palace. As late as 1821 the French performing troupe les Viol Frères did their act for the ladies of the harem, and spread their threadbare rug upon the floor of a vast chamber, before an invisible audience. An odd sensation it was for them, performing to a blank screen; but when Claude, the youngest and most agile of the brothers, finally made his terrific acrobatic leap and somersaulted to the top of the human pyramid, he found himself looking over the screen; his eyes met those of a voluptuous odalisque, the merest glimpse of whom meant death; his confidence wavered, the pyramid shook, and they collapsed in confusion of bruises and muffled curses.

The Turks were an earthy people. They adored picnics. They loved to escape the confines of the city and eat as one might in paradise, in the shade of trees, with running water close at hand. Many travellers were struck by the romantic beauty of an Ottoman cemetery, always well sited, perhaps on the slope of a hill dotted with slender cypress trees, the gravestones tilting, untended, but all expressive, so the visitor thought, of eternity, and decay.

Lady of the Baths; a public hamman or bath-house was a feature of all Ottoman towns, along with a mosque and bedsten (market)

Busbecq cites several examples of the essential harmony which ruled Ottoman life: above all, he observes their cleanliness, both at home, where they used the hammam, and in camp, where rubbish and excrement were always buried. They had no scruples against eating meat – 'they declare that the sheep is born for the butcher's stall; but they do not tolerate that anyone should take pleasure in its agony'. The Prophet once cut off his sleeve rather than disturb a cat, and the Turks protected animals by law. When Greece achieved its independence in the nineteenth century, Edward Lear found the Turkish border town of Larissa thick with storks, all seeking Ottoman sanctuary from the neighbouring Greeks, who preferred to shoot them. Songbirds were kept in cages, of course, but there was a place near the Atmaidan in Constantinople where you could pay to have a bird released, and a Venetian goldsmith was once roughed up by the crowd when for a joke he pinned a living bird to the lintel of his shop. Men came through the streets with smoking offal on a stick, which you could buy to throw to the stray dogs, and to Baron Wratislaw's amusement all the cats of the city came prowling out for their regular evening charity. In Sivas, someone had set up a charitable foundation whose sole purpose was to provide food for the birds when the snow lay thick on the ground.

The fauna of the empire was overwhelming. There were jackals and hyenas whose urine was much prized as an aphrodisiac. There were bears who could climb trees after you, and wolves which roamed Balkan villages in winter. In Greece the swallows were believed to be so crafty that they arrived each year on the back of storks. In Serbia flies could kill a horse ('the smallest fly that ever I did see, covered with a thin Fluff, or Down', Rycaut reported in amazement). The Albanian flea, on the other hand, 'has been called "the biggest and fattest in the world" '. The croaking of Edirne's frogs could drive the most reluctant sultan away from the city and back to his palace in Istanbul; itself a city where the very skies were so thick with life that if you stood in the street and tossed a scrap of food into the air, ten to one it would never hit the ground. The English traveller Fynes Morison met Europe's first giraffe in the city in 1597: 'he many times put his nose in my necke, when I thought my self furthest from him, which familiarity I liked not', he reported rather churlishly. In the 1770s one old admiral, who maintained very strict order in the fleet and closed down taverns, kept a tame lion which he took for walks, amused by the way it frightened the Mufti, the chamberlain and various 'effeminate eunuchs' who were obliged to visit him. Eventually the lion grew ferocious, and took to biting Europeans; when it turned on its master, too, the sultan confined it in the royal menagerie, where Horace Walpole saw it in the 1790s.

Busbecq discovered his lodgings to be infested with weasels, snakes, lizards and scorpions. Pleased by the amusement the weasels gave him, he brought in monkeys, wolves, bears, stags, common deer, young mules, lynxes, ichneumons, martens, sables, and a pig 'whose society, according to the grooms, is very good for the horses'. He had eagles, crows, jackdaws, strange kinds of ducks, Balearic cranes and partridges that hung about his feet and pecked his satin slippers. (The lynx fell in love with one of Busbecq's men, and eventually pined away from grief at his absence; while the Balearic crane fell for a Spanish soldier Busbecq had ransomed. It followed his every move, searched for him with piercing cries if he ever went out, knocked at his door with its beak, and on his return 'would spread its wings and rush to meet him with such absurd and ungainly movements that it seemed to be practising the figures of some outlandish dance or preparing to skirmish with a pygmy. As though this were not enough, it finally made a habit of sleeping under his bed, where it actually laid him an egg.') Suleyman celebrated the capture of Buda by tracking down all the beasts in the royal hunting ground, and it took him two visits with hounds and falcons to exterminate every bear, tiger, jackal, boar, gazelle, panther and hyena in the park, with countless pheasants, partridges and pigeons.

The cities were full of animal noises, the screech of gulls, the flapping of storks, the swish of kites, the barking of dogs, the mewing of cats; and you may still hear for yourself that the cockerels of Turkey do not 'cockadoodledo' at all, but follow the drawn-out cadence of the muezzin. The noises of Constantinople were the howling of dogs on the shore, the flutter of birds' wings as they were released from cages by pious men, three Bulgarians having an argument, porters running uphill and shouting a warning, the chink of coins in the market, the bubbling of coffee in the bazaar, the notes of a lute drowning the Sweet Waters of Asia, the bray of a bumpkin, a Christian's apology. The cry of hawkers, the spitting of camels, the flapping of wet fish, the clatter of pattens, the call of the muezzin, the chanting of the Mass, the clash of Anatolian cymbals, the thunder of tugs, the flute, trumpet, horn and kettledrum of the Mehter bands, the special yell of the deli.

The call of the muezzin sounded over Eger and Sarajevo and

Istanbul; over Sofia and Bursa and Mosul; but Hungary was the pounding of hooves; Arabia, the wind; Epirus, shots in the street; Ragusa, the running of oars through a galley port; the Balkans, the echo of a loosened stone on a hillside; Attica, the drone of bees; Sarajevo, the groan of a camel; Mecca, the murmuring of the faithful at prayer; Gallipoli, the wingbeats of storks in flight; the Danube, the crash of rocks; the plains of Konya, the skirl of cymbals; the Rhodopes, the wail of pipes; Athos, male chants; Salonica, the lamentations of Jewesses at a funeral; Serbia, the grunting of pigs in oak woods; Ankara, the bleating of goats in the herbage; all highlands, the clanking of sheep bells; all low-lands, the snorting of buffalo; all palaces, the growl of a panther; every city, the yelping of dogs.

Into this cacophony one might throw the clamour of the dead and gone, whose monuments littered the landscape and gave it the feel of a silently gibbering madhouse, full of baffling claims and inexplicable characteristics. Some, like the pyramids, or the standing men of Anatolia, were vast and peculiar. Others, like the columns of Athens, seemed to a traveller like Evliya Celebi to be scarcely of this world, so perfectly were they fitted together.

Pierre Gilles, an antiquarian who first visited the capital in 1544, made a fruitless search for the remains of the old Stoa Basilica of the Byzantine emperors, and stumbled across the Cistern instead:

> Through the inhabitants' carelessness and contempt for everything that is curious, it was never discovered except by me, who is a stranger among them, after a long and diligent search. The whole area is built over, which made it less suspect that there was a cistern there. The people had not the least suspicion of it, although they daily drew their water out of the wells that were sunk into it. By chance I went into a little house where there was a way down to it and went aboard a little skiff. I discovered it after the master of the house lit some torches and rowed me here and there across the pillars, which lay very deep in the water. He was very intent on catching his fish. . . .

But in Balkan fields stood rum old stones whose regenerating properties were respected by everybody. There were shrines to Christian saints which received not only Muslim adulation, but Muslim priests and caretakers. Muslim or Christian, everyone around Skopje knew the place where an inscribed stone lay buried, and knew that if ever it were dug up the rain would never stop. By the river in Athens young girls left salt, honey and bread on a plate on the first night of a new moon, murmuring some forgotten words and wishing for 'a pretty young man': at the very spot, classicists averred, where a statue of Aphrodite had once stood. There were whole lost cities into which no one ventured at night, and to which the Turks, in their last, febrile moments, were to add Ani, and the Montenegrins Stari Bar. In Egypt there was the Valley of the Kings, tombs into which Pietro della Valle had himself lowered; and Istanbul was itself a charnelhouse of the past, with its Roman cisterns and Byzantine mosques and eerie, serpent-twined columns.

The government protected such things when it had the power and the wherewithal. 'Let the man be a reprobate who sells a slave, injures a fruit-bearing tree, and makes lime from chiselled marble,' was a saying attributed to the Prophet. An Ottoman governor was dismissed in 1759 for blowing up a column in the temple of Olympian Zeus in Athens for his mosque; and it was not a Turk but an officer from Lombardy, under a Venetian general, who demolished the Parthenon with a lucky shot, leaving the ruins to be crawled over, tapped at, and transported piecemeal by high-paying Europeans like Lord Elgin. Western tourists in Rhodes were flattered to see, above the lintels of old doorways, the arms of French and German and Italian nobility, for they imagined these had been preserved by the Turks out of respect for the bravery of the Knights; but in fact the Turks seldom bothered to alter what they found, and beyond a little whitewash in the churches they squatted in old buildings in picturesque confusion, and treated palaces and hovels they inherited as practical shelter, with no more thought of repairing or improving a palace than they would a roomy and convenient cave. 'Whatever castle or fortress they take', wrote Belon du Mans, 'remains in the state in which they found it', the Turk 'esteeming it an egregious folly', adds Sandys, 'to erect sumptious Habitations, as if hee were to live forever'.

Anatolia, Thrace, Thessaly and Bulgaria were the homelands, long since under Ottoman rule, where Ottoman power was absolute. To the buffer states, the Principalities, Transylvania, Crimea, the Porte contributed nothing more than political legitimacy to vassal rulers in return for warriors and food. Hungary – ever *sui generis*, since the Magyars settled it in the ninth century and planted the dialect and looks of Central Asia into the midst of Slavic Europe – Ottoman Hungary was neither quite buffer state, nor yet a place where an Ottoman might feel at home. In Hungary for almost 150 rather fruitless years the Ottomans were pitted against the Habsburgs, and by the seventeenth century it was a no man's land where Muslims were rare and lived huddled in towns if they valued their lives; where instead of the usual tribute from the Habsburg Emperor, the Pasha of Buda once received a bag of teeth drawn from the jaws of captive Ottoman officers; a costly, end-of-the-world sort of place, bankrolled by Egyptian revenues, mocked by its own great river, the Danube, whose banks were so puddled with marsh and swamp that the cattle ranched on the puszta could not be ferried away, and were herded instead into Austria, to feed Vienna. Sixty thousand steers might be sold in a year, and the profits of the trade did as much as the endless warfare to turn the Hungarian Plain into the desolate grassland it is today.

At the other extreme there was Dalmatia, a coast pitted with 'ravines, crevasses, precipices, caves, valleys, defiles, dens and holes in the ground', as Kritovolos had it, infested with ne'er-do-wells who crisscrossed the borders for gain or plunder, cocking a snook at the Great Powers and their solemn treaties. When the Venetians proudly introduced Paul Rycaut to some new converts in the 1660s, he found them in such a cheerful muddle that they pictured Muhammad as the Holy Ghost, read the Gospels while circumcising their children, and drank wine like true Christians, all through Ramadan, only carefully leaving out the spices. Uskoks on the Catholic side, armatoles on the Ottoman, their exploits were sung in peasant houses not because they were decent but because they were brave. The ballads were collected and published in Venice in 1756, with this warning: 'These songs will not be to everyone's taste, for there is little variation among them, all of them containing the same words, such as: hero, knight, horseman, galley slave, serpent, dragon, wolf, lion, falcon, eagle, falcon's nest and sword, sabres, lances, Kraljevic, Kobilic, Zdrinovic, necklets, medallions, decrees, heads chopped off, slaves carried away, etc. May those who find them pleasing sing them; may those who do not, go off to sleep.'*

Villagers who lived on either side of the border in Dalmatia, like the Hungarian peasants, frequently paid tax, or tribute, or protection money several times over to whichever side arrived to levy payment; but they paid not only the Venetians and the Ottomans, but the uskoks, too. Invariably they found the uskoks gave better value. The bandits tried not to kill the goose that laid the golden eggs, but from an imperial point of view their constant

* *The Pleasant Conversation of the Slavic People* by Andrija Kacic-Miosic, Venice, 1756.

raids discouraged major settlement, and the Ottomans made a stern effort to suppress them. An ordinance of 1588 forbade any subject of the Porte to pay ransom, in hopes of undermining the basis of the uskok economy. But kidnapping was better than bloodshed for everyone, so the men on the spot – sworn enemies, of course, and 'evil dustlike misbelievers', to a man, according to the Turks – arranged a hasty conference, swapped gifts, mingled their blood, and 'went to sleep in a bed, in one another's arms'.

Everyone found the uskoks insupportable. The Venetians loathed them when they took to the sea, with a pirates' nest at Zante in the Adriatic – the 'Gulf of Venice', as the Venetians styled it, where any bullying was for them to do; and at last the Habsburgs, too, grew tired of parrying Ottoman complaints. For half a century they had been sheltering the uskoks, and lifting from them the profits of their raids – money paid, as the uskoks pointed out, 'for fear of our valour', but in the mid-seventeenth century they stopped responding to uskok appeals. The Habsburgs now preferred to see the *Militärgrenze*, their armed line of defence, held by sturdy yeoman soldiers, after the German fashion: men who grew all their own vegetables, and fought to protect their wives and children, but who cut no dash, and never inspired one of the repetitive old songs.

PART III

Hoards

18

Hoards

Polarities had long governed the Ottoman world: the division of the world between peace and war, the choices offered by the law, the distinction between the public world and the harem; the claims to rule on two seas, and two continents. But the stunning polarity of the empire is the historical distinction that comes into focus in the early seventeenth century, between the empire's early genius for lightness and speed, and its later reputation for lumbering sloth. It is a very *weighty* empire which emerges, baroque and swagged in its more exuberant phases, but sagging, too, once the first shock of containment has been absorbed.

There exists in the Turkish military archives an inventory of the contents of Adale castle, which the Ottomans took from the Habsburgs in 1670, a year after it was built on an island of the Danube near the Iron Gates. Here are the elements of a terrific war, or at least a major engagement, one of those 'hot skirmishes' old Knolles often talks about: 94 bronze cannon (6 burst); an unspecified number of ladles and powder horns; 3,311 infidel muskets (11 cracked); 3,173 bombshells; 26,018 hand grenades;

17,813 cannon balls; various moulds for casting lead bullets; 6,531 shovels; and 5,850 hemp sacks and bags. But actually the inventory does not bring a hot skirmish to mind at all. All the elements of war are there, bar war itself; and in the entries for fishing tackle and fourteen saucepans you can conjure up the little garrison instead, a hundred men for so many shovels; picture them waiting on the borders, like a hundred other garrisons in the empire, living on fruit and nuts, some fields of corn, rye and wheat, and sturgeon from the river. They grew vegetables, and probably kept bees, and possibly ran a stall or two in the nearest bazaar.

Patience was always the virtue that westerners selected, when they wished to damn the Turkish character with faint praise: they meant inanition. The classic pose of Turkish verse is, forget the lies peddled in the mosques, the great and the beautiful of the past are dead and dust, we are all mortal; let's go down to the tavern and drink red wine. In all their poetry, writes Nermin Menemencioglu in his *Turkish Verse*, 'they used the same repetitive vocabulary: the names of the same birds, animals, trees, flowers, jewels, scents, elements of nature, heavenly bodies, colours, human features, described by identical adjectives. The beloved is a moon-faced, almond-eyed beauty with a cypress-like figure. Her cheeks are rose or tulip, her locks hyacinth, her eyebrows two bows, her eyelashes arrows, her teeth pearls etc. Her waist is thinner than a hair and her ruby lips are the Fountain of Youth.' Turkish 'divan' poetry was little more than a rearrangement of the same inventory, like *The Pleasant Conversation of the Slavic People*, or the memorialist's list of foreign infestations in the capital.

A man sent to investigate the strange behaviour of the Mullah of Jerusalem, who had been much annoyed by the barking of dogs and buzzing of flies, 'found the whole city busy in catching flies, and stringing them on a long thread, that they might be told with more ease'. Everywhere one comes across stashes of men, goods and treasures in the years after the 1590s. People count their blessings and number their grievances: and they arrive not light and untrammelled, but lugging their pedigree, and jealous of advantage. The empire seemed to juggle with its stock, piling it up here, treasuring it up there, and bending its arm secretively, as it were, across the pages of its own history.

In the Balkans, travellers noted, people had devised all manner of ways to detect buried treasure: will-o'-the-wisps, eerie lights glowing on a moonlit night. An Austrian actually found six gold ducats in the stomach of a Turk killed at Vienna in 1683, whom he hoicked over the palisade on the end of a pike; afterwards they 'made it a common practice to dive into the Entrails, of as many as they took: Examining their Bowels like the ancient Augurs . . .' A ransom – 3,000 gold purses – was discovered cemented under Kara Mustafa's bath after he had been executed for his failure at Vienna. The garden of another disgraced grand vizier yielded three buried chests, eighteen bags with 60,000 sequins, and a chest full of precious stones. He had acquired them legally, as it happened; but it did look odd. 'Not everyone', remarked the bailio cheerfully, 'could raise such radishes.' The sultans themselves were not immune. Ahmet III used to return presents to the shop where they had been bought and exchange them for cash. Murad III threw all the coin he could lay hands on into a pit under his bed, and finally had the palace decorations melted down and made into coin, minted and stamped with his own name, for hiding in his pit. Sultan Mustafa hurled money into the sea, saying the fishes needed money to spend; and Ibrahim (whose ill-omened name was never again used by the House of Osman) strewed his beard with pearls and jewels.

Even the sea, lapping against the walls of the Sultan's palace, was becoming a grisly oubliette. The empire's hopes of Mediterranean dominion were lost down there, with the 200 Ottoman ships that sank at the battle of Lepanto, which was not only the largest sea battle in history, but claimed a record number of wrecks for a single engagement. Venetian doges tossed their rings to the waves, in the ceremony which was known as their Wedding of the Sea; but Sultan Ibrahim arranged his own sort of Divorce by Water when he had all the women of his harem sewn alive into sacks and thrown into the Bosphorus.* And come a coup in the palace, you were able to reckon the severity of the purge, for 'every night a cannon sounds to indicate that another unfortunate has been tossed to the waves'.

After the girding ceremony at Eyup, after the visit to Mehmet II's tomb, it was the custom for a sultan to make an inspection of the relics and mementoes of his ancestors which were piled in careless abundance in the palace vaults. The Treasury would be decorated with precious and curious items, many of them displayed against carpets hung upon the walls. In the same vein, the Sultan was always summoned when 200 bags of gold had accumulated in the fourth hall of the Treasury. Down in the basement, marked by the distribution of largesse to the head treasurer and his team, the Sultan received halva and sherbert, and watched the gold being transferred into coffers. There Ahmet I was heard to murmur that that life was a transitory thing, praising God who had given them such blessings.

By the seventeenth century the vaults were a cross between a reliquary and a jumble sale. Windowless, they smelled of lamp oil and incense, camphor and old cotton. Joseph's turban and Abraham's crown were bundled up in coffers among the clothes of sultans long dead. The mantle of the Prophet was stored there, to be dipped in water at Ramadan, bottles of which were sent round under the Treasury seal to favoured dignitaries; also his beard ('three inches long, of light brown colour, and without grey hairs'), his decayed tooth, and the impression of his foot in stone. Then there were the swords – the sacred sword of the Prophet, Omar's twin-bladed sword, the swords of sultans, and the surrendered weapons of defeated kings. One single trunk was found to contain tables, shields, water vessels, guns, plates, china and a variety of musical instruments. There were bolts of cloth, belts, boots and shoes; napkins and old cushions, raincoats, kaftans, sofa covers and prayer mats, and hundreds of ornaments for the

* One of them floated free. She was picked up from the water by a European ship, and ultimately caused a sensation in Paris.

royal turban. In the middle of one hall stood a dais covered by a tapestry worked in gold thread, showing Charles V enthroned, with a globe in one hand and a sword in the other, receiving the homage of grandees; and on the tapestry lay European books, vellum maps, and two actual globes, one terrestrial, the other celestial.

All the letters and gifts that sultans had ever received from the kings of France – 'his brothers and old friends', as the French ambassador put it – had been placed in a gilt casket with a suitable identifying inscription on the lid, and it is tempting to picture Suleyman's successors rereading the plaintive missives dispatched by Francis I to the Grand Seigneur at his most superb. If you looked very carefully you would see Murad IV's 'silver pellets, thrown by him with that violence, as to stick in an iron door'; and a lot of the treasure, as visitors liked to note, was dusty. 'Rustem gathered all this,' read one approving inscription carved in stone, above the entrance to an empty cavern. The outer walls of the Privy Chamber were festooned with the weapons Selim had used when he took Egypt, 'in a pitiful state', Tavernier noted, pitted with rust. The observation chimed with the regrets of the people, who could only dream of their forebears' strength, and of those javelin marks on the Atmaidan.

An Austrian who visited the palace in the sixteenth century left it, according to Ottoman reports, 'astonished, bewildered, stupefied, and completely enraptured'. In 1640, though, a palace memorandum suggested that they show off the silverware, give the gate-keepers silver-plated batons, silver over the Chamber of Petitions and the vizier's council hall, and set the janissaries to fence when a foreign envoy was to be received. The authorities moved the Prophet's standard from Damascus, where it had always been kept, for the 1593 campaign against the Austrians. They brought it out again for the campaign of 1594, and then abandoned all pretence of sending it home; it was kept, with all the other treasures, in the palace in Constantinople.

Presumably the ceremony by which gold was transferred to the vaults when it reached a certain sum did not happen very often now, for in 1688 the French ambassador could report that 'the most important occupation of the Sultan's treasurer was to look for new slave girls and to dress them'. In Mehmet IV's harem apartments, he wrote, 'the number of women reached four thousand, including those in his mother's as well as in his lover's service. Although the plague often devastated such a multitude, their number never fell below two thousand, owing to the careful and continuous recruitment of replacements. All these women were slave girls and even the lowest-ranking ones cost some four or five hundred thalers. They wore the most expensive clothes, belts and fasteners studded with gems, earrings and several strings of pearls. Each mistress of the sultan had the power to free and give in marriage any slave girls who were in her service or who aroused her jealousy. When these freed women left the palace they took with them all the precious stones and money they had managed to accumulate there.' Thomas Dallam allegedly glimpsed them through a little grate in a wall in 1599, believing they were boys until he noticed their plaits, and 'britchis of scamatie, a fine clothe made of coton woll, as whyte as snow and as fine as lane; for I could desarne the skin of their thies throughe it'. His terrified guide 'made a wrye mouth, and stamped with his foute to make me give over looking; the which I was verrie loth to dow, for that sighte did please me wondrous well'.*

The women could hope either to get on, by producing an heir, or to get out. A woman's chances of bedding the Sultan, though, were extremely remote. Merely to catch the Sultan's fancy was hard enough, for the majority of sultans were essentially family men, and many jealousies had to be allayed, and friendships forged, before a girl was allowed to catch his eye. The most important woman in the harem was the Sultan's mother, who was allowed to call him by a name other than Padishah – Aslanim, 'My Little Lion'. She, of course, strove to keep his attentions focused on her protégées; and the machination of these women to promote their own sons to the sultanate, the struggle of the

* Dallam was an organ maker who was sent in 1599 to present the Sultan with an organ from Queen Elizabeth I.

queen mother and her daughters-in-law with the mothers of rival princes, and between lowly newcomers anxious to ingratiate themselves, made the atmosphere of the harem one of poisoned indolence in which pseudo-tasks were eagerly pursued and everyone sought something to do, some rank – to wash the Sultan's underwear, or to care for the clothes and jewellery of the more favoured women. Hardly surprising, then, that sultans turned a bit cracked. Sultan Ibrahim, apparently, rode his girls like horses through rooms lined in fur from ceiling to floor.

In 1609 Ahmet I, who had started the stultifying practice of imprisoning princes in the Cage, began to plunder his empire to create his Blue Mosque. He began work in spite of the warnings of the holy men that a mosque should only be built with the spoils of conquest. The Ahmediye became the first mosque of the empire, the people's favourite, and is one of the sights of Istanbul today. It has six minarets, which the holy men claimed were uncanonical. The court of the mosque was the biggest in the empire. Yet it seemed to suffer from its own bulk, too, as if the weight of it all had flattened and compressed elements which had come more gracefully to the neighbouring Sulimaniyye, the mosque Sinan had built for Suleyman half a century before. The drum of the Blue Mosque was smaller; the tensions less acute, the patterns less absolutely regular. The entire output of the Iznik tile factories was consumed in its decoration, yet most of the blue interior is only pretending to be tiled, and on close examination reveals itself as stencil work. It was full of ostrich eggs; most mosques were – they were brought back from the Holy Land by pilgrims. It was crammed with lamps. Everywhere there were glass bowls – one containing a little rigged galley, another a model of the mosque, and the rest 'a great many knacks of that nature', Thévenot said. The tiles – not all of which were made to fit, and many of them simply plundered from other buildings – were used in bushel-loads – 21,043 in the gallery above the main door alone. So greedy for materials was this mosque that it gobbled all the stone, marble and tiles the empire produced, and building work elsewhere was suspended. And within twenty years an expressive change had come over the iridescent tileware of Iznik. The glowing reds turned brown, the greens slipped into blue, the whites lost their ovular clarity, turning dirty and mottled; and the glazes became gritty. Anatolian tileware never regained its earlier perfection.

Constantinople in the 1790s

Constantinople was very tightly packed, and building plots grew zanier by the year. The shores of the Bosphorus were lined with the palaces of successful pashas – Cantemir tells us he snapped one up cheap during an invasion scare in 1684, and after his exile he heard it had gone to a sister of the Sultan. 'Suppose we combine mosque, minaret, gold, cypress, water, blue, *caiques*, seventy-four, Galata, Tophana, Ramazan, Backallum, and so forth, together . . . your imagination will never be able to depict a city out of them,' wrote Thackeray in 1853, when he thought it droll to make a 'remarkable catalogue' of things embedded in the labyrinthine fabric of the city which he didn't have time to see. Lady Mary Wortley Montagu, who was there in 1717, attempted to describe at a glance all that she did see – an 'agreeable mixture of gardens, pine and cyprus trees, palaces, mosques and public buildings, raised one above the other', and by her own admission she fell on 'a very odd image, [which] gives me an exact image of the thing: a cabinet adorned by the most skilful hands, jars showing themselves above jars, mixed with canisters, babies [small cups] and candlesticks'.

Was there ever a general more rococo than Shishman, who distinguished himself in war with the Poles at the end of the seventeenth century, and who had a French surgeon scoop his fat out every year, until he finally popped? Was there ever a piling up of years and wives and progeny to equal the achievement of a Venetian of Smyrna, so old that his age seemed to stand for the state of the parties, the country he served and the country he lived in: he was 115 when he died in 1713.* In 1717, after his failure against the Russians at Witowa, the Swedish King Charles XII was forced to flee south, and he arrived in Constantinople as a refugee. For over a year he remained in the city, attempting to work up a Turkish alliance, and to arrange a safe passage back to Sweden. His enemies bayed for his extradition but the Ottomans, in their stiff fashion, blandly refused to give him up. Fate had sent them the Swedish king, and erected the curious diplomatic circus which surrounded him; it was not for them to intervene, and no pleas or threats could change their minds.

Kicking his heels in exile, Charles developed an interest in archaeology. He arranged to purchase an Egyptian mummy like those the traveller Pietro della Valle had seen when the locals lowered him into a burial pit at the end of a rope. As soon as the mummy arrived in Constantinople, though, the authorities intervened. Of course the Egyptian sands were stuffed with mummies no one had ever bothered either to examine or to protect, but they did not like the king's enthusiasm. The more they thought about it, the better it seemed that the mummy should not be taken away at all; it was whispered that the very fate of the empire might depend on preserving it. So they confiscated the mummy, and when Lady Mary Wortley Montagu visited the capital in 1717 it was still languishing, like a very old reprobate, in the notorious Turkish dungeon, the Castle of the Seven Towers,

* In Smyrna, after shipwrecks, piracy, Ottoman avanias (extortionate taxes) and crippling insurance rates for Venetian ships had left not one Venetian trader in the port, Francesco Lupazzoli was born in 1587. He died in 1702. His sinecure as consul was created for him at the end of the 1647–69 war, as a typically cheap Venetian reward; he was already in his eighties. By 1678 only three Venetian merchants traded in Smyrna. The 1680s war forced his retirement: but at its end, in 1699, he bounced back, fit and 112. He ate fruit, bread and water, with some soup and roast meat, and avoided stimulants, milk, snuff and tobacco. His name, Lupazzoli, 'Lone Wolf', was singularly inappropriate for a man who had racked up 5 wives, 24 legitimate children – the last born when he was 95 – innumerable alliances and 105 bastards.

where, incidentally, there was a huge pile of salt laid up by the Byzantines and untouched since the Conquest.

The Swede was only one of the kings mouldering in the capital; Thokoli, a Hungarian pretender, once lived there on a wine-seller's licence and a pension of five dollars a day 'in one of the Vilest streets in the Town . . . His Countenance much changed, pale, & Fallen, & his Feet Swelled, so that his enemies scorned him.' During abortive peace negotiations in 1689, both the Turks and the Austrians declared their contempt for him; the Austrians asked that he be handed over as a rebel; but the Turkish envoy explained that he had not travelled so far to become Thokoli's assassin. The Dutch ambassador, acting as mediator, pointed out that the Turks used him like a dog. 'Ay, Tekeli is indeed a dog,' the envoy answered; 'a dog that lies down or rises, that barks or is quiet, according to the Sultan's bidding. But this dog is the dog of the Padishach of the Ottomans; and at a sign from him the dog may be metamorphosed into a terrible lion.' In 1697, anyway, the authorities remembered him. He was stricken with gout, and was just heading off to the baths when they 'threw him into a Carr like a Log to make him a King'.

Ottoman artillery parks were a jumble of cannons, some of them immensely old, like the medieval brutes of solid iron which defended the Bosphorus and fired granite balls weighing five hundred weight and which in 1805, after a proper clean-up organised by the French military attaché, managed to drop one smack into a British frigate, so saving Constantinople from a naval bombardment; others new, but unreliable; some captured from Russia, or Austria; but all of them of perfectly random bore. The soldiers had no single calibre of musket, either, and they carried a whole range of bullets to be matched to their guns in the pandemonium of war. Perhaps nothing was more redolent of *ancien régime* than the sight of an imperial galleon hoving to when it was time for the men to eat. The anchor was weighed, the oars were shipped, the sails were furled: and a dozen little fires might be seen springing up in every cranny of the ship, in the fo'c'sle and on the poop, a cluster of men around the mast, or stirring a pot beneath a companionway on the main deck, each little party in a world of their own, and appreciatively sniffing the good smells emanating from their own mess.

Whatever clarity had once shone through the empire from its silent centre to its most turbulent frontier, was defracted and mottled like the colours on the Iznik tiles. Darker and darker did

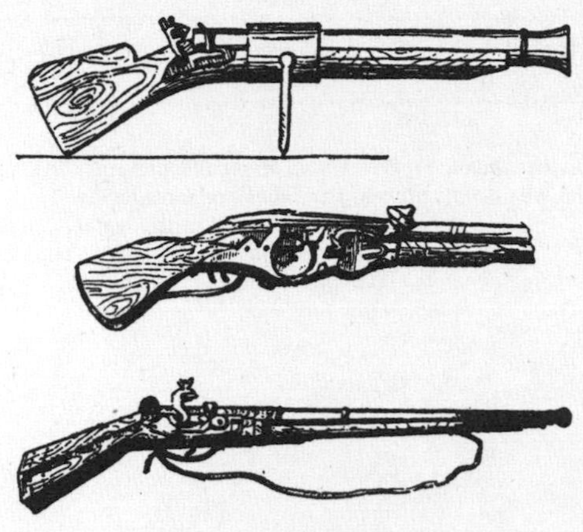

Turkish guns

the empire seem: more impenetrable its gloom; more helplessly reserved and secretly bewildered its functionaries; more groping and local its arrangements. Each new tax spawned an office to collect and assess it. Even the impeccable surveys of the conquest years and after, which measured the swag and kept it equitably distributed, were largely abandoned in the seventeenth century, so that the empire's wealth became a half-forgotten hoard itself, whose size could only be guessed at. While the names of fifty thousand janissaries might be found on the payroll, pay books had long since been traded like gilts and the number of men ready or willing to answer a call-up was a conjecture only proved – and usually dismally – by the actual event: for war without success was an expense even the spahis preferred to avoid.

In 1593 John Sanderson compiled a list from information given to him locally to show the population of Istanbul, which arrived at a total of 1,231,207 inhabitants; but what is really interesting about this list is the way the census is framed.

Viziers (I say Viseroys) 6;

the list* began, then:

Muftie 1
Women and children of all sorts, christians, Jues, turks
etc 600,000

* As an illustration of *ancien régime* logic, it recalls the entry Alexander Herzen saw being made when he was doing time in the Siberian bureaucracy:

No of persons fallen in the water 2
No of persons saved 2
TOTAL 4

19

Koprulu and Vienna

The Ottoman royal line seemed like a Juggernaut against the fractured and random genealogies of the other servants of the empire, but there were other families, all the same. The descendants of the Prophet's sister were all known as emirs, and were entitled to wear distinctive green turbans. They were allowed to be judged, but not punished, by men. They remained, Cantemir tells us, 'Men of the greatest Gravity, Learning and Wisdom' until they turned forty, when they would become 'if not quite Fools, yet they discover some sign of levity and stupidity.' The descendants of the vizier who had concealed news of Mehmet I's death, working his corpse like a puppet, enjoyed the title of khan, and resolutely kept away from affairs of state 'for fear of losing everything. They have greatest honours paid them by the Sultan, who visits them twice a year, eats with them, and lets them visit him, when he will rise a little from his seat and say peace be with you, and even ask them to sit down.'

Out in the provinces lived descendants of the old chieftains who had spearheaded the invasions. As late as the nineteenth century Muslim landowners in the valley of the Vistritza, surrounded by feudal retainers, claimed that their lands had been in the possession of their ancestors for more than six hundred years, perhaps as a result of a politic change of faith. In many ulema families, traditions of learning and piety had been handed down from father to son for generations. Endowments were often managed by the descendants of the founder: the gatekeeper at the Church of the Holy Sepulchre in Jerusalem, for example, remains to this day a descendant of the Muslim appointed to the office in 1135, and may say that his family has seen the Ottomans come and go. Above all the Girays, traditional khans of the Crimean Tartars, had the blood of Genghis in their veins and were, by persistent report, heirs to the empire if the Ottoman line should fail.

Family loyalties had always existed among the kapikullari, in spite of the slave theory. Suleyman's young Grand Vizier, Ibrahim, looked after an old Greek sailor who often arrived roaring drunk outside his house. Ibrahim would lead him home, the handsome, smooth-shaven youth, counsellor to the foremost sovereign of Islam, shepherding his drunken old father through the streets of Constantinople. People thought well of him for it, and made no effort to see in the younger man the faults of his father, for they did not hold much by heredity, having proved again and again how carefully selected men could be trained to the pitch of perfection. Family bonds could be carried too far. Suleyman's last Grand Vizier, Sokullu, was a Serb by birth; he did much to preserve the Sultan's mystique by keeping alive the memory of Suleyman's grandeur through the reign of the jovial and worthless Selim the Sot, and into that of his successor; but he was an arrant nepotist, and went so far as to create a Serbian patriarchate for the benefit of a relative. People remembered this when Sokullu was assassinated in 1579 on his way to the council chamber, and they thought it on the whole a just reward.

In the seventeenth century the pressure to admit the sons of slaves into palace service became irresistible. In 1638 the boy tribute was formally abandoned, and a few years later, in the 1650s, the empire acquired a sobriquet, such as Venice – *La Serenissima* – enjoyed, or the possibly ironic *La Humillima*, 'Most Humble', by which the Knights of Malta chose to designate their irreducible presence in Valetta. From now on she was known as Baba Ali, or 'High Gate', *La Sublime Porte*. The new name indicated, perhaps, that the Ottomans were settling to the Mediterranean world; but it marked a shift in the balance of power, too, from the Sultan himself, the Grand Turk, to his more anonymous officials, for the Gate in question was in fact the residence of the Grand Vizier. With the boy tribute formally abandoned the way was cleared for the establishment of dynasties; and for fifty years after 1656 the government was controlled by the most famous dynasty of the lot, so sure of itself that one of its members went so far as to contemplate the destruction of the Ottoman line as a means of renovating the flagging energies of the empire.

Its founder was one of the very last tribute boys, and his career to 1656 was a traditional one. By shrewd alliances and steady service in both Constantinople and the provinces he had reached the position of governor of Tripoli. By the age of seventy-one Ahmet Koprulu was living 'a private and stoical life at Constantinople, in expectation of even the smallest Bashalic. Indeed he enjoyed the name and honour of a Basha', but he had few friends in the capital. He was not rich. He found it hard to keep up the retinue expected of a pasha of his rank, and avoided public appearances.

Only death could free the Kapikulu from his duty of obedience. In 1656 the summons came from the Valide Sultan Turhan, mother of the young Mehmet IV. For the past eight years, grand viziers had followed one another in rapid succession as the factions jostled for position and the office became sacrificial – fourteen grand viziers rolled over as first Kösem and then, after her murder in 1651, Turhan herself clung to the reins of power. The Venetians, in defence of Crete, were blockading the Dardanelles. Shipping was at a standstill and the link with Egypt – commands from the Porte, and grain from the Nile – was broken. On 4 March 1656 the army in Constantinople revolted over pay – further debasement of the coinage was one consequence of the political friability – and demanded the heads of thirty high officials. Turhan gave way, and the unfortunate men were hanged at the gate of the Blue Mosque.

In desperation, Turhan turned to Ahmet Koprulu. Before accepting the position of Grand Vizier, Koprulu demanded written guarantees that the Sultan would not listen to any court gossip and that no one would countermand any order he might give. Turhan surrendered her regency to him, and the young Sultan Mehmet left Constantinople for the freer atmosphere of Edirne, where he and his successors were to remain for fifty years. Koprulu promptly demonstrated his grim efficiency by executing the pasha who had abandoned Tenedos to the Venetians, suppressing the spahi revolt and purging the corps. But he also beat the Venetian fleet, broke the blockade of the Dardanelles and allowed a return to Tenedos and Limnos. The rebellious George II Rakoczi, Prince of Transylvania, was summarily replaced by a more amenable ruler.

Evliya Celebi's patron, Melek Pasha, was governor of a Black Sea province at the time, and he soon received a letter. 'It is true', Koprulu wrote, 'that we were raised together in the imperial harem, and are both protégés of Sultan Murad IV. Nevertheless, be informed from this moment that if the accursed Cossacks pillage and burn any one of the villages and towns on the coast of Ozu province, I swear by God Almighty that I will give you no quarter and will pay no heed to your righteous character, but I will cut you into pieces, as a warning to the world. Be wary therefore, and guard the coasts. And exact the tribute of grain from every district, according to the imperial command, in order that you may feed the army of Islam.'

Melek had suffered a brief spell as Grand Vizier himself. Consequently he was not at all offended by the tone of the letter, it rather buoyed him up. Koprulu, he reminded Evliya, 'is not like other Grand Viziers. He has seen much of the hot and cold of fate, suffered much from poverty and penury, distresses and vicissitudes, has gained much experience from campaigning and he knows the way of the world. True he is wrathful and contentious. If he can get rid of the segban vermin in the Anatolian provinces, restore the currency, remove the arrears, and undertake overland campaigns – then I am certain that he will bring order to the

Ottoman state. For as you know,' Melek added mildly, 'breaches have occurred here and there in this Ottoman state.'

In 1665 Koprulu sent the first ever Ottoman ambassador to Vienna, marching into the infidel city under a forest of standards and banners, to the sound of kettledrums and to the consternation of the people. Koprulu was convinced that the breaches could be repaired if only the empire could recapture the military manner, which Koprulu, and others, saw as the real cause of the empire's former success.

In the 1640s when Sultan Ibrahim launched his crazed search for ambergris, and furs, two men in the empire dared to cross him. One was a judge in Pera who, dressed as a dervish, declared: 'You may do three things: kill me – and I shall die a martyr; banish me – there have been earthquakes here recently; or fire me – but I resign.' The other was a soldier, a janissary colonel adored by his 500 men, who had served in the longest and most bitter siege, of Candia, the capital of Crete, that the Ottomans ever conducted. Black Murad was met off the boat by a treasury official demanding amber, furs and money. He rolled his eyes, 'bloodshot with wrath'. 'I have brought nothing back from Candia but gunpowder and lead,' he thundered. 'Sables and amber are things I know only by name. Money have I none and, if I am to give it to you, I must first beg or borrow it.' He escaped a ruse to murder him, and was apparently instrumental in the deposition of the Sultan.

Men like these were Koprulu's natural allies. Many of the abuses he attacked so vigorously were symptomatic of changes over which he had no control, but the terrible old man took them for the cause, and went about rooting them out with murderous energy and application. He was remembered, not as subtle or far-sighted, but as a stern traditionalist, whose notions of reform were fierce and corrective. Fiscally rigorous, he controlled expenditure and regularised tax income so that the soldiers received their pay in full, and even on time, and when he died, at eighty-five, in 1669, the empire's books were very nearly balanced.

The Venetians in 1644 had allowed a Maltese fleet with Ottoman prizes to anchor off the southern shore of Crete. They had received a boy captured by the Knights of Malta on board the flagship of the pilgrimage fleet, supposed by the knights to be the Sultan's son.* Ibrahim, mad as ever, was all for going against Malta; but his advisers suggested Crete itself, to be taken by surprise. Venetian apologies for the error were graciously received, and a fleet which left the Dardanelles on 30 April 1645 sailed with the avowed object of taking Malta from the knights. Surprise was a dependable weapon in the Ottoman arsenal; when once asked where the army was headed, Mehmet II himself had replied: 'If a hair of my beard knew my schemes, I would pluck it out.'

The Venetians were old hands at the game, and not easily duped. For over two hundred years they had been shuffling diplomacy with war, and in the slow war of attrition they seldom overplayed their hand. They had beefed up the Cretan garrisons, and raised the militia. The Ottomans soon overran the entire island nonetheless, reaching the walls of Candia in July 1645. Here the Venetians resolved to make a stand; and they stood so redoubtably that a generation passed without the Ottomans being able to take the citadel. In 1648 a Venetian fleet imposed a blockade on the Dardanelles. The military humiliation which called forth Ahmet Koprulu also sealed Sultan Ibrahim's fate. 'Traitor!' he cried to the men who came to announce his deposition. 'Am I not your Padishah?' 'Thou art not Padishah, for as much as thou hast set justice and holiness at nought, and hast ruined the world. Thou hast squandered thy years in folly and debauchery; the treasures of the realm in vanities; and corruption and cruelty have governed the world in thy place. You have made yourself unworthy, by leaving the path in which your ancestors walked,' their leader retorted. Several days before the fatwa allowing Ibrahim's execution was issued by the Mufti, a few hours before sunset on 8 August 1648, the principal dignitaries of the

* His mother was wetnurse to Ibrahim's legitimate son, and Ibrahim was said to have openly preferred him. He was only at sea in the first place because the Chief Black Eunuch, scenting scandal, wanted him away from the court. The Venetian governor of Crete, who disbelieved the rumour, had him brought up in Venice, where he became a monk and was known as Padre Ottomano.

empire paid homage to Sultan Mehmet IV – a few admitted at a time lest a crowd should frighten the eight-year-old boy.

The Candian siege dragged on, through the minority of the new Sultan, the appointment of Ahmet Koprulu in 1656, and the succession of his son as Grand Vizier. Fazil Ahmet, 'Breaker of the Bells of the straying and blasphemous nations', reined back the ferocity of his father's rule, and gave the empire a decade of wise and mild leadership; he was able to spend three years between 1666 and 1669 personally conducting the siege, and running the empire at the same time. The Venetians had chosen to make Crete the proving ground for Venice's desire to maintain the status of a great power, but when, in desperation, they tried to buy the Ottomans off, Fazil Ahmet answered curtly: 'We are not money-dealers. We make war to win Crete.'

The beleaguered garrison hung on until their citadel was a termite nest. Volunteers came from all over Christendom; the Turks pressed the assault with brilliant engineering – a skill in which they excelled, until they forgot it entirely, and had to be retaught by the French in the nineteenth century the principles of parallel trenches which they themselves had invented. In the last three years of the war, 30,000 Turks and 12,000 Venetians were killed. There were 56 assaults and 96 sorties; both sides exploded exactly 1,364 mines each. But on 6 September 1669 Morosini – destined to be known as Morosini the Peloponnesian for his reconquest of the Greek peninsula – surrendered on honourable terms, and Crete became Ottoman.

It was, however, one of the last extensions of Ottoman power: the very last, perhaps, in the settled world. To the north, in that vastness of the expiring steppe north of the Black Sea, Poland, Russia and the empire struggled to master the Cossacks, and to enfold Podolia and the Ukraine in their own dominions; and here the Ottomans seemed at first successful. By 1676 they had forced the Poles, under their king, Jan Sobieski, to cede the entire region; the great fortress of Kaminiec was theirs, and the horsetails were planted in the black earth of the Ukraine; but Fazil Ahmet died three days after the treaty was signed. The Cossacks of the steppe brought their flirtation with the Ottomans to an end, more impressed with the efficiency of Russian arms. The vizierate passed to a protégé of the Koprulu family, Kara Mustafa, 'Black Mustafa', whose face had been disfigured in a city fire.

In June 1683 the war train paraded through the streets of Edirne, then headed upriver to Sofia and Belgrade. Carried along with it was the Sultan, Mehmet IV, a man more familiar with the pleasures of the chase than the arts of war. At Belgrade he stopped to hunt while his great army pressed on up the Danube, into the heart of Central Europe, under the command of Kara Mustafa, a man, in the words of a near contemporary, 'no less valiant than wise; warlike and ambitious'. A Hungarian rebel had called for Ottoman aid; the Habsburgs seemed suspiciously eager for peace.

Kara Mustafa made the fateful decision at the outset of the campaign not to name his destination. Austria and Poland hurriedly promised to aid each other in the event of an attack. As soon as Ottoman troops crossed into Habsburg territory, the emperor requested Polish assistance.

In Vienna there was pandemonium. A Habsburg army sent forward to engage the Turks had rapidly retreated in the face of what seemed like a tidal wave of men. Perhaps a quarter of a million Ottoman soldiers had been amassed for this extraordinary campaign; and with them – around and before them, swelling their ranks and fanning out with terrifying effect – rode the Tartars who had joined the army of their overlord from their distant home in the Crimea. Everyone feared them, the Turks no less than the Christians; they looked after their own interests.

News of the Turkish advance reached Vienna in garbled bulletins. Early reports of what was in fact a skirmish at the rear of the retreating Austrian army which had required the intervention of its commander, the Duke of Lorraine, came out as news of a ghastly rout. People began packing. The Emperor Leopold was very prone to take the advice of the last person he had spoken to; he now tried to determine whether his imperial duty was to remain in the city and risk the enemy, or to retire. When he was finally pressed to leave with the imperial family on 7 July, the royal party found itself sneaking along between the night-fires of Tartar encampments.

The city's fortifications had been improved over the years, but not urgently; now stocks of grain in the city were examined, the crown jewels were removed for safe keeping, and the fortifications were reinforced by teams of city burghers and labourers. Money to pay the troops and men in the city was raised partly from loans made by departing grandees, partly by sequestering the assets of the Primate of Hungary, who was living safely elsewhere. On 13 July the city commander, Stahremberg, had the glacis, or outer wall, cleared of houses which had grown up around it over the years, in defiance of the law, in order to give the attackers no cover.

He was just in time. By the next day, Kara Mustafa was encamped before the city. Behind the glorious order of the camp, the magnificence of the tents themselves, and the quiet industry of the men, lay a brilliant feat of organisation, perfected over centuries; established now with such finality that to the men on Vienna's walls it seemed as if the Turks meant to erect another city beside it. Vienna had taken a thousand years to grow; the Ottomans eclipsed it in two days. Kara Mustafa had a garden planted in front of his own quarters – a succession of tents, of silk and cotton, strewn with rich carpets, with lobby tents and sleeping tents and latrines and public meeting rooms, as gorgeous as any palace.

Immediately, the Turks began digging towards deep trenches, often roofed in timber and earth, which allowed them to approach the walls under cover. This digging made the siege memorable: the methodical extension, inch by inch, of a network of tunnels and trenches. The besieging army had very little artillery, and none heavy enough to penetrate the defensive walls: because the walls would have to be breached for an assault to succeed, all depended on laying mines. Meanwhile the Turks' light cannon fired on the city. Stahremberg escaped serious injury when he was hit on the head by a piece of stone. The paving stones inside the city were dug up, partly to soften the effect of cannon balls falling in the street, and partly to help repair the walls. Yet even in these desperate circumstances, when it seemed the fate of Christendom hung in the balance, the commander found himself having to warn Viennese women from stealing out of the city and trading bread for vegetables with the Turkish soldiers.

To deal with the Turkish mines, the defenders resorted to furious sallies, in which a group of soldiers would rush out and attempt to damage as much of the enemy earthworks as possible. The classic response, though, was to countermine, and the defenders in this case had to invent the science for themselves, taking warfare away from noise and light and into the quiet bowels of the earth: listening for the sound of digging; making their own tunnels, hoping to break into the enemy tunnels – ghastly hand-to-hand fights in tight little holes underground. It was then, according to legend, that the city bakers saved Vienna: for early one morning, standing beside their bread ovens, they heard the tell-tale noise of Turkish tunnellers, and alerted the defence in the nick of time; which feat they commemorated by baking little crescent buns, or croissants.

And for those above ground, the waiting. On 12 August an eerie hush fell over the city and the camp; both sides waiting, listening. Early that afternoon there was a huge uprush of earth and stone as a Turkish mine silently laid beneath the outer moat threw up a huge causeway against the ravelin wall, up which fifty men could march abreast. Soon Turkish standards were planted on the wall. The fall of Vienna could not be long in coming.

Away from the city, Tartar and Turkish horsemen harried the countryside. The Austrians sent frantic pleas to the Polish king, Jan Sobieski, and to the German princes. Some of the princes struck good bargains – the Habsburgs, in effect, bought their troops, and saved them the expense of keeping standing armies at home. The Elector of Saxony made the mistake of promising aid before negotiating terms, and never forgave himself. In Poland, Jan Sobieski began a weary round of bargaining with his over-mighty nobility, many of whom were in the pay of France, which viewed the storm breaking around its old Habsburg enemy with profound and scarcely Christian satisfaction.

As summer turned to autumn, the Christian coalition slowly came together: agonisingly slowly for the people of Vienna, who had been left with no means of communicating with the outside world – no system of flags or fires had been established before the Turks cut the lines of communication with the court and the army. But meanwhile the inaction of the Grand Vizier became curiously apparent. The outer walls were breached; the inner walls were crumbling; now, if ever, was the time for the blood-curdling general assault that Ottoman troops were accustomed to make as soon as a breach appeared: when eager volunteers would fling themselves forward, wear down the enemy's defences, and, martyring themselves in their hundreds, provide a slippery footing for the fresh professional troops who closed in for the kill. Nothing of the sort was happening now; always the eerie, slow, methodical trenching and mining.

Kara Mustafa has been roundly criticised ever since for this slowness to attack. Perhaps he was over-confident of victory; certainly he is said to have disbelieved reports of a meeting between Lorraine and the King of Poland, with their armies a few days' march away. If Kara Mustafa had been a better general, or Stahremberg less energetic, or Sobieski less chivalrous, or if the French had rattled their sabres on the Rhine with a little more vigour to pin down the German princes, Vienna would have become an Ottoman bridgehead from which to soften and break down the resistance of Central Europe. When the King of Poland did see the Ottoman camp he wrote that 'the general of an army, who had neither thought of entrenching himself nor concentrating his forces, but lies encamped as if we were hundreds of miles from him, is predestined to be beaten'.

The Grand Vizier seems to have believed that the city was on the point of surrender. A city stormed, according to Muslim law, was to be given over to plunder for three days and nights before authority stepped in – to take possession of the ruins. A city which surrendered, however, was inviolate, and everything in it belonged to the state. The Grand Vizier doubtless hoped to bring the wealth and revenues of Vienna and its dependencies into the service of the sultan, rather than squandering them on the soldiers and inheriting a desert. Meanwhile, however, the Christian allies were moving up, presenting poor Emperor Leopold with yet another difficult decision. Should he head the army? Would it not be better to avoid riding amongst all these warlike princes and remain, instead, imperially aloof? As ever, unable to make either decision, he took both at once, and so dithered on the Danube, halfway between Vienna and his new headquarters at Passau. It didn't matter: the German armies were already ahead of him. By early September they had begun taking possession of the heights north and west of the city, from which the Christian troops could survey both the spires of Vienna and the gorgeous pavilions of the Turkish encampment.

On 4 September, a mine blew a big hole in the inner wall of the city; whole lengths began crumbling. Belated assaults were launched with increasing ferocity upon these breaches; but overnight the citizens did their best to repair the holes, and fought back with equal ferocity, although the effects of the siege were beginning to tell. Butcher's meat had run out; vegetables were scarce; families sat down to donkey and cat. The elderly and weak began dying, and disease stalked the unpaved streets. Even Stahremberg fell ill.

Kara Mustafa should never have allowed the enemy to occupy the ridges surrounding his camp virtually unopposed, and he ought to have spared some of his sappers for digging trenches around the camp, to help break a cavalry charge and to give his own musketeers cover. Perhaps he relied on the broken ground, the endless dips and hollows and ravines which broke the hillsides.

On the night of the eleventh, the Germans were in position to the north of the city, with the Danube to their left. In the morning the battle began, the German infantry advancing from one ridge to the next in the wake of their big guns. Co-ordination was difficult. Whole companies of men vanished for hours on end into some ravine, and horsemen and infantry became hopelessly entangled.

The Turks put up an improvised but furious resistance, and the battle raged until noon, when a sort of lull occurred, occasioned partly by the expectation of the Poles' arrival on the Christian right wing. At one o'clock a shout of triumph – or relief – came from the German wing as they saw the Poles emerge onto the plain through a narrow defile, and make their way forward against stiff Turkish opposition.

There was a brief discussion among the Christian commanders over whether the battle should be pressed today, or not; everyone was for going on. 'I am an old man,' said one Saxon general, 'and I want comfy quarters in Vienna tonight.'

He got them: the Turkish camp, suddenly stormed, collapsed. Kara Mustafa himself fled, with most of his money and the sacred standard of the Prophet. The hapless sappers in the trenches turned to find themselves assailed from the rear. Sobieski at the head of the Polish army broke into the camp while the German regiments strove to catch up: Sobieski and his men secured most of the booty of that day. Never had a Turkish camp been so suddenly overthrown.

The besieging army was routed and chased down the Danube all the way to Belgrade, and the Ottomans suffered their first decisive loss of territory to a Christian foe. Kara Mustafa must have hoped to reach his sovereign in Belgrade, in order to explain the débâcle to Sultan Mehmet in person. It was a bitter blow to learn that the Sultan had already departed for Edirne. Less than noble in defeat, Kara Mustafa blamed, and executed, scores of his own officers. It was from Edirne, a few weeks later, that an imperial messenger reached the Grand Vizier. Kara Mustafa did not wait to read the command. 'Am I to die?' he asked. 'It must be so,' the messengers replied. 'So be it,' he said, and washed his hands. Then he bowed his head for the strangler's bowstring.

Kara Mustafa's head, as custom required, was delivered to the Sultan in a velvet bag.

The Koprulu family, though, survived the disgrace, and two more scions of the dynasty were to be invested in office. The last to hold the vizierate, Amdjazade Huseyin Pasha, died in 1703, ill and despondent: he had cut unnecessary taxes and drastically reduced the numbers of palace men and janissaries on the payroll, combing the timar registers for irregularities; he had managed to steady the currency; but he left office beset by enemies who gathered around the Grand Mufti himself.

Hereditary rank was no substitute for the stern-minded meritocracy of former years. The Koprulu line had already grown degenerate when the bookish and etiolated Nuuman Koprulu became obsessed with a fly he imagined had settled on the end of his nose, 'which indeed flew away when he scared it, but returned again immediately to the same place'. All Constantinople's physicians made efforts to cure him of the delusion, but it was Le Duc, a French physician, who solemnly agreed that he saw the fly, and made the pasha take a few 'innocent juleps, under the name of purging and opening medicines; at last, he drew a knife gently along his nose, as if he was going to cut off the fly, and then shewed him a dead fly which he had kept in his hand for that purpose: whereupon Nuuman Pasha immediately cried out "this is the very fly which has so long plagued me": and thus he was perfectly cured.'

An inordinate number of places preserve the memory of the Turkish wars, like bladderwrack left by a receding tide. In Austria you may hear the *Türkenglocken*, peals which once were rung to warn of an impending akinci raid. In German museums you may find the whips and scourges by which wandering men allayed the Great Fear. In Transylvania, churches are built like fortresses, and it was the custom, well into this century, for every local family to deposit, each year, a flitch of bacon or sack of flour in the storerooms built within the walls, against the possibility of a Tartar raid.

Kosovo was so often a theatre of war that even now it rumbles with discontent, and the Albanians who moved or returned there after the great exodus of Serbs to Austria in the seventeenth century retain a prickly and dangerous hostility to the Serbs who govern them now. Men in the Serbian army that passed through in 1911 stooped to unlace their boots, and crossed it barefoot so not to disturb the souls of their fallen forebears. A huge pile of masonry, approached by 234 steps, now sits atop the pass at Sumla in Bulgaria, to commemorate the passage of Soviet armies in the spring of 1944; but its purpose was to evoke the memory of Russian armies in the autumn of 1779, when Diebitsch avoided the pass and wound his way around almost to Edirne, with a force that everyone supposed, from its martial confidence as much as anything, to amount to 100,000 men, so that the Turks sued for a disastrous peace whose terms gave rise to the Crimean War half a century later, while in fact Diebitsch led an army of perhaps 13,000, wasted by disease.

Often the scene of battle is softly commemorated, by people who have long since forgotten the terror of the day: in St Gotthard, the battle of 1674 is remembered in a café sign; and Vienna 1683, the great lost opportunity for Ottoman arms, is remembered in a croissant: the head of the Grand Vizier Kara Mustafa, who besieged the city, lies somewhere in the vaults of the Kunsthistorisches Museum, where it used to be displayed on a cushion, in a cabinet, before curators in our lily-livered age chose to hide it from the public gaze.

The sixteen years of war which followed the reverse at Vienna were full of military disasters for the Ottoman Empire. The Austrian armies expelled the Ottomans from Hungary. Venetian troops, led by that Morosini who had surrendered nobly at Candia, took the Peloponnese. In 1687 a defeat at the hands of the Austrians at Mohacs, the scene of Suleyman's great victory in the previous century, rebounded on the pleasure-loving Sultan Mehmet IV, who was deposed in favour of another Suleyman, his brother. On 20 August 1688 the citadel at Belgrade surrendered to the Austrians; Nis a year later; and in this crisis, with the enemy circling for a push into the heart of the Balkans, the Ottomans rallied under a new Grand Vizier, brother to Fazil Ahmet, Fazil Mustafa. He managed to push the Austrians out of Serbia, but he died gloriously (if ineptly), sword in hand, at the battle of Peterwaradin in 1691. Suleyman II had died that year; his successor Ahmet II was to die of grief and shame in 1695; and at last, in 1699, the belligerents accepted a peace, mediated by the English ambassador to the Porte.

The treaty of Karlowitz was signed on the general principle of

The mule that carried the Koran to Mecca; after Selim (the Grim) captured Mecca and Medina, the Ottomans managed the annual pilgrimage of believers across the Arabian deserts

'uti possidetis': that matters should be fixed as they stood. The Habsburg emperor was recognised as sovereign of Transylvania, and most of Hungary. Poland recovered Podolia and her fortress at Kaminiec. Venice retained the Peloponnese, and made gains in Dalmatia. Russia was a reluctant party to the peace: she kept the Sea of Azov behind the ear of the Crimea, and lands north, which she had seized in 1696. The empire which barely a generation earlier had challenged Vienna lost half its European dominions at a stroke; and what perhaps was worse, her cover was blown, her weakness revealed, and her importance, in the world's eyes, was now almost wholly diplomatic.

20

Austria and Russia

In 1643 the Ottomans retook Baghdad from Persia; in the 1660s the Koprulu grand viziers finally destroyed Venetian power in the Levant, and took Ukraine; in 1711 Peter the Great and his army were holed up on the River Pruth, and sued for an abject peace; even in the 1730s the Austrians, hoping for a whirlwind victory like the one Prince Eugene had won for them twenty years before, were driven out of Belgrade instead. Sometimes it seemed that by a convulsive effort the empire could shake off lethargy and confusion, and discover some of its old direction.

But the troughs from which the Ottomans climbed were deeper every time. In 1674 they lost their first land battle against the Habsburgs at St Gotthard. Then came the crushing failure at Vienna in 1683; a string of defeats culminating in the humiliating treaty of Karlowitz in 1699; the no less disastrous treaty of Passarowitz, in 1718; the inescapable rise of Russian power in the eighteenth century, and the indefatigable resistance of Persia. These were hammer blows the empire sought to deflect by a variety of retreats: into diplomacy, safer territory, nostalgic fantasy, or selfishness. People moved to carve themselves out a place in an enterprise which struggled, first to maintain the status of a lofty power, then against failure, and lastly against disintegration, as the effort to pull together and recoup grew harder with the years.

The treaty of Belgrade in 1739, and treaties with Persia in 1748, gave the empire almost half a century of unprecedented peace. When the Ottomans chose to break that peace with a new series of Russian wars in 1784, they were roundly defeated, and the exercise proved only how fantastic all their expectations had become, and what little use they had made of this respite. By the end of the eighteenth century, Russian armies could lunge at Edirne; Napoleon took Egypt in 1800; and the integrity of Ottoman dominion, such as it was, was maintained as much by the bickerings of foreign diplomats as by any active policy of the state.

Some say that the causes of Ottoman decline are to be sought on the periphery, which no longer provided the empire with fresh blood; others blame it on the behaviour of the palace. Old-fashioned historians observed that the warrior blood of early sultans had been diluted, drop by drop, by the foreign slave-girls of the harem; as late as 1911 Professor Libyer computed the falling-off, and declared that the Ottoman Sultan possessed no more than one part in a million of Turkish blood (another historian corrected him by factoring in the Turkish odalisques, and thus arrived at a sum of about 1/16,000). But they also point to the entry of Muslim boys into the slave caste of the empire. Some see the empire's nemesis not in western imbroglios but in the perpetual struggle with Shi'ite Persia, which promoted a stale orthodoxy and beggared the treasury. Foreign historians tend to blame the international forces of capitalism – their capital, their force – and suggest that the West reduced the empire to a peripheral producer of raw materials. Turkish historians repatriate the faults: they demonstrate that western trade had a negligible influence on the empire until the nineteenth century. But the military experts, taking the last Ottoman siege of Vienna in 1683 as a moment of reckoning, suggest that Austria and Russia were beginning to learn lessons that the Ottomans themselves had already started to forget.

War provided an excuse to raise more taxes, a full quarter of which were spent on the Sultan and his palace. War took the janissaries and the spahi cavalry off the streets. War brought the Ottoman Empire into the field, kindled some of the old flame, and set the elderly mechanism creaking and whirring into life again. Success or failure at the march's end was really beside the point; and wars continued to be punctiliously waged even when Ottoman armies journeyed, not as a glorious caravan to lands of booty, but to dismal and near-inevitable defeats.

Both Austria and Russia benefited from coming late to the imperial feast: they were able to arrange their command structures, their tax-gathering efforts, and their technology to suit the modern style of warfare. The superiority of massive infantry divisions backed by mobile field artillery over medieval cavalry charges and heavy bronze siege cannon had been proved in Central Europe during the Thirty Years' War, when the strategy had been imported from France and Italy. It demanded much more from the state, for while knights who took revenues from their own lands were satisfied with the plunder they could seize from others, and remained, in essence, marauding hordes, the new style of warfare demanded huge discipline, systems of co-ordination, and a massive investment of funds – training, wages and supply. This in turn called for a very efficient tax system, encouraging the growth of a sophisticated bureaucracy backed by military force: if the countryside was to be milked, it had to be held hard.

The Russians eventually turned out to be very good at this. With their seemingly limitless reserves of manpower, they were quick to settle, cultivate and tax newly conquered lands, which paid for the army moving up ahead. Because they were moving on the whole into underpopulated territory, north and north-west of the Black Sea, their conquests had greater homogeneity than the Austrians could impose in Central Europe, or the Ottomans had ever considered imposing on the Balkans when they slipped in their horsemen as one link in the tax system. The passage of Ottoman armies, not composed of disciplined conscripts but of predatory horsemen and hired guns, and the high-handed attitude of the privileged janissaries towards peasants, did nothing to encourage settlement on the Ottoman frontier. Austria and Russia used armies as a palisade behind which people could be settled for tax and cultivation, which financed the next advance. The Ottomans left settlement to private initiative.

The support mechanisms which the Ottomans had excelled at establishing from early times were now looking old-fashioned. The guild-bound artisans of Constantinople were not up to manufacturing *matériel* and arms on the scale that modern war demanded. The tax system was fairly rudimentary, and nothing in Ottoman experience or training prepared them for the business of managing the enormous funds a modern state was obliged to raise, protect and disburse for war. Ottomans did not, on the whole, engage in trade; they worked in administration; their minorities, Greeks, Jews and Armenians, separated from them by a gulf of culture and sympathy, traditionally looked after the money side.*

The Austrian years were dominated by Prince Eugene of Savoy, who brought drill and discipline, promotion by merit and a clear command structure to the Austrian armies. Within a few years the Austrians were able to inflict regular defeats on the Ottomans with armies no larger than before.† Under Eugene, the Austrians had taken Belgrade and Nis; in 1697 they had defeated Sultan Mustafa IV in person at Zenta, on the lower Tisza, thwarting Ottoman efforts to recover the middle Danube, and created the conditions by which the Habsburgs gained Hungary and Transylvania in the peace of Karlowitz in 1699. Following a resumption of war, the treaty of Passarowitz in 1718 established Habsburg rule over Serbia itself, and it might have seemed that the Austrians were poised to sweep the Ottomans back into Asia. But 'pride spread the veil of negligence over the eye of sagacity', as an Ottoman historian once wrote. Eugene's brilliance and daring so overawed his junior officers that when he was dead, and they had

* The Ottomans had originally encouraged them, successfully, as a counterweight to the Italian monopoly of Levantine trade.

† His men, however, were frequently encouraged to get drunk before battle, better to face the terrifying janissary bands and warcries.

the command, they fatally sought to imitate his daring, while possessing none of his brilliance. Trying to repeat history without Eugene in the campaigns of 1734–6 they found themselves losing most of their gains to Ottoman armies which, if not brilliantly generalled, and no longer splendidly equipped, were very obdurate. The treaty of Belgrade in 1739 overturned many of the decisions of Passarowitz, and Serbia was returned to the empire.

The spirit of victory now moved decisively to Russia. The Tsars began to develop a sort of scientific rhythm to secure and settle the great steppe, which extended south of Muscovy to the northern shores of the Black Sea; after which they could reach out with both arms to encircle the so-called Turkish lake. By 1774, when Russia inflicted the humiliating treaty of Kucuk Kainardji on the Ottomans, Austria's own twin-headed eagle seemed to peer uncertainly now east, now west; and in token of her confusion she was working as Russia's poor relation, in the field at least. Austrian armies suffered one of their most terrible defeats near Slatina in 1788, when the order to halt one night was mistaken, by men further down the column, as the shout of 'Allah!' Believing the Turks had sprung an ambush, the troops panicked. The drivers of the ammunition carts lashed their horses to full speed, and at the terrible sound of their wheels, which sounded to the infantry like the charge of enemy cavalry, the soldiers fell out of line and clustered together in terrified huddles, firing wildly in all directions. At daybreak, without an enemy in sight, the corpses of 10,000 Austrian soldiers lay scattered across the snow.

The momentum of Russian victory, though, was slow to gather. At the beginning of the eighteenth century the Russians were harassing and nibbling at the frontiers of the Crimea, where the treaty of Karlowitz had given them a toehold. They had, as the Tartar chief informed the Sultan, begun to intrigue with his orthodox flock, reaya, the Tsar casting himself in the light of a redeemer. The Swedes, at war with Russia, urged the dangers of the bear. In 1710, accordingly, the Grand Mufti issued a fatwa licensing war against Russia as not only justifiable but necessary. Thirty thousand janissaries were enrolled; the Kapudan Pasha readied the fleet, and the Russian ambassador was clapped up in the Castle of the Seven Towers, by way of declaring war.

Peter the Great secured his advance into Ottoman realms by buying the favour of the two hospodars, of Wallachia and Moldavia – but Prince Brancovich of Moldavia was playing a deep game, and when Peter's army had crossed the River Prut to begin its advance through the principality the Tsar found that the supplies he wanted were not forthcoming. His men were already suffering from hunger and disease, and he boldly determined to push on and capture a vast stockpile of weapons and food which the Ottomans had made for themselves further south. The Ottomans had undoubtedly benefited from the unpalatable defeats registered by the treaty of Karlowitz twelve years before, and had been spurred into making improvements in their army and intelligence. While Peter marched down the right bank of the Prut, believing the Grand Vizier's army still far away, the Ottoman army was even now advancing up the left bank to meet him. Ten thousand Crimean Tartars had brushed aside an advance guard which attempted to prevent them crossing, and very soon the entire Russian army found itself holed up between the Prut and a marsh. From the opposite bank the Ottoman guns prevented any soldier from approaching the river, and after two days of desperate fighting the Russians were unable to break the Turkish encirclement.

On 21 July 1711, Peter signed a treaty promising to keep within his own dominions in future, and to retreat from Azov, which had given him an entry into the Black Sea. Entirely at the mercy of the Grand Vizier, he was allowed to withdraw on astonishingly light terms. Peter himself never re-opened hostilities with the empire in his lifetime;* but the project was only deferred, and in 1774, when the situation was reversed – when the Russians had swept victorious right up to the Balkan passes, and the Vizier discovered that he had just 8,000 men to defend the Bulgarian pass at Sumla and sued for peace, the Russian general Romanzoff

* In 1718 Tsarina Catherine's favourite general, Prince Golytsin, led an army of a million men out from Moscow to drive the Turks into the sea, but without supplies, so that 400,000 starved to death without ever leaving Russian territory.

delayed putting his signature to the treaty for four days, allowing it to fall on the anniversary of the treaty of the Pruth, to expunge the memory of that humilating reverse.

The treaty of Kucuk Kainardji, signed on 21 July 1774, was very different from the treaty extracted from Peter some sixty years before; it mirrored, rather, the treaty of Karlowitz signed with the Austrians in 1699, when the Ottomans were forced to give way in Central Europe. In 1774 they lost control of the northern shore of the Black Sea. Kucuk Kainardji made the Crimean Tartars independent of the Sultan, an obvious preliminary to their absorption into the Russian Empire, which took place ten years later. The Sultan was permitted to retain his role as Caliph, but this was a shadowy title at best (Selim the Grim, who had allegedly earned it by his conquest of Arabia and the Holy Cities, had not used it himself; its importance rose only as the temporal authority of the Sultan waned). The Principalities, Moldavia and Wallachia, were returned to the Porte, but the Russian ambassador was given the right to make representations on their behalf. Russian merchant ships were allowed access to Ottoman waters, which meant that for the first time since the Conquest, foreign ships might pass through the Bosphorus. The Russian ambassador was entitled to represent the interests of a new church that was to be built in Constantinople, as well as its ministers; and by sleight of hand this became, in the end, a claim by the Tsar to act as ultimate protector of all his co-religionists in the Sultan's realms.

At St Gotthard, in 1674, the Ottomans had suffered their first true defeat on an open field ('Who are these young girls?' the Grand Vizier wanted to know when he saw the French cavalry advancing, with shaven faces and powdered wigs: but 'Allons! allons! tue! tue!' was a cry the Turks did not forget). The Austrian general in command during that engagement wrote later of the tremendous courage and obstinacy displayed by the Ottoman troops, but he was astonished, too, by their inexplicable failure to make use of the pike, which he called 'the queen of weapons'.

The Ottomans did have a horrid arsenal to draw on all the

same, from jabby little daggers to a sinister militaristic version of the long-handled scythe; yet a century later it was not the pike but the bayonet that Ottoman armies lacked. In the summer of 1774 General Suvarov appeared as Russia's genius, and the bayonet's devotee. 'The ball is a fool – the bayonet a hero!' was one of his maxims. He taught his soldiers to attack instantly and decisively: 'attack with the cold steel – push hard with the bayonet!' His soldiers adored him, and he never lost a single battle. He joshed with the men, called the common soldiers 'brother', and shrewdly presented the results of detailed planning and careful strategy as the work of inspiration. He announced the capture of Ismail in 1791 to the Tsarina Catherine in a doggerel couplet, after the assault had been pressed from house to house, room to room, and nearly every Muslim man, woman and child in the city had been killed in three days of uncontrolled massacre, 40,000 Turks dead, a few hundred taken into captivity. For all his bluffness, Suvarov later told an English traveller that when the massacre was over he went back to his tent and wept.

21

Ayan

As the institutions of empire fell into disarray, the kapikullari addled their single-minded devotion to the Sultan's cause. With the Sultan in their grip, power became something they quarrelled over mercilessly, falling into factions, advancing their protégés, and stabbing each other in the back. The world they made for themselves was far more frightening and uncertain than the world Mehmet had made for them, in which they had been at the mercy of the Sultan's will.

In Constantinople, the poet wrote, 'are the ranks of glory and honour / Anywhere else life is frittered away.' The sultans believed otherwise; in the latter half of the seventeenth century they abandoned their palace in Constantinople for the security and pleasaunces of Edirne, where they could hunt in the parks. In 1703, though, the mob marched on Edirne; they deposed Mustafa II on 22 August, and released his younger brother from the kafes where he had lived for the past sixteenth years. Ahmet III was then installed in the palace, which had become a prison where he exclaimed against the practice of sending forty pages to attend him in his bedroom. 'I do not feel at all comfortable if I have to change my trousers,' he complained; 'I must ask my sword-bearer to dismiss them, keeping only three or four men so that I might be at ease in the small room.'

'The rumour of the Sultan's death has spread down to the very children; and a riot is expected, accompanied by a sack of shops and houses as usual,' wrote the bailio in 1595. 'I have hidden the embassy archives and brought armed men into the house . . .' When a coup, or a mutiny, or a massacre closed down the shops, sealed the bazaars, and silenced the talk in the cafés – 'sad it is to see the aspect of this city', wrote Emo, the bailio in 1731 – and when soldiers patrolled the empty streets, and the nights were punctuated by the boom of cannon, signalling that some unfortunate had been tossed to the waves – the atmosphere was oppressive and tense.

The panache and abandon of the empire in its golden days had given way to the stifling confinement of the Cage, the stagnation of the borders, the dark warren of streets, the pent-up hours of the harem. All this resembled slavery of the galley; and it fostered and irritated the idea of nationhood – until the empire seemed a prison of the nations, too.

It was Rycaut in the seventeenth century who called the Ottoman court 'a Prison and Banniard of Slaves, differing from that where the Galley-slaves are immured, only by the Ornaments and glittering out-side and appearances: here their Chains are made of Iron, and there of Gold and the difference is only in a painted shining servitude, from that which is a squalid, sordid and a noisome slavery.'

The Kiosk of Processions was built into the palace walls, from where the Sultan was expected not only to watch the colourful parades of guildsmen, but to listen to the complaints of the multitude. The officials could do nothing to close this aperture upon the wider world, and although they curated the Sultan according to their own lights, and arranged the manner in which he was displayed to the public gaze, through the blanket of court ceremonial they could always hear the terrible baying of the mob outside and the thunder of the cauldrons overturned, the bass notes of popular power and discontent.

From the high window of the Kiosk traitors and criminals were thrown to meet the fury of the mob; and so were officials who had incurred their displeasure. On April Fool's Day 1717, Lady Mary Wortley Montague wrote: 'The government is entirely in the hands of the army and the Gran Signor as much a slave as any of his subjects . . . Sh'd a reflection on [a minister of state's] conduct be dropped in a coffee house (for they have spies everywhere) the house would be razed to the ground. But when a minister here displeases the people in three hours time he is dragged even from his master's arms. They cut off his hands, head and feet . . . while the Sultan (to whom they all profess an unlimited adoration) sits trembling in his apartment, and dare neither defend nor revenge his favourite.'

Again and again, the designs of the Porte were thwarted by the rabble. Again and again, the state stamped down on all the symptoms of dissent: in 1712 the newfangled coffee houses were closed, as notorious centres of unrest; in 1756 a number of janissaries who had been caught smoking had pipes stuffed up their noses and were led in derision through the streets of the capital. But the mutinous *Kaffeeklatsche* were soon in full swing again, and the soldiery clung insolently to their pipes and pouches.

The empire swarmed with the dispossessed, churned up in the chaos and devaluations of the early seventeenth century. Ever since the borders had closed, the ruling classes had turned to squeezing the lower orders for the plunder and riches which warfare no longer seemed to bring.

'This miserie abroad will make us love our owne Countrie the better when we come thither,' an Englishman consoled himself in 1612, after making a trip through the eastern reaches of the Ottoman Empire. No longer was it perfectly safe to travel the Sultan's highways. The poor felt their poverty more keenly, perhaps; but on the way to Jerusalem from Aleppo in 1604, an English traveller found a village so poor that when he gave them his bread they 'blessed God that there was bread in the World'. As taxes rose, ordinary country folk ran away or surrendered their rights to some powerful local ruler. Increasingly they turned to piracy and banditry. All over the Balkans, men melted into the woods and vanished into the mountains to prey on travellers and villagers, and at least once the government considered torching the forests of Chalkydike near Thessalonica to flush them out.* The exploits of klephts or heyducks were sung in ballads like those of the uskoks before them, and the bandit way of life itself became traditional: and though inevitably – armed and desperate – bandits were instrumental in furthering the nationalist rebellions which broke out from the late eighteenth century, at heart they belonged to the decline of the old order, not the eruption of the new – very like the *armatoles*, or local police, whose business it was to round them up.

It was often hard to say who was klepht and who was armatole, for both sprang from local stock, and were involved in the game of protection and intimidation. Many of them wanted nothing better than a fair deal and a quiet life. Urquhart was finally seized by brigands in northern Greece in 1835, but in four hours flat he had them pleading that times were very bad when honest men had to turn to this sort of work to make a living (and they actually turned on a curmudgeonly Albanian colleague who seemed intent, notwithstanding, on slitting Urquhart's throat and taking all his money). 'Woe is me! I've married a robber!' shrieked the heroine of a Balkan play when the simple herdsman she had married put on his guns. 'Now every man is become a robber,' he grimly pointed out. But bandits were bandits, too.† Robert Curzon in Albania could only think that 'the natives do not shoot so much

* The woods were as full of hives as men – until even the bees began to experience overcrowding, and were sent to sea 'in little yachts, in which the swarms cruise about in the adjoining gulfs of classical renown; rifling the sweets of their respective coasts, and exhibiting that superiority over their continental neighbours which is always assumed by a maritime people'.

† The Swedish artist Otto Magnus von Stackelberg was taken by Albanian bandits in northern Greece, who entertained him by singing:

> There were forty brigands, sitting on Olympus
> forty cold nights long.
> Their jackets rotting on their bodies
> were smeared with black blood.
> Bo! Bo! the night and the moon.

at Franks because they usually have little worth taking and are not good to eat'; and shortly before the First World War Noel Buxton, MP, pretended to the Turkish Ambassador that he was going to the Balkans as a cure for a weak throat. 'It is not a very good place for throats,' the ambassador replied drily.

The grander the larceny, the more eagerly the authorities sought to negotiate. When pashas themselves stooped to criminality, it could not be long before criminals, in their turn, were being made pashas, and in the provinces by the end of the eighteenth century it was often unclear who was the bandit and who the governor, so complex and negotiable had Ottoman rule become.

In Constantinople the rulers of the empire kept a weather eye on the rise and fall of cliques and households, but they lost interest in distant provinces, over which they were losing direct authority. The old system of timariot soldiery led by the local *sancakbey* had been replaced by cash revenues remitted to the Porte by the *beylerbeyi*, men who controlled whole regions, and were in a better position to oversee the business of raising revenues. So much for theory. The money was an irresistible temptation: many compounded timars and hass revenues dropped out of the system altogether, and were attached by sleight of hand to various offices and persons in authority, from beylerbeyi and their provincial aides to the innermost functionaries of the court – the Black Eunuch and his harem women not excepted.

If at times the provincial rulers did their best to elude the grasp of Constantinople, they still required its mantle of legitimacy. Sultans – or their ministers – used an unpredictable network of personal alliances to secure the loyalty of their more powerful subordinates. Pashas were given royal brides, so that the old seventeenth-century Sultanate of the Women is sometimes called the 'Sultanate of the In-laws'.* Hasan Pasha in 1720 declared himself lord of Babylon: 'seized the province after fifteen years of deriding and eluding the Porte,' the bailio wrote, and 'reigns as a

* The continuity of Ottoman rule in Buda, for example, was provided less by the four pashas who ruled there in the late seventeenth century than by Atike, Mehmet IV's younger sister, who married each of them in succession.

sovereign, although he sends each year the customary tribute to the Gran Signor. So great is the dissimulation of this Government that it does not declare him a rebel and constrain him with force, but communicates with him, shows confidence in him, and honoured him a short time ago by creating his son Pasha at the premature age of seventeen.'

Hajji Ali Haseki's governorship of Athens in the late eighteenth century was so tyrannical that a joint deputation of Greeks and Turks made their way to the Grand Vizier in Istanbul to protest, and a band of farmers threw their ploughshares at his feet and begged to be given land elsewhere. Hajji Ali was dismissed, but he was the lover of the Sultan's sister, and he bribed his way back into the governorship a few years later, banishing his Turkish opponents, stealing land, forcing men to labour for him, and driving half the population of the city to flight. An Athenian abbot who attempted to register his protests in Constantinople met Ali there by mischance, and took coffee with him; he soon realised his mistake when 'his beard fell off and his teeth were injured'. It was the death of the Sultan's sister which caused Hajji Ali's downfall; he was exiled to Kos, and finally beheaded.

Often the Porte would simply stipulate a sum it expected to receive in dues, and leave it to the local notable to apportion the taxes in his locality, so that a system which had once operated only in very remote and awkward places became general in the seventeenth century. All sorts of people were drawn into this devolution of power – priests, kadis, traditional chiefs like the Serbian knez or the kapitanos of Muslim Bosnia, truculent officials. The central authorities also began ridding the capital of as many janissaries as they could, posting them to garrisons around the empire; when their pay faltered they began to impose themselves in familiar style upon the local town. They were especially common in Bosnia and Serbia, but by 1792 more than half the male population of Salonica was enrolled in some janissary regiment. All these local power groups formed a dangerous counterweight to the corruption and timidity of the central authorities, whose governors in the provinces were apt to behave like guests of honour, benign spectators to the show.

The fertile chaos of appointments and usurpations, frequently winked at by the central authorities, led to the emergence of local dynasties of *ayan*, Lords of the Valleys:* as if the state itself was too exhausted to climb the mountains and traverse the passes which divided them all, in such a corrugated and ridged terrain.

Ali Pasha the Albanian, one of the most absolute and terrifying of the ayan, ruled his pashalik as a monarch for twenty years. Born locally in Janina in 1745, he carved out lands for himself by trickery, daring, terror, cruelty and cheek which straddled much of southern Albania, northern Greece, and Macedonia, and he freely negotiated with foreign powers on his own account. Sometimes you feel that his whole career was darkly devoted to wreaking vengeance on the Suliotes, who had once abused his mother, a real witch; sometimes, that he was a modern tyrant, working in difficult times, who made the roads good and understood trade. He winningly asked Henry Holland to stay on as his physician, and to name his fee. Of course Holland declined, so Ali asked him instead for a good undetectable poison. He enjoyed a kind of popularity, preventing anyone from oppressing his people except himself; while he and the Porte together successfully pretended that he was just the man they meant to have, and in the perfect spot. Whether he used the Porte, or defied it, it was only in the early 1820s that the rupture between them became open and unavoidable. The old Lion of Janina was still firing on his enemies, exhorting his troops, and swearing a terrible vengeance, as Ottoman soldiers came pouring into his house; and he was so magnificent that they shot him dead, not face to face, but by firing muskets through the floorboards.

Under these conditions, as ordinary people grew poor, others became significantly rich. For every village enserfed, there were individual villagers who rose through soldiering, tax collection, moneylending, trade, muleteering, or the amassing – at the expense of the peasantry – of hereditary estates. The economic

* No one, by now, could count themselves lords of the hills, which were riddled with bandits.

convulsions of the seventeenth century gave way, in the eighteenth, to increased trade and unequal prosperity: conditions of social turmoil and demographic change which were mirrored, perhaps, in the more lively movement of the plague from city to city in the wake of troops and trade.

The plague epidemic generally began in Constantinople in April and May, climaxed in August and subsided in October: ships took it to Cairo and Alexandria, caravans to the Balkans. War spread pestilence: in 1718 the Tartars brought it to Belgrade; in 1738 a Russian army contaminated in Moldavia carried plague across the Ukraine, while Austrian armies diffused it through the Banat and Hungary. Sometimes it arose unexpected and unexplained, devastating in a season whole cities which had considered themselves safe for generations. Always it seemed to strike hardest at regions already reeling from crop failures, earthquakes, or the passing of the army. In contrast to sixteenth-century population growth, the seventeenth century saw numbers shrink, with the decline most pronounced in the countryside as people fled for security to the towns. There, unfortunately, they were likely to meet the plague; but in the Balkans the proportion of Christians in cities grew enormously, nonetheless.

A German had noticed in 1553 that almost every house appeared to be of the same value as the next, and 'of wood, single storeyed, built directly on the ground and on a level with it, without underground cellars' (lawless Albania was an exception: here houses were shaped like towers, and the living quarters were approached through a trapdoor). By the end of the eighteenth century the Greek village of Ambelikya, which produced the dye called Turkey red, was home to a group of dye merchants with branches in Vienna and London; their grand and ornate houses still survive. In 1787 a Greek businessman of Siphnos left his wife and children shares in olive trees, a vineyard, three ships and a boat; in mischief or wisdom, he saw to it that his wife got the stairway down to the river, and one daughter the iron pier at the bottom.

The growth of a money economy had been presaged at the end of the sixteenth century by the army's demand for professional paid infantry; but while the Ottomans themselves developed sticky fingers, they were not clever with money. 'They are great wits at times,' della Valle wrote in the early 1600s, 'but in business we always make them pause, because, do what they wish, they know far less about it than we others do.' Whatever funds they possessed were spent on climbing the ladder. Service in the bureaucracy, the army and the mosque was their defining role as a ruling caste – for they were not a nation, or a geographical entity. Of course there were exceptions – like the governor who argued that a pasha ought to engage in trade, to lessen the burden on the people – but Turks with any pretensions were *rentiers* through and through, and always hoping for promotion and rewards they used their money to attain positions enabling them to carve off a slice of the wealth that was being created under their noses.

Unlike the aristocracies of the West, who ultimately moved into trade, finance and production, the Ottomans still saw wealth as plunder, to pile up in glittering heaps. War tended, overall, to serve and stimulate the economies of Western Europe, but in the Ottoman Empire it was the other way about.* The economy served war. The Ottomans made requisitions as they had done when the empire's wealth was spread at the Sultan's disposal, and most fighters could sustain themselves. So there was a market price, and a requisition price, and the best producers suffered most. Culturally the Ottomans were cut off from the people in their empire who were parlaying their labour into capital, and their capital into a good return. Increasingly the minorities invested in trade, production and even land – people who by definition had no role in the political process. The Ottoman state did not see promoting trade as its business, nor, by the eighteenth century, would it have had enough influence to do so; so that the endeavours of home-grown capitalists remained, by the standards of Western Europe, relatively small-scale: great riches were never very secure in the empire anyway. Stealth and intrigue allowed the Ottomans and their minorities to benefit from each other, to

* The seventeenth-century population explosion made trouble for the Ottomans, as much as its subsequent contraction.

an extent; and who you were always counted for less than who you knew.

In the days of his power Ali Pasha of Janina had been unpredictable. His charisma, like his cruelty, was satanic: Byron was utterly charmed by him, and wrote to tell his mother so. And he at last gave Henry Holland a strongly worded passport, ordering his people to treat the traveller as they would Ali himself. The sanction for this was not the Koran, nor the Sultan, nor the judgement of the court. At the bottom of the scroll, dark and weird and more quixotic than any of these, flared out the terrible incantation, 'Do this, or the Snake will eat you.'

'The empire will be destroyed', wrote Mustafa Ali (1541–1600), when 'our descendants will say that kanun is what they decide.' But actually it shuddered on, patched and strung together, exploding here, reviving there, into an age when western visitors, far from marvelling at the system, sought to surprise their readers by finding evidence of any system there at all. Among them, though, were a handful of romantics who observed that the random and sporadic violence of the Ottoman Empire, while regrettable, was as likely to be offset by acts of random generosity and wisdom. Urquhart, who travelled widely in Albania in the 1830s, thought that the flexibility of Ottoman rule contrasted favourably with conditions in the West, where the relentless cruelty and ugliness of industrialisation had the full backing of the law. He believed that the personal nature of power in the empire supplied it with automatic checks and balances, and encouraged a perpetual dialogue between power-holders. When Urquhart pondered the childish ease with which rebel chiefs and rivals were invariably lured to their own doom, he concluded that revolts originated with a person, rather than with a principle, and that the betrayal of every rebel leader was 'the result of the same daring and decision upon which alone their authority depends'. Negotiation was always the order of the day; complaints were aired, grievances addressed, and a resolution invariably found that was agreeable to all the parties. How preferable, he thought,

The Fountain of Ahmet III: built in 1728, this exquisite fountain reflects the spirit of imperial benevolence

to the blind injustice daily inflicted on his own countrymen by the grindings of an implacable system.

If men were not perfect, the Ottomans felt, there was much to be said for having men in power who took a pecuniary interest in everything that went on around them. An official who sold offices, a farmer of taxes, a commissar discreetly on commission or simply a predictable judge* would have made his pile already, and his 'eye was full', content with a little gentle squeeze that made him thoroughly reliable. It was only men who declared their honesty who frightened everyone. For a certain length of time they would hold themselves aloof: justice deferred, business at a standstill, while everyone knew that their resolution was bound to fail, on salary; and then they became very rapacious indeed, to make up for lost time.

* 'They tell us of some rare examples in Turkey of uncorrupt judges,' Porter wrote. 'I have heard of one, but I have known none.'

22

Shamming

'Decline' is perhaps a bankrupt term for describing the Ottoman experience in those years. The old system grew more complex and differentiated after the shocks it received in the early seventeenth century; more purposeless and ordinary and modern. The timar cavalry were degenerating largely because the empire was turning itself into a cash-based society. Power in the provinces lay ever more in the hands of the local notables: their understanding of conditions was invariably more acute, and they relieved the central authorities of the burden of providing effective government in every case. The state was broken into cliques, which excited much bitter comment from those who lost out; but patronage, here as elsewhere, was a form of meritocracy: one man sent the brilliant ten-year-old Ali Corlulu Pasha to court, to extend his networks, 'as a spacious theatre, in which his virtues might shine; and, by being his patron, enlarge one day his fortune'. He was Grand Vizier between 1706 and 1710. Eighteenth-century scribes wrote on poorer paper than their seventeenth-century predecessors, but with greater detail and accuracy. Men of the pen seemed to be taking over from men of the sword – and so they were in every major European state.

Only peasants, everywhere, were the losers, as the world shifted from the quiet of medieval agrarianism into a more busy, bossy, opportunistic age. In the empire they were pressed by the growing class of landowners who compiled the peasants' smallholdings into large estates; by ranchers who drove them off with threats and sabotage – like stopping their access to water; or by the nomads who began pushing into regions where settlement was already in decline.

New compartments were added to society, blurring the old simplicities which had placed the reaya on the one hand and the Ottomans on the other, with a thin layer of holy men and merchants in between. But a society which could sustain landless sharecroppers, moneylenders, local bigwigs, independent artisans, and dynasts at every level of state service, was recognisably closer to the kind of society into which modern Europe, too, was evolving.

The problem lay with the Ottomans themselves. The ancient formulas, the old practices, the shape and direction of the Ottoman state underwent no parallel development. 'May the stretching shadow of the Sultan's grandeur and authority be extended from the reaches of the width and breadth of the world to the highest heaven, and may the cordons of the tent of his prosperity and majesty be firmly tied to the God-given tent pegs,' an Ottoman ambassador wrote sanctimoniously in 1776, as he set off to negotiate a deservedly humbling treaty with the Russians. It seemed hardly necessary to add that 'the effect of his auspicious accession to the throne was a bounteous gift of spring to the rose garden of the world', but the ambassador did so; unaware of course that this particular bounteous gift of spring was to die fighting with his own officials in 1807, leaving his kaftan, spattered with blood, to hang as a chilling memento of Ottoman decay in the Topkapi museum.

The gap between theory and reality grew wider with every passing year. Too many people owed their living, not to the real world, but to the sham of it, from the Sultan down, in his sham omnipotence; through the government, with its pretence of controlling the empire; the janissaries in the guise of soldiers, the ulema, in the sham of everlasting Islamic victory; governors, in the sham obedience from which they derived their legitimacy. Thousands of people came to work in the palace every day, but only about twenty of them performed significant tasks. Dozens of provincial governors were seconded from the palace whose real job was to keep their nargiles alight and their noses clean. They counted themselves lucky to live peaceably within their own four walls, and left the task and rewards of government to some local cabal or gang of bully-boys, received fanciful instructions from Constantinople and gave fictitious answers. Athens fell gratefully under the protection of that powerful arbiter of harem affairs, the Chief Black Eunuch, and sometimes managed to get unpopular governors dismissed; and on one such errand a merchant called Dimitri Paleologus spoke so well that the Chief Black Eunuch drew a silver inkwell from his secretary's belt and gave it to him, saying, 'Take this inkpot, and from today I appoint you governor of Athens.' Doubtless the Chief Black Eunuch, who had never left the harem, let alone seen Athens, was pleased by his own perspicacity and style; but poor Dimitri, who lived in the real world, was appalled. He was killed as soon as he returned to Athens, by a league of outraged Turks and jealous Greeks.

The veil of fantasy was tough and widely spread. Anyone who could get a handle on power or money in the real world could generally parlay it into the style of the sham world, too, and any number of imperious local tyrants were escorted by horsetails and janissary guards, lording it over the Balkans whenever the regular army was off the scene, 'marching like princes in cloth of gold and silver; their handsome Tartar horses groomed by their concubines, who followed them to the field dressed in man's apparel'.

Double-entry thinking, though, was a waste of talent, and produced an insurmountable backlog against which all energies frittered themselves away. Nothing was more impressive, Eliot thought, than the air of industry and importance surrounding a pasha at his work: the corridors lined with petitioners and summonees; the pasha himself dealing with a dozen bits of business all through the interview; a vast amount of scribbling and dictation from which he is unable to tear himself away. But Eliot knew better. 'Though the Turks write inordinately, they take no care of their papers, and as a rule merely stuff them into bags and throw them away after a month or two.'

Even the economy of the Turkish language, which can express 'I love' in one word and 'I really do love' in another, had suffered from the Ottoman taste for erudite allusions – the hallmark of an educated gentleman. It became involuted and obscure: its references secondary and arcane, its allusions merely allusions to allusions. Of course all those terrified slaves had gibbered in their native tongues: Ottoman Turkish was a creaking make-believe so truffled with Arabic and Persian, written so inappropriately in vowelless Arabic that many years later 'it was said that during the Turco-Greek war many Turkish soldiers wrote to their families in Anatolia, saying that they were wounded and requesting remittances, but that these requests, when written down by a professional letter-writer and deciphered by the village sage, were thought to be a statement that the sender of the letter was well and saluted his friends'.

At a minor level there was a lot of fibbing and pretence, all the more obvious now that every European diplomat maintained a string of inside informers. Pork was forbidden in Constantinople, but foreign ambassadors bought permission to bring pigs into Pera for Carnival on the sly: the pig was run into town by night, and whisked through the streets to the embassy by rushlight. Europeans reported unanimously that high-ranking Ottomans flocked to their table for wine and went off half tipsy, and when challenged would say, like the Mufti of Aleppo, with becoming hauteur, that the prohibition did not apply to great men who knew when to stop. Busbecq remembered an old fellow who used to shout violently on the point of raising a glass to his lips, to warn his soul 'to betake itself to some distant corner of his body so that it would not participate in the crime he was about to commit'. Edward Dodwell's sketching picnics on the Acropolis in 1805 were constantly interrupted by the arrival of the Athenian governor, who referred to his artistic new friend as 'Pig, Devil and Buonapartist . . . and seldom failed to drink a greater part of our wine: observing that wine was not good for studious people like us'. As for Byron, he wrote in his Athens journal: 'The Voivode and the Mufti of Thebes supped here and made themselves beastly with raw rum, and the Padre of the Convènt being drunk as we, my *Attic* feast went off with great *éclat*.'

But Muslims in liquor, like lascivious priests, are humbug's stock-in-trade, and the tulipomania which swept the court in the 1720s reveals a more material flight from reality. The tulip was the emblem of the Ottoman royal house, worked into textiles and inlay, and celebrated in poetry: the romantic tulip of Central Asia, that is, a lyre-shaped flower with pointed petals. For a brief period at the end of the seventeenth century the tulip's sway in the Ottoman garden was challenged by melons and cucumbers; but under Ahmet III in the 1720s it came back into favour with a frenzy which recalled, in its less sordid aspects, the tulipomania of mid-seventeenth-century Holland.

The Dutch mania had been a speculator's bubble. In Turkey tulipomania came to symbolise the hedonism of the court. Sultan Ahmet III had so many children that with all the births, circumcisions and daughters' weddings a permanent holiday atmosphere reigned in the Seraglio. 'Let us laugh, let us play, let us enjoy the delights of the world to the full,' wrote the court poet Nedim, a particular favourite of Sultan Ahmet's. Grizzled old kapudan pashas stooped tenderly over the bulbs with little trowels; the head gardener laid his executioner's tools aside, and dazzling were the nightly displays in the palace in the fleeting growing season. The French ambassador described such an evening at the house of Grand Vizier Damad Ibrahim Pasha in 1726:

> When the tulips are in flower, and the Grand Vizier wishes to show them to the sultan, care is taken to fill the gaps where the tulips have come up blind, by flowers taken from other gardens and placed in bottles. Beside every fourth flower is stood a candle, level with the bloom, and along the alleys are hung cages filled with all kinds of birds. The trellises are all decorated with an enormous quantity of flowers of every sort, placed in bottles and lit by an infinite number

of glass lamps of different colours. These lamps are also hung on the green branches of shrubs which are specially transplanted for the fête from neighbouring woods and placed behind the trellises. The effect of all these varied colours, and of the lights which are reflected by countless mirrors, is said to be magnificent. The illuminations, and the noisy consort of Turkish musical instruments which accompanies them, continue nightly so long as the tulips remain in flower, during which time the Grand Seigneur and his whole suite are lodged and fed at the expense of the Grand Vizier. . . .

For ten years the whole of Constantinople gave itself over to illusions of fairyland. Giant turtles bearing flickering candelabra paddled through the Seraglio grounds. 'Sometimes the court appears floating on the waters of the Bosphorus or the Golden Horn, in elegant caiques, covered with silken tents; sometimes it moves forward in a long cavalcade towards one or another of the pleasure palaces . . . These processions are made especially attractive by the beauty of the horses and the luxury of their caparisons; they progress, with golden or silver harnesses and plumed foreheads, their coverings resplendent with precious stones.'

At the back of it all, though, lay policy desperate and inspired: it was all the handiwork of a single Grand Vizier, Damad Ibrahim Pasha, who feverishly worked the silken threads. Damad Ibrahim assumed office in 1718, and after Ahmet had kept his Grand Viziers turning over every fourteen months for twelve years it was a credit to his capabilities that he stayed in office until 1730. He waved his Sultan away on a froth of loveliness and poetry; presented his Sultan with the cynosure of pleasure-domes in Sa'adabat, the 'Palace of Happiness', upon the shore of the Golden Horn known as the Sweet Waters of Europe; and threw his own lavish party to celebrate his wedding to the Sultan's sister. But behind the dazzling displays he was hard at work upon affairs of state; desperately papering over the cracks which had widened in the humiliations of Karlowitz in 1699 and Passarowitz in 1718.

So, ironically, the so-called Tulip Period of Ottoman history refers not merely to the sensual abandon of the court, but to the administration's first efforts to form a more sober view of the West. It was not only in their search for more and more lovely blooms that the Ottomans sent to Holland and to France; nor idle fancy that saw Sa'adabat modelled on the French château of Marly. In 1719 Ibrahim sent an ambassador to Vienna, and in 1721 to Paris, with instructions 'to make a thorough study of the means of civilisation and education, and report on those capable of application.'

These inspired a little burst of Frankishness, in deference to the old French ally – French gardens, décor and furniture, matched by an equivalent French mode for *turqueries*. But in 1720 a French renegade also organised a fire brigade in Istanbul. In 1729, more significantly, a Turkish printing press was allowed, for the very first time, to operate in Constantinople. It was run by Ibrahim Muteferrika, who was born in Kolozsvar in 1674 and destined for the Calvinist ministry, but was taken into slavery in 1693 and sold in Constantinople. He converted to Islam and made a career for himself in government service. With the help of Said Celebi, the son of the ambassador to France, he petitioned the Grand Vizier Damad Ibrahim for permission to establish his press, and succeeded in getting the ulema's approval to print books of a non-religious nature. Initially he received Jewish help; later type and presses were imported from Leiden and Paris. Seventeen books in all were published between 1729 and 1742, when the works closed down, including a Turkish grammar in French, an account of the ambassador's French sojourn, a treatise on syphilis and one on the tactics of European armies.

The lovely illusions of the palace, as well as the more realistic approach to the West, all came to a bloody end, of course. Damad Ibrahim did what he could to suppress grim news arriving in Istanbul from the Persian front, but not everyone can be fooled all of the time. In 1730 popular opinion at last drove the Sultan and his Grand Vizier to gather an army at Scutari, on the Asian shore, and there, instead of marching out, they dallied in disgraceful parley with Persian negotiators in an effort to bring the war to a close.

An Albanian called Patrona Ali, a janissary dealing in second-hand clothes, led a street rebellion that September, denouncing the Sultan's luxuries and infidel ways. Sa'adabat was destroyed by his mob. The Sultan hastily served up the Grand Vizier Ibrahim to the bowstring, but he was soon deposed himself, and returned to the Cage in favour of his nephew, Mahmut I, who was girded with the sword of Osman on 1 October 1730. For several months Patrona wielded immense power, stumping into the palace every morning while the elegant functionaries of the court waited, cowering, and the janissary rolls leaped from 40,000 to 70,000 men. Patrona stuck to his rags and common ways for longer than anyone had expected; but power did finally go to his head. When he demanded to have a butcher who had once lent him money appointed Hospodar of Wallachia his charisma shrivelled up. He lived a few days more, and then was ambushed in the palace by men who had despaired at last of his ability to rectify the system.

The Ottomans were a very swaggering people, like Texans of the old school, and their Ottoman sense of caste remained singular, as ever. No longer drawn from peasant stock, but from boys to the manner born, the ruling class became fiercely insular. Nothing could dent their pride. They supposed that everything in their empire was not only bigger, but more harmonious and more interesting than elsewhere. 'The hosts of the Padishah are the most powerful force in the world; but unfortunately they do not have enough to eat,' a visitor was told at the beginning of this century. A near-unbroken series of defeats at the hands of infidels suggested, to subtler minds, the possibility that something might be learned from them (in 1805 the Ottoman ambassador to France was writing sniffily, 'I have not yet seen the Frangistan that people speak of and praise'), but the open expression of curiosity was considered bad form, like the invasion of the harem, and Urquhart noticed that whereas the Greeks would rush at you with such eagerness for news that they asked the question in three languages in a single breath – 'Ti mandata – ti chaberi – ti nea?' – the Turks maintained a measured *politesse*, and waited to be told a thing before they asked. The kapikullari preferred to find the reasons for failure in some unwonted deviation from the old routine. Again and again they grappled with these abuses; matters improved; vigilance relaxed; and the same abuses increased a hundredfold, and had to be repressed with greater effort, until at the very last the system cracked, like a piston head.

Until then, though, all the cabals, factions, rivalries and bitter jealousies that seemed to rend the kul from top to bottom and from side to side were only the feuds that might plague any old and very haughty family. 'Give me the seal, you foolish boy!' roared the Chief Black Eunuch in a moment of crisis; and the hapless Grand Vizier of the moment, a man, one would have said, of eminence and age, meekly gave way as one might to a terrifying and wrinkled mother-in-law.

They possessed, *contra mundum*, all the dignity of an old family. Louis XIV's ambassador sought an audience with the Grand Vizier to inform him of his master's victory over the German princes of the Rhine. Old Koprulu, the Grand Vizier, withered him with this reply: 'What does my master care, if the Dog worry the Hog, or the Hog the Dog, but that his Head is safe?' Louis XIV received the same kind of dusty answer from the Ottoman ambassador at his court; for when he condemned the attitude of the Dutch, who had lately overthrown their prince, his ally, 'we Ottomans,' the ambassador said, 'are accustomed to overthrow our princes.'

French hauteur – which froze the assembled diplomatic corps of all Europe – broke like foam on the granite pride of the Ottomans, who maintained their French friendship with excruciating magnanimity, and proffered them the trade concessions, called Capitulations, which they so ardently desired. The French, of course, were more used to handing out this kind of treatment themselves. The French ambassador in the days of Mehmet III had to be carried, raving, from Istanbul, and died in an asylum in Sévigny, victim of his own unbending sense of decorum. The outgoing ambassador had left him a memo on protocol in which he playfully recorded that he had done what no man, native or foreign, had ever done, and carried a blade into an audience with the Sultan. In point of fact it was no more than a tiny dagger, almost a toy, which he had carried in his hose; but his successor was not aware of this. Naturally he was not about to retreat from a privilege accorded thereby to his master the King of France; but when he turned up at the palace wearing his sword and refused to disarm, he was turned away; and no amount of bluster, argument, persuasion and beseeching was of any avail. For several years he lived on in Istanbul, worrying at the point, unable to meet the Sultan, until his mind finally gave way.

But the British ambassador Porter would have advised him to steer clear of the whole thing: the reception of ambassadors struck him as so humiliating that he could only suppose that nobody had ever dared mention it to their respective governments before, and force a change in proceedings. In fact Venetian reports since the fifteenth century had talked of little else, and Porter was merely one of the first ambassadors conscious of his country's swelling power *vis à vis* the fading grandeur of the Porte. His Britannic Majesty's Ambassador found himself crammed into a waiting room 'fit for a Polish Jew'; in the second court of the Seraglio he was asked to wait on a rain-soaked bench, and when he finally reached the audience chamber the Sultan sat at an angle to him, and all the talk was conducted with a Grand Vizier. He was obliged to sit again, for hours, while a divan of which he could not follow a word took place. Mounted at last and ready to head for home, he found himself obliged to wait in the saddle while the Grand Vizier, and all his retinue, assembled and proceeded to ride out first.

From the seventeenth century the empire went into its shell. It went its own way, and maintained its proud ignorance of the West as the manners and mores of the two Europes diverged. Each supposed itself, for lack of better evidence, superior. The western powers made a point of their science, and quarantine stations were sniffily established all around the empire.* The great influx

* In 1995 fastidious Macedonian border guards made us trample up and down in a tray of disinfectant when we emerged from incorrigible Albania, under the eye of a man in a white coat.

of renegades was over: fewer westerners were willing to make the crossing and turn Turk; and the Turks themselves were far less willing to adopt them. The man sent to hunt down old manuscripts for Louis XIV in Constantinople had been taken up by one of the janissary regiments when his money ran out; it was hard to conceive of this happening now. It had been a matter of course to meet old janissaries speaking broken German, and every embassy took the risk of seeing a number of its men turn Turk – Wratislaw, for instance, saw a Cretan Italian in his suite tear off his hat, trample it, cut it into pieces and fling the lot into the Danube, to signal his meaning to the Turks. Foreign experts were a rare sight now, and the Porte no longer demanded that they convert; on the contrary, it desired them to remain apart.

Although their hospitality was superb ('I am not an innkeeper,' a Turk would say if a traveller offered to pay for his entertainment, whereas Greeks tended to follow up a friendly visit by presenting a bill), at an official level the Ottomans came to mistrust the western powers, and felt an insult keenly. It was recalled that while the Turkish ambassador was introducing the French to the civilised pleasures of drinking coffee,* the French were landing a shipload of false coin in Istanbul, whose circulation caused an insurrection. Nettled pride made them spiky and unpredictable, and there followed 'a time hazardous for foreign diplomatists, when the French ambassador was struck in the face, and beaten with a chair; that of Russia kicked out of the audience chamber; the minister of Poland almost killed; and the Imperial [i.e. Austrian] Interpreter bastinadoed'.

In 1774, after their disastrous defeat at the hands of the Russians, ambassadors were exchanged to hammer out the detail of the treaty of Kucuk Kainardji. Much of the negotiation on the border, as it turned out, involved the meeting that was to occur. The Russian wanted an upholstered chair. 'Since we are not accustomed to chairs, disposing of an upholstered chair in this area is difficult,' he was told. 'This time, however, it has been arranged.

* Coffee replaced spices as the staple of Egypt's trade with the West soon after – the spices were carried by European ships around the Cape.

The chair . . . has been brought from the voivode of Moldavia on condition that it be returned.' Would the local Ottoman governor cross the river and escort the Russian over? No: he was governor first, broker of the meeting second; and in his gubernatorial hat, he pointed out, 'whatever time they desire to cross to this side is of no consequence to me. It is up to them.'

The ambassadors met on a raft moored in the middle of the river. The Russian had insisted on sitting on Mehmet Pasha's right; unable to overcome this, the pasha recorded that he had organised 'a subtle procedure by which outwardly there would be no perception of left and right', with the Russian seated in such a way that 'to those entering from the Ottoman side it appeared that the Russian side was on the left'.

Discussions over, the Ottoman ambassador was taken to a quarantine station, built of pine, he reported, with gardens, wallpaper and tiled stoves. His Russian escort, instructed to tell Catherine the Great what gifts the Ottomans had brought, so that she could match them, suggested that the Ottoman ambassador should not stay overlong in quarantine, but simply let them fumigate his goods one by one. Mehmet Pasha rumbled him, pointing out that no ambassador before had been quarantined. As he wrote in his report, 'The general says – "I speak out of real affection for you. Our empress is horrified at the thought of disease. Your acquiescence would please her . . ." He terminated his words with some Frankish cliché such as, "My friendship for you is joined to faithfulness and is beyond description." *He was unable to achieve his aim.*'

Ottoman pride was perhaps ridiculous because it was misplaced; but it was certainly real. The pasha brought before the conqueror of Egypt in 1802 was superb. 'I shall take care to inform the Sultan of the courage you have displayed in the battle, though it has been your mishap to lose it,' Napoleon told him courteously. 'Thou mayst save thyself the trouble,' he replied. 'My master knows me better than thou canst.'

In happier days to follow, the French emperor Napoleon III and his empress, Eugénie, spent a week in Istanbul as the Sultan's guests in 1862. The Empress was so taken with a concoction of

Symbol of the Ottoman ruling house

aubergine purée and lamb that she asked for permission to send her own chef to the kitchens to study the recipe. The request was graciously granted by their host, and the chef duly set off with his scales and notebook. The Sultan's cook slung him out, roaring, 'An imperial chef cooks with his feelings, his eyes, and his nose!'

The dish went down in Turkish culinary history as Hunkarbegendi, or 'the Empress was pleased'; but Eugénie never got the recipe.

23

Borderlands

By the eighteenth century the calcifying empire appeared encrusted with peculiar polities that had grown up in the vacuum of initiative, waiting in vain to be reorganised and digested by the central authority. They achieved a sort of ramshackle permanence instead, like eccentric lodgers in a rambling country house. There was the monkish republic of Athos. There were chartered Greek monasteries like that of St Catherine in Syria, to whom Mehmet the Conqueror, if not the Prophet himself, had promised liberties in perpetuity (the Patriarch had no charter when he found himself defending his right to a church in Constantinople, but he dug out an old janissary who had been present at the Conquest, and who backed him up). As late as 1755 under the very walls of the Seraglio there stood a row of houses which were finally slated for demolition to create a firebreak. All the owners consented, except an old lady who 'declared she would not part with hers; it had been a property in her family for several generations, and no money could compensate the infinite value it was of to her . . . The men in power cried out and abused her; but the injustice appeared too violent to dare take it by force; the house stood; and when it was asked why the sultan did not use his authority?

take it, and pay the value? the answer was, 'Tis impossible, it cannot be done, it is her property.'

While the Ottoman approach to her dependencies seemed characterised by inertia, the Ragusans, typically, moved on unassisted. In the late sixteenth century they were put to the squeeze by a shrewd manoeuvre of the Venetians and the Jews to establish Split, instead, as the major gateway to the Balkans from the west. Ragusa's response was to take control of the carrying trade, and for a while the republic possessed the largest merchant fleet in the world.* The Ragusans still maintained their merchant *plazzae* in every town of consequence in the empire, and still pleasantly mourned each execution in the city, performed by an imported Turkish executioner, but gradually they slipped from the Ottoman embrace. They remained so robustly oligarchical that in all 500 years of Ragusan self-government only one monument to a nobleman was ever erected, which in any case commemorates not so much a man as a moment. The Ragusans sent Nikolica Bunič to the Pasha of Bosnia, to refuse him a loan. The pasha, they reasoned, might kill the messenger; but he was no longer capable of threatening Ragusa. 'To violence you will reply with renunciation and suffering,' they told Nikolica Bunič. 'Promise nothing, give nothing, suffer everything. The Republic is watching you. There you will meet a glorious death, but here the land will be free. Be united and reply that we are free men, that this is tyranny and God will judge them.' The Ragusans had gauged the business with typical exactitude; and to mark Nikolica Bunič's martyrdom a small tablet was placed posthumously, instinctively hidden from the vulgar gaze, in the Hall of the Grand Council.

Napoleon finished off Ragusa as he had finished off Venice, though without quite the same relish. He never muttered of being an Attila to this republic, nor described its main square as the drawing room of Europe: in 1807 he had his decree annexing it to the province of Illyria read out by an NCO. Like Venice, Ragusa was tossed to the Austrians when Napoleon fell, but if Venice whirled with gaiety to compensate, the Ragusans replied

* And some of the largest ships, too, *argosies*, or *ragusea*.

with a spiny honorability which was not at all Venetian, but owed everything instead to the mountain codes that flourished at her back. The best families of the republic vowed not to marry or have children while under foreign occupation; and by 1918, when the Austrians were at last forced out in favour of the new Yugoslavia, they had all died out.

Up the coast the Montenegrins remained largely independent though the centuries, suffering Turkish rule on their more accessible lower slopes but rejecting it successfully higher up. 'We found the enemy so numerous', three Montenegrin scouts reported in 1711, 'that had we all three been turned to salt, we should not have been enough to salt their soup. But their army is only a pack of one-legged, one-handed cripples.' No one could conquer Montenegro; a big army would starve there, and a small one never stood a chance. Their men sniped from the rocks with carbines three yards long, their women triggered off landslips, and their children fetched ammunition and used their catapults. They made the Turks look clumsy, and the Albanians effete; they were all over six foot tall, preternaturally handsome, and they considered the cruellest jibe to be 'I know your people: all your ancestors died in their beds.' When the last of the Black Princes left in 1516, the Montenegrins entrusted their government to Bishop Babylas, partly because he was pious and wise, and partly because he was a terrific warrior. Their enthusiasm for Orthodoxy was unbounded, and in the eighteenth century they were far more prone than any other Balkan people to listen to the promises of Russian agents: being so remote, perhaps, the Montenegrins had a weakness for novelties. In 1493, with Cyrillic type brought from Venice, the first printing works in the Slavic world had been established here of all places, a mere twenty years after Caxton's; but quite soon they melted down the lead for bullets. The barrack-like palace they built for their prince in 1830 is called the Biljarda, after the billiard table which the prince-poet-bishop had brought up by mule train. In the late eighteenth century they were so smitten by all things Russian that they temporarily cast their bishop prince aside in favour of a dwarfish adventurer who persuaded them that he was none other than the Tsar Peter III,

Catherine the Great's murdered husband, come to lead them in an all-out battle against Muhammadan superstition. In 1766 they made him their ruler, under the name Steven the Small. The Russians were as embarrassed as the Ottomans, and there was general relief when in 1773 the Porte managed to get him poisoned by a Greek servant. With this exception, the Montenegrins continued to be ruled by the Vladikas until 1851, at first an elective, then a hereditary line of fighting bishop princes – the succession passing from uncle to nephew, since the bishops were celibate; in 1851 Dnilo II dropped the ecclesiastical title to marry, and was assassinated.

Until the 1970s, at least, there remained black-skinned Montenegrins at Ulcinj, descended from sixteenth-century slaves, for as long as Ottoman rule lasted nominally in these parts (until 1878) Ulcinj was a nest of corsairs – Moroccan, Albanian, Turkish and Serbian – who came in 1571 with the Bey of Algiers, to have a crack at Venice.

The Jews were sustained by a sense of destiny and loss. On their arrival in Salonica from Spain in the early sixteenth century, they had built themselves synagogues named after Castille or Catalonia, Aragon, Toledo or Cordova; and men who had saved their fortunes from the wreck, like Don Señor Benveniste, son of a former finance minister in Spain, founded schools and libraries, academies which offered courses in astronomy and mathematics and philosophy; and printing presses turning out philosophical, theological and religious treatises. Their style of cookery, their dignified bearing, the dazzling cleanliness of their appearance, the way they began a story – 'era'n buenos d'un rey', 'it was in the good days of a king' – betrayed their Spanishness. When a Spanish senator paid a visit to Salonica in 1904 he was naïvely overjoyed, not only to find himself prattling away on the street in his own tongue, but to feel, in his bones, so perfectly at home.

Salonica, though, had already failed. It failed, curiously, just as and when Spain itself had failed: there was a curious equivalence between the two empires, Spanish and Ottoman, whose sixteenth-century skirmishes for power in the Mediterranean and in Central

Europe seemed so pivotal, and yet so utterly irrelevant a century later. Both empires hit their stride at the same time; both seemed invincible; and yet they began their decline together from the seventeenth century and both became proud, weak and helplessly particularist. Between the two leviathans, like a midget referee, was Venice, whose bailio in Madrid was quite as busy as his colleague in Istanbul: her stock sank, too, as the protagonists lost their punch, and the avid spectators of the sixteenth century drifted out. If the modern period has a starting date, it might be the moment at which the political colossi of the Renaissance world bowed out: the Spanish Armada thwarted, Ottoman designs on Persia and Europe checked, and Venice declining into a backwater, far from the hungry adventure of the Atlantic.

So it was with the Jews. When the Ottomans took Crete in 1669 and finally drove the Venetians from their seas, that branch of trade, so useful to the Salonicans who dealt in Balkan surplus, dried up. Years of Ottoman rule had already sapped the community of much of its old sophistication. The Spanish Jews had grown rich with Spain, and mastered its heady rhythms; but the Ottoman Empire – after a few bright decades, in which Jews did serve as bankers, traders and go-betweens – had disappointed them. Some began to emigrate from the empire to more dynamic countries like Holland and England (Salonica had 40,000 Jews in 1660; thirty years later, perhaps 12,000). They were leaving a tremulous and disintegrating community, further from the pulse of Europe, larger, poorer and more inward-looking.

Jewish Merchant

But it was still lively. Messianic tremors ran through the Jewish community; abstruse rabbinical disputes divided them; and all over Europe the year 1666 was awaited as a turning point in the history of the Jews, the year, some believed, when the chosen people would be redeemed and the House of David would re-establish itself in the Holy Land. In 1654 Sabbatai Levi, the son of a Smyrniot commercial agent, arrived in Salonica bearing a document which proclaimed him as the Messiah. The troubled community welcomed him with a fortnight of feasts and processions, giving themselves over to a frenzy of joy in which Christians as well as Jews participated, while the Messiah sang love songs and danced about hugging the scrolls of the Law. Cooler heads arranged for his departure. In 1661 he could be found living in the lap of luxury, supported by a government official in Cairo, organising his marriage to Sarah, a Jewish girl orphaned at the age of six by Chmielnicki's Cossacks in Poland. Raised by nuns, she had escaped to Amsterdam, and from there, moving to Leghorn, she proclaimed that she was destined to become the bride of a new Messiah. She was beautiful and charismatic and a thorough reprobate. Sabbatai's reputation soared to new heights when they married.

In Smyrna on New Year's Day 1666, to the sound of trumpets in the synagogues and the acclamation of the crowds, Sabbatai Levi proclaimed the coming of the Saviour, and an end to troubles. Orgies and merrymaking replaced, for a short while, the feasts and fasts and days of prayer hitherto incumbent on believers, while the Messiah tossed whole kingdoms and empires to his followers. Orthodox Jews were outraged.

Eventually the Ottomans arrested him. In a personal interview with Mehmet IV, Sabbatai rather lamely agreed to 'turn Turk' and become a Muslim. His enthusiastic following evaporated; but some diehards shadowed their leader, and maintained such a perfect faith in him that they followed his esoteric example and embraced Islam while waiting for their Saviour's return.

Some years later Sabbatai Levi died in exile, in Dulcigno. The followers of his cult hung on. Over the years, as ostensible Muslims, they lost their Spanishness and spoke Turkish among themselves; but neither Muslims nor Jews would have anything to do with them. In well-hidden Salonican synagogues they maintained their esoteric Hebrew rites, as prone to argument and dissension as any cult, so that by the end of the nineteenth century about 18,000 of them, mostly rich businessmen and merchants, formed three separate groups. They never intermarried, but they did liaise. Every morning, right up to the Greek conquest of Salonica in 1912, seven men would stand by the city gates shading their eyes to see if the Messiah was coming up the road.

As merchants and go-betweens, the Jews were finally outstripped by the Greeks, who watched them like hawks – in Athens, well into the nineteenth century, Jews were permitted to stay in town for only three days ('God preserve you from the Hebrews of Salonica, and the Greeks of Athens . . .'). The Greeks were 'crafty, subtle and acute', travellers agreed; 'their bad fortune hath not been able to take from them . . . much natural Subtlety or Wit'. 'The Greek in his cups is lively, enterprising, and desperate, he is noisy and quarrelsome, he wants to fight, to kill, and to dethrone the Ottoman monarch, that he may restore the empire to the Christians,' recalled Elias Haneschi in 1784. 'I like the Greeks,' Byron wrote, 'who are plausible rascals, with all the Turkish vices without their courage. However some are brave and all are beautiful.'

Greek Merchant

There were Greeks scattered throughout the empire, not just in the Greek peninsula; they had been in Anatolia, of course, since ancient times, when Alexander's conquests had made demotic Greek the lingua franca of the Levant, the medium of trade, government and scripture. The later development of the Byzantine Empire had put Greek on a solid footing in the Balkans and across the Middle East; and under the Ottomans Greek was an administrative language, the language of power, like Ottoman Turkish; so you did not need to be born Greek to become, to all intents and purposes, a Greek yourself. There was a natural tendency to identify any educated Greek with a person on the make. With a desk job in the church or the government of the Principalities, Porter said, 'ostentatious pride, empty vanity, contemptuous insolence, acts of tyranny and oppression, attend their prosperity: Deposed, you see them dejected, pliant, base, grovelling, even to most abject servility.' A Greek doctor was only a Greek who could not wangle himself a proper job. Porter knew one who sold lion's urine as a cure for infertility; it was his own. 'Any common servant to a physician of any tolerable reputation, after a few years' service, were it only in beating the mortar . . . thinks himself sufficiently skilled in the medicinal art to stand on his own bottom, and kill by diploma.'

Athenian dress

Greeks succumbed to whirlwind cravings. Their devotions were sensual. The church kept them together as a people, with saints' days and services, ceaselessly celebrating deaths, births, weddings, baptism, forever edifying the language. Outside church they were frequently accused of irreligion, but the charge was unfair; they were capricious and changeable, and what moved them at one moment was tossed aside by the quicksilver shift from solemnity to merriment.

Just like the Montenegrins they were followers of fads, and possessed the enthusiasm which leads to trade, with 'a natural Dexterity in all the little Matters they undertake'. Sturdy moralists were driven to despair. 'They do not know the difference between good and evil,' snapped a sixteenth-century Athenian noblewoman; 'a people without religion, decision or shame, wicked and reckless, with mouths open for insults and reproaches, grumbling, barbarous tongued, loving strife and trouble and gossip, petty, loquacious, arrogant, lawless, crafty, inquisitive and wide-awake to profit by the misfortune of others.' But the Greeks didn't mind her peddling her prejudices; they weren't at all offended; and after her death at the hands of a Turkish gang, the Athenians beatified her as St Philothei, and made her the city's favourite saint.

The Greeks, after all, were a very broad community, entertaining every shade of opinion and embracing every layer of society. There were learned, religious and reformist Greeks, like the Patriarch Loukris, a Cretan, who attempted to establish a bridge between Orthodoxy and the Reformation. There were poor Greeks such as you see nowadays whacking octopuses to death on seaside rocks, prior to turning them inside out. There were very rich Greeks, in administrative competition with the Jews, who lived in palaces in Constantinople. There were Greeks of doubtful origin who lived in an atmosphere of Byzantine splendour and deceit, ruling the Principalities with archaic ritual and timid devotion to the Porte. There were Greeks who established a New Town for themselves in western Anatolia, with boulevards and theatres. There were angry Greeks, and complacent Greeks, shepherd Greeks, island Greeks, Albanian Greeks and Bulgarian Greeks, and above all there were Greeks of one sort or another all along the empire's coasts: in Smyrna and other cities along the Anatolian seaboard, on the islands of the Aegean, around the Peloponnese and the Greek peninsula. So they always had the sea, the very essence of caprice. By the mid-eighteenth century the Greek community in Marseilles was one of the richest in Europe; the French consul in 1764 believed that the Greeks had 615 ships and employed 37,526 sailors. After Russia and the Ottoman

Empire signed the treaty of Kucuk Kainardji in 1774, the Greeks were allowed to trade under the Russian flag, and they soon controlled the Black Sea, their dominance extending over all Balkan import and export, and across the eastern Mediterranean. The French felt the squeeze in the Levant. The British went so far as to call for their elimination, with self-interested venom, and also a certain righteous indignation – for the Greeks were a piratical lot, and some economists have suggested that Greek wealth was founded on capital seized on the high seas.

Greeks had the church: Mehmet the Conqueror saw to that, his arrangements for the Orthodox millet, or community, making the church a powerful instrument of state control. Ecclesiastics enjoyed state backing. By the sixteenth century the upper echelons of the church hierarchy were stuffed with men who had purchased their office and recouped the cost from those below – ultimately the hapless Orthodox peasant, paying his tithe. A Greek-speaking aristocracy of sorts developed around the Greek patriarchate sited in the Phanar quarter of Constantinople; and they proved very loyal to the authorities who put them in power. Entry to the club was reserved for Greek-speakers. The Phanariots were proud of their Hellenic institutions, and regarded themselves as heirs to the glories of ancient Greece. Prince Cantemir, the author of the *History of the Turks*, proudly sketched the amenities of the Phanar quarter, which included an academy, he says, where philosophy was taught in all its branches, in pure uncorrupted Greek. By the eighteenth century the Phanariots controlled five of the most important posts in the empire. They supplied the Patriarch, and the hospodars of the two Principalities, Wallachia and Moldavia. In the old days there had never been any special need for interpreters, since Ottoman officials themselves spoke a variety of tongues; but once the officials were selected from officials' sons, then Ottoman Turkish, Arabic and Persian were the only languages they knew, and foreigners were encouraged to make use of the imperial

Greek sailor

dragomen, or interpreters. Both the Dragoman to the Porte and the Dragoman of the Fleet were Phanariot Greeks.

The Phanariots monopolised these jobs, and also the dubious

Phanar houses

reputation that went with them. Foreigners and Ottomans alike tended to regret the influence of the dragomen, who effectively controlled the increasingly important avenues of communication between the Porte and the world beyond, and thrived in an atmosphere of hints, promises, bribes, and concocted misunderstandings: 'In Pera sono tre malanni: Peste, fuoco, dragomanni!'

Eleven Phanariot families provided the hospodars who were sent to squeeze the Principalities. The Patriarch and his underlings worked to bring the whole Orthodox world under Greek tutelage, so that the Pec patriarchate, re-created by Sokullu Mehmet as a vehicle for a relative, was suppressed after the Austrians cannily invited the Serbian Patriarch to enter their dominions (and their control) with 37,000 Serbian families. The Bulgarian See of Ohrid in Macedonia, though long since hellenised, remained autocephalous until 1767, when it was finally abolished. Old Slavonic disappeared from the liturgy: in 1825 the Metropolitan Ilarion set fire to all the Slavonic books he found in the old library of the Bulgarian patriarch in Turnovo; and the Phanariots squeezed Greek and non-Greek with impartial zest, demanding payments for consecrating priests, or saying prayers, or blessing a new church. Their power rested on the threat of excommunication, of course: which incidentally stoked the vampire legend, most Orthodox believing that the body of an excommunicant would not decay so long as the devil had its soul. Their theology was not very distinguished, but they remained such implacable foes of western Christianity that in 1722 the Pope was anathematised, for the umpteenth time, for the crime of wearing shoes embroidered with a cross.

The Greeks and the Ottomans were united in their dislike of the Catholic West. Venice wrested the Peloponnese from the Ottomans in 1699, but although she brought prosperity to the region she failed to win the hearts of the Greek population: Greek merchants complained that the wealth all ran into Venetian pockets, everyone resented the arrival of Catholic priests and Venetian attacks on the Orthodox church, comparing their plight with the freedom of worship enjoyed by their fellows across the Ottoman border, and the Ottoman army which invaded the Peloponnese in 1718 drove out the Venetians with the help of the local population.

Unfortunately for the Phanariots, their cosy arrangement with the Porte was disturbed by the rise of a rival vision of Orthodox power, one that was not quiescent and Byzantine, but martial and increasingly wedded to a classical vision of the Greeks. Soon after his defeat on the Pruth in 1711, Peter the Great had moved to bring the Russian church under his personal supervision, turning it into an arm of the state. His agents, secular and divine, began to circulate through the Sultan's Balkan territories, presenting the Greeks with the dream – which only the Tsar could realise for them – of a Christian Constantinople risen again, proud at least, if not necessarily quite free.

The Russians inevitably fanned the flames of mistrust, raising hopes they were not strong enough to fulfil, and fears which they had no desire to allay. In 1770 the Orloff brothers were sent to the Peloponnese to whip up support for the Russian fleet, but they found the Greeks less resolute and united than they had expected, and left cursing their greed and inertia. The Peloponnesians, for their part, had expected to see more men and ships, and felt betrayed. The much-vaunted rebellion went off at half cock: several thousand Greeks took up arms and managed to seize Navarino, but the Russians had by then lost interest in the project. The Ottomans, of course, were thoroughly alarmed. The Ottoman governor was only able to quash the revolt by calling in the Albanians, who cheerfully set about massacring the population until they were ejected by an Ottoman army in 1779.

The treaty of Kucuk Kainardji in 1774, which the Tsarina understood to place 'Orthodoxy under our Imperial Guardianship in the places whence it sprang', extended Russian protection to Greek shipping; and the Philiki Hetaira, a secret society devoted to the overthrow of Ottoman rule in the Balkans and the cause of Greek independence, was founded in the Russian Black Sea port of Odessa in 1814, moving to Constantinople, with Russian consular aid, in 1817. Phanariots were divided. It was a Phanariot officer, Alexander Ypsilantis, serving as aide-de-camp to the Tsar, who led a Greek raid on Bucharest and Jassy in 1821, hoping to light the fires of rebellion. His raid was a dismal failure; the rebellion failed to ignite; and Ypsilantis fled to Austria; but the fear it inspired in Constantinople provoked a Muslim backlash against Greek establishments in the city; despite the refusal of the Grand Mufti to sanction any action against the Greek community, the

Sultan himself was convinced of his patriarch's involvement in the insult.

The tragedy of the Phanariots is encompassed in the life and death of Patriarch Gregory. In the midst of the anti-Greek rioting, Gregory anathematised Ypsilantis and his agents, reminding his flock of the gratitude they owed the Porte for preserving the faith from the corruptions of western Christendom. But the Ottomans hanged him all the same when his own brother, a Peloponnesian bishop, placed himself at the head of the rebels. His body was given to a group of Jews, who were told to cut it up and feed it to the dogs; rumour suggested that they sold it back to the Christians for 100,000 piastres, but it may be that they cast the corpse into the Bosphorus where, shortly afterwards, it bobbed to the surface. A Greek sea captain grappled it aboard his ship, before continuing on his way to Odessa with a cargo of grain. There Gregory was given a martyr's funeral, and became the very thing he had never wished to be, a beacon for Hellenic hopes.

On the Black Sea the Giray dynasty of Tartar khans – descended from Genghis himself – retained their sovereignty over the wild horsemen of the Crimea, whom they brought to campaigns in eastern Europe. Their loyalty to the Sultan increased as Russian pressure on them mounted in the eighteenth century. Now and then they might be unleashed against recalcitrant vassals such as the territories of modern Romania across the Danube, Wallachia and Moldavia; but the closer they identified themselves with the Ottoman military machine the more anachronistic they appeared. By the late eighteenth century the empire was run by subtle diplomats who were prepared to sacrifice them to Russia if it allowed them to pluck a treaty from the years of Russian intervention in the Balkans, and in 1774 the Porte gave the Crimea an independence it did not want. Russia annexed the peninsula ten years later, and gradually marginalised the Tartars in their own lands. Most of them left for Ottoman territory west of the Black Sea, becoming famous throughout the empire as messengers and guides; some 50,000 remained in the Crimea, but so far on the fringes of Russian patronage and society that in 1940 they greeted the Germans as their liberators, enlisted in their armies, and were ultimately scattered wholesale across the eastern USSR by Stalin.

The war that might have brought Moldavia and Wallachia into the narrowest orbit of the Ottoman system was never waged. The boyars proved very pliant, with Tartar prodding, happy to use the ceaseless Ottoman demand for sheep and grain as a means of enserfing their peasants, passing on the squeeze; while the Ottomans did not mind how the Principalities governed themselves, provided that they maintained the tribute payments and supplied the Ottoman authorities with foodstuffs at the stipulated price. Troops intervened, where necessary, to ensure successions, and punish laggardly hospodars; but the Ottomans maintained no garrisons in the country, and relied on the subjection of the people to the Orthodox church, and the subjection of the church to their own appointed patriarch in Istanbul. The rulership was sold off to the highest bidder every few years, so that the incumbent, who was always an Orthodox Christian, ground his people hard to recoup the purchase price.

Only when the native hospodars began leaguing with the Russians in 1711 were they replaced by the more biddable Phanariots of Istanbul, who pretended to a Byzantine style, but maintained the grind; so that the peasants, feeling the double standard where it hurt the most, devised a special cart, with runcible shafts, to be driven away in either direction at the first sign of trouble, and took to eating that dreadful maize mush, mamaliga, knowing it was one grain that rapacious tax officers would not seize, finding there was no market for it (like the Irish potato).

The way people were beginning to huddle together for security potently illustrates the collapse of Ottoman order. An intricate pattern in the lost Ottoman world had linked the borders to the palace, the centre to the sentinel; its subsequent caricature was the alliance between the palace bureaucracy and the fierce montagnards from Albania. The Grand Vizier Ahmet Koprulu was Albanian himself, and amid the faithlessness and opportunism of the empire's servants he had recognised the franker opportunism and loyalty of the Albanians – who were mostly Muslims, and whose oath of loyalty, or *besa*, was considered binding and final, so harshly etched was the mountain honour code, the so-called Law of Lek, by which they were raised. But a multitude of Albanians soon infested every major city of the empire – 11,000 in Constantinople joined Patrona's rebellion in 1730. Lady Mary Wortley Montagu, peering from her lumbering purdah carriage, fancied their soldiery immensely, in their gleaming white blouses. Byron adored them a century later, as much as they were detested by his Greeks – quite understandably, too, for whenever their luck ran out they would merrily sing that they had their 'musket for vizier, and their carbine for pasha', and go off to terrorise their neighbours. They were especially dangerous to the Greeks, whose various rebellions from the last quarter of the eighteenth century they were detailed to quash; a task they performed in a leisurely way, cheerfully describing Missolonghi – the longest and bloodiest affray of the last Greek rebellion in the 1820s – as their bank.

It was as if the Albanians, infesting every city in the empire, or the 20,000 Moroccans in Cairo, or the 200,000 Crimean Tartars who from 1774, pressed by the Russians, came pouring into the Dobruja west of the Black Sea, were hoarding themselves. The eighteenth century saw a rush to the cities, a flight from the land, and a staggering drop in the population – in the Balkans from perhaps 8 million in Suleyman's day to 3 million by the 1750s. In times of trouble huge numbers made the Haj to Mecca, suffering the predations of the Bedouin; efforts to drive them away from the Syrian desert marches, and the Yörük and Kurdish nomads further towards them, came to nothing. Bosnian Muslim colonists in Hungary started to pull back into safe Ottoman territory, where they proved very independent; Serbs began moving north into the Habsburg Empire, where they proved rather pliant. The Austrians employed them as border warriors. The Russian invasion of the Principalities in 1736 sparked a peasant exodus over the Habsburg border which persisted with the resumption of Phanariot rule three years later: Mavrocordato, the Prince of Wallachia, ushered in all manner of liberal reforms in the 1740s, but for the peasantry the liberal extension of freedom was combined with the liberal extension of insoluble debts, and amounted to the same slavery as the naked oppression of the past. As for the eternally ruthless boyars and the court, the experience of abandoning one style, Byzantine, anachronistic, exploitative and avowedly corrupt, in favour of a flirtation with the *philosophes*, modern, Frenchified, exploitative and corrupt, did nothing to improve their world standing, and gave rise to the old jibe that the Romanians are not a nation but a profession.* So when the Russians came again in 1769, 1774 and 1812, with higher hopes and fancier propaganda, perhaps 200,000 Bulgars crossed the Danube to join them.

The Ottomans always found it harder to impose their system on co-religionists. They could do little more in the eighteenth century than send out governors and garrisons, and make judicial appointments; Egypt and Algiers, Syria and Tunisia, stuck to their old ways, at best supplying the empire with a fixed sum in tribute, but more often in default. In Tunisia, the tradition of a peripatetic ruler, the Mahalla, was so entrenched and efficient that the Ottomans appointed a governor to Tunis, and a Bey of the Camp to supervise the interior. Mecca kept its sherif. The Egyptian Mamelukes continued to recruit from the slave markets of the Caucasus. Long before the janissaries of Constantinople grew corrupt, the corps was going its own way in the Middle East: in 1577 the Porte complained to the governor of Damascus that janissary vacancies were not being given 'to good capable young men from Rum, following my command, but to rich and favoured natives and foreigners', and by 1659 the governor was obliged to look on while the local janissaries and a task force from the capital slugged it out for power in the streets. In Tunisia, the vacancies went to Turkish half-castes; in Algeria, on the other hand, the Turks were so isolated that they continued recruiting troops from the Levant – Smyrna especially – until the nineteenth century.

But even a city as close to the seat of Ottoman power as Aleppo, and as important to its caravan routes, had to be governed with

* Later reinterpreted to cover the hordes of Romanian (and often gypsy) violinists who serenaded European restaurant goers in the 1920s and 1930s, and are back again at last.

tact and flexibility. Thirty miles beyond the city boundaries the untameable Bedouin roamed the fringes of the desert: they were kept in check, where possible, by a so-called Prince of the Arabs – as prickly and demanding as any of his fellows, but ideally more powerful – appointed by the governor. Within the city, lacking any real military clout, the governor worked through a divan made up of local notables – financiers, concessionaires, tax farmers, landowners and members of the powerful ulema. On the streets, too, he had to hold the ring between sherifs and janissaries, who brokered power. The sherifs were all theoretically descendants of the Prophet, and one of their tasks was to keep the family records: their numbers seemed to swell, however, whenever their power was threatened by the janissaries, who as everywhere else had become a hydra of privilege among the ordinary artisans of the city. By his handling of this ancient rivalry the governor was not only enjoined to keep the peace, but also to recoup the hundreds of thousands of piastres he had shelled out to receive the appointment in the first place, in the knowledge that after a year at best another well-greased palm in Constantinople was likely to secure his replacement.

With the decline of the Ottoman navy in the seventeenth century, and the effective retreat from the western Mediterranean, the North African coast grew increasingly independent, and its rulers, always happy to celebrate a distant Ottoman victory in Europe, or to send congratulations on the birth of an Ottoman son in the most grovelling and acceptable style, blandly ignored orders that flooded out of Istanbul. Of course Islamic loyalty counted for something. In the sixteenth century the North African Moriscos, forever dreaming of Andalusia, were delighted to see the Ottomans engage in their naval struggle with the Spaniards, and however politically independent they became, the people of North Africa were glad of Ottoman victory, and proud of their association with Islam's spearhead. A Damascene diary records the grand prayers offered up on Mount Qasiyun in December 1667 for the victory in Crete: prayers for the Sultan, the Pasha, his retinue, and the soldiers of the faithful, 'a grandiose affair and a day the like of which was never seen . . . I think that among the inhabitants of Damascus only a hundred or so . . . didn't go onto the mountain, being handicapped or bakers. Despite that, I heard that most of them prayed themselves, too, for victory and conquest.'

When Selim took the keys to the Holy Cities in 1517, and pledged himself and his successors to the protection of the Haj, he appears to have inherited the mantle of Caliph as well; but there is nothing to show that either he or his son took the title very seriously. It was technically in abeyance, and if anything it was applied to the Ottoman sultans as a complimentary gesture, *ex officio*, to the man who best embodied Islam's hopes, and whose overweening military success lent credence to the faith. Most of the world's Muslims performed the entire pilgrimage under Ottoman jurisdiction, and as the great caravan crossed the deserts it followed the Ottoman imperial camels which went out each year; drank water provided by the Ottomans; and relied on the organisational abilities of the Ottoman governor of Damascus, who devoted three months to it every year. Only much later, when sultans were losing ground and subjects to the infidels, did the caliphal claims come into play; and it was the Russians, filching the Crimea from the Ottomans in 1774, who tossed the Sultan this dubious compensation, and wrote it into their treaty.

'Your slave has been brought up under the shade of your empire,' Muhammad Bey of Tunisia wrote to the Sultan in 1855; but only on the occasion of proclaiming himself a sultan too.* Algeria had enrolled in the empire rather by accident, when the Algerians turned to Barbarossa for help and Barbarossa turned to the Porte; after Lepanto in 1571 it became clear that the Ottomans were not going to win the western Mediterranean and the relationship cooled almost to nothingness. The last communication of the Dey of Constantine with the Sublime Porte was also unusually humble: it was in 1837, and the French were poised to reduce his city as they had taken Algiers seven years before. 'The enemy of God marches on us . . . We do not have the power to attack without the help of God and the Sublime Porte . . . This land is

* The French, however, occupied Tunisia in 1881.

yours, these people are yours also, we are the faithful and obedient servants of your Imperial majesty,' added the Bey in desperation: it must have been the first the Sultan knew of it.

Egypt proved very hard to keep under control, although its grain and revenues were so important to the empire. The Mamelukes, largely Circassian slaves recruited into the administration and army, continued the recruitment system devised by Ibrahim Pasha in the 1520s; by the start of the seventeenth century the Mameluke beys were powerful enough to depose Ottoman governors, and only dissunion and rivalries allowed the Porte to regain a measure of control later that century. Even then, Mameluke weakness tended to enhance the power of the local military. When an Ottoman pasha was deposed and imprisoned by the leading bey in 1740, the Porte insisted on his reinstatement. 'A watery command', as the Ottomans said themselves: when the beys held firm, they sent a replacement, Ali Pasha, who had served as Grand Vizier in Constantinople. His emollient address before the court which heard the reading of the firman confirming his investiture ran:

> I have not come to Egypt to sow discord between the emirs, nor dissension among the inhabitants. My mission is to safeguard everyone's rights. The Sultan, our master, has ceded me the territory of this country – and I in turn make it over to you. Only, do not make difficulties for me in the paying of dues.

24

The Auspicious Event

On 7 April 1789, fifteen years after the disastrous treaty of Kucuk Kainardji had opened the way to Russian intervention in Ottoman affairs, Sultan Abdulhamid I died of a stroke, and was succeeded by his nephew Selim. Selim had spent his life in Cage confinement like all other sultans, but he had been allowed an education (his musical compositions are occasionally aired today on Istanbul radio). His young cousins, Mustafa and Mahmut, took his place in the Cage, where they enjoyed similar freedoms; they were later to rule as Mustafa IV and Mahmut II. Selim had few illusions about the empire's glaring weaknesses.

By the end of the eighteenth century the empire's military prowess had dried up. Her existence was to be prolonged only by the reluctance of the Great Powers to see her carved up and delivered to their own enemies. At Tilsit, where Napoleon and Tsar Alexander met in 1807 to share out the world, they divided up the empire between them – unable quite to resolve the problem of Constantinople itself, which the Russians wanted as the capital of a restored Byzantine Empire; the French would only agree to this if they might have control of the Dardanelles. Within a few years the French would have burned Moscow, and Russian guns would have laid Paris open, while 'the house of Othman proceeded to complete its fourth century of unbroken dominion at Constantinople'.

The empire in those Napoleonic years was tugged into strange alliances: now with the Russians, now with the French. In 1798 a joint Russo-Ottoman fleet sailing to assist France's enemies on the Italian coast produced the sublime spectacle of the forces of the Russian Tsar and of the Sultan-Caliph co-operating in support of the Pope. In 1805, with the aid of the British, Ottoman troops landed all along the Syrian coast and retook Acre. In Serbia in 1810, they allied with the reaya, the Christian peasantry, against the janissaries. In 1826 they called in the Egyptians to quell the nationalist rebellion in Greece.* In every one of these encounters, their allies praised the fighting spirit and martial qualities of the Ottoman troops, disparaged their commanders, and despaired of their training, organisation and equipment. 'They march in heaps, fight without order,' Rycaut had noticed in 1699; Napoleon called them 'an Asiatic rabble' and, when not seeking their help, was content, as at Acre, to have his Ottoman prisoners led out to a field and shot. And when the British were threatening to sail up the Dardanelles to impress upon the Porte the desirability of not acting with the French in 1805, the reaction of the French adviser in the city was to sort out the ordinance in the Bosphorus forts, while the Ottoman vizier had the forts painted very white, to give his enemies the impression that they were all newly fitted up.

Selim called up a sheaf of memos on the origins of his state's decline, and reopened the old correspondence with the King of France. Not every effort towards reform had been abandoned in the eighteenth century. Count Bonneval arrived in 1729, and in 1731 he asked to reform the Bombardier Corps. A school of geometry opened for him in 1734. It was soon closed down when the janissaries began to grumble, but it appears to have reopened secretly in 1759. In 1773 a new maths school was established for

* During which campaign, it is said, Ottoman gunners created the first cigarette, rolling the baccy in their touch papers after their clay pipe was shattered by enemy fire; and so bequeathing to the footsloggers of the world the supreme comfort of military life.

the navy, with the help of a French officer, Baron de Tott, and a Scots renegade called Campbell, known as Ingiliz Mustafa. One of Selim's first acts was to develop a new Artillery Corps along lines laid down by Baron de Tott. When the janissaries resisted all efforts to reform their training and discipline Selim developed, side by side with them, a New Order infantry who were trained by western officers, and even accoutred in European style.

The Sultan was neither a fool nor a coward, but he lost confidence when the leaders of the established army, with ulema support, rebelled in Edirne on 20 June 1806. The New Order troops were taken from their commanders and placed under the command of a rebel, Alemdar Mustafa Pasha. A year later the janissaries and the religious students of Constantinople stormed the palace, and seventeen New Order officers were handed over to the mob, who stuck their heads on poles outside the palace walls. Once again, the sacrifice was vain: on 29 May 1807 the Grand Mufti answered the rebels' demands with a fatwa deposing Selim. The unhappy Sultan was returned to the Cage in favour of Mustafa IV, who was already mentally ill. Once again the janissaries, true to form, went on the rampage through the streets, killing anyone still wearing the New Order uniform, and looting with impunity.

But two years spent with the remnants of the New Order troops on the Danube had swung Alemdar Mustafa Pasha round to Selim's orginal position on reform. On 1 July 1808 he marched his army into Constantinople, secured the city and, surrounding the palace on 7 July, demanded Selim's restoration. Mustafa had sufficent sense to secure himself as the sole surviving male of the House of Osman: Selim, after a furious struggle, was stabbed to death by the Chief Black Eunuch and his men in his mother's apartment. When Alemdar forced his way into the second court of the palace bellowing for Sultan Selim, he was met by Mustafa, coldly commanding his men to show the *seraskier* the body. Mustafa must have supposed, by then, that his brother Mahmut too had been murdered on his orders; but when Alemdar's soldiers had seized Mustafa the youth emerged from his hiding place. The Grand Mufti was persuaded to issue a fatwa deposing Sultan

Mustafa, and Mahmut II, aged twenty-three, was proclaimed Sultan.

Not for eighteen years was Sultan Mahmut II in a position to deal with the open scandal of the janissary corps. For years he had been quietly appointing loyal men to high office; the janissary aga was one of his supporters, and a troop of artillerymen, some 10,000 strong, had been raised independently of the janissaries, and drilled along western lines. In eighteen years Mahmut had managed to break the power of the overweening barons of Anatolia and the Balkans by exploiting a series of fortuitous deaths, a rash of family quarrels, and judicious force: the heads of Ali Pasha of Albania and his sons were being displayed in a neat circle at the gate of the Seraglio.

Alemdar, his liberator, champion and first Grand Vizier, had not lasted very long. In November 1808, barely five months after his dramatic entry into the capital, Alemdar fell victim to janissary wrath. He had attempted to reinstitute Selim's army reforms by creating yet another modern army, the so-called Segbani Cedit. Besieged by the janissaries in the Porte he retired to a powder magazine which exploded with massive loss of life, Alemdar's included. The Segbani Cedit held off the rebels from the Topkapi, with the support of the navy, whose erratic firing from ships on the Golden Horn did little to cool the rebels' ardour, but started house fires which swept through the city, killing thousands. Supported by the angry mob, the janissaries put the palace under siege, stopping the water supply. In this crisis, Mahmut had Mustafa strangled, as Mustafa had so recently had Selim stabbed to death. At length, as the last living Ottoman prince, Mahmut signed an agreement with the janissaries, mediated by the ulema, which allowed him to keep his throne in return for disbanding the Segban Cedit. Despite guarantees of safe conduct, these loyal soldiers were hacked to pieces as they left the palace, and various other notables who had supported them were murdered.

Upon the overthrow of Selim, and Alemdar's intervention, the ulema had largely supported the janissary reign of misrule, preferring conservative anarchy to innovation and reform; but by 1826 the janissaries had managed to alienate these powerful allies, and even the common people of the capital were against them. The janissaries robbed shopkeepers. They extorted protection money. They opened their own shops and forced suppliers to bring them stock at ridiculously low prices. They muscled in on respectable trades and turned them into rackets, delivering a hundred bricks for the price of a thousand. They respected nobody. They spread their cloaks on the ground at Easter and made Christians pay to walk across them. They sang obscene songs to the guitar as the Friday procession to the mosque passed by, and robbed the kadi of Istanbul. Janissary watchmen set fire to houses, looted them and raped the women. In the countryside they descended on villages like brigands. Above all, they were quite incapable of fighting, even when the battle was not being waged against modern armies, but against infidel rebels in Greece.

The long struggle with the Greek rebels at Missolonghi, begun in 1822 and brought to an end in 1826, was the culmination of forty years of Balkan repression and misrule. The Serbs, under Kara George, had been the first nation to raise the standard of revolt in 1804, though theirs was, at least initially, sponsored by the Ottoman government, which had lost control of Serbia to a janissary junta stationed in Belgrade. The idea of rousing the nations of south-eastern Europe to break from Ottoman rule had sprung up everywhere in the final quarter of the eighteenth century – among admirers of the French Revolution of 1789, among Philhellenes like Byron, and principally in Russia, where the court had long cherished the hope of creating an Orthodox empire under Russian tutelage, and perhaps even of restoring a Russo-Byzantine empire in Constantinople. Catherine the Great had gone so far as to have her grandson, Constantine, tutored in Greek and groomed for the office of Byzantine Emperor as soon as the Greeks should demand him. In 1771, however, a Russian attempt to trigger off a rebellion in Greece fell apart amid recriminations and reprisals: the Greeks had failed to fight, the Russians had failed to support them, and after thousands of Muslims had been slaughtered the Russians backed off, and left the Greeks to the tender mercies of Albanian irregulars.

The Napoleonic Wars, in which the Porte was harried from one unsuitable alliance to another, saw the empire's extremities twisted and wrung by all the powers in combat. Egypt suffered a French invasion in 1798; and when Mehmet Ali finally beat off the French, the British showed signs of meaning to replace them. Part of the Dalmatian coast fell under French suzerainty; and the Ionian islands, in the western Aegean, remained British protectorates for fifty years.* The Russians invaded the Principalities, and gave great encouragement to the Serbian rebels, who were able to pluck a promise of autonomy from the peace concluded in 1812. Revolutionary aspirations – for glory, for country, for equality – were spread abroad by the belligerents' propaganda; and local rebellions were increasingly marked by nationalism. Greek aspirations resurfaced. The Hetira was the first of those shadowy organisations which were to thrive in the Balkans throughout the nineteenth century, of which IMRO, the Bulgar-inspired Macedonian terrorist organisation whose follower Gavrilo Princip fired the fatal shot at Sarajevo in 1914, was the most notorious.

The most impressive feature of Ottoman rule was its opposition to the thin inadequacies of national identification. The Ottoman system made no national distinctions; and truly there were few to be made with any clarity. Language was a very uncertain indication of nationality. The men of Koritza, for example, looked identical, lived in the same round huts, and wore the same blue robes though different groups of them spoke Greek, Vlach and Albanian. With Greek and Turkish the only official languages of the empire, you could easily find Albanian families in the capital who only spoke Turkish; notional Bulgars who had nothing but Greek. Race was meaningless. Southern Albanians looked more like Greeks than Albanians from the north, whose language they shared – and when the Greeks did achieve independence they adopted as their national dress the outfit Byron had admired as

* During which time they were governed by the delightful Lord Newgate, who founded a university in which everyone was attired in Attic costume, and who was to be seen in Pall Mall wearing purple buskins, yellow leggings and snow-white robes in the 1820s.

the epitome of Albanian elegance. Every man could be made, the Ottomans believed; the claims of nationality were merely spurious; and as a western observer drily remarked, 'one is tempted to believe that wherever there are three Bulgarians, two will combine against the third, and the third call in foreign assistance'.

Nationalism was a pretence, like the construct of the empire which it came to overthrow. As soon as nationhood became the cry, the principles on which each nation based its identity could be cobbled together *ad hoc* from a smorgasbord of history, religion, middle-class notions of propriety, brigand notions of honour, foreign intervention, Ottoman inanition, military audacity, energetic tyrants, slothful pashas, ambitious professors of philology, greed, despair, and ridiculous youthful heroism. The Albanians only developed a sense of nationhood by the skin of their teeth, mobilising a scratch army of philologists and forgotten national heroes just in time to prevent their country being completely overrun by Greece and Serbia shortly before the First World War. The Bulgarians took Ottoman architecture of the late nineteenth century and smugly recaptioned it as National Revival Style; and almost every visitor to independent Greece complained that the Greeks seemed to have grafted all that was tinniest about the West onto a residue of all that was underhand and disagreeable in the Ottoman world. Politics in the successor states was generally unsavoury; the peasants found themselves oppressed by law, not chance, as Urquhart had predicted; and a shoal of German aristocrats were drafted in, to rule over countries which could ill afford their style, among people whose language they could not speak.

It was Sultan Mahmut, though, who called in foreign assistance first. Egypt, it is true, remained in name a vassal state, and was ruled by a cunning Albanian, Mehmet Ali, in the imperial manner; but under Ali everything had changed, and by the 1820s Egypt was the most progressive and efficient state in the entire region. In 1801 Ali had rebuffed the French; five years later he repulsed the British; in 1811 he overcame the Egyptian notables and suppressed a fundamentalist Arab revolt in the Wahhab. The ulema were delighted: they had hated the infidels, mistrusted the

Mamelukes and resented Wahhabite control over the Holy Cities. Ali, though, went further. Egypt had been occupied by the French for three years, and French administration had proved startlingly efficient by Ottoman standards. With the revenues of a rich country nimbly gathered into his hands, and little to fear from Constantinople, Mehmet Ali had begun to modernise and westernise his country. The army he inherited refused to reform, and in 1823 Ali had turned, instead, to peasant conscripts, the Egyptian fellahin, drilled by French officers left behind after Napoleon's adventure. The national army – a wholly new concept in the Ottoman Empire – soon showed its paces in Greece, under his son Ibrahim Pasha. In 1825, as the struggle for Missolonghi entered its third year, Ibrahim landed at Modon in the southern Peloponnese, defying the prognosis of Greek seamen who declared that an Egyptian army could not hope to cross the sea in winter, and brought 10,000 men with horses and artillery to sweep up the rebels of the Peloponnese. In April 1826, having crossed the Gulf of Corinth, the Egyptians finally dislodged the defenders of Missolonghi – where Byron had died in 1824.

With that, it was reasonable to suppose that the Greek affair was over. Mahmut's tasks were now to deal with his overmighty Egyptian vassals, and at the same time provide himself with an army as modern and well-disciplined as theirs. In May 1826 the Grand Vizier, leading jurists and senior army officers meeting in the house of the Sheikh ul-Islam hammered out a decree which foisted a great number of reforms on the Janissary Corps. The Grand Vizier, himself a respectable old soldier, briskly described a corps riddled with adventurers and with Greeks, all of them afraid of war. Their faith, he added tactfully, was weak; in them the spirit of gazidom was dead; and they neglected the old laws of discipline. These were charges which the ulema themselves could support, and when the decree which stipulated prayers, discipline, regular training, punishment, pensions, systems of promotion, numbers and organisation of the corps was finally read out, with a rider that all evil or blind men who muttered or frustrated the Sultan's order should be punished, the Sheikh ul-Islam actually cried out: 'Aye! And severely!'

Drawn up in the courtyard of the janissary aga's residence the janissary officers, after an awful pause, surged forward to put their signatures to the decree, and swear obedience. As soon as the first reorganised regiment began to drill, the janissaries began to foment their inevitable mutiny. Various officers were with them, despite their signatures on the decree; and if they failed to revolt immediately it was because, according to janissary tradition, a revolt had to be signalled by the overturning of the cauldrons.

A month passed. On the night of 15 June 1826, three days before the Sultan had demanded that the janissaries should parade before him in western uniforms and to western drill, the janissary conspirators began assembling, in twos and threes, upon the Atmaidan. The cauldrons were lugged from the barracks and piled up. By morning a huge crowd had spilled out of the Atmaidan and various detachments of janissaries were prowling the streets, calling for blood. The Grand Vizier was told that they refused to perform 'infidel' exercises, and that they demanded the heads of the men responsible for the decree: by their pyramid of cauldrons the janissaries believed, it seems, that their mutiny was already successful. The Grand Vizier only replied that Allah would crush them.

Mahmut was kept informed of the course of events at his summer palace up the Bosphorus, and before long he was back in the palace, where the pashas and ulema together urged 'Victory or death!' The Sultan himself unfurled the black banner of the Prophet, while criers went out across the city, and to Pera and Uskudar, calling on loyal citizens to rally to his cause. It was hardly necessary. In the first court of the palace, a near riot had to be quelled by an equerry when latecomers discovered that all the weapons in the armoury had been handed out already to the medrese students.

The unfurling of the standard disturbed the janissaries, who sent a group of officers to negotiate the terms of a pardon while at the same time they moved to block off all approaches to the Atmaidan. The Grand Vizier dismissed the delegation; two cannon riddled a company of janissaries by the Horhor fountain with grapeshot. Fleeing to the Atmaidan, the janissaries moved back to their barracks *en masse* and barracaded themselves in, using heavy stones, and abandoning many of their companions still roving the streets. It cannot be known how far the rebels supposed the authorities would go, for no one survived the barrage of artillery which now rained down on the door of the barracks. Before long the building was on fire, and those who survived the shelling perished in the flames.

There were still many janissaries hiding out in parts of the city. Some are supposed to have taken refuge in the stoke-holes of the Constantinople baths, where they survived on food smuggled to them by stubborn well-wishers.* Some reached the Belgrade forest in a suburb of Constantinople, where long ago Mehmet the Conqueror had settled large numbers of Serbs during his repopulation of the capital. Loyal officers toured the city in disguise, pointing out janissaries for the executioner. The bodies of hundreds of soldiers were flung under the Janissary Tree on the Hippodrome. Part of the Belgrade forest was torched to smoke them out. Perhaps 10,000 men were killed on the first day. The city was placed under effective martial law, and on Friday 16 June 1826 the firman abolishing every vestige of the Janissary Corps was issued from the divan and read from the mimbars at noon prayers. Tartar cavalrymen were sent to the provinces, with orders to the governors to remove every cauldron from the janissary units stationed under them, as government property, and to chase the soldiers out of the country. Their very name was never to be mentioned again.

Janissary headstones, topped by the cocky turban of the order, were knocked over. Perhaps a thousand men were executed, including notorious criminals and rebel ringleaders, but the ordinary janissaries, on the whole, survived by keeping their heads down and looking for menial jobs. Addison found a couple of former janissaries, who had broken their silence, in a lunatic asylum in the 1830s, and many years later a former janissary was found living in Damascus, making walking sticks. He presented

* They allegedly composed the threnodies which can still be heard, the songs of the Men of the Stoke-Hole, the Kulhan Beyler, lamenting the great old days of janissary power.

one to the governor every year and claimed to be 150 years old. His memory of events was excellent up to 1826, after which he remembered nothing at all.

In return for their support the ulema were given a new mosque, the Divine Victory; the Sheikh ul-Islam received the former palace of the janissary aga; and the Bektashi dervish order was formally, but ineffectively, abolished. Historic tekkes where the dervishes assembled were converted into mosques, and their dervishes were either exiled or joined other heterodox movements. In the long term this may have been a loss to the Ottoman government, for Sufis preached, on the whole, a disregard for the manifest conditions of this world, and their influence was stabilising.

A further ironic consequence of the destruction of the janissaries, the so-called Auspicious Event, was Greek independence. The arrival of Egyptian troops in Greece had finally prompted the intervention of the Great Powers. Unprovided now with even the shadow of an army, the Sultan lost his navy, too, at Navarino off the Peloponnese, on 20 October 1827. After Navarino the ease with which the Sultan could be browbeaten by the allies – Russians invaded both eastern Anatolia and Thrace, and took Edirne in August 1829 – led inevitably to an independent Greece, established under western auspices in 1830; a Greek kingdom was proclaimed in 1833.

The episode set the framework in which the great Eastern Question was posed: Russia had always been seeking to move south, in her famous desire for a warm-water fleet – a prospect nobody else welcomed. Austria thought principally of protecting her own polyglot empire in Central Europe, a policy which would ultimately make Hungary and Bosnia into bastions of Austrian influence. But Napoleon's pretensions in the eastern Mediterranean, where the French hoped to capitalise on their old traditions of trade, had triggered Britain's fears for her overland connections with India. Both had come to perceive the potential benefit of a ring of client states, first in the Egyptian mould, and now in the Greek: states sufficiently small to be easily influenced, sufficiently multifarious to preserve easy checks and balances in the region, and sufficiently westernised to offer both markets and supplies to European commerce and manufacture. After the victorious Russian advance through Moldavia and into Thrace, it was Anglo-French intransigence that prevented the Russians from establishing an overt Balkan hegemony. In the peace of 1830 the Greeks got independence, Moldavia, Wallachia and Serbia were given autonomy, and Russia had to be satisfied with Bessarabia.

As the price of his own assistance to the Porte in Greece, Mehmet Ali of Egypt demanded powers which the Porte was unwilling to give, but powerless itself to resist. Along with his radical reforms of the military, Ali had modernised the Egyptian administration, encouraged the development of new industries, and confiscated Mameluke and vakif lands which the state then apportioned to the peasants, who were told what they were to grow, and how. Ali was chasing western markets, and he opened Egyptian society to the West, sending students to Europe, and creating a new, secular education system. His success gave Sultan Mahmut a powerful model to follow, until it almost seemed that the two rulers were engaged in a race to westernise the societies they controlled. Only Ali's Egypt, however, fitted the western, national ideal.

An Egyptian army under Ali's son Ibrahim took Syria and Palestine in the summer of 1832, and approached Constantinople in early 1833 to force Mahmut to accept Mehmet Ali's terms. The Sultan turned to the only other military power capable of resisting them: the arch-enemy, Russia. Russian troops occupied Constantinople in the spring of 1833, as the Sultan's protectors; Ibrahim was bought off with a treaty that left him and his father in control of the Middle East; the Russians wrung an agreement that closed the Bosphorus to foreign warships in time of war, to the alarm of the British and the French; and the entire episode set up reverberations of absurdity and dependence which were to echo for the remainder of the empire's days.

25

The Bankrupt

In an address to new medical students in 1838, the Sultan declared: 'My purpose in having you taught French is not to educate you in the French language; it is to teach you scientific medicine and little by little to take it into our language,' and it did seem that the Sultan had the power to sift even the language from the ideas it tended to express. After the destruction of the janissaries, Mahmut was free to institute reforms wherever he pleased. With his loyal bombardiers, he no longer had to fear the rage of the mob, who could be dispelled by the customary whiff of grapeshot. This drew the ulema's teeth and enabled Mahmut to start taking control of charitable foundations, something not contemplated since the days of the Conqueror almost four centuries before. Mahmut didn't actually dispossess these vakifs, it is true; but he put them on file and had their revenues collected centrally, as a first step. By the end of 1826 the only bastion of ancient privilege beyond challenge in the empire was the person of the Sultan himself.

But as Count Helmuth von Moltke, who in 1835 was brought from Prussia to train the army, pointed out, it was one thing to demolish the old structure, quite another to build a replacement acceptable to all the groups who now leaned upon the Ottoman regime: the ulema, the European powers, the restless minorities, the Muslims, the traders, the agriculturalists, the nationalists and the imperialists. 'It was indispensable for him . . . to clear the site before setting up his own building,' von Moltke wrote. 'The first part of his great task the Sultan carried through with perspicacity and resolution; in the second he failed.' It was hardly to be wondered at. Everyone had their own plans for the site, and the ramshackle and extended edifice of power seemed in retrospect to have hung together well, and housed its inhabitants more snugly than anything which succeeded it.

Von Moltke's contemporary Augustus Slade* put the case against reform: 'Hitherto the Osmanley paid nothing to the government beyond a moderate land-tax, although liable to extortions, which might be classed with assessed taxes. He paid no tithe, the vacouf [vakif] sufficing for the maintenance of the ministers of Islam. He travelled where he pleased without passports; no customs-house officer intruded . . . no police watched . . . His house was sacred. His sons were never taken from his side to be soldiers, unless war called them. His views of ambition were not restricted by the barriers of birth and wealth: from the lowest origin he might aspire without presumption to the rank of pasha; if he could read, to that of Grand Vizier; and this consciousness ennobled his mind, and enabled him to enter on the duties of high office without embarrassment. Is not this the advantage so prized by free nations?'

Certainly the Sultan's plans ran ahead of his subjects' ability to fulfil them. In 1821, when all Greeks were under suspicion, the Dragoman of the Sublime Porte was executed and the authorities looked about for a Muslim to replace him, in an office which had been a Phanariot perk since the eighteenth century. The difficulty was finding any Muslim with knowledge of a foreign language. For weeks the correspondence piled up, before the post could be

* Slade's critique of the *Tanzimat*, or reform, influenced the Young Ottoman movement of the 1860s and 1870s, along with the works of Rousseau, Adam Smith, Montesquieu and the Koran.

filled by a convert who founded a dragoman dynasty. Mahmut had to begin with schooling, which until now had been controlled by the ulema, and was narrowly religious; without openly challenging the medrese, he opened a range of primary and secondary schools with a secular curriculum, and a number of technical colleges to receive their alumni.

Westernisation had to be imposed against all the instincts of his Muslim subjects. Two generations of reform, beginning with Mahmut's uncle Selim, had produced a certain number of men with an understanding of western ways, or the enterprise would never have got anywhere at all; but von Moltke soon discovered how slender a resource they were. 'A Turk will concede without hesitation that the Europeans are superior to his nation in science, skill, wealth, daring and strength, without its ever occurring to him that a Frank might therefore put himself on a par with a Muslim,' he reckoned. 'The Colonels gave us precedence, the officers were still tolerably polite, but the ordinary man would not present arms to us, and the women and children from time to time followed us with curses. The soldier obeyed but did not salute.'

Mahmut II began to reorganise his government along bureaucratic lines, in an effort to replace personalities and old traditions with more anonymous offices and committees, whose voices were less powerful as a result. The Grand Mufti was pushed into an office and had all his fatwas drawn up by committee. The new schools were kept out of the hands of the ulema and entrusted to a Ministry of Education, while the legal system was placed under a new Ministry of Justice. Even the grand vizierate was abolished for a while, before its use as a pillory for unpopular measures was recognised once again.

Mahmut died on 1 July 1839, in the midst of the so-called Eastern Crisis: Ibrahim Pasha had defeated an Ottoman army in Syria, and Mehmet Ali had announced his intention of ruling Egypt as an independent sovereign. Mahmut's sixteen-year-old successor, Abdul Mecit, fathered the last four Ottoman sultans; he also forged the link between domestic policy and Great Power approval which was to dog their sultanates. In 1839, in return for the powers putting pressure on Mehmet Ali to accept a hereditary governorship of Egypt, he issued the Rescript of the Rose Chamber, a reformist charter which was proclaimed in the lower gardens of the Topkapi Saray to an audience of ministers and foreign ambassadors. It called for the abolition of tax farming, security of life, property and honour for all, universal conscription, fair public trials and equality for every subject before the law. It even dared to use the word 'innovation', which spelled heresy for the devout: had not the Prophet said: 'Every novelty is an innovation, every innovation is an error, every error leads to Hellfire'?

The foreigners swung into action: in 1840 the British chased Ibrahim Pasha from Syria and bombarded Alexandria. Mehmet Ali pulled his troops out of Crete and Arabia, accepted hereditary governorship, and died within months of his son Ibrahim in the winter of 1848–9. In 1850 his grandson Abbas Hilmi met the Sultan on Rhodes, and did homage to him. Four years later a crisis broke out in another region of the empire, when the Russians refused to evacuate the Danubian principalities which they had occupied in 1848. Mindful of Russian ambitions to control the Bosphorus and the Black Sea, the French and British joined the Ottomans in declaring war on Russia in 1854. The Crimean War was brought to an end by the treaty of Paris on 30 March 1856, making few changes to the borders and binding all the signatories 'to respect the independence and the territorial integrity of the Ottoman Empire', which was rather more generous on paper than the treatment meted out to another old-fashioned and limping empire, China, at the time. But China was not, as yet, the scene of superpower rivalries, nor entramelled like the Ottoman Empire by western economic demands, and up to her eyes in debt. The war, the costs of the *Tanzimat*, or restructuring, ushered in by the Rescript of the Rose Chamber, and Abdul Mecid's fancy for glamorous palaces and parties forced the empire into a series of ruinous loan issues on the European markets.

While Urquhart once met an old Albanian bey who seemed glad of a change, and was 'tearing out his eyes learning French', the reforms scandalised traditionally minded Muslims. The concentration of government power, along with the rising cost of living, when the westernised élite were expected to have dining chairs, and wear tailored clothes, and keep a carriage, made corruption almost irresistible. For pious Muslims the new dress code was not only an affront to taste. From 1829 only the ulema were permitted to wear robes and the turban – but the turban was a mark of a believer, and people passing in the street were no longer sure how to salute one another without risk of blasphemy. It looked, from the outside, more orderly; it spread confusion from within. Visitors continued to remark on the ineffable courtesy and apparently instinctive good manners they encountered – the practice of 'a gentleman to comport himself towards another gentleman, as in Europe he would comport himself to a lady' – but increasingly they found them only among the older Turks, less and less among the young, and hardly at all among the Greeks.

The political reforms themselves were sometimes well-intentioned, sometimes mere sleight of hand. Outside Istanbul, they were often ignored, or misunderstood, or just inapplicable. The idea of equality before the law, regardless of faith, made no sense in traditional Muslim terms, and merely brought authority into disrepute. Henry Holland had been glad to receive Ali Pasha's passport, with its terrible injunction, 'Do this, or the Snake will eat you', in 1814; he felt that, like Ali Pasha himself, it was irregular but practical, and it saw him through to Monastir; but when Edward Lear stuffed his pockets with all manner of official passports and letters patent for Albania in 1848 he soon discovered that almost anything would do, down to a 'bill from Mrs Dunsford's Hotel at Malta'. The more liberal institutions were constantly being short-circuited by the peremptory actions of the Sultan. Exile was the unfailing penalty for anyone who took to the letter of reform too enthusiastically, and failed to observe its peculiarly Ottoman spirit. A whole generation grew up, deliberately infused with western attitudes, but constrained to sort them, all the time, into the acceptable and the dangerous, to recognise instinctively which order was really to be obeyed, and which was but a 'watery command'. As Eliot put it, 'no reform is clamoured for which does not already figure in the statute book'.

As the empire opened itself up to reform it began erecting public clocks, in an effort to graft on what was punctilious and punctual about the successful West. These great towers stand as a symbol of Ottoman reform, lonely as lighthouses in every Ottoman city. Very often they were erected outside mosques, or across the square. They were ambiguous because they were built, for the most part, by the Armenian Balian family, royal architects, and their Armenian assistants; and something of the ambiguous relationship between the Armenians and the Ottomans may be seen in these edifices. For the Armenians then as now were a people without a country; the only Christians without a useful proximity to Christendom; scattered and industrious and frequently poor, debarred by their faith and customs from full Ottoman citizenship, but lacking champions abroad.

Of the Balian clock towers there are some which resemble minarets, several like pagodas, with decorated eaves, and others like campaniles. Some were made of wood, and others, heavy and fat, of stone, plonked atop older monuments like the Koprulu's Gate in Istanbul, or the fifteenth-century medrese at Merzifon. Often the clock itself resembles an afterthought, a round face in a square hole, or a sort of spiky mushroom which has grown up beneath a well-head, and driven the little canopy uncomfortably high. But whatever bits and pieces of the Ottoman heritage they appropriate, none of them really belong to it – least of all to the mosques which they so frequently shadow. They stand close, but still apart; rather in the attitude of a mute to the pasha he has come to bowstring.

The harder the empire tried to secularise time – to bring it up to date, and make it open and available to all – the more absolutely ordinary it became. There was always, as Bagehot explained of the British Empire, an impressive as well as an effective dimension to rulership: and the faster the Ottomans built clocks for their people, the more disputatious and querulous those people grew, and the louder the bells tolled for the Ottoman state. 'Oh, the Turkish time!' wrote J. F. Fraser in 1906: for it sometimes seemed that the measurement of Ottoman time proved nothing but its laggardliness, that it only pointed to a world slipping inexorably behind. 'The day begins with sunrise. That is 12 o'clock. But the sun does not rise at the same time every day. So the Turk – who happily has much spare time – is constantly twiddling the lever of his cheap Austrian watch to keep it right. Nobody is ever sure of the time. The very fact that the Turks are satisfied with a method of recording time which cannot be sure unless all watches are changed every day, shows how they have missed one of the essentials of what we call civilisation . . .'

And nothing more succinctly demonstrates the loss of cohesion, and the rise of the private man and the discrete institution, or better evokes the way in which an atmosphere of *sauve qui peut*, such as had only existed in an interregnum, became permanent, than the little *Almanach à l'Usage du Levant* which the British consul in Istanbul consulted on 9 December 1898. There he discovered that the Greeks were lagging a fortnight behind, and believed it to be 27 November. The Bulgars and Armenians agreed with the Greeks, but the Jews were well into their fifth millennium, the Muslims were living in the fourteenth century and the Ottoman government, too, although broadly quattrocento, followed a calendar which seemed two years out of date. It was the month of December; or November; or Kislev or Rejeb or Tehreni-sani. It was the 9th of the month, or the 25th, the 26th, or the 27th. On a Friday all the Muslim business of the city shut down: the Sultan went to the mosque in a landau,* where prayers were said in his name. On Saturday the synagogues were full. On Sunday all the Balkan races in the city – the Serbs, Bulgars and Greeks – and all the Franks on Pera, and the Armenians, too, attended their churches. But on a Thursday the Ottoman government itself was closed for business, French style. An almanac would be useful, thought the consul, 'to the Pasha and the Rabbi; to him who speaks Bulgarian and to him who speaks French; to

* Bravely, for he was sure he was going to be shot.

Turkish almanac

him who thinks that the sun sets at 4.30, and to him who considers that mid-day is twenty-three minutes past seven'.

The nineteenth century was not kind to the Ottomans. Their cities were muffled in a sort of greyness, which went unrelieved by pageantry and showing off now that the guilds were breaking up. The palace itself was less showy and more secretive, and the army, in drill khaki and kepis, rather less eye-catching than before.

Inevitably, people in the outer world began to appreciate what they were already beginning to lose. Men like Disraeli perceived a sort of political honesty in the empire, or at least a tolerant conservatism. French writers and poets were to remain fascinated by the Levant, perhaps treating it as a storehouse of emotions squeezed out from rational society, extremes of feeling and indolence; perhaps sensing, as artists might, their kinship with a world that maintained a rich inner life combined with material poverty and a total lack of influence on the world stage. But while a host of artists arrived to record, heighten, distort, interpret and refurbish the scenery, colour and costume of the East, more hard-boiled observers threw up their hands in despair.

By then you could say – as many did – that the empire was a rather ugly place, a pastiche of western styles. Its architecture descended to the gimcrack. The Stambouline, the black frock coat adapted from European dress in the 1820s, was a hideous confection: its tails were economically but inelegantly short, and its high round collar and tight sleeves gave its wearer the look of a struggling insect. When Captain Nolan, of the Light Brigade, considered the effect of French training on the cavalry, he found only that the Turks had lost the benefit of their old ways without mastering the advantages of the new: 'Buttoned up in close jackets and put into tight pantaloons the men, accustomed to sit cross-legged, and to keep their knees near the abdomen . . . are always rolling off, and get frequently ruptured.'

The fez, made in Austria to a design imported from Tunisia, was neither fish nor fowl: yards of muslin might have made it the basis of a turban; with a brim you could have turned it into a sort of Spanish hat; as it was, it was a truncated hybrid of both. The view over Istanbul was not improved when in 1888 a French company blasted a railway line along the Marmara shore, demolishing the great sea walls and slicing into the wooded lower gardens of Topkapi Palace. 'Alas,' said an old servant, 'in that grove of boxwood every Wednesday night the king of the jinns holds council. Where will he go now?'

But Topkapi, in whose harem labyrinth he had hidden from the murderous janissaries, had come to symbolise all that was crazed and rotten in the state Mahmut II inherited. When, at last, true power was his, he determined to escape the warren which, like the janissaries, had begun by expressing the Sultan's grandeur and had been smothering sultans notwithstanding for two hundred years. Angrily he compared Topkapi to the palaces of European monarchs. 'None save a rogue or a fool could class that palace . . . hidden beneath high walls, and amid dark trees, as though it would not brave the light of day, with these light, laughing palaces, open to the free air, and pure sunshine of heaven,' he growled. 'Such would I have my own, and such it will be.'

The sultans embarked on a frenzy of palace building: it was very expensive and it did not make them happy, for all of them dragged the terrible burden of their line from one palace to the next.* The Armenian Balian architects built every one, as they

Palace of Dolmabache

built the clock towers, too, and a mosque which was both Moorish and Turkish, part Gothic, part Renaissance and overall French Empire. Topkapi was finally abandoned for Dolmabache in 1853 – 800 feet long, with 285 rooms and the world's heaviest chandelier. Ciragan Saray (now a five-star hotel) was topped out

* All sorts of ceremonial and traditional accretions stuck to the Ottoman line as they rolled on through the centuries, including a number of curses: one at least uttered by a sultan on his own descendants.

in 1874. Yildiz Saray was a complex of pavilions and living quarters that were raised intermittently throughout the mid-nineteenth century. Kucuksu Kasri went up in 1856–7, a little rococo holiday palace by the Sweet Waters of Asia. Beylerbeyi Saray was commissioned by the burly, fun-loving Abdul Aziz in 1865. Sunshine and laughter eluded even him: he was deposed in 1876 and apparently slit his wrists with a pair of scissors a few days later, in Cirigan Saray, where the unfortunate Murad V – who briefly succeeded him – lived out the remainder of his days in imperfect secrecy: his death was officially mourned in 1884, but really he survived until 1904. By the end of the century the Sultan, his brother, had moved definitively to Yildiz, where he reigned among night terrors and revolvers; took coffee in a mock-up of a real street café whose other tables were staffed with his own bodyguard; and from which he only emerged when absolutely necessary, confining his Friday procession to a quick dash to a mosque especially built for him just beyond the palace gates.

Spending became an international issue. After the first Ottoman loan was floated in London in 1854 it was no longer the Ottoman peasant to whom the sultans had to answer for their extravagance. There were no janissaries now to growl at the dissipation of the court. Only the exigencies of the foreign bond market could check the lavish spending; and in 1875 the empire was forced to declare bankruptcy. In return for restructuring the debt, foreign parties demanded extraordinary access to the levers of Ottoman power and finance; they insisted on reform; and they warned the Sultan to take steps to control the situation in Bulgaria, where rebellion had slipped across from Bosnia, and was being furiously repressed by bands of irregulars, the notorious bashi bazouks.

In 1876 the theology students in the capital revolted, probably with the backing of a liberal ministerial party led by Midhat Pasha, darling of the reformers. Abdul Aziz was deposed by fatwa and promptly committed suicide* – a shock which the new Sultan,

* His body was examined by sixteen foreign and Turkish physicians, all but the doctor from the British Embassy agreeing on a verdict of suicide.

Murad V, well versed in European and Turkish affairs, with an interest in science and literature, took badly. Years of seclusion, and a partiality for wine, this mysterious death and the assassination of several ministers in cabinet by a Circassian infantry captain drove Murad over the edge. Within four months, in the midst of foreign war and domestic crisis, mad Murad had been returned to seclusion; and shortly before the noonday prayers on 7 September 1876 Abdulhamid II was girded with the sword of Osman.

Meanwhile the Great Powers convened a meeting in Constantinople, to hammer out an agreement on the integrity of the Ottoman Empire, and to urge as a corollary Bulgarian reforms. Abdulhamid appointed Midhat Pasha as Grand Vizier and on 19 December, to the boom of cannon, he proclaimed a constitution along Belgian lines, which undercut the conference entirely: it broke up a few weeks later. Midhat Pasha did not outlast it: when the foreigners had quit the city Abdulhamid ordered him from the country. The vaunted constitution produced an assembly – seventy-one Muslim deputies, forty-four Christians and four Jews – which met for the first time in March 1877 and was soon plunged into the crisis of a Russian war. On 20 January 1878 the Russians, having broken through the Shipka Pass, took Edirne. Facing muted criticism in parliament, Abdulhamid dissolved the assembly.

With that, the so-called Young Ottoman movement – inspired by a desire for a return to simple Islamic pieties, while recognising no contradiction between liberal democracy and the founding tenets of the faith – lost credibility, and largely withered away. The Sultan was forced to sign an armistice at San Stefano so disastrous for the Ottoman Empire, and so favourable to the victorious Russians, that Britain insisted on its revision a few months later at Berlin; but to even moderately pious Muslims, it looked as if Islam had been decisively rejected by the West. The Sultan was not invited to attend, and Bismarck, Disraeli and the Russian minister thrashed out a settlement. Part of Bulgaria, all of Romania, Serbia and Montenegro, became independent. Russia took control of north-eastern Anatolia, and received a massive war indemnity, the modern equivalent of plunder. At a stroke, the Ottoman Empire lost nearly half its territory, and a fifth of its population.

Abdulhamid himself survived this reverse: survival was his consuming passion. His opponents were driven into exile, bought, or locked up, while he took modernisation into his own hands. He recognised the benefits of science and education, just as long as neither became a tool against himself, and used the new telegraph, as Eliot observed, to full advantage: 'It is no longer necessary to leave a province to the discretion of a governor, and trust that he will come home to be beheaded when that operation seems desirable. With the telegraph one can order him about, find out what he is doing, reprimand him, recall him, instruct his subordinates to report against him, and generally deprive him of all real power.' It was hardly surprising that many country mullahs viewed the telegraph with deep suspicion, and argued fiercely against having the voice of Satan pass anywhere near their mosques. Sadly for Abdulhamid, the telegraph provided the revolutionaries with the means of delivering him an ultimatum in 1906; and the telegraph operators themselves – with eyeshades, Morse, perfect French and an unusually deep knowledge of the empire's affairs – were thoroughly disloyal.

Abdulhamid imposed a sultanic despotism on the people, linking the claustrophobia of the *ancien régime* with all the modern apparatus of security. *The Swiss Family Robinson* was banned because the Robinsons' dog was called Turk. An Ottoman dictionary of 1905 defined the word 'tyrant' as an American bird. Newspapers were forbidden to mention assassination: Empress Elizabeth of Austria died of pneumonia, President Carnot of France of apoplexy, US President McKinley of anthrax, and the King and Queen of Serbia simultaneously of indigestion in 1903. While Abdulhamid's mad brother, his predecessor Murad V, remained under lock and key in Ciragan Saray, the Sultan announced that he had died, and his name was never mentioned in the press – Murads I and II could not be referred to directly. Abdulhamid did away with all sorts of pomp: he would settle visitors down on the sofa beside him and light their cigarettes.

He was the first sultan to receive a Christian woman at his dining table. He spoke good French, although he craftily conversed with foreigners through a dragoman. So monstrous was his morbidity that he refused to hear Sarah Bernhardt when she came to Pera, because she mimicked death so well; and electric light was forbidden in the empire, everyone said, because he had mistaken the word 'dynamo' for 'dynamite'.

But it needed more than electric light to dispel the gloom. In 1898 the Turkish poet Tevfik Fikret portrayed the decay of Constantinople in his ode 'Mist':

> Once more a stubborn mist has swathed your horizons . . .
> Veil yourself and sleep forever, whore of the world!

To foreigners especially the empire seemed an enjoyably creepy sort of place. Queer tales abounded of abductions, of white slavery, pale hands glimpsed through the grilles which covered upstairs windows, persistent whispers of strange sights to be avoided on the Bosphorus on moonless nights. A whole class of literature sprang up in Europe to deal with the Unspeakable Turk: everyone wanted to hear about harem maidens, ravishings, eunuchs, and slaves with their tongues slit guarding abominable secrets. In that year of European revolution, 1848, a German traveller ferried across the Danube found Belgrade filled with exiles and runaways, its darkest alleys hideaways, its gestures conspiratorial and subdued. In Khimara Lear caught the tone perfectly, being introduced to a crowd of people crammed together in a big low-lit room. As they came forward to shake his hand, three or four 'gave me so peculiar a twist or crack of my fingers, that I was struck by its singularity. . . . I shortly became aware that I was among people who, from some cause or other, had fled from justice in other lands.

'Of these was one who, with his face entirely muffled excepting one eye, kept aloof in the darker part of the chamber, until having thoroughly scrutinised me, he came forward, and dropping his capote, discovered to my horror and amazement, features which, though disguised by an enormous growth of hair, I could not fail to recognise. "The world is my city now," said he; "I am become a savage like those with whom I dwell. What is life to me?" And covering his face again, he wept with a heart-breaking bitterness only life-exiles can know.'

Certainly savagery marked the Ottoman Empire's dying decades; the last half of the nineteenth century saw the empire, as it fell, reacting badly to an era of Christian triumphalism. This may explain the relatively low rate of emigration to the United States, and the generally high return rate.* As the borders were driven back, some seven million Muslims moved with them into the rump: Crimean Tartars down the western coast of the Black Sea, Circassians along the east and south; Balkan villagers and townsmen. Fears and jealousies quickened. No longer the complacent rulers of a docile flock, the Ottomans were baffled and afraid when the people rose in nationalist revolt. Massacre became the stock response to threat; the authorities made little effort to check the atrocities; and the frenzied blood-lust of the Turks in retreat is still a delicate subject. Excesses were committed by all sides; the arrival of Protestant missionaries, singing 'Onward Christian Soldiers', among the once-quiet Armenians alarmed the Ottomans into thinking that the process which had turned their Bulgarian, Greek or Serbian reaya against them was about to be repeated. The bitterness and betrayal spiralled into pogrom, and every rumour was magnified, every incident was taken for the whole truth; terrified peasants in arms became the butchers of thousands.

The Sultan was not above using circumstances to his own advantage. When it became clear that the western powers had no intention of letting the empire 'imprison' its minorities any longer – its western minorities, at least – he launched out on a new tack, by which he became Caliph of the Muslim world – vaunting a pan-Islam to match the pan-Slavic rhetoric of Russia. It was in this guise – a clever one, disquieting to the British in India, the French in North Africa, and the Russians on the Black Sea;

* One Hajji Ali, a Lebanese, did develop a camel corps in America for Secretary of War Jefferson Davis. He was known as Hi Jolly and his tomb, a pyramid topped with a camel, still stands in Quartzite, Arizona.

disquieting to his own domestic opposition, secular, westernised and progressive – that he became very friendly with the German Kaiser, an emperor without an empire. Much Ottoman state business fell into German hands, most of the Ottoman army was placed under German officers, and railways were built with German capital (except the branch line to Mecca, which was financed by subscription, and at that time was the only railway in the world built by Muslims, with Muslim cash).

The army eventually put an end to the pretensions of the Sultan Caliph. The army, of course, contained a very high proportion of 'advanced' types: scientists, linguists, mechanics, themselves related to businessmen and administrators in civilian life. It seemed to know, far better than the Ottoman government any longer knew, what values it stood for, and where to stand for them, too: it was predominantly Turkish, and largely modern in outlook.

In 1906 a group of Macedonian army officers mutinied in Salonica – a city which was to be lost to the empire within seven years. They called themselves the Committee of Union and Progress, and the first victories of the CUP were greeted with wild enthusiasm. In the capital Armenians, Turks, Greeks and Jews went about hugging one another, each filled with hope and fellow-feeling. The poet rushed out a sequel to 'Mist': 'A bursting brightness like the dawning sun', he wrote. In the autumn of 1908 elections were held again, in which the CUP won all but one of the seats in the Chamber of Deputies.

Some of the old grace died hard, even in an age of juntas and telephones. 'One district in Stamboul', H. G. Dwight recalled later, 'brought its voting urn to the Sublime Porte on the back of a camel. Five great fishing caiques, with their splendid in-curving beaks, their high poops gay with flags and trailing rugs, their fourteen to twenty costumed rowers . . . made a water pageant that reminded one of state days in Venice. . . . Near the head of the procession, led by an Arab on a camel, rode a detachment of men representing the different races of the empire, each in the costume of his "country". And later came a long line of carriages in which imams and Armenian priests, imams and Greek priests, imams and Catholic priests, imams and Jewish rabbis, drove two and two in the robes of their various cults.'

Muslim Turks, however, formed a scant majority in the Chamber: they had 147 seats, the Arabs 60, the Albanians 27, the Greeks 26, the Armenians 14, the Slavs 10 and the Jews 4. Within six months an Islamic backlash – with shadowy support from the throne – inspired a coup. It was suppressed when the CUP abandoned its civilian dress and marched the Third Army into Constantinople. On 27 April 1909 a hastily convened assembly voted to depose Abdulhamid. The Grand Mufti provided the necessary fatwa, and while Abdulhamid was dispatched to Salonica by rail his brother Mehmet Resat, who was enormously fat, struggled with some difficulty into the belt holding Osman's sword.

The presence of the army at the heart of Ottoman political life did not, however, prevent military disaster in the field. Italy launched an attack on Libya in 1911. A Balkan coalition of Greece, Bulgaria, Serbia and Montenegro launched an attack on the empire by invading Albania on 8 October 1912; six months later the Bulgarians were forty miles from Istanbul. Arguments over the division of the victors' spoils, though, prompted Bulgaria to launch a surprise attack on her erstwhile allies on 29 June 1913. The Second Balkan War was over in a month; Bulgaria was defeated, and Enver Pasha – military darling of the CUP – led an army to recapture Edirne.

The kind of government the CUP committee fostered was modern, populist, Turkish and authoritarian all at once. Women, for instance, were admitted to university, and Turkish was made the obligatory medium of every school. Opponents – traditional Muslims, linguistic minorities, sultanic reactionaries – were consequently imagined around every corner. More and more the CUP found it impossible to direct affairs through a succession of weak mouthpieces, and were dragged out into the open where the only solution they could offer to the doubt and confusion was an increasing intimidation, and the cloak of war.

Fairly inevitably, they brought Turkey in on the wrong, the

losing, side: the entire army was, after all, the beneficiary of Abdulhamid's pro-German policy, and Enver Pasha, one of the CUP triumvirate, had been trained in Berlin. The Austrian annexation of Bosnia Herzegovina in 1908 had pushed Russia, the Ottomans' most rapacious foe, into the Triple Entente with France and Britain. The Ottoman army was trained and re-equipped under Prussian auspices. The navy, which was very much less significant, had been run with British help; but the British were lukewarm supporters of Ottoman power, and at the outbreak of war they commandeered two ships on slipways on the Clyde, for which Turkish crews had already been sent out, and the money paid. A secret alliance between Germany and the empire was signed on 2 August 1914, and did not remain secret for very long. The war saw Ottoman troops engaged against the Russians in the Caucasus and eastern Anatolia, against the British on the Persian Gulf, in Syria and Palestine, against the Greeks in Thrace. It brought Gallipoli, that stubborn defence of Turkish soil against the Allies in which 100,000 died and which created, curiously, two resonant justificatory myths of nationhood; for Australians tend to date the crystallisation of a national consciousness from the death trap into which the British imbroglio led them, while the Turks fought for their homeland, and were ably led by Mustafa Kemal.

As the First World War drew to a close the empire slipped away. Mehmet V Resat died of a heart attack on 2 July 1918, Damascus and Beirut fell in October, and on 13 November an Allied fleet occupied Istanbul, by the terms of an armistice in which the Ottomans surrendered unconditionally.

The Greeks, who had come out on the allied side in time, were given control of Izmir and the Anatolian hinterland at Paris in 1919; by July 1920 Greek armies had overrun western Anatolia, captured Bursa, and occupied Thrace. British pressure prevented the Greeks from capturing Istanbul, which remained under Allied occupation, but the Ottoman government, under Allied auspices, was forced to sign the treaty of Sèvres in August 1920, which largely recognised Greek conquests and put the straits between the Black Sea and the Mediterranean under international control, like the Danube.

Whatever authority the Ottomans still possessed now withered. In Anatolia three months before, a Grand National Assembly of the Turkish nation had met and elected as president Mustafa Kemal Pasha, the military hero and the backbone of armed resistance to the Greeks. When Greece opened a new offensive in 1920 it was halted by the Nationalist army, and in 1922 Kemal led a rout of the Greek forces, who fell back in confusion on Izmir and took to flight. On 13 September 1922 Izmir itself suffered a catastrophic fire, and on 11 October an armistice was signed, leaving only Istanbul's status to be defined by a subsequent peace treaty.

The act of parliament separating the sultanate and the caliphate was passed on 1 November 1922, shortly before Sultan Vahideddin was informed that his office had been abolished. The caliphate was formally bestowed on Crown Prince Abdul Mecid Effendi, but two years later Turkey's capital was moved to Ankara, a republic was declared, and the caliphate abolished.

Belief in the empire had long since leached away when the First World War swept out Europe and ushered in our own century of dictators and massacres. The Ottoman Empire by then was one of the cobwebs; one of the crazy hopeless causes; and a new polity had arrived to take the shrunken place of an empire which had long since ceased to possess a rationale. In its days of greatness, the Ottoman enterprise had been conquest; its gift, by and large, peace and prosperity on terms familiar and appreciated by everyone. Even in stasis and decline it had preserved for the people of the empire at least some of the peace and some of the prosperity of former times; it had kept at bay some of the elements of modernity, maintained an appreciation of the old ways, kept up the traditional way of life. Dignity and honour flourished in their old circuits. Trouble was couched in familiar terms. The Serbs who walked barefoot through Kosovo in 1911 were matched by the Turks who reaped the corn and filled the byres when they marched through enemy lands at harvest time; and even the King of the Jinns held court, until the eleventh hour.

In 1896 Edmondo de Amicis walked down to the new steel-built Galata Bridge, where today the Turkish restaurateurs beguile you with fish and napery, and the traffic which is slowly reducing Istanbul rumbles overhead. Tourists peek into the fishtanks. A minion, staring vacantly up one of the great waterways of the world, cuts up another lemon. Now and then a tug, or a trawler, comes chugging up the Golden Horn.

There in 1896 de Amicis saw 'all of Constantinople pass in an hour'.

> A mussulman woman on foot, a veiled female slave, a Greek with her long flowing hair surmounted by a little red cap, a Maltese hidden in her black faletta, a Jewess in the ancient costume of her nation, a negress wrapped in a many-tinted Cairo shawl, an Armenian woman from Trebizond, all veiled in black – a funereal apparition . . . Then the Syrian, clad in a long Byzantine dolman, with a gold-striped handkerchief wrapped around his head; the Bulgarian, in sombre-coloured tunic and fur-edged cap; the Georgian, with his casque of dressed leather and tunic gathered into a metal belt; the Greek from the Archipelago, covered with lace, silver tassels, and shining buttons. From time to time it seems as though the crowd were receding somewhat, but it is only to surge forward once more in great overpowering waves of colour crested with white turbans like foam, in whose midst may occasionally be seen a high hat or umbrella of some European lady tossed hither and thither by that Mussulman torrent . . . Every tint of skin can be found, from the milk-white Albanian to the jet-black slave from central Africa or the blue-black native of Dafur . . . While you are trying to make out the designs tattooed on an arm, your guide is calling your attention to a Serb, a Montenegrin, a Wallach, an Ukrainian Cossack of the Don, an Egyptian, a native of Tunis, a prince of Imerzi . . . An expert eye can distinguish in that human torrent the distinctive features and costumes of Caramania

> and Anatolia, of Cypress and Candia, of Damascus and Jerusalem – Druses, Kurds, Maronites, Telemans, Pumacs, and Kroats . . . No two persons are dressed alike. Some heads are enveloped in shawls, others crowned with rags, others decked out like savages – shirts and undervests striped or particoloured like a harlequin's dress; belts bristling with weapons, some of them reaching from the waist to the arm-pits; Mameluke trousers, knee-breeches, tunics, togas, long cloaks which sweep the ground, capes trimmed with ermine, waistcoats encrusted with gold, short sleeves and balloon-shaped ones, monastic garbs and theatre costumes; men dressed like women, women who seem to be men, and peasants with the air of princes . . .

The glories of the Levantine world were only Ottoman tradition; and the centuries of peace and discretion of an imperial kind were over. On 4 November 1922 the last Sultan accepted the seals of office from his ministers, seals of a power which had been wielded in his name for six hundred years. Frightened and alone, he asked the British high commissioner for safe passage from Istanbul. He died at San Remo on 15 May 1926, and was buried in Damascus. The last Caliph died in Paris on 24 August 1944. He was buried in Medina.

Epilogue

For hundreds of years street dogs prowled, fought, and lay snoozing in the sun, forcing pedestrians to step over them as best they could, or pass by in the gutter, and every visitor from della Valle onwards heard them howling on the Pera shore at night. The Ottomans considered dogs unclean, but they accepted their presence in the divine plan, recognised their habits, and never called them strays. For centuries the dog's meat men sold skewered offal for the pious to give out, and whelping bitches were sure to receive a porridge of scraps even in the city's dankest quarters. It was not unusual for a Turk to leave a small bequest for feeding the dogs in his street; but the Armenians and Greeks often fed them poisoned meat on the sly.

The dogs kept the Ottoman cities relatively clean and wholesome, converting the rubbish into the shit scooped up by the tanners' men, for processes noxious and arcane; in Constantinople Byron claimed to have seen two dogs actually tucking into a dead body under the Seraglio walls, though in Bursa, that exquisite city, they left the cleaning chores to jackals, who scavenged in the streets by night. Thornton was not alone in finding them very loyal to their doggy parishes in the capital, rather like Stambouliots themselves: they never crossed the line, even 'in the attack on the passenger, whom they deliver over at their frontier to be worried by the neighbouring pack'. There is evidence to suggest that by the late nineteenth century there were 150,000 dogs in Istanbul alone: one for every eight inhabitants. But the dogs were not attached to people; only to the few blocks or streets they considered home.

They suffered the odd upheaval. Nasuh Pasha, Grand Vizier to Ahmet I, had all the street dogs sent over to Asia in boatloads, 'from concealed motive'. After the loss of Buda, the imperial greyhounds were turned loose 'and suffer'd to run without a Master through all the streets of Constantinople', as the Sultan sought to disassociate himself from an image of indolence and hunts. The fortunes of these aristocratic hunting dogs were closely bound up with those of their janissary masters, and vice versa: the name the reformist Grand Vizier Alemdar Pasha gave the new modern army he raised in 1807 meant 'dog-handlers'. Outside the city walls dogs worked, of course: like the Hungarian condor, or the vast Carpathian sheepdog. Macedonian shepherd dogs were no doubt descended from the brutes who killed Euripides at Pella; and the Albanian dogs were a law unto themselves, seeming to obey the same harsh codes as their masters, who protected them with the absolute loyalty for which Albanians were notorious. 'I remembered first a serious bit of advice given me by a British consul,' recalled J. F. Fraser, who was attacked by 'two brutes of goat-dogs' outside Ohrid in the early 1900s, 'never to shoot a dog belonging to an Albanian goatherd unless you are prepared immediately afterward to shoot its master before he has time to shoot you.'

The dogs of the cities – Salonica, Istanbul – were your true curs, sly, lazy, lively, flea-bitten and battle-scarred. Edward Lear disliked them. 'Such vile beasts they are, like old, mangy wolves: if I were Sultan for but one day wouldn't I send for 10 boat loads of dogs' heads!!' Right up to the Crimean War – the war through which the West made its overwhelming entry into the Ottoman world, snapping up its concessions, availing itself of its hans, sneering at its benighted superstitions, and pushing its loans –

Ottoman street dogs maintained their ancient purity, and were alike in every town and city in the empire. Perhaps they were nomads at heart. Legend had it that they came to Constantinople with the Turks in 1453; and their indolent behaviour ever after recalls Eliot's observation that the nomad seeks rest when he stops, not dancing. They were about the size of a collie, fierce-looking, tawny, with bushy tails and pointed ears. (The Crimean War brought all manner of foreigners into the empire, and left the breed underfoot slightly more erratic.) Like soldiers on furlough they lived rakishly, snoozing in the sun by day, and howling by night.

Very few people ever seem to have been bitten by one of these dogs; though when one English gentleman, impressed by their intelligence, tried to rear a litter of puppies in London, they grew savage and had to be put down. Probably they only gave up their territory to move in congenial company, perhaps recognisable in an American gypsy's lament for the coming of the automobile, recorded in New York in the 1950s by Joseph Mitchell: 'And the yellow gypsy dogs that we don't even have no more, they would lie down under the waggons and scratch their fleas. These *gajo* dogs you see in New York, the women practically nurse them, I despise those dogs. When they bark, yah-yah, they don't even sound mad. They sound sick. A yellow gypsy dog, even a baby one, when he barked he sounded like an old bear.'

In their own country they observed the proprieties, and never thought of going into shops or restaurants, preferring to wait patiently in the sun for some well-wisher to bring them something to eat. A terrier brought over from England once escaped from its mistress's hotel, dashed into the street, and was guarded by all the street dogs of the neighbourhood; they even made up a posse to rescue him from a neighbouring pack when he was foolish enough to cross the line, and brought him safely back to the hotel. At the end of the nineteenth century a dog on Davey's street was so very thin, and super-long, that everyone knew her as Sarah Bernhardt. One day she became very ill; a doctor friend of Davey's gave her some medicine, and from that day on she remained unswervingly attached to him, and 'in a hundred ways she showed her appreciation of his medical skill', including dragging him away by the coat to admire her new litter in a box around the corner.

They had, you might say, a rather static view of the world; and the forces of modernity certainly could find no place for them. Mahmut II finished off the janissaries, refashioned all his pashas as ministers, brought in the fez and the Stambouline, and had the dogs swept off the streets of Constantinople and shipped out to an island on the Sea of Marmara. It *was* all window dressing, though: the ministers became pashas again, the Grand Vizier was restored, and the dogs swam back.

In the last years of the empire, a French firm offered half a million francs to turn 150,000 street dogs in Istanbul into gloves. The Sultan – very hard pressed for cash – nobly refused. But the Ottoman world was relentlessly changing. In 1888 the famous Pera Palace Hotel opened to service the needs of passengers off the Orient Express from Venice, which arrived at the newly built Sirkeci station on the Golden Horn. Traffic in the city became speedier, and mechanical. The street dogs now loafed about tram-lines, fell asleep beneath the wheels of stationary omnibuses, and flopped down in the path of speeding cabs. They became three-legged, and worse.

By 1918 the Sultan no longer possessed any authority. Women were going to university, a military cabal still ruled the empire, the First World War was just ended, and in Turkey another war – for Turkey itself – was about to begin. The Board of Hygiene, too, had all but done its work. The drains were laid. There were asphalt roads, and pavements, so that mud and garbage had become discrete items to be picked out and avoided, except by the dustbin men who rode up and down the streets on collection day on smart new Davis refuse lorries from America. Mangy and lazy, three-legged and obtrusive, the dogs of Istanbul were rounded up again. It took five days, with nets and bait and leashes. They did not shoot or poison them, or get in touch with the enterprising French glove company, for perhaps within the empire's shrunken breast there remained a suggestion of that modesty which shrinks from forcing violence on the world, an echo of those Turkish curves. The dogs were locked up in an old tramp steamer and transported, howling and fighting, to a waterless island off the southern Marmara coast, where they were turned loose. And this time they never tried to swim back.

Ottoman Sultans

1	Sultan Othman I, Ghazi the Victorious, son of Erthogrul Shah	1300–1326
2	Sultan Orkhan, Ghazi the Victorious, son of 1	1326–1360
3	Sultan Murad I, Ghazi the Victorious, son of 2	1360–1389
4	Sultan Bayezid I, Ilderim the Thunderbolt, son of 3	1389–1403
Interregnum		1403–1413
5	Sultan Mohammed I, son of 4	1413–1421
6	Sultan Murad II, son of 5	1421–1451
7	Sultan Mohammed II, el-Fatih, the Conqueror, son of 6	1451–1481
8	Sultan Bayezid II, son of 7	1481–1512
9	Sultan Selim I, Yavouz the Ferocious, son of 8	1511–1521
10	Sultan Suleyman I, el-Kanuni the Legislator, the Magnificent, the Sublime, son of 9	1521–1566
11	Sultan Selim II, Mest, the Drunkard (or Sot), son of 10	1566–1574
12	Sultan Murad III, son of 11	1574–1595
13	Sultan Mehmet III, son of 12	1595–1603
14	Sultan Achmet I, son of 13	1603–1617
15	Sultan Mustapha I, son of 13	1617
16	Sultan Othman II, son of 14	1617–1622
15	Sultan Mustapha I, son of 13	1622–1623
17	Sultan Murad IV, Ghazi the Victorious, son of 14	1623–1640
18	Sultan Ibrahim, son of 14	1640–1648
19	Sultan Mehmet IV, son of 18	1648–1687

20	Sultan Suleyman II, son of 18	1687–1691
21	Sultan Achmet II, son of 18	1691–1695
22	Sultan Mustapha II, son of 19	1695–1703
23	Sultan Achmet III, son of 19	1703–1730
24	Sultan Mahmud I, son of 22	1730–1754
25	Sultan Othman III, son of 22	1754–1757
26	Sultan Mustapha III, son of 23	1757–1774
27	Sultan Abdulhamid I, son of 23	1774–1789
28	Sultan Selim III, son of 26	1789–1807
29	Sultan Mustapha IV, son of 27	1807–1808
30	Sultan Mahmud II, The Reformer, the Great, son of 27	1808–1839
31	Sultan Abdul Mecid, son of 30	1839–1861
32	Sultan Abd-ul-Aziz, son of 30	1861–1876
33	Sultan Murad V, son of 31	1876
34	Sultan Abd-ul-Hamid II, son of 31	1876–1909
35	Sultan Mehmet V Resat	1909–1918
36	Sultan Mehmet VI Vahideddin	1918–1922
37	Abd-ul-Mecit II, Caliph only	1922–1924

An Ottoman Chronology

AD 330 Roman emperor Constantine the Great founds new imperial city, Constantinople or Byzantium. While the Roman Empire in the west collapsed under barbarian invasion, its eastern portion, based at Constantinople, prospered. Christian, Greek-speaking, its culture spread across Russia and southeastern Europe.

537 Emperor Justinian builds St Sophia in Constantinople.

c. 570 Mohammed born in Mecca; died 632. Within a century, Mohammed's Arab followers had defeated armies from Persia, the Byzantine Empire, Latin Christendom, China and India, and had spread the Prophet's faith, Islam, from the Atlantic to the Himalayas. Samarkand in Central Asia fell to them in 710; Cordoba in Spain a year later. But Moslim unity was split between rival followers of the Prophet since 656, and the Islamic world was increasingly divided between local dynasties.

1054 Schism between eastern and western church (healed 1965).

1071 Seljuk Turks rout Byzantines at Manzikert, opening way for Turkish settlement of Anatolia.

1069–99 First Crusade.

1204 Fourth Crusade sacks Constantinople and divides Byzantine Empire between Latin powers.

1261 Byzantine Emperors return to Constantinople.

1280 Osman, founder of the Ottoman dynasty, born.

1349 Ottomans cross into Europe.

An Ottoman Chronology

1346–53	Black Death sweeps Europe.
1361	Ottomans take Edirne.
1402	Bayezit the Thunderbolt taken prisoner by Tamerlane at Ankara.
1402–13	Interregnum.
1448	Second battle of Kosovo consolidates Ottoman rule in Balkans.
1453	Mehmet the Conqueror takes Constantinople.
1454–81	Greece, Trebizond and Crimea conquered.
1492	Columbus 'discovers' the Bahamas.
1517	Selim the Grim takes Syria and Egypt.
1519–22	Portuguese Magellan circumnavigates the world.
1520	Luther launches attack on Roman church.
1521	Suleyman the Magnificent takes Belgrade.
1523	Suleyman takes Rhodes, key to eastern Mediterranean.
1526	Hungarian resistance overthrown at Mohacs.
1529	First siege of Vienna.
1566	Suleyman dies, leaving Constantinople as Europe's biggest city (½m inhabitants).
1571	Ottoman fleet destroyed at Lepanto.
1606	Treaty with Austria gives Hapsburg Emperor titular equality.
1607	Virginia colonised.
1609	Work begins on the Blue Mosque.
1618–48	'Thirty Years' War' in central Europe.
1622	Janissaries depose Osman II.
1623–40	Murad IV restores order.
1644	China's decaying Ming dynasty swept away by Manchurian Qing dynasty.
1644	Execution of Charles I of England.
1645–69	Siege of Venetian Candia, capital of Crete.
1683	Second siege of Vienna leads to Ottoman rout.
1699	Peace of Karlowitz: loss of Peloponnese, Hungary, Podolia, Azov to Christian enemies.
1703	Peter the Great founds St Petersburg.

An Ottoman Chronology

1720–30	First Ottoman ambassadors sent to western capitals.
1730	Patrona rebellion against taxation and western influences; Ahmet III deposed, Tulip Period ends.
1739	Peace of Belgrade returns Belgrade to Ottomans; Russians forced to sign separate peace.
1757	Clive's victory at Plassey establishes British in India.
1769	War with Russia renewed.
1774	Disastrous Treaty of Kucuk Kainardji with Russia.
1776	American Declaration of Independence.
1779	Russia annexes Crimea.
1789	French Revolution.
1799–1815	Napoleon Bonaparte reshapes map of continental Europe.
1815	Congress of Vienna.
1826	Massacre of the janissaries by Mahmud II.
1828	Fez introduced, along with judicial, military and administrative reforms on more western models.
1830	Greek independence.
1839	'Noble Rescript' promulgated, a liberal charter of reform. All creeds and races declared equal.
1853–56	Crimean war pits Turkish, English and French troops against Russia.
1861–5	American Civil War.
1868	Meiji Restoration in Japan.
1875	Empire declares bankruptcy. Balkan uprisings.
1878	Treaty of Berlin – to which Ottomans are not invited – establishes partial Bulgarian autonomy.
1895	Armenian massacres. Last Ottoman province in the Balkans, Macedonia, succumbs to civil war.
1908	Mutiny in Monastir, calling for restoration of the constitution. Committee of Union and Progress triumphs. Bulgaria declares independence. Crete unites with Greece.
1909	Muslim counter-revolution thwarted. Sultan deposed. Constitutional manarchy declared.
1911	Republic in China.

1912	Serbia, Greece and Bulgaria launch joint assault on European Turkey.
1913	The victors turn upon each other; Turkey recaptures Edirne.
1914	Turkey enters World War I on German side.
1918	Armistice. CUP leadership flees. Civil War erupts, followed by war with Greece in Anatolia.
1918–21	Mustafa Kemal secures boundaries of a Turkish state.
1922	Deposition and exile of last sultan.
1923	Turkey proclaimed a republic.

Glossary

aga military commander, leader
akinci mounted raiders
armatole policeman
asper small coin
ayan notable, local leader, in the later empire

baba (*lit.* father) holy man
bailio Venetian ambassador to the Porte
besa Albanian given bond, or promise of loyalty
bektashi an order of dervishes, linked to janissary corps
bey, beg commander/general
beylik estate of a bey
beylerbey (*lit.* lord of lords) a provincial governor

chaush equerry

deli mad
derbendci people guarding a mountain pass
dervish member of a sufi brotherhood, following a defined spiritual path
divan (*lit.* a low couch) council
dragoman interpreter

emir chieftain, greater than bey

fatwa judgement of a mollah, i.e. legal ruling
firman imperial decree
futuwwa Muslim chivalric brotherhood, cross between a guild and a masonry, with emphasis on chivalric conduct

gazi warrior of the faith

Haj annual pilgrimage to Mecca
Hajji someone who has performed the pilgrimage
hammam bath
han inn
harem (*lit.* forbidden) the private family quarters
hass revenues of a great official
heyduck Balkan irregular, usually in Habsburg service
hospodar ruler of one of the principalities, Moldavia or Wallachia

imam leader of prayer
ixarette signed language, which became court language

janissary (*lit.* new troop) the empire's crack infantry corps

kadi Muslim judge
kafes the so-called Cage, or group of harem apartments, reserved for heirs to the sultancy
kanun imperial law
kapudan pasha (*lit.* captain pasha) Admiral
kisilbas (*lit.* red-head) Shi'ite heretics known by their distinctive red head-dress
khan lord
kapikulu, pl. *kapikullari* slave(s) of the Porte
kulliye complex of educational and charitable institutions surrounding a mosque
klepht Balkan bandit

Mahdi (*lit.* the rightly guided one) supposed to rule before the end of the world
Mameluke (*lit.* slaves) rulers of Egypt
medrese Islamic college, usually attached to a mosque
meydan, *maidan*, *atmaidan* rough piece of open ground
millet religious community
mufti Islamic juror
mullah Islamic dignitary, scholar

nargile pipe

otak tent

pasha high civic or military official
pashalik territory under a provincial pasha's rule

reaya (*lit.* flock) the non-government subjects of the sultan

sekban military auxiliaries
sancakbey commander of a sancak, or district
saray palace
selamlik men's apartments
saraglio from *saray*, palace
sipahi imperial horseman

tanzimat restructuring
tekke dervish lodge or monastery
timar military stipend
timariot horseman holding a timar
tughra imperial cognomen, an elaborate signature

ulema doctors of religious law, the sharia
uskok Dalmatian bandit

vakif charitable endowment
valide Sultan Queen Mother
vizier royal minister
voivode Hungarian governor

Gazetteer

Bursa – Brusa
Candia – Crete
Candia, Crete – Iraklion
Circassia – Caucasus
Coron – Koroni
Dalmatia – coastal Croatia
Edirne – Adrianople
Ephesus – Efes
Epirus – ancient country of north-western Greece
Karaman – medieval Turkish emirate in south-eastern Anatolia
Lepanto – Navpaktos
Missolonghi – Mesolongion
Modon – Methoni
Navarino – Pylos
Nicaea – Iznik
Podolia – region of southern Ukraine
Ragusa – Dubrovnik, a Croatian port on the Adriatic
Salonica – Thessalonica / Thessaloniki
Sarajevo – Bosna Saray, Bosnia
Scutari – Uskudar
Skopje – Uskub
Smyrna – Izmir
Split – Spalato
Thessaly – region of central Greece
Thrace – south-eastern Europe, divided between Bulgaria, Greece and Turkey
Wallachia – south-western Romania

Bibliography

A. D. Alderson, *The Structure of the Ottoman Dynasty*, Oxford 1956
Sonia P. Anderson, *An English Consul in Turkey*, Oxford 1989
Anon., trans. James Whittle, *A Visit to Belgrade*, London 1854
Philip Argenti, *Chius Vincta (1566)*, Cambridge 1941

Franz Babinger, *Mehmed the Conqueror and His Time*, Princeton NJ 1978
Thomas M. Barker, *Double Eagle and Crescent*, New York 1967
Ottavio Bon, ed. Godfrey Goodwin, *The Sultan's Seraglio*, London 1996
John L. C. Booth, *Trouble in the Balkans*, London 1905
Catherine W. Bracewell, *The Uskoks of Senj: Piracy, Banditry and Holy War in the Sixteenth-Century Adriatic*, Ithaca and London 1992
Ernle Bradford, *The Sultan's Admiral*, London 1969
Fernand Braudel, *The Mediterranean and the Mediterranean World in the Age of Philip II*, Vols I & II, London 1972
George Bull, ed. and trans., *The Pilgrim: Travels of Pietro Della Valle*, London 1990
Noel Buxton, *Europe and the Turks*, London 1912

Dmitrius Cantemir, trans. N. Tindal, *The History of the Growth and Decay of the Othman Empire*, London 1734–5
Lavender Cassels, *The Struggle for the Ottoman Empire 1717–1740*, London 1966
George Castellan, *History of the Balkans*, Boulder, Col. 1992

R. Chandler, *Travels in Asia Minor 1764–5*, London 1817
Paul Coles, *The Ottoman Impact on Europe*, London 1968
Sir Edward S. Creasy, *History of the Ottoman Turks*, London 1877
J. A. Cuddon, *The Companion Guide to Yugoslavia*, London 1974

Thomas Dallam, *Early Voyages and Travels in the Levant* (Hakluyt Society), London 1893
Richard Davey, *The Sultan and his Subjects*, London 1897
James C. Davis, ed. and trans., *Pursuit of Power; Venetian Ambassador's Reports 1560–1600*, New York 1991

Sir Charles Eliot, *Turkey in Europe*, London 1900

E. S. Forster, trans., *The Turkish Letters of Ogier Ghiselin de Busbecq, Imperial Ambassador at Constantinople 1554–1562* (trans. of 1633 edition), Oxford 1927
J. Foster, ed., *The Travels of John Sanderson in the Levant 1584–1602*, London 1931
John Foster Fraser, *Pictures from the Balkans*, London 1906
John Freely, *Istanbul, The Imperial City*, London 1997
Philippe du Fresne-Canaye, ed. M. H. Hauser, *Le Voyage du Levant (1573)*, Paris 1897

H. A. Gibbons, *The Foundation of the Ottoman Empire 1300–1403*, Oxford 1916
H. A. R. Gibbs and H. Bowen, *Islamic Society and the West*, London 1957
Fatma Muge Gocek, *East Encounters West*, Oxford 1987
Daniel Goffman, *Izmir and the Levantine World*, Seattle and London 1990
Godfrey Goodwin, *A History of Ottoman Architecture*, London 1971
The Janissaries, London 1994

Annie Jane Harvey, *Turkish Harems and Circassian Homes*, 1871
Joan Haslip, *The Sultan: The Life of Abdul Hamit II*, London 1958
Elias Hebesci, *The Present State of the Ottoman Empire*, London 1784
Klara Hegyi, *The Ottoman Empire in Europe*, Budapest 1989
J. C. Hobhouse, *Journey through Albania 1809–10*, London 1813

Halil Inalcik, *The Ottoman Empire; The Classical Age 1300–1600*, London 1973
ed. *An Economic and Social History of the Ottoman Empire 1300–1914*, Cambridge 1994
Insight Guides, *Turkey*, Hong Kong 1989
Norman Itzkowitz and Max Mote, trans. and ed., *Mubadele – An Ottoman–Russian Exchange of Ambassadors*, Chicago 1970

Barbara Jelavich, *History of the Balkans*, 1983

Kemal Pasha Zadeh, trans. and ed. A. J. B. Pavet de Courteille, *Histoire de la Campagne de Mohacz*, Paris 1859
Lord Kinross, *The Ottoman Centuries*, London 1897
M. Faud Koprulu, *Origins of the Ottoman Empire*, New York 1992
Carl Max Kortepeter, *Ottoman Imperialism during the Reformation*, New York 1973
Kritovolos, trans. Charles T. Riggs, *History of Mehmed the Conqueror*, Princeton 1954
Ibrahim Metin Kunt, *The Sultan's Servants; the Transformation of Ottoman Provincial Government 1550–1650*, New York 1983

Edward Lear, *Journals of a Landscape Painter in Albania, Illyria &c.*, London 1852
Bernard Lewis, *The Emergence of Modern Turkey*, London 1960

Istanbul and the Civilisation of the Ottoman Empire, Norman, Oklahoma 1963
Raffaella Lewis, *Everyday Life in Ottoman Turkey*, London 1971
A. H. Libyer, *The Government of the Ottoman Empire*, Cambridge, Mass. 1913

Molly Mackenzie, *Turkish Athens*, Ithaca 1992
Noel Malcom, *Bosnia: A Short History*, London 1994
Robert Mantran, *Histoire de l'Empire Ottoman*, Paris 1989
Istanbul dans la Seconde Moitié de XVIIe Siècle, Paris 1962
La Vie Quotidienne à Constantinople au Temps de Soliman le Magnifique, Paris 1965
William McNeill, *Europe's Steppe Frontier, 1500–1800*, Chicago 1964
Nermin Menemencioglu, ed., *The Penguin Book of Turkish Verse*, London 1978
R. B. Merriman, *Suleyman the Magnificent*, Cambridge, Mass. 1944
Lady Mary Worley Montagu, ed. Malcolm Jack, *Turkish Embassy Letters*, London 1993
Frederick Moore, *The Balkan Trail*, London 1906
G. Muir Mackenzie and A. P. Irby, *Travels in the Slavonic Provinces of Turkey-in-Europe*, London 1987

Gubu Necipoglu, *Architecture, Ceremonial and Power: Topkapi Palace in the Fifteenth and Sixteenth Centuries*, New York and London 1991

Baron I. M. D'Ohsson, *Tableau Generale de l'Empire Ottoman* (7 vols), Paris 1788–1824

Alexander Pallis, *In the Days of the Janissaries*, London 1951
Alan Palmer, *The Decline and Fall of the Ottoman Empire*, London 1992
M. N. Penzer, *The Harem*, London 1936

D. E. Pitcher, *An Historical Geography of the Ottoman Empire*, Leiden 1972

Pollo, *History of Albania*, London 1981

Sir James Porter, *Turkey, Its History and Progress* (2 vols), London 1854

Leopold von Ranke, *History of Servia*, 1853

Clarence D. Rouillard, *The Turk in French History, Thought and Literature 1520–1666*, Paris 1941

Steven Runciman, *The Fall of Constantinople 1453*, Cambridge 1965

Sir Andrew Ryan, *The Last of the Dragomans*, London 1951

Sir Paul Rycaut, *The History of the Turkish Empire 1623–77*, London 1687

Johannes Schiltberger, trans. J. B. Telfer, *Bondage and Travels of Schiltberger in Europe, Asia and Africa 1396–1427* (Hakluyt Society), London 1879

Karl August Schimmer, *The Sieges of Vienna by the Turks*, London 1847

Stanford J. Shaw, *History of the Ottoman Empire and Modern Turkey* (Vols I & II), Cambridge 1976

Between Old and New: The Ottoman Empire under Sultan Selim III, 1789–1807, Cambridge, Mass. 1971

Mary Shay, ed., *Ottoman Empire from 1720–34 as Revealed in Venetian Dispatches*, London 1944

John Stoye, *The Siege of Vienna*, London 1964

Thomas Thornton, *The Present State of Turkey*, London 1809

Nikolai Todorov, *The Balkan City, 1400–1900*, Washington 1983

David Urquhart, *The Spirit of the East, or Pictures of Eastern Travel*, London 1839

Lucette Valensi, *The Birth of the Despot, Venice and the Sublime Porte*, Ithaca and London 1993

A. J. B. Wace and M. S. Thompson, *The Nomads of the Balkans*, London 1914

Andrew Wheatcroft, *The Ottomans*, London 1993

Sir J. Gardner Wilkinson, *Dalmatia and Montenegro* (2 vols), London 1848

Paul Wittek, *The Rise of the Ottoman Empire* (Royal Asiatic Society), London 1963

A. H. Wratislaw, *Adventures 1599*, London 1862

Acknowledgements

Bellini's portrait of Mehmet II, page ii, is used with the kind permission of the National Gallery, London. Illustrations on pages xvii, 117, 142, 180, 198, 236, and 268 are used with the kind permission of the British Museum. The James Robertson photograph on page 255 is used with the kind permission of the Scottish National Portrait Gallery. The Colossus of Rhodes woodcut on page 85 is by Jean Cousin and taken from Thevet's *Cosmographie de Levant* (Lyon, 1556). Antoine Melling's engraving on page 125 is from *Voyages Pittoresque de Constantinople et des rives du Bosphore.* Illustrations on pages 58, 104, 108, 191 and 276 are by Thomas Hope, taken from *Pictures from Eighteenth Century Greece* (Athens, 1985), with kind permission of the Benkai Museum and the British Council.

The chapter heads and section breaks are the emblems of various janissary regiments, taken from Marsigli, Stato Militare dell'Impero Ottomano, published at The Hague in 1732.

I would like to thank Norman Stone, the K. Blundell Trust, Jenny Uglow and Alastair Langlands, whose dining-room table was sequestered by the Ottomans for a year, like Toulon in 1543.

Index

Abbasid caliphs 7
Abdi xv*n*
Abdul Aziz, Sultan 311
Abdulhamid I, Sultan ('the Damned') 168, 289
Abdulhamid II, Sultan 308, 311, 312–14, 315–16, 317, 318
Abdul Mecid I, Sultan 303, 304
Abdul Mecid II, Caliph 319, 321
Acre 290
Adale castle: inventory 209–10
Adrianople *see* Edirne
Ahmed the Broken-Mouthed, Grand Vizier 49
Ahmet I, Sultan 166–7, 168, 212, 215, 323
Ahmet II, Sultan 235
Ahmet III, Sultan 211, 245–6, 260, 261, 262–3
Ahmet Koprulu *see* Koprulu, Ahmet, Grand Vizier
akinci bands 77
Albania/Albanians 77, 91, 151–2, 189, 248–9, 254–5, 283–4, 295, 305; aqueducts 108; dress 107, 108, *108*; fleas 199; houses 252; invasion (1912) 317; language 107–8, 294; medicine 107, 108; religion 192, 193; songs 194, 248*n*
Alemdar Mustafa Pasha, Grand Vizier 291, 292, 323
Aleppo 173–4, 259, 285–6
Alexander, Tsar of Russia xv, 289
Alexander VI, Pope (Rodrigo Borgia) 156–7
Algeria 287; Algiers 124, 126, 285, 287
Ali Pasha, Grand Vizier 256, 288
Ali Pasha, Lion of Janina (Albania) 251, 254, 292
Ali, Mehmet, of Egypt 294, 295–6, 300, 303–4
Ali, Mustafa (historian) 51, 54–5, 254
Ambelikya, Greece 252
Amdjazade Huseyin Pasha, Grand Vizier 233–4
Amicis, Edmondo de 320–1
Amouritzes, George 47
Anatolia 7, 8, 20, 25, 181, 195, 203
animals 198–201; *see also* dogs, street
Ankara 20, 201; battle (1402) 26–7
armatoles 248
Armenians xv, 92, 240, 306, 308; Balian clock towers 306; Christians 27, 95, 306; dress 96; massacre (1895) 315
army, Ottoman xiv, xv, 65–77, 177–8, 182, 223–4, 225, 239–40, 316; auxiliaries and volunteers 74–5, 76–7; camps 70–2; cavalrymen *see* spahis; European training 301–2, 309; infantry *see* janissaries; Salonica mutiny (1906) 316; weapons 218, 239, 244
Arumanians 93
aspers 175
Athens/Athenians 17, 51, 193–4, 201, 202, 203, 250, 258, 259–60, 277; dress 276; Jews 275
Athos, monks of 109, 201, 269
Atike 249*n*
Austria 238–41, 243–4; Long War 164, 177, 178; *see also* Habsburg dynasty

Index

Avars 12
ayan 251
Azerbaijan 92, 164, 182*n*
Azov 162, 163

Babylas, Bishop 271
Babylon 249–50
Baghdad 7, 65, 171, 237
Baki (poet) 159
Balian architects 306, 310
Balkans 12–21, 91–2, 111, 187, 190, 201, 284; Second Balkan War 317; *see also* Albania; Bosnia; Bulgaria; Montenegro; Serbia
Baltoghlu 34, 35, 36–7
bandits 179, 204–5, 248–9, 251*n*
Barbarossa (corsair) 126–8, 287
'Battle of the Torches' 164
Bavaria, Dukes of 23*n*, 113
Bayezit I, Sultan 20*n*, 21, 22–3, 24, 25–7, 28, 66, 149, 150
Bayezit II, Sultan 98–9, 121, 124, 155, 157
Bayezit, Prince 89, 169
bazaars 110, 118–19, 182, 196
Bedouin, the 94, 192, 284, 286
Bedreddin (mystic) 9–10, 134
Beg, Yaga 158
Bektashi order of dervishes 9, 57, 299
Belgrade 16, 77, 84, 112–14, 118, 228, 235, 237, 314; siege (1456) 48–9, 77, 86; treaty (1739) 238, 241
Benveniste, Don Señor 272
Berlin, treaty of (1878) 312–13
Bernardo, Lorenzo 165–6
Bernhardt, Sarah 314
Besma Sultan 137
beylerbeyi 74, 249
Biddulph, William 140
Black Eunuchs 176, 249, 291
Black Sea 21, 122, 124, 129, 161, 278, 282, 304
Bonneval, Count 290
Borgia, Alexander *see* Rodrigo VI, Pope
Bosnia/Bosnians 17, 77, 106, 187, 192, 250, 270, 284, 299, 311
Boucicault, Marshal 24
boy tribute system 56–8, 59–60, 66, 95, 116, 172, 222, 223, 238
Bragadino (Venetian commander) 160
Brancovich, Prince of Moldavia 242
bridges 135–7, 143
Broughton, Consul at Algiers 126
Brown, Edward 185, 195
Buda 15, 23, 86, 87, 113, 123, 152, 185, 200, 203; bridges 136
Bulgaria/Bulgars 12, 15, 16, 22, 143, 187, 193, 203, 234–5, 242–3, 280, 285, 294, 295, 308, 311, 312; horsemen 109, 120
Bunič, Nikolica 270
bureaucracy 69, 71, 174, 175, 192
Bursa 8, 14, 112, 200, 318, 322; Green Mosque 10, *112*, 150
Busbecq, Ogier Ghiselin de 45, 60, 71, 84, 94, 97, 118, 149, 152, 165, 175, 187, 188, 193, 194, 195, 198, 199–200, 259
Buxton, Noel, MP 249
Byron, Lord 107, 131*n*, 188, 189, 254, 260, 275, 284, 293, 294, 296, 322
Byzantine Empire 7–8, 12–18

Cacca Diabolo (corsair) 126
Cage, the 168–9, 170, 171–2, 215, 245, 246
calendars 152–3, 308
calligraphy 20*n*, 140
camels 72, 109, 114
Campbell (Ingiliz Mustafa) 291
Candia (Crete), siege of (1645–69) 225, 226–7
cannon, use of 32, 34, 35, 218
Cantacuzenos *see* John V, Emperor
Cantemir, Dmitri 51, 131, 171, 195, 216, 221, 278
capitulations 120, 264
Caspian canal 161, 162
Catherine II ('the Great') 242*n*, 244, 267, 293
Cavendish, Lord Harry 188
Celali revolts 179
Celebi, Evliya 106, 115, 141–2, 151, 170, 196–7, 201, 224
Celebi, Musa 171
Celebi, Said 262

Cem 85, 155–7
cemeteries 198, 201, 202
Cervantes, Miguel de 126, 163
Chalcocondyle (chronicler) 70
Chandler, R. 142
charitable foundations 142–3, 301, 302
Charles II of Anjou 45
Charles V, Holy Roman Emperor 83, 84, 86, 87, 88, 127, 161, 213
Charles VI, King of France 25
Charles VIII, King of France 156, 157
Charles XII, King of Sweden 217
Charrah, Syria 193
Chendereli, Kara Halil 57
Chesterton, G. K. 163
Chians/Chios 100–6
Christians/Christianity 5, 9, 10, 18, 20, 59, 95–6, 128, 140, 141, 144, 189, 252; Armenian 27, 95, 306; Orthodox 12–13, 16–17, 278, 280–1, 283; shrines 202; *see also* crusades; Knights of St John
Cigalazade Yusuf Sinan Pasha 125
cigarettes 290*n*
Cihangir 155
Circassians 107, 312, 315
cities/city life 110–11, *see specific cities*
clocks 152, 153, 176–7, 306–8
cloth industry 119, 140
clothes 96, *104*, 131, 145, 186, 189, 305, 309; Albanian 107, 108, *108*; Greek 96, 111
coffee drinking 111, 247, 266
coinage 55*n*, 19, 119, 174–5, 223, 266
Columbus, Christopher 122, 137*n*
Committee of Union and Progress (CUP) 316, 317–18
Comneni, the 13, 48*n*
Company of St John (joint stock company) 122
Constantine XI, Emperor 30, 33, 37, 38, 39, 40, 41, 42, 45
Constantinople (Istanbul) 12, 13–14, 22, 23, 28, 44–7, 54, 55, *55*, 80, 91, 110, 111, 115–16, *117*, *123*, 150–1, 216, *216*, 243, 287, 289, 318, 319, 320–1; Ahmediye mosque 215; Atmaidan 182, 196; Bayezit mosque xi, xii, *xii*; Blachernae Palace 34, 42–3, 51; Blue mosque 215; Castle of the Seven Towers 217–18, 242; Ciragan Saray 310, 311, 313; Cistern 202; and Committee of Union and Progress 316–17; decline 161, 165, 182–3; dogs 200, 322–6; Dolmabache Palace 310, *310*; French influences 262, 264; guilds 94, 196–7, 240; Hagia Sophia 42, 46; Kukucsu Kasri 311; noises 200; plague 138, 165, 252; population (1593) 219–20; siege and fall (1452–3) 29–43, 149; Sulimaniyye mosque 215; Topkapi Palace 51–4, 115, 134, 245, 246–7, 309–10; tulipomania 260–1; vaults 212–13; Yildiz Saray 310–11
Contarini, Bernardo 80–1
Coron 122
corsairs 124, 126–8, 271, 287
Cossacks 161, 224, 227
costumes *see* clothes
Crete 192, 193, 223, 225, 226; siege of Candia (1645–69) 225, 226–7, 273, 286–7
Crimean Tartars 74, 77, 93, 106–7, 162, 163, 222, 242, 243, 282–3, 284, 315
Crimean War (1853–6) xv, 235, 304, 323, 324
Crusades 6, 13, 23–5
Cumans 12
CUP *see* Committee of Union and Progress
Curzon, Robert 248–9
Cyprus 122, 159–61

Dallam, Thomas 214
Dalmatia 187, 204, 294
Damad Ibrahim Pasha, Grand Vizier 260–1, 262–3
Damascus 112, 118, 213, 287, 298, 318
Danishmends 19
Danube, River 23, 25, 48, 113, 118, 195, 201, 203–4, 209

Dardanelles, the 14, 223, 224, 289, 290
Davey, Richard 324–5
David, Trapuzuntine emperor 47
Davut Pasha 170
deli 65
della Valle, Pietro 46, 71, 75, 182, 196, 202, 217, 253, 322
Demetrius, Peloponnesian despot 48
dervishes 15; Bektashi 9, 57, 299; Mevlevi ('whirling') 142
Devlet Giray, Khan 162
Diebitsch, General 235
Disraeli, Benjamin 308–9, 312
divan, the 133
Dnilo II, King of Montenegro
Dodwell, Edward 259
dogs, street 322–6
Doria, Admiral Andrea 83
dragomen (interpreters) 278–9, 302–3
dress *see* clothes
Dubrovnik *see* Ragusa
'Dubrovnik Elbow' 98
du Fresne-Canaye, Philippe 152, 170
du Mans, Belon 106, 203
Durham, Edith 151–2
Dusan, Steven, Kraal of Serbia 16, 20
Dwight, H. G. 316

economy 174–5, 178–9, 251–4, 311; *see also* taxation; trade
Edirne (Adrianople) 15, 16, 43, 46, 119, 228, 291, 299, 312, 317; cannon casting 32; frogs 118, 199; royal parks 118, 245
education 130, 303, 313, 317
Eger, Hungary 138, 200
Egypt/Egyptians 63–4, 78, 122, 192, 195, 202, 238, 266*n*; grain 84, 121, 223; Mamelukes 64, 285, 288, 296; under Mehmet Ali 294, 295–6, 300, 303–4
Eliot, Sir Charles: *Turkey in Europe* 134, 143, 189–90, 258–9, 306, 313, 324
Emo (bailio) 246
Enver Pasha 317, 318
Ephesus 27
Epirus 200
Eugene, Prince of Savoy 113, 115, 166, 240–1
Eugénie, Empress 267–8
Eyup 79–80, 212

Fazil Ahmet Koprulu *see* Koprulu, Fazil Ahmet, Grand Vizier
Ferdinand, Duke of Austria 86–7
Ferdinand, King of Spain 99
Ferhad Pasha 167
fez, the 309
Fikret, Tevfik 316; 'Mist' 314
France/the French 23–4, 45, 127, 132–3, 138, 143, 155–7, 169, 213, 234, 262, 263, 264, 266, 267–8, 287, 289–91, 293–4, 309, 318
Francis I, King of France 82, 144, 213
Fraser, J. F. 190, 306–8, 323
fratricide, law of 55, 168–9
futuwwa brotherhoods 8

Gallipoli 14, 15, 17, 25, 201, 318
gazi 5, 10, 11, 19, 67
Gennadius the Scholar 46, 95
Genoa/Genoese 14, 49, 100, 105, 121–2, 174; and siege of Constantinople 31, 33, 35, 36, 37, 41, 44
George II Rakci, Prince of Transylvania 224
George of Trebizond 47
Georgians 116
Georgius de Hungaria 65–6
Germany 301–2, 316, 317–18
Gheg chieftains 92
Gibbon, Edward 10, 131*n*
Gilles, Pierre 201–2
Giray dynasty of Tartars 222, 282
Giurgiu: Danube bridge 136
Giustiniani, Giovanni 33, 41, 100
Giustiniani, Monsignor Timoteo 104
Giustiniani, the 100–1, 105
Golytsin, Prince 242*n*
Gonzaga, Julia 127
Grant, Johannes 33, 38
Greece/Greeks xv, 96, 192, 193, 194, 240, 266, 275–82, 290, 316–19; and Albanians 284, 294; and birds 198, 199; brigands 248; Byzantine 7, 8, 10, 12, 14–15, *see also*

Constantinople, siege of; independence 294, 295, 299; *see also* Athens; Chians/Chios; Missolonghi; Phanariots
Gregory, Patriarch 282
Gritti, Alvise 64
Gritti, Doge Andrea 45, 123
guilds 9, 94, 110, 116, 118, 143, 196–7, 240
Guns, siege of (1532) 88

Habsburg dynasty 82, 86, 127, 164–5, 182, 203, 205, 228, 230, 236, 240, 284
Hacivet (puppet) xi–xii, 131
Haj, the 6, 192, 287
Hajjis: costumes 96
Halil Pasha, Grand Vizier ('the Greek') 30, 38, 39, 44, 55, 57
Haneschi, Elias 63, 275
hans (hostels) 110, 143, 188
harem (Seraglio) 52, 111, 131, 176, 197, 211–12, 214–15, 249; *see also kafes*
Harvey, Mrs A. J.: *Turkish Harems* 132
Hasan (janissary) 149
Hasan Pasha 249–50
Hasan, Uzan 150
Haseki, Hajji Ali 250
Hellespont, the 14–15
Helly, Jacques de 24
Hetira (secret society) 294
heyducks 248
Hill, Alban 127
Hilmi, Abbas 304
Hobhouse, J. C. 97
Holland, Henry 109, 189, 251, 254, 305
horses/horsemen 3, 4, 60, 67–8, 109, 120, 150, 177, 178, 195; *see also* spahis
hospitality 96, 134, 143, 266
houses, private 111, 133
Hungary/Hungarians 16, 38, 77, 78, 192, 194, 203–4, 299; battle of Nicopolis (1396) 23–5, 77; falls to Suleyman 84–7; houses 111; and treaty of Karlowitz (1699) 235, 236, 240; *see also* Belgrade; Buda; Eger; Habsburg dynasty
Hunyadi, Janos 48, 49, 77

Ibn Battuta 6
Ibrahim, Sultan ('the Mad') 168, 169, 211–12, 215, 225, 226
Ibrahim, Grand Vizier 63–4, 123, 136, 139*n*, 152, 222, 288
Ibrahim Pasha 296, 300, 303, 304
Ilarion, Metropolitan 280
IMRO 294
Innocent VIII, Pope 156
Ionian islands 294
Ipsir Mustafa Pasha 173–4
Iran *see* Persia/Persians
Isa, Prince (Bayezit's son) 26, 27
Isabella, Queen of Hungary 86, 87
Islam (Muslims) xiii, xiv, 5–7, 9, 10–11, 17–18, 23, 139, 143–4, 192–4; and boy tribute system 56–7; and charity 142–3; Koran 21, 39, 55, 94–5; Mecca 50; and trade 116; and women 57; *see also* Haj; mosques
Ismail, capture of (1791) 244
Istanbul 55*n*, *see* Constantinople
Ivan the Terrible xv
Ivan III, Grand Duke 48
ixarette (sign language) 53, 169, 170
Izmir, Anatolia 27, 318, 319
Izmit, kadi of 171
Iznik tileware 109, 119, 215–16

Jami, Nur ud-Din 142–3
janissaries 9, 21, 48, 51, 57, *58*, 58–9, 62, 66–7, 71–2, 115, 132, 140, 165, 171, 178–82, 191, *191*, 219, 250, 263, 286; agas 75; at Belgrade 48–9, 77, 113–14; at Constantinople 32, 35, 41; reforms and massacre 290–4, 296–9
Jerusalem 192, 210; Church of the Holy Sepulchre 222
Jews 5, 95, 96, 98–100, 160, 182, 189, 197, 240, 277, 308; in Salonica 100, 109, 187, 201, 272–5
John V, Byzantine Emperor (Cantacuzenos) 14, 15, 18*n*
Joseph, Rabbi 23

Jovius 81
Juan, Don, of Austria 161

Kaaba, the 50
Kacic-Miosic, Andrija: *The Pleasant Conversation of the Slavic People* x, 204
kadis 22, 75, 115, 116
kafes (the Cage) 168–9, 170, 171–2, 215, 245, 246
Kaffa 49, 103, 162
kapikulu 57, 62
Kara George 114, 293
Kara Mustafa, Grand Vizier 63, 113, 211, 228–9, 230–3, 235
Kara Yusuf 26
Karagoz (puppet) xi-xii, xvi, 131
Karaman 17
Karavulik 4
Karesi 14
Karlowitz, treaty of (1699) 105, 235–6, 237, 240, 242, 243, 261
Kasim Pasha 162–3
Kastamonu: clothes washing 109
Keduk, Ahmet 157
Kemal Pasha, Mustafa 318, 319
Khalifa, Hajji 165
Kilic Ali Pasha 125–6
Kinglake, Alexander 124, 186
klephts 248
Knights of St John of Jerusalem 24, 27; on Malta 82, 102, 161, 222–3, 226; on Rhodes 45, 63, 82, 84–5, 155–6, 203
konak 137
Koprulu, Ahmet, Grand Vizier 105, 223, 224–5, 226, 227, 264, 283
Koprulu, Fazil Ahmet, Grand Vizier 132, 227, 235
Koprulu, Fazil Mustafa, Grand Vizier 235
Koprulu dynasty 223, 233, 237
Koprulu, Nuuman 234
Koran 5, 21, 39, 55, 94–5
Kos, Karoly 139
Kosem, Valide Sultan 171, 183–4
Kossovo 234, 319; battle (1389) 12, 16, 21; battle (1448) 18
Kritovolos 47, 90, 150, 204
Kucuk Kainardji, treaty of (1774) 241, 243, 266–7, 277–8, 281, 287
kul 56, 60–3, 145, 165, 174
Kunt, Ibrahim Metin 176*n*

La Brocquière, Bertrand de 66, 118
Ladislas, King of Hungary 23, 24, 25
language(s), Ottoman 92, 130, 188–9, 259, 294; Greek 263–4; sign 53, 169–70
La Quira, Madame 167
Larissa 198
laws 82–3, 94–5, 130–1, 134, 143, 153; of fratricide 55, 168–9
Lear, Edward 91*n*, 97*n*, 107*n*, 110–11, 134, 188, 198, 305, 314–15, 323
Le Duc (French physician) 234
Lemnos 193
Leo X, Pope 81
Leopold, Emperor 228, 232
Lepanto: battle (1499) 122, 124; battle (1571) 126, 128, 161, 163, 211
Levi, Sabbatai 274
Libyer, A. H. 238
Longo, Giovanni Giustiniani *see* Giustiniani, Giovanni
Lorraine, Duke of 228, 231
Louis I ('the Great'), King of Hungary 15
Louis II, King of Hungary 85, 86
Louis XIII, King of France 132
Louis XIV, King of France 143, 169, 264, 266
Loukris, Patriarch 277
Lupazzoli, Francesco 217*n*
Luther, Martin 18, 84
Lutheranism 88*n*

Machiavelli, Niccolò 172
Magyars 12, 203
Mahmut I, Sultan 263
Mahmut II, Sultan ('the Reformer') 282, 289, 292, 295, 296–7, 300, 301–3, 309–10, 325
Mahona/Mahonesi 100, 101–3
Malta 225–6; Knights *see* Knights of St John of Jerusalem
Mamelukes 64, 285, 288, 296

Index

Manuel, Prince 17–18
Manzikert, battle of (1071) 7
Marmara, Sea of 14, 32, 33, 106, 194
marriage customs 52, 92–3
Marseilles: Greek community 277
Marsigli, Comte de 70
Matthias, King of Hungary 77
Mavrocordato, Prince of Wallachia 284
Mavrocordato, Alex 105
Mecca 6, 78, 192, 201, 285; Kaaba 50
Medina 6, 143, 192
Mediterranean Sea 7, 121, 124–5, 194
Mehmet I, Sultan 26, 28, 155, 221
Mehmet II, Sultan ('the Conqueror') xv, 10, 18, 28, 29–49, 51–7, 66, 80, 86, 95–6, 115, 119, 121, 143, 150, 155, 226, 269, 278
Mehmet III, Sultan 54, 166, 168, 264
Mehmet IV, Sultan xv*n*, 54, 65, 214, 223, 224, 227, 228, 233, 235, 274
Mehmet V Resat, Sultan 317, 318
Mehmet VI Vahideddin, Sultan 328
Mehmet Pasha (ambassador) 267
Melami, the 9
Melek Pasha 224–5
Menemencioglu, Nermin: *Turkish Verse* 210
Mevlevi dervishes 142
Michael the Brave 164
Michael of the Pointed Beard 8
Midhat Pasha 311, 312
millets 95, 192
Missolonghi 284, 293, 296
Mistra, court at 16
Mitchell, Joseph 324
Modon 122
Mohacs, battle of (1526) 85–6, 112
Mohammed *see* Mehmet
Moldavia, Principality of 74, 77, 118, 119–20, 164, 176, 203, 242, 243, 278, 280, 282, 283, 284, 294, 300
Moltke, Count Helmuth von 301–2, 303
Monastir: bridges 136
Mongols 7, 8
Montagu, Lady Mary Wortley: *Turkish Embassy Letters* 71, 133, 142, 145, 188, 216, 217, 247, 284
Montenegro 193, 202, 271–2, 312
monuments 137
Morison, Fynes 199
Morosini, Francesco 59, 72, 118, 227, 235
Mortamama (corsair) 126
mosques 19, 52, 80, 138–40, 215–16, 310
Mostar bridge *135*, 135–6
Mosul 200
muftis 115
Muhammad, Bey of Tunisia 287
Murad I, Sultan 17, 19, 20*n*, 21, 25
Murad II, Sultan 19, 28, 30, 44, 56, 121
Murad III, Sultan 151*n*, 154, 160, 162, 163, 166, 211, 313
Murad IV, Sultan 54, 169, 171, 196, 213, 224
Murad V, Sultan 311–12
Musa, Prince (Bayezit's son) 26
Mustafa I, Sultan 170–1, 211
Mustafa II, Sultan 245
Mustafa IV, Sultan 240, 289, 291, 292
Mustafa, Kara *see* Kara Mustafa, Grand Vizier
Mustafa, Prince (Bayezit's son) 26–7
Mustafa, Prince (Suleyman's son) 89, 158
Muteferrika, Ibrahim 262
Mysri Effendi 9*n*

Nabi (poet) 46, 139*n*
Naima (historian) 166
Napoleon Bonaparte xv, 239, 267, 270, 289, 290, 294, 296, 299
Napoleon III 267
Nasi, Joseph 160
Nasuh Pasha, Grand Vizier 323
Nauplia 122
Navarino, battle of (1827) 299
navy, Ottoman 118, 121–9, 163, 211, 218, 219, 286, 299, 318
Naxos, Joseph Nasi, Duke of 160
Nedim (court poet) 260
Nevers, Jean de 23
Newgate, Lord 294*n*

Nicaea 14
Nicholas V, Pope 31
Nicopolis, battle of (1396) 23–5, 77, 85
Nis 12, 21, 177, 235; battle (1387) 16
Nolan, Captain 309
nomadism 92–4
Notarias, Lucas 43
Nur Banu Sultan 160

Obravitch, Milosh 21
Ohrid 280; Lake Ohrid 120, 190
Omar Pasha 174
Orhan, Sultan 6–7, 10, 14, 15, 17, 18, 19, 21
Orloff brothers 281
Orthodox Church 12–13, 16–17, 278, 280–1, 283
Osijek, Yugoslavia: bridge 136
Osman I, Sultan 6, 7–9, 10, 12, 19, 21, 50, 80, 169
Osman II, Sultan 170
Osman III, Sultan 171–2

pageantry 195–7
Paleologi, the 13, 48
Paleologus 103*n*
Paleologus, Dimitri 258
Palestine 300
papermaking 256
Passarowitz, treaty of (1719) 237, 240, 241, 261
Patrona Ali 263, 284
Pechenegs 12
Peloponnese, the 48, 77, 235, 236, 280, 281
Pera 14, 31, 33, 37, 111, 121, 122, 138, 225, 259, 279, 314, 325
Persia/Persians (Iran) 7, 65, 70, 78, 89, 130–1, 140, 164, 171, 237, 238, 262–3
Peter the Great 131*n*, 237, 242, 243, 281
Peterwaradin, battle of (1691) 235
Phanariots 177, 278–80, 281–2, 283, 284, 302
Philiki Hetaira (secret society) 281
Philothei, St 277
Piali Pasha, Admiral 101–4
picnics 197
piracy 248; *see* corsairs
plague 138, 165, 214, 252
Podolia 151, 236
poetry/poets 43, 46, 131, 139*n*, 156, 157, 159, 210, 245, 260, 314, 316
Poland 230–3, 236
Pomaks 193
Porter, Sir James 116, 195–6, 255*n*, 265, 276
Portuguese, the 137*n*, 161–2
Postel (antiquarian) 143
Princip, Gavrilo 294
Principalities *see* Moldavia; Wallachia
printing 262, 271
Ptolemy 49

Quiclet, M. 114, 115

Ragusa (Dubrovnik)/Ragusans 16, 31, 44, 97–8, 109, 174, 201, 270–1
Ramadan 153, 196, 204, 212
Ramberti, Benedetto 45–6
reaya 5
Reis, Piri 137*n*, 162
Reis, Seydi Ali 137*n*
Rhodes 63, 84–5, *85*, 122, 155–6, 203
Rhodopes, the 193, 201
Richelieu, Cardinal 132
Rizzi, Antonio 31
Roe, Sir Thomas xiv
Romania/Romanians 109, 282, 285, 312
Romanzoff, General 243
Roxelana (wife of Suleyman) 83, 89, 160
Rudolf, Emperor of Austria 96*n*
Russia/Russians: and Caspian canal project 161, 162; 18th century 129, 236, 237, 238, 239–40, 241–3, 257, 266–7, 281, 293–4; 19th century 289–90, 304, 312–13, 315; *see also* Ukraine
Rustem 183, 213
Rycaut, Sir Paul 68*n*; *The History of the Turkish Empire* 58, 60, 68, 75, 76, 98, 107, 119, 124, 179, 183–4, 190–1, 199, 204, 246, 290

Safiye Sultan 160
St Catherine's monastery, Syria 269
St Gotthard, battle of (1674) 235, 237, 243–4
Salonica (Thessalonica) 16, 17–18, 119, 250; army mutiny 316; Jews 100, 109, 187, 201, 272–5
Sanderson, John 219–20
Sandys, George 53, 118, 186–7, 203
Sarajevo 114–15, 138, 200, 201
Sarakatsans 93
Saxony, Elector of 230
Scanderberg (George Castriota; Iskander Beg) 77
Scheder's Chronicle: *Constantinople* 55
Schweigger, Salomon 52
Scutari 136, 166, 262–3
Selaniki (historian) 183
Selim I, Sultan ('the Grim') 4, 78, 79, 80, 91, 122, 157*n*, 169, 213, 243, 287
Selim II, Sultan ('the Sot') 54, 89, 159, 160, 163, 166, 168, 222
Selim III, Sultan 138*n*, 171–2, 289, 290–1, 303
Seljuks, the 8
Serbia/Serbs 16, 77, 192, 199, 201, 294, 298; under Austrian rule 113, 240–1, 280; independence 312; and janissaries 250, 290; under Kara George 114, 293; and Kossovo 12, 16, 18, 21, 234
Sèvres, treaty of (1920) 318–19
sherifs 286
Sherley, Sir Thomas 128
Shi'a Muslims 6, 70, 90–1
Shishman, General 216–17
Shishman of Bulgaria 17, 22
sign language (*ixarette*) 53, 169–70
Sinan (architect) 62*n*, 136, 215
Sivas 26, 199
Skopje 152, 202
Slade, Augustus 302
Slatina, battle of (1788) 241
slaves 21, 97, 106–7, 163, 222, 245; boy tribute system 56–8, 59–60, 66, 95, 116, 172, 222, 238; *kul* 56, 60–3, 145, 165, 174
smoking 133–4, 247, 290*n*
Smyrna 111, 140, 217, 274, 277, 285
Sobieski, Jan, King of Poland 227, 230, 231, 233
Sofia 21, 200
Sokullu Mehmet, Grand Vizier 159, 161, 163, 183, 222, 280
spahi (cavalrymen) 19–20, 67, 75, 76, 140–1, 178
Spain 124, 272–3; expulsion of Jews 98–100, 273
Split 270
spy network 72
Stackelberg, Otto Magnus von 248*n*
Stahremberg (commander of Vienna) 229–30, 231, 232
Stalin, Joseph 283
Stambouline, the 309
steppes 3–4
Sufis 141–2
Suleyman I, Sultan ('the Magnificent') 53, 54, 63, 79–89, 112, 122, 123, 127, 136, 144, 153, 154, 155, 158–9, 160, 169, 175, 200
Suleyman II, Sultan 172, 235
Suleyman, Prince 17, 26, 27
Sumla pass, Bulgaria 234–5, 242–3
Sunni Muslims xiv, 6, 91, 192
Suvarov, General 244
Syria 25, 111, 193, 269, 285, 290, 300; *see also* Aleppo; Damascus
Szitvarok, treaty of (1606) 178

Tahmasp, Shah 169
Tamerlane the Great 25–7, 140
Tanzimat (reforms) 301–3, 304–5
Tartars 25–6, 177; *see* Crimean Tartars
Tavernier, Jean-Baptiste 213
taxation 68–9, 120, 173, 179, 192, 219, 225, 233, 239–40, 249, 250
tents 70–2
Thackeray, William Makepeace 138, 186
Thessalonica *see* Salonica
Thessaly 203
Thévenot, Jean 215
Thokoli (Hungarian pretender) 218
Thomas, Peloponnesian despot 48
Thornton, Thomas 322
Thracc 7, 15, 203

Tilsit, treaty of (1807) 289
timar/timariots 67–8, 179, 249, 256
time, concept of 151, 151*n*, 152–3, 154; *see also* clocks
Timoni, Emmanuel 105
Tirana: mosque 138
Tisza, battle of (1596) 166
Topal Recep Pasha 171
Tott, Baron de 138, 291
Toulon 127
trade 97, 110, 116, 118–20, 140, 161, 162, 186, 253, 264
treasure, buried 210–11
Trebizond 47, 122, 150
tughras 20*n*
tulipomania 260–1, 262
Tunisia 124, 285
turbans 96, 221, 305
Turhan, Valide Sultan 223–4
Tursun Bey 46, 70
Tvrtko, King of Bosnia 17

Ukraine 227, 237, 252
Ulcinj, Montenegro 271
ulema 5, 19, 153, 171, 182, 222, 262, 292–3, 295, 296, 299, 302, 305
Urquhart, David 91*n*; *The Spirit of the East* 91, 248, 254–5, 263, 295, 304–5
uskoks 204–5

vakif (endowments) 143, 301, 302
Varna, battle of (1444) 44
Vavassore, Giovanni: *Constantinople 117*
Venice/Venetians xv, 45, 49, 121, 150, 211; ambassadors and visitors 59, 60, 64, 66, 81–2, 165–6, 175, 176, 189, 265; and Chios 105–6; and fall of Constantinople 31, 33, 34, 37, 44; and loss of Crete 129, 223–7, 273; and fall of Cyprus 159–61; and Dalmatian *uskoks* 204, 205; battle of Lepanto (1571) 125–6, 128; losses in the Levant 122, 124; and Napoleon 270; and the Parthenon 203; and the Peloponnese 235, 236, 280; printing 271; in Smyrna 217; trade 14, 116, 120, 122–3, 217*n*
Victor II, Pope 13
Vienna 225; first siege (1529) 87, 123; second siege (1683) 70, 211, 228–33, 235, 238
Vigenère, Blaise de 54
Viol Frères, Les 197
Vistritza valley 221–2
vizier 62
Vlach, the 74, 93–4, 136
Vlore: mosque 138

Wallachia, Principality of 24, 25, 77, 74, 109, 118, 164, 176, 203, 242, 243, 263, 278, 280, 282, 283, 284, 294
Walpole, Horace 199
weather conditions 194–5
'Women, Sultanate of the' 160, 176, 249
World War, First 318
Wratislaw, Baron A. H. 61, 96*n*, 125, 144, 186, 190, 196, 199, 266

Yörük tribes 92–3, 284
Young Ottoman movement 302*n*, 312
Ypsilanti, Prince 177
Ypsilantis, Alexander 281–2

Zaganos Pasha 39
Zapolya, John, Voivode of Transylvania 86
ziamet 68
Zoë, Grand Duchess 48